STUDIES IN EVANGELICAL HISTORY AND THOUGHT

Evangelicals Embattled

Responses of Evangelicals in the Church of England to Ritualism, Darwinism and Theological Liberalism, 1890-1930

STUDIES IN EVANGELICAL HISTORY AND THOUGHT

A complete listing of all titles in this series will be found at the close of this book.

STUDIES IN EVANGELICAL HISTORY AND THOUGHT

Evangelicals Embattled

Responses of Evangelicals in the Church of England to Ritualism, Darwinism and Theological Liberalism, 1890-1930

Martin Wellings

Foreword by John Walsh

First published 2003 by Paternoster

Paternoster is an imprint of Authentic Media,
9 Holdom Avenue, Bletchley, Milton Keynes, MK1 1QR, U.K.
and
P.O.Box 1047, Waynesboro, GA 30830-2047, U.S.A.

09 08 07 06 05 04 03 7 6 5 4 3 2 1

British Library Cataloguing in Publication Data
A record for this book is available from the British Library.

ISBN 0–84227–049–4

Typeset by Profile
Printed and bound in Great Britain
for Paternoster
by Nottingham Alpha Graphics

STUDIES IN EVANGELICAL HISTORY AND THOUGHT

Series Preface

The Evangelical movement has been marked by its union of four emphases: on the Bible, on the cross of Christ, on conversion as the entry to the Christian life and on the responsibility of the believer to be active. The present series is designed to publish scholarly studies of any aspect of this movement in Britain or overseas. Its volumes include social analysis as well as exploration of Evangelical ideas. The books in the series consider aspects of the movement shaped by the Evangelical Revival of the eighteenth century, when the impetus to mission began to turn the popular Protestantism of the British Isles and North America into a global phenomenon. The series aims to reap some of the rich harvest of academic research about those who, over the centuries, have believed that they had a gospel to tell to the nations.

Series Editors

To my parents

Contents

Foreword

Understandably, church historians often prefer to focus on the 'heroic' phases in the life of their church or religious grouping rather than tell the story of other periods which were marred by stasis or controversy. Thus historians of Evangelicalism in the Church of England have tended to be more comfortable with the eras of Henry Venn and John Newton, Simeon and Wilberforce, than with some subsequent decades. The late Victorian and Edwardian Evangelicals certainly had their successes (in home missions, in the pioneer work of CMS, for example) but they had to meet new challenges too, from ritualism, Darwinism, and the new biblical criticism. Martin Wellings' admirably clear and fair-minded study shows how they dealt with these unsettling issues. Many Evangelical leaders were not content merely to withdraw into pained isolation (as modern historians too easily assume): on the contrary, with integrity and intelligence they grappled with the problems facing them. Their responses were not uniform, or easily grouped. There was no tidy division between accommodationists and conservatives. Instead, there was a spectrum of responses from Evangelicals who sought to hold fast to the biblical revelation and to the faith of their forefathers while recognising the existence of advances in knowledge and shifts in religious sensibility. Wellings describes the painful but thoughtful re-positionings and reassessment which resulted, provoking some disarray, but also much hard thinking. This is an important work which dissects sensitive issues with calm and balance. It should be of value not only to evangelical readers but to many historians of modern culture.

John Walsh,
Jesus College, Oxford

Acknowledgements

This study is a revised and updated version of my Oxford DPhil thesis on late nineteenth century Anglican Evangelicalism. There are four areas in particular in which I would like to express thanks for help received in the original research, and in the subsequent writing of this book.

The first is financial. I am grateful to the British Academy for the award of a Major State Studentship, which made my course of research possible, and to the Rector and Fellows of Lincoln College, Oxford, who elected me to a Senior Scholarship for two years, and very kindly extended this for a further year.

Secondly, I have benefited academically from the help of many people. The staff of the Bodleian Library provided the lion's share of the material on which this study is based, while coping with a major reorganisation and extensive renovation. Librarians and archivists at the Cambridge University Library, the Henry Martyn Library at Westminster College, Cambridge, the Central Library of the Selly Oak Colleges, Lambeth Palace Library, Pusey House, King's College, London and the British Library have also greatly assisted my research. I owe special thanks to Mr Brian Dyson, the Archivist at the University of Hull, to Mr Peter Scott of the BCMS, to Miss Rosemary Keen of the CMS and to Mrs Ruth Ward, the Secretary of the Bible League, for taking particular trouble to find material for me, and, in one case, for kind hospitality.

My work has been furthered by conversations with or letters from the Revd Professor G.W. Bromiley, the Revds J.S. Reynolds, A.T. Carver, J.F. Balley, Dr A.F. Munden, Dr Ian Randall, Dr Alan Wilson, Canon P. Hinchliff, L. Hickin and Dr W. Stott. Mr Hickin's memories of the AEGM were very valuable, and material lent by Dr Stott helped to fill the gap created by the refusal of the PRS to let me consult the records of the FEC. Dr Clive Marsh and Dr Martin Davie have provided a source of theological expertise on which I have been able to draw on several occasions. Dr David Bebbington, the external examiner for my thesis, has been an inspiration and encouragement – and a friend – to me, as to many other students of evangelicalism.

My final academic debt is to my supervisor, Dr John Walsh, who provided careful and scholarly guidance throughout the course of my original research, and who has graciously written a foreword for this book. I hope he will regard the finished product as at least a first step towards the mapping of the *terra incognita* of late nineteenth century Evangelicalism.

Thirdly, my thanks are due to Jeremy Mudditt at Paternoster Press for editorial support and expertise, and to Robert Parkinson for guiding me through the technicalities of wordprocessing. Dr John Vickers generously undertook the compilation of the index, thus ensuring that this would be done to the highest standard.

The final area of gratitude is personal. Research can be a lonely undertaking, and I would like to conclude by thanking those who have supported me, either by taking an interest in my work or by providing friendship and thus helping me to retain a sense of balance in the midst of academic pressures. Above all, I am grateful to my parents for their constant encouragement. My late father saw the completion of the DPhil, but, sadly, not of this book. It is to him and to my mother that this work is dedicated.

Martin Wellings,
Kidlington,
July 2002.

Abbreviations

BW	*The British Weekly*
C	*The Churchman*
CC	*Chronicle of Convocation*
CM	*Churchman's Magazine*
CT	*The Church Times*
DNB	*Dictionary of National Biography*
DP	*Davidson Papers*
G	*The Guardian*
KCA	*King's College archives*
JEH	*Journal of Ecclesiastical History*
MC	*Modern Churchman*
ODCC	*Oxford Dictionary of the Christian Church*
R	*The Record*
RCED	*Royal Commission on Ecclesiastical Discipline, 1904-06, Minutes of Evidence and Report*
SCH	*Studies in Church History*
T	*The Times*
TransVI	*Journal of Transactions of the Victoria Institute*

Notes on the Text

In the present work 'evangelical' has been used to refer to adherents of the evangelical movement (as defined in the Introduction) regardless of their denominational affiliation; 'Evangelical' refers to those who practised their religion within the Church of England; 'churchman' refers to members – clerical or lay, female or male – of the Church of England.

CHAPTER 1

Introduction

'As concerning this sect, we know that everywhere it is spoken against.' (Acts 28:22)

'An army of illiterates generalled by octogenarians.' The damning description of the Protestant opponents of Prayer Book revision in the 1920s, quoted, if not coined by Hensley Henson, has been widely used as an epitaph for the Evangelical school in the Church of England in the first decades of the twentieth century.[1] Historians of the period, dazzled by the spectacle of exuberant, self-confident Anglo-Catholicism or by the daring speculations of theological Modernists, have been inclined to dismiss the Evangelicals as a spent force, if not to ignore them altogether. Some Evangelicals, moreover, proud of the late twentieth century strength of their movement, have used the perceived decline of the earlier years as a foil to magnify later successes. Historiography, then, has not been kind to late nineteenth and early twentieth century Anglican Evangelicalism. Randle Manwaring's chapter headings are telling: 'Into battle', 'The defensive years', 'Through the Waste Land', 'Continuing nadir'.[2] Adrian Hastings' judgment is equally severe: 'Never was Evangelicalism weaker than in the 1920s – in vigour of leadership, intellectual capacity, or largeness of heart.'[3]

In their critical analysis, modern historians have reflected some strands of contemporary opinion on the position of the Evangelical school. An article in the *Spectator* in August 1888, for example, declared that the Evangelical movement 'has lost its hold on the educated classes, and has scarcely any influence over the masses.'[4] In his splenetic *Annals of the 'Low Church' Party in England, down to the death of Archbishop Tait* (1888), W.H.B. Proby summarised Evangelical history from the middle of the nineteenth century to the time of writing as an 'Immoral Period', marked by pastoral inefficiency and the persecution of innocent ritualists.[5] Twenty years later the *Church Times* and the

Methodist Recorder each commented on the imminent collapse of the Evangelical school.[6]

Although such charges provoked indignant rebuttals and appeals to an impressive catalogue of achievements, Evangelicals themselves were quite prepared to scrutinise and debate their own policies and practices. Furthermore, this internal debate took place against a background of strenuous activity at parochial level, often overlooked by historians and polemicists. Evangelicals in this period continued to gather large congregations and to sustain busy churches in a wide range of geographical and social settings. They supported an army of Christian workers and an enormous number of missionary and philanthropic societies. Although regularly lamenting their lack of influence in the wider councils of the Church, they were not without representation in the clerical hierarchy. It is too easy, then, to underestimate the Evangelicals, to ignore their constructive work or to see the ultra-conservatives who emerged in the 1920s as the sole authentic representatives of the school. This beguiling path has been made much more tempting by the disappearance of Liberal Evangelicalism since the 1960s, leaving the heirs of the ultra-conservatives as the residuary legatees of the whole history of the tradition.

In a perceptive article published nearly sixty years ago in the *Cambridge Historical Journal*, Charles Smyth described the history of nineteenth century Anglican Evangelicalism as 'a territory which remains to a remarkable extent unmapped.'[7] Although some of the *terra incognita* of Evangelical history has been charted in recent years, the later part of the nineteenth century and the first decades of the twentieth still remain comparatively unexplored, at least in detail. The older histories by Moule, Balleine, Russell and Elliott-Binns devote little space to the period after 1890, while Anne Bentley's comprehensive (and sadly, unpublished) thesis concludes with the Lincoln Judgment of 1892.[8] Manwaring begins his account in 1914, Hastings in the 1920s. There are overviews by Kenneth Hylson-Smith and Roger Steer, a chapter in David Bebbington's seminal and panoramic *Evangelicalism in Modern Britain* (1989), and a fine study of Evangelical spirituality by Ian Randall, but still no thorough scholarly published account of the years between the trial of Bishop King and the collapse of Prayer Book revision in 1928.[9]

Given the breadth of the field to be covered, it has been necessary to place a strict limit on the scope of the present work. It focusses on Evangelical responses to four challenging contemporary developments: ritualism, the higher criticism of the Bible, Darwinian biology, and the modification of traditional credal orthodoxy by 'liberal' theologians. These four issues are examined in depth, and attention is also given to a series of conflicts within Evangelical institutions which arose, in part, from the pressures placed on Evangelicalism by ritualism and by 'modern thought'. An inevitable consequence has been the omission from this study of many central Evangelical preoccupations, such as mission at home and abroad, the education debate, the issue of disestablishment and the quest for reunion between the Church of England and the Protestant Free Churches. The non-controversial aspects of Evangelical parochial and devotional life are also not treated here.

Apart from the constraints of space, two reasons may be given for the focus on ecclesiastical and theological controversy, on 'Evangelicals embattled', rather than Evangelicals engaged in the broad field of positive Christian work. First, contemporary Evangelicals would not have accepted the simplistic division of their activity into 'negative' polemics and 'positive' pastoral and evangelistic work. Taking a stand for truth and wrestling with the issues of modern thought were constructive aspects of the total missionary task, even if they sometimes entailed controversy and led to some protagonists losing sight of the constructive purpose in the heat of the battle. Second, the conflicts discussed in this book did much to determine the shape of twentieth century Evangelicalism, and to pose with uncomfortable sharpness fundamental questions about Evangelical identity. If nothing else emerges from this study, it is hoped that it will promote a greater understanding of the sheer diversity of Anglican Evangelicalism, and a recognition that, historically, there is more than one legitimate Evangelical identity.

Defining Evangelicalism

In his paper 'Evangelical religion', published in *Knots Untied* (1874), J.C. Ryle observed that whereas everyone recognised the existence of an Evangelical party within the Church of England, many were uncertain as to its precise tenets.[10] The broader evangelical movement has suffered from the same problem, and one consequence of the evangelical renaissance of the second half of the twentieth century has been a burgeoning of definitions of evangelicalism.[11] Among the various analyses produced by historians and theologians, the most persuasive and influential proposal has been crafted by David Bebbington, who suggests that evangelicals share a theology and spirituality characterised by four features: biblicism, conversionism, crucicentrism and activism.This quadrilateral, he argues, accommodates the evolution of evangelical beliefs in dialogue with contemporary culture – whether evangelicals were conscious of cultural influences, or not. It also respects differences of emphasis and varying interpretations of the core beliefs.[12] It will be seen later that Evangelicals who shared convictions about the centrality of the Cross and the authority of Scripture might disagree strongly about the mechanics of the atonement and theories of inspiration. Grayson Carter's refinement of Bebbington's general picture, defining the Evangelical school as evangelicals 'who practised their piety within the State Church', [13] approximates to the working definition used in this book, although it is important to emphasise that the Evangelical attachment to the Church of England was one of principled commitment to a Protestant establishment, not mere Erastianism or coincidence.[14]

The phenomenon of Evangelicalism, however, entailed more than shared beliefs. Another defining characteristic for most, if not all, Evangelicals was involvement in, commitment to, or at least tacit support for, a range of Evangelical institutions. The Evangelicals maintained three weekly newspapers: the mainstream *Record*, the more popular *Rock* and the ultra-Protestant *English Churchman*, as well as the monthly review, the *Churchman*. They operated patronage trusts, schools and theological colleges. They met in local clerical and lay associations and in national gatherings like the annual Islington Clerical Meeting and the great May Meetings at Exeter Hall. Above all, they subscribed to a galaxy of societies: the institutional expression on the national and international stage of Evangelical activism. Through these voluntary societies Evangelicals sought to spread the gospel, strengthen the Church and alleviate social needs. Many were comparatively small, appealing only to sectional interests and enthusiasms. Some, however, were enormously influential, and pre-eminent among them all was the Church

Missionary Society (CMS), founded in 1799. A snapshot of the CMS in 1900 offers an insight into the might and extent of Evangelicalism in the middle of the period under discussion.[15]

The income of the CMS in 1900-01 was £350, 492. Although this represented a fall from the centenary year's record figure of £404, 906, nonetheless it was nearly three times the income of the SPG. Of the eight hundred rural deaneries in the Church of England, only fourteen failed to contain at least one parish supporting the CMS, and between a third and a half of the parishes in each diocese made a contribution to the Society. Of course, gifts varied considerably. In some parishes there was a single donation, perhaps from the incumbent. Wivenhoe, in Essex, for example, produced one gift of ten shillings, while the £7 17/8 raised by Sacombe, Hertfordshire, included £5 from the incumbent. Relatively modest totals, however, might include many small contributions through subscriptions or collecting boxes. The CMS report also reveals the social spectrum of Evangelical parishes. Clifton Parish Church raised £674 8/1, including £150 from a sale of work, while Christ Church, Gipsy Hill, produced £1910. St Peter's, Islington, one of the poorest parishes in London, nonetheless raised £155 for the CMS, and £286 came from the working-class parish of Christ Church, North Brixton.[16] This may be set against Brightlingsea with its £28 19/6 in one box from the Hon Mrs Bateman, and £116 5/ from Stanstead Abbots, with subscriptions from the Buxtons of Easneye. Clearly there were particular Evangelical strongholds. Forty of the fifty parishes in the deaneries of Sheffield and Eccleshall, for instance, supported the CMS, and the rural dean and archdeacon of Sheffield, J.R. Eyre, was a prominent Evangelical. Likewise W.H. Barlow, vicar and rural dean of Islington, presided over a deanery in which most parishes were in Evangelical patronage and in which most supported the CMS. It is striking, however, to observe the breadth of CMS support, in urban, suburban and rural parishes, from Wales and the West Country to Essex and East Anglia, and into the highly industrialized areas of Lancashire and Yorkshire. Evangelicals could make good their claim to have active support in five thousand parishes – about a quarter of the Church's total.[17]

The CMS reserved the honour of patron of the Society for a member of the Royal family. Queen Victoria headed the list of life governors, the archbishop of Canterbury was vice-patron, and the vice-presidents included all the English and Welsh diocesans, and many Irish, suffragan and colonial bishops. The president of the Society was Sir John Kennaway, Bt, MP, and a sprinkling of peers, baronets and MPs joined the clerical dignitaries as vice-presidents. Evangelicalism reached into the English élite, from the earls of Chichester and Harrowby through Kennaway and the Buxtons to millionaire businessmen like W.D. Cruddas, financial director of Armstrong, Mitchell and company.[18] The social spectrum extended through clerical dynasties like the Moules, Knoxes and Chavasses, lawyers like the Inskips, and legions of retired officers, to small businessmen like John Kensit, stationer and sub-postmaster before he became a Protestant agitator, and the myriad subscribers with their CMS boxes in East Ham, Eccleshall and Eastbourne.[19]

When Proby penned the preface to his *Annals of the 'Low Church' Party*, even he was forced to admit that although the Evangelical school 'has not a *moral* position in the Church, yet it has an *historical* one.'[20] Evangelicals, in other words, made up an acknowledged part of the mosaic of the contemporary Church of England. They were well-represented in the parishes. Despite frequent complaints about 'partisan patronage', there were Evangelical bishops, deans and other dignitaries in the Church hierarchy.[21] In their parochial work, in their voluntary societies and in their rapport with the faith and spirituality of a Protestant nation, the Evangelicals were stronger than they are often given credit for. They were, however, anxious about the beliefs and practices of Anglo-Catholicism, and uneasy about aspects of 'modern thought'. Addressing these issues in the four decades after 1890 stretched the doctrinal and institutional unity of Evangelicalism to breaking point, as will be seen below.

Notes

1 H.H. Henson, 'The Composite Book', *Edinburgh Review* 245 (London), April 1927, 240.

2 Randle Manwaring, *From Controversy to Co-existence. Evangelicals in the Church of England 1914-1980* (Cambridge, 1980).

3 Adrian Hastings, *A History of English Christianity 1920-2000* (London, 2001), 200.

4 *Spectator* (London), 25 August 1888, 1153.

5 W.H.B. Proby, *Annals of the 'Low Church' Party in England, down to the death of Archbishop Tait* (London, 1888), ii, chapters 53-73.

6 *R*, 19 November 1909, 1172; 21 April 1911, 362.
7 C. Smyth, 'The Evangelical movement in perspective', *Cambridge Historical Journal* 7 (Cambridge, 1941-3), 160.
8 H.C.G. Moule, *The Evangelical School in the Church of England* (London, 1901); G.W.E. Russell, *A Short History of the Evangelical Movement* (London, 1915); G.R. Balleine, *A History of the Evangelical Party in the Church of England* (London, 1908); L.E. Elliott-Binns, *The Evangelical Movement in the English Church* (London, 1928); A. Bentley, 'The transformation of the Evangelical party in the Church of England in the later nineteenth century', Durham PhD thesis, 1971.
9 K. Hylson-Smith, *Evangelicals in the Church of England, 1734-1984* (London, 1989); R. Steer, *Church on Fire* (London, 1998); D.W. Bebbington, *Evangelicalism in Modern Britain. A History from the 1730s to the 1980s* (London, 1989); Ian M. Randall, *Evangelical Experiences. A Study in the Spirituality of English Evangelicalism 1918-1939* (Carlisle, 1999).
10 J.C. Ryle, *Knots Untied* (London, 1874), 1.
11 Alister McGrath, *Evangelicalism and the Future of Christianity* (London, n.d.), chapter 2; Boyd Hilton, *The Age of Atonement* (Oxford, 1988), citing the 1991 edition, 8; Mark A. Noll, 'Revolution and the rise of evangelical social influence in North Atlantic societies', in Mark A. Noll, David W. Bebbington, and George A. Rawlyk (eds) *Evangelicalism. Comparative studies of popular Protestantism in North America, the British Isles, and Beyond, 1700-1990* (New York, 1994), 129-30; M. Wellings, 'What is an evangelical?', *Epworth Review* (Peterborough), September 1994, 45-53.
12 Bebbington, *Evangelicalism*, chapter 1.
13 Grayson Carter, *Anglican Evangelicals. Protestant Secessions from the Via Media, c. 1800-1850* (Oxford, 2001), 7-8.
14 P. Toon, *Evangelical Theology, 1833-56. A Response to Tractarianism* (London, 1979), 5.
15 *CMS Proceedings* (London, 1901), 3-310; *Clergy List* (London, 1900), 550-616; Frederick Burnside (ed.), *Official Year-Book of the Church of England, 1900* (London, 1900).
16 *R*, 8 November 1907, 986; J. Cox, *The English Churches in a Secular Society. Lambeth, 1870-1930* (Oxford, 1982).
17 *R*, 4 January 1907, 1.
18 David J. Jeremy (ed.), *Dictionary of Business Biography* (London, 1984), i, 860-1.
19 *Burke's Peerage and Baronetage* (London, 1969-70[105]), 431-7, 1470-1; *DNB 1941-50*, 421-3; M. Wellings, 'The first Protestant martyr of the twentieth century: the life and significance of John Kensit (1853-1902)', *SCH 30* (Oxford, 1993), 347-58.
20 Proby, *Annals*, i, v.
21 *Rock*, 22 March 1889, 9.

CHAPTER 2

Ritualism: The Causes of the Controversy

'If any man preach any other gospel unto you than that ye have received, let him be accursed.' (Gal. 1:9)

In November 1896 an article appeared in the *Churchman* on the subject of 'The Religion of the Oxford Undergraduate'. After surveying the religious scene, the author, the Revd E.N. Bennett, declared that 'the only instance of the *odium theologicum* one can remember happened in a football match between Wycliffe Hall and Cuddesdon, when a stalwart forward of the former club, with a zeal recalling the vigorous orthodoxy of the Councils period, repeatedly uttered a loud shout of "No Popery!" as he charged over his antagonists.'[1] It will be suggested that in the closing decades of the nineteenth century and the first years of the twentieth century the *odium theologicum* was not confined to the football field, nor was the shout of 'No Popery!' a harmless relic of byegone days. This was the period of the last great Victorian anti-ritualist campaign,[2] one in which ritualism was denounced from pulpits and platforms across the land and in which the press regularly reported on the 'crisis in the Church'. The purpose of this chapter is to explore the causes of the conflict between Evangelical Churchmen and ritualists, and to explain why it was so bitter.

It should be noted from the outset that Evangelicals held no monopoly on opposition to ritualism, nor was the agitation which marked the period confined to Anglicans. Evangelicalism was not synonymous with popular Protestantism, although Evangelicals cherished their place as heirs of the Reformation. Many of the accusations levelled against the ritualists by Evangelicals could come with equal force from other Anglicans or from Protestant Nonconformists, but it should become apparent that Evangelical hostility was especially deep, first, because the conflict was rooted in fundamental theological convictions, which gave it an ideological edge; secondly because ritualism touched issues basic to Evangelical piety and experience; and thirdly because theology and piety met in a battle over the identity of the Church of England. The antipathy between Evangelicalism and ritualism, therefore, was not coterminous with the agitation of the late 1890s which was dubbed the 'crisis in the Church': it both pre- and post-dated it. Since this study concerns Evangelical Anglicanism rather than general opposition to ritualism, it will place a major emphasis on theology as a cause of conflict and also explore the debate about the origins, identity and position of the Church of England. Before turning to the *odium theologicum*, however, a brief account should be given of the rise of Anglican ritualism.[3]

Ritualism in the Church of England

Many aspects of the history of the Victorian Church have been subject to revision in recent scholarship, and the development of ritualism is no exception. In place of an interpretation which emphasized discontinuity between the Oxford Movement of the 1830s and 1840s and ritualists later in the nineteenth century, it has been argued, especially by Nigel Yates, that ritual innovations and ecclesiological developments were taking place even before the publication of the *Tracts for the Times*. On this analysis, Tractarians, ecclesiologists and ritualists overlapped as elements of a broader picture of High Churchmanship in the second quarter of the nineteenth century. Tractarian theology, the work of the Cambridge ecclesiologists, the influence of romanticism and contemporary aestheticism, the appeal of Roman Catholic models, the quest for effective means of outreach to the unchurched and a reappropriation of the Catholic heritage of the Church of England fed the mid-century evolution of ritualism.[4]

The spread and distribution of ritualism, however, were far from uniform. Yates' investigation of the period 1845-74 has shown that ritualism was represented more strongly in southern dioceses than in the north of England, and that there were far more ritualists in rural parishes and small towns than in major centres of population. London had its ritualist strongholds, as did several South Coast ports and resorts like Brighton and Bournemouth, but Bradford, Salford, Sheffield and Portsmouth among the major towns and Eastbourne and Southport among the resorts were virtually untouched by the movement. The last quarter of the nineteenth century brought some changes, for instance with the work of G.C. Ommanney in Sheffield and R.R. Dolling in Portsmouth, but ritualism remained predominantly rural rather than urban. Despite the hardy myth of the ritualist slum priest, moreover, most of the successful ritualist churches in London were in the suburbs, not the slums.[5] Among the strongest bastions of ritualism were those district churches which had been Tractarian or Anglo-Catholic from their foundation and where, therefore, the congregation knew of no other tradition.[6] Churches like St Alban's, Holborn and St Peter's, London Docks came into this category, and it was here that incumbents were able to introduce the most extreme services with the support of their congregations and opposition only from Protestant parishioners and the Church Association. Ritualist incumbents in older parishes and in rural areas were less likely to succeed in promoting drastic liturgical changes without parochial obstruction. Thus J.E.B. Munson's study of the distribution of ritualism at the turn of the century indicates that although 57% of ritualist clergy were to be found in rural benefices, only 21% of those who used incense, an index of extremism, were rural incumbents. Users of incense were concentrated in the towns, with 27% in Greater London.[7] In terms of geographical distribution, although Bishop Westcott's claim that 'the Oxford Movement had nothing more than an academic hold at any time over the North of England' was something of an exaggeration, nonetheless only 80 of the 559 churches referred to the 1904 Royal Commission on Ecclesiastical Discipline were within the Northern Province.[8]

Ritualism was not a static phenomenon, so a major cause of Protestant concern was the steady spread of practices formerly regarded as extreme to the more moderate churches, combined with a move to still more elaborate services by the extremists. Alarmed Evangelicals traced the 'Romeward Drift' through the pages of the English Church Union's *Tourist's Church Guide*, published at regular intervals as a handbook to guide people to 'Catholic' services. The *Guide* increased its coverage from 2581 churches in 1882 to 8689 in 1901, with a corresponding display of 'levelling up', illustrated in the following table[10]:

Year	1882	1892	1901
Churches listed	2581	5043	8689
Vestments	336	1029	2158
Incense	9	177	393
Lights	581	2048	4765
Eastward position	1662	3918	7397

Levelling up drove, and was driven by, the ritual debate. Thus the celebrant's eastward position at the eucharist, controversial in the 1880s as indicative of sacerdotal leanings, was declared legal by Archbishop Benson in the Lincoln Judgment and thereafter was more widely adopted, even by some Evangelicals. By the early 1900s the party of advance was pressing for recognition of the full eucharistic vestments, which, the bishops claimed, were in use in 4000 churches in 1914.[11] By then the campaign had moved on to permit perpetual reservation of the sacrament for purposes of adoration, with episcopal attempts at regulation, vigorously promoted by Charles Gore, [12] being challenged by a memorial to Convocation from one thousand clergy rejecting any restriction on devotions to the blessed sacrament.[13] Ritualism was aggressive and advancing in this period, and Evangelicals complained that the ritualist camel, having intruded its nose into the Anglican tent, was trying to expel the rightful inhabitants.[14]

The figures from the *Tourist's Church Guide* serve to show the spectrum of ritualist practice, ranging from adherence to Anglo-Catholic theology with a minimum of ceremonial to adoption of medieval or Roman usages. The Romanisers were a comparatively small section of the Anglo-Catholic party, but they were vocal and determined, and the extravagance of their views brought them publicity. Evangelical propagandists were prone therefore to concentrate on the antics of the extremist minority and to assume that they spoke for the majority of Anglo-Catholic sympathisers.

Both the mood of the advanced party – Ronald Knox's 'Ultramarines' – and the bewildering variety of contemporary ritualism[15] (sometimes seen as homogeneous by hostile Evangelicals) is illustrated in Compton Mackenzie's trilogy of novels *The Altar Steps*, *The Parson's Progress* and *The Heavenly Ladder*. Mackenzie, born in 1883, was brought up by an Anglo-Catholic nanny, and Father Dolling was a family friend. He witnessed John Kensit's protest at the veneration of the Cross at St Cuthbert's, Philbeach Gardens on Good Friday 1898, worked with Sandys Wason, whose promotion of benediction provoked episcopal censure, and became a Roman Catholic in April 1914.[16] The trilogy appeared between 1922 and 1924 and the novels offer a fascinating insight into an Anglo-Catholic world of saintly High Churchmen, ecclesiastical politicians, cautious incumbents gradually introducing vestments and ceremonial, out and out Romanisers and medieval faddists, colliding as much with each other as with the bishops or the Protestants. Mackenzie captures the spirit of the extremists, the 'spikes', impatient of their cautious colleagues and taking a dare-devil delight in introducing yet more outrageous or ostentatiously Roman ritual in defiance of public opinion and episcopal rebuke. Mackenzie's hero, Mark Lidderdale, who tries to make a Cornish parish 'Catholic' overnight in the teeth of local opposition, found his counterpart in fact in the young vicar who told his horrified churchwardens: 'You are going to have everything Roman, except the Pope.'[17] The 'spikes' were men of high ideals and deep conviction, crusaders for what they regarded as Catholic truth in a sadly maimed church. Like most crusaders, they despised compromise and were in danger of relishing the battle more than the cause for which they fought. Nothing less than the Mass would satisfy them (and some went further and called for reunion with Rome), and Evangelical Churchmen realised that mere ceremonial adjustments would not suffice; the very nature of the Church of England was at stake.

Much of the popular opposition to ritualism was provoked by the rapidity and tactlessness with which changes were made.[18] Evangelicals shared this natural dislike of innovation, but their quarrel with the ritualists was more substantial. Liturgical changes had doctrinal implications, and on a whole range of theological issues the Evangelicals were at enmity with the Anglo-Catholic beliefs propagated and illustrated by ritualism.

Issues of doctrine

Source material for the doctrinal opposition to ritualism on the part of Evangelical Anglicans is plentiful and may be divided into several categories. There are the systems of dogmatic theology produced by Evangelical scholars, most notably E.A. Litton's *Introduction to Dogmatic Theology on the Basis of the Thirty Nine Articles* (1882, 1892) and H.C.G. Moule's *Outlines of Christian Doctrine* (1889), together with the more popular handbooks *The Catholic Faith* (1904) by W.H. Griffith Thomas and *English Church Teaching* (1897), edited by R.B. Girdlestone. Alongside these general works are the manuals devoted to specific issues: Griffith Thomas on Holy Communion and Hay Aitken on baptism. Books of sermons and addresses also cover aspects of the ritual controversy, as do collections like J.C. Ryle's classic exposition of Evangelical principles, *Knots Untied* (1874), and the manifestoes of Evangelical groups in the early twentieth century : Denton Thompson's *Central Churchmanship* (1911), the Liberal Evangelical volumes *The Creed of a Churchman* (1916) and *Liberal Evangelicalism* (1923), and the conservative counterblast *Evangelicalism by members of the Fellowship of Evangelical Churchmen* (1925). Last, but not least, letters and articles in the Evangelical press and speeches at clerical meetings took up the doctrinal cudgels and attacked the perceived errors of ritualism.

Turning to the conflict itself, Evangelical Churchmen of all shades of opinion often described it as a clash of two mutually incompatible systems. Litton, arguably the most learned dogmatician produced by the party in the second half of the nineteenth century, stated in the preface to his exhaustive *Introduction* that Christian theology could be divided into two schools, the Roman and the Protestant, and that Anglo-Catholicism was only the 'mutilated counterpart' of Romanism. There was, claimed Litton, no *via media* between the two systems, between the Roman religion of the Incarnation and the Protestant religion of the Atonement.[19] The same point was made by Prebendary Webb-Peploe, preaching for the Protestant Reformation Society in July 1902. According to Webb-Peploe, 'In their aim, their desire, their intention, these two systems are absolutely contrary, the one to the other. One leads to a clear intercourse with God by Jesus, and Jesus only; the other man as an interferer as between God and the soul… hinders the soul from drawing nigh to its God.'[20] As might be expected, the ultra-Protestant Church Association was still more forthright: 'The two types of doctrine set forth at the present time [i.e. ritualism and Protestantism] were entirely irreconcilable and wholly contradictory.'[21]

Although the doctrinal battle was often conceived and described in terms of complete and incompatible systems, it is possible to draw out the most contentious points, and five key areas of conflict may be identified. These were the rule of faith, justification, the Church and its ministry, the sacraments, and mechanical and spiritual approaches to religion. These areas inevitably overlapped to a large extent, but it is possible to examine them separately and in some detail to show how the Anglo-Catholic and Evangelical understandings of the Christian faith brought them into bitter opposition.

Scripture

Much religious controversy may be traced to debates concerning the rule of faith, seeking to determine the source of ultimate authority.[22] Both doctrine and practice depend upon the resolution of this question, and it formed the starting point for the dogmatic theologies produced by Evangelicals in this period, from Litton and Moule through Girdlestone and Griffith Thomas to T.C. Hammond's *In Understanding be Men* (1936), the theological handbook of conservative Evangelicalism in the student movement. On this most basic question the Evangelicals and Anglo-Catholics were in profound disagreement.

To Evangelicals, the Anglo-Catholic answer seemed closely akin to the Roman one. It affirmed the inspiration of the Bible, but placed alongside Scripture the tradition, both written and unwritten, of the Church. Scripture, it was claimed, was unsystematic and difficult to understand; indeed, most heresies had arisen due to the misuse of private judgment by the ignorant. The Bible was therefore to be read under the direction of the Church, since the Holy Spirit had inspired the Primitive Church to write the Bible and the Spirit still indwelt the Church to guide its interpretation of Scripture. The parish magazine of St Andrew's, Worthing, exemplified the ritualist point of view thus in December 1893: 'The Church did not give us the Bible that we might *each take his own religion from it*. We *take* our religion from the Church, which is living; then we *prove* it, if we will, from the Holy Bible.' The ritualist maxim was 'The Church to teach and the Bible to prove, ' with the corollary that if the Bible ever failed apparently to support the Church's teaching, the individual's understanding of the Bible must be at fault and should be corrected.[23]

This view of the rule of faith was deeply repugnant to Evangelicals. The supremacy of Scripture was an integral part of the

Evangelical creed, held by all shades of opinion within the party. J.C. Ryle set out the traditional Evangelical position in his sermon at the consecration of St Agnes', Liverpool, when he affirmed that 'The Bible is the only infallible guide.'[24] The absolute supremacy of Holy Scripture was the first of the five distinctive marks of Evangelical religion highlighted in *Knots Untied.*[25] From J.C. Ryle in 1874, the conservative tradition may be traced to the 1920s, when the same adherence to the Bible as the sole rule of faith appears in the doctrinal standards of the Bible Churchmen's Missionary Society (1923)[26] and of the Inter-Varsity Fellowship (1927).[27] Nor was this loyalty to Scripture the preserve of the conservative Evangelicals. Herbert Ryle, son of the bishop of Liverpool and an ecclesiastical moderate, addressed the Islington Clerical Meeting of 1900 on 'The Protestantism of the Church of England'. The first principle adduced by Professor Ryle was that 'Holy Scripture is the one absolute standard of Christian doctrine and conduct.'[28] Later, as bishop of Exeter, Ryle applied this principle in his censure of Plymouth ritualism for its unscriptural teaching.[29] The Liberal Evangelicals of the 1920s were less enthusiastic in proclaiming the supremacy of Scripture, because they feared that veneration for the book was in danger of obscuring the figure of Christ, but nonetheless they placed the written Word second only to the Living Word as the ultimate authority in religion.[30]

The liberal disquiet at what some were prepared to call bibliolatry[31] indicates that Evangelical adherence to the Bible was emotional as well as logical and dogmatic. Evangelical religion was soaked in Scripture, while prayer and Bible reading were the staples of Evangelical piety.[32] Scripture was a converting agency for Evangelicals, much as the sacraments were for the Anglo-Catholics. If Mark Lidderdale hoped to bring his people to Christ through the real presence and the sacrament of the altar,[33] J.C. Ryle attributed his own conversion to hearing Ephesians 2:8 read aloud in an Oxford church,[34] an experience which was echoed regularly in the annual reports of the Bible Society. Litton gave a theological underpinning to this emotional commitment to Scripture by explaining that the primary evidence that the Bible is the Word of God is to be found in the internal witness of the Holy Spirit. The Spirit in the Word and the Spirit in the heart 'answer one to the other as sound and echo, or voice to voice.'[35] Anglo-Catholics made the sacraments an extension of the Incarnation; H.J.R. Marston came close to making a similar claim for Scripture.[36] Put more simply, and at the risk of sounding trite, Evangelical Christians loved their Bible. It was to them the Word of God, the message of salvation, the source of guidance, assurance and hope. Ritualism, by apparently downgrading Scripture, struck not only at Evangelical theology, but at the emotional roots of Evangelical piety. As will be seen later, the Bible was one thread in a web of associations which held together Evangelical religion, a Protestant reading of Reformation and post-Reformation history, and English liberty. To disparage Scripture was to lay impious hands on one of the most cherished of Evangelical idols, and, as Hensley Henson warned Lord Halifax, to risk 'provoking… the Bible-venerating sentiment of the people'; people whose Protestant Evangelicalism was primarily emotional and experiential, rather than dogmatic.[37]

Confronting the ritualist point of view, many Evangelicals merely asserted that the Bible alone was the rule of faith, citing Article Six, 'that sheet-anchor of our Church', [38] as their authority. Others deployed arguments to prove the Anglo-Catholic theory to be mistaken. The claim that the Church was older than the Bible was refuted by making the obvious point that the Old Testament considerably pre-dated Christianity. It was emphasized, moreover, that the Anglo-Catholic hypothesis confused the mechanics of the process by which the gospel writers had collated and transcribed the New Testament with the original reception of the revelation which the books contained. It was undeniably true that the former process was carried out by the early Church, but the material which later formed the New Testament consisted of the original teaching of Jesus and the Apostles, teaching which was instrumental in calling the Church into being. Walter Abbott posed the question in a sermon on 'The Church and the Bible: Their Relative Authority': 'As the Word printed is identical with the Word written, so the Word written is identical with the Word spoken. Was the Church before the *Word spoken*?'[39] The Evangelical case for the priority of Scripture as the sole rule of faith thus rested on the assumption that the text of Holy Scripture was an accurate record of the original divine revelation which had created the Church. This creative revelation existed before the Church and was therefore superior to it, so the Church was the keeper of and witness to Scripture, but neither its maker, nor its author.[40]

Alongside the supremacy of Scripture, Evangelicals placed its perspicuity. The Anglo-Catholic teaching that an infallible interpreter was needed to clarify the opaque message of the Bible was met by the assertion that Scripture was quite clear enough to convey its message. What use was a revelation, asked Litton, if it was incomprehensible to all save the experts? If an infallible interpreter be required, who is to interpret the interpreters? While admitting that the Bible contained difficult passages, Litton held firmly to the belief that 'on all the essential points of faith, morals and discipline, Scripture is sufficiently perspicuous, it being presupposed that the reader brings with him a willingness to receive what it seems plainly to teach.' The basic hermeneutical principle was 'Scripture is its own authentic interpreter,' since as a uniquely inspired book it required a uniquely inspired interpreter, and no such figure existed outside the canon. Furthermore, the diversity of Scripture made it possible to use the insights of one author to explain those of another.[41]

Scriptural sufficiency was another basic Evangelical principle. Again, Article Six could be used to prove that the Bible contained all things necessary to salvation. J.C. Ryle launched a powerful attack on those who sought to supplement Scripture in a sermon entitled 'Pharisees and Sadducees', in which the ritualists appeared in the guise of the Pharisees, making void the Word of God and burying it beneath their traditions.[42] The main charge was that the ritualists obscured the gospel by adding to it, and that they failed to observe the proportions of Scripture in their dogmatic teaching. In other words, they emphasized certain truths about which the New Testament said little and neglected others about which it said a lot. According to the Evangelicals, the whole sacramental and sacerdotal emphasis of Anglo-Catholic theology and ritualist practice illustrated this, for it rested on comparatively slender New Testament foundations, while still holding the chief place in their teaching. This distressed Evangelicals like Handley Moule, for whom fidelity to the gospel meant not merely doctrine based on Scripture, but also reflecting the scriptural priorities of justification and holiness, while keeping questions of sacraments and Church order in their proper, and subordinate, place.[43]

It was not uncommon for Evangelicals to suggest that the ritualist rule of faith had been adopted for devious purposes. Griffith Thomas spoke for many when he criticised Gore's *The Body of Christ* for devoting 240 pages to a theological review of eucharistic doctrine and only 20 pages to a study of the relevant biblical passages.[44] The assumption, implicit here, but explicit in other Evangelical works, was that Anglo-Catholics knew their beliefs to be unscriptural and therefore had concocted a theory of 'Catholic' tradition to justify them. Canon Barnes-Lawrence expressed this suspicion when he complained of the 'vague and nebulous' Church to which the Anglo-Catholics always seemed to be appealing.[45] Although the accusation of deliberate deceit was unfair, it is not difficult to see how the charge might be made to seem plausible, since ritualists were prone to disregard the legal and liturgical rulings of the Church of England in favour of the authority of a very imprecise 'Catholic' tradition.

Evangelical Churchmen did not accept this definition of catholicity, nor were they prepared to abandon the term 'Catholic' to the ritualists. F.G. Llewellin, writing in the conservative volume of essays *Evangelicalism by members of the FEC* (1925), appended a footnote to the word 'Anglo-Catholic' : 'We have throughout put the term "Anglo-Catholic" in inverted commas because from our point of view the teaching of the school so designated is not English in its outlook, nor truly Catholic in its dogmatic assertions.'[46] Griffith Thomas devoted two chapters of *The Catholic Faith* to a consideration of true catholicity, giving some weight to the teaching of antiquity and to the test of the Vincentian Canon, but concluding that the vital component was fidelity to Apostolic teaching, as recorded in the New Testament. Catholicity was 'the development of Apostolic Christianity as represented in and safeguarded by the New Testament.'[47]

It can be seen therefore that the Evangelicals denied the catholicity of ritualist doctrine and practice. H.E. Ryle referred to 'the revival of medievalisms under the misused name of Catholicity', [48] and this encapsulated the position of those Evangelicals who did take antiquity seriously, the most prominent of whom was Henry Wace, dean of Canterbury from 1903 to 1924. Wace's ideal of the Church of England will be considered later, but it may be noted here that his churchmanship included a reverence for the primitive Church and a conviction that his Church stood close to the model of antiquity.[49] Unlike the founders of the Oxford Movement, the ritualists were prepared to borrow from the medieval Church and from contemporary Rome under the guise of 'Catholic' practice. Wace denied their right to do so, and as one step in the campaign against ritualism, promoted a declaration that no practice could even be admitted for consideration as Catholic if it did not derive from the first six centuries of the Christian era. Like Llewellin, Wace disliked the term 'Anglo-Catholic' and regularly referred to members of that school as 'Anglo-Romanists' instead.

There was, therefore, a basic conflict between the Evangelicals and the Anglo-Catholics on the source of authority in religion. The Evangelical position was the Protestant one captured in Chillingworth's oft-quoted dictum, 'The Bible and the Bible only is the religion of Protestants, ' while the Anglo-Catholics added tradition to Scripture as the rule of faith, and placed both under the inspired interpretation of the living Church. The stage was thus set for further divergences on other doctrinal issues.

The way of salvation

The second broad area of theological controversy, the doctrine of justification, continued to position Evangelical anti-ritualist polemic within the traditional categories of Protestant-Roman Catholic debate. In 1917 the *Record* published a series of articles by 'An Old Evangelical' under the general heading of 'Principles and Policies'. The second of these, which appeared on 20 September, set out what the author regarded as the two vital areas of principle at the heart of the Reformation: the doctrine of justification and the interpretation of the Lord's Supper.[50] Both were contentious issues between the Evangelicals and the ritualists.

Justification, as 'An Old Evangelical' observed, was a major source of dispute in the sixteenth century Reformations. Luther was widely credited with making the claim that adherence to justification by faith was the mark by which a church stands or falls ('*articulus stantis vel cadentis ecclesiae*') and Evangelical Protestantism accordingly saw the battle as one for the integrity and heart of the gospel.[51]

Dogmatic theologians were accustomed to divide justification into three parts or causes, the formal, the meritorious and the instrumental. All agreed that the meritorious cause of justification was the work of Christ, but differences appeared over the other two elements.

On the formal cause, the Roman Catholic position was that justification was creative. Grace, it was claimed, was infused into the soul at baptism, and this divine provision made sinners just and enabled them to work out a righteousness of their own. Inherent or infused righteousness made the individual worthy to be accounted just by God. Against this understanding, Protestantism affirmed that justification was entirely declaratory, that God counted the sinner to be righteous solely because of the merits of Christ imputed to human beings. No infusion of grace could make people merit justification, not least because as soon as grace touched the human soul it lost some of its efficacy through contact with human sin. As Litton remarked, so long as human beings were visibly imperfect, it was impossible to make inherent righteousness the formal cause of justification, for people were palpably unrighteous and sinful.[52]

The instrumental cause was also a source of division. Rome emphasized baptism, the rite which infused a seed of grace into the soul. Protestantism, on the other hand, maintained that faith alone was instrumental in securing to the individual the salvation won by Christ on the cross – hence Luther's choice of justification by faith as the keynote of a healthy church. The Reformer's judgment of its significance was supported by considering the consequences which the rival views of justification brought in their train. They affected the interpretation of baptism, the role of the Church, priesthood and eucharist, the doctrine of assurance and the place of sanctification. The Roman plan of salvation began with baptism and left Christians building up their own righteousness, with the assistance of the sacraments, to merit justification. Under the Protestant scheme, justifying faith was the key, and holy living was a consequence, not a cause, of acceptance by God. In Litton's words, 'The Romanist teaches forgiveness of sin through sanctification, the Protestant sanctification through forgiveness of sin.'[53]

The significance of this long-established antagonism for the ritual controversy was that Evangelicals assumed that the Anglo- Catholic school embraced the full Tridentine doctrine of justification. It has already been seen how Litton dismissed Anglo-Catholic theology as mutilated Romanism, unworthy of independent consideration. From the very beginning of the Oxford Movement Evangelicals had identified the Tractarians with Roman Catholic doctrine, and thus endeavoured to reply theologically in terms of the dogmatic categories of Reformed polemic. G.S. Faber, C.P. McIlvaine, James Garbett and C.A. Heurtley set the trend for Litton and Moule to follow. Litton in particular worked through the standard areas of debate in his lengthy section on 'The Order of Salvation', discussing effectual calling, conversion, justification, formal cause, justifying faith and assurance.[54] As late as 1902 reference was made to Newman's *Lectures on Justification* (1838) as an expression of the Tractarian belief that 'Baptism, not faith, is the primary instrument of justification.'[55] This was seen as the root of the whole sacerdotal system.

Few Evangelicals engaged with ritualism on the level of the debate about formal, meritorious and instrumental causes. Many, however, resolved the issue into simpler terms: the approach of the individual soul to God. This, like veneration of the Bible, was integral to Evangelicalism at an emotional as well as a theological level; it represented the experience of those who called themselves Evangelicals, and it summed up the essence of the gospel which they felt impelled to proclaim at home and abroad – the direct access of the soul to God through Christ, without any human mediator. Like the supremacy of Scripture, it was a tenet held across the spectrum of Evangelical opinion from traditionalists like J.C. Ryle to the modernisers like Theodore Woods and his co-authors in *The Creed of a Churchman*.[56]

Ritualism seemed to undermine this basic principle in a number of ways. The most controversial was through its revival of the practice of auricular confession. This was associated especially with Pusey, who was reputed to have taken up confession at an early stage of the Oxford Movement, and with the Society of the Holy Cross, which was responsible for the manual *The Priest in Absolution*, which provoked an uproar when it was denounced in the House of Lords in 1877. Setting aside the moral objections to the confessional, Evangelicals were quick to point out that the system imposed a barrier between the penitent sinner and God, thus obstructing 'the directness of every man's access to God, by himself and for himself.'[57] Evangelicals saw no harm in people seeking spiritual advice from the clergy; indeed, personal dealing with souls was regarded as essential, but there was a world of difference between what one Evangelical called his 'consultational'[58] and the compulsory confessional imposed by some Anglo-Catholics as a preliminary condition for confirmation and promoted as a vital element of the spiritual life.

A second obstruction came in the shape of the invocation of the saints and prayers to the Virgin Mary. A.H. Stanton's *Catholic Prayers for Church of England People* (1891), a popular ritualist manual which had sold sixteen thousand copies of its fifth edition by 1901, advocated imploring the aid of saints, monks and hermits, as well as setting out the 'Hail Mary', Litany of the Blessed Virgin and Rosary of the Blessed Virgin.[59] Walter Walsh cited examples of hymns and prayers to Mary, Joseph and other saints in an appendix to his *Secret History of the Oxford Movement*, while in 1913 the National Church League complained to the archbishop of Canterbury about a volume entitled *St Swithun's Prayer Book*, which included a prayer beginning 'I confess to God Almighty, to Blessed Mary Ever-Virgin, and to all the Saints...'.[60] That most moderate of Anglicans, Herbert Ryle, attacked both practices as unscriptural, unprimitive, uncatholic and disloyal to the Church of England. Worst of all, they undermined that 'direct communion between the soul of man and the Divine invisible Father [which] lies at the root of all genuine religion.'[64]

The final obstruction to the believer's communion with God, in the opinion of Evangelicals, arose from the very style of ritualist worship. The Evangelical ideal of worship was corporate and congregational, a meeting of Christian believers to praise God and share in fellowship one with another. Ritualism, it was claimed, produced elaborate services which reduced the laity to the status of spectators and rendered the proceedings incomprehensible by the introduction of inaudible prayers and interpolations from unauthorised books. Simplicity in worship was not merely a question of aesthetics, but of theological principles and of loyalty to the Prayer Book's purpose of a 'Common Prayer' intelligible to all.[62]

Church and ministry

The third aspect of doctrinal controversy centred on the Church and its ministry. It was here that Anglo-Catholic theology received its most colourful expression, and thus on this field that the ritual controversy raged most fiercely.

The Anglo-Catholics took up the Tractarian understanding of the Church as a visible divine society, whose continuity and doctrinal integrity were preserved by the episcopate, which stood in lineal descent from the Apostles. On this understanding, episcopal ordination was essential to a valid ministry, and therefore to the celebration of the sacraments. This position was cogently argued by Charles Gore in *The Church and the Ministry* (1888), by Walter Lock in *Lux Mundi* (1889) and by R.C. Moberly in *Ministerial Priesthood* (1897) and, although always controversial, rose to a new prominence in the aftermath of the Kikuyu Conference.[63]

The conference was a missionary gathering held in June 1913 at a Church of Scotland mission station in East Africa, and it was attended by sixty Protestant missionaries of various denominations, including Anglican CMS clergymen. Bishop Willis of Uganda presided, and plans were drawn up for increased co-operation between the different societies in the face of the challenge of Islam. After the deliberations had been concluded, Holy Communion was celebrated by the bishop of Mombasa, according to the rites of the Church of England, and the elements were administered to all the delegates.

Kikuyu provoked an immediate and hostile reaction from Frank Weston, the Anglo-Catholic bishop of Zanzibar, and from Weston's mentor Charles Gore. Weston complained to Archbishop Davidson and lodged a charge of heresy against the bishops of Uganda and Mombasa, while Gore, in *The Basis of Anglican Fellowship in Faith and Organisation* (1914), insisted that the Church must uphold episcopal ordination, restrict celebration of the sacraments to episcopally ordained priests and enforce episcopal confirmation as an essential prerequisite for receiving Holy Communion.[65]

Evangelical Churchmen had never accepted the Tractarian doctrines of the visible Church and the apostolic succession. William Goode, the foremost Evangelical scholar of the mid-nineteenth century, wrote, 'Both the Roman and Tractarian systems are founded upon one and the same fundamental error; namely that the true Church of Christ must be a body of individuals united together by external and visible bonds of union and communion, under the government of those ordained in succession from the Apostles as their bishops and pastors.'[66] Evangelicals were careful to separate the visible Church from the true Church, and to apply the New Testament notes of unity, catholicity and holiness only to the latter body. This case was argued by Henry Wace in a series of papers in the *Record* in 1889, subsequently published in a collection entitled *The Church and Her Doctrine* (1891). Wace clearly had Gore's *The Church and the Ministry* in mind as he wrote, and his reply followed traditional Evangelical lines. The true Church, he claimed, is a holy society united by virtue of its members' union with Christ. This society is not visible, first, because the institutional churches include nominal Christians; second, because the Church on earth has been obviously divided at least since the Great Schism; and third, because Christ did not establish his Church on Tractarian principles. 'The question is, ' wrote Wace, 'whether, as Mr Gore says, "Christ did not encourage His disciples to form societies; He instituted a society for them to belong to as the means of belonging to Him, "... or whether Christ and His Apostles were commissioned to invite men primarily to union with Him through His Spirit, and, as a consequence of that union, to union with each other.'[67] Griffith Thomas put the difference more succinctly: 'It is Christ Who places us in the Church, not the Church who places us in Christ.'[68] The Anglo-Catholic doctrine of the visible Church tended, in the eyes of Evangelicals, to place a human institution between the individual and God, and thus to obstruct that direct communion which was a hallmark of the Reformation and a keynote of Evangelical piety. It also seemed to tie salvation to membership of a visible ecclesiastical body, and therefore to challenge justification by faith. This was regarded as erroneous and unscriptural, as well as being the first step on the road to the persecution of dissenters, as Church history demonstrated.

Alongside the visible Church, Anglo-Catholicism placed the apostolic succession. Newman had made this the foundation of the Church's authority in the first of the *Tracts for the Times* and from it flowed the conclusion that episcopacy was of the *esse* of the Church. Gore's judgment was that 'no ministry except such as has been received by episcopal ordination can be legitimately or validly exercised in the Church.'[69]

Evangelicals were quick to point out the practical consequences of this theory. On the one hand it condemned English Nonconformity, the Church of Scotland and the Reformed Churches of Europe to the 'uncovenanted mercies of God', because these bodies lacked the essential note of episcopacy in the apostolic succession. On the other hand it brought the Church of England into communion or fellowship with Rome, Moscow, Constantinople and the episcopal churches of the East, described by Canon Hay Aitken as 'some of the most ignorant, superstitious, and even degraded types of Christians throughout the world.' This could produce ridiculous results, since it compelled English Churchmen to treat Roman Catholics in Europe as part of the true Church, while condemning them in England as agents of the 'Italian Mission', so 'A Frenchman at Boulogne is a good Catholic; at Folkestone he is a schismatic.'[70]

The attempt to confine grace to episcopal channels was strenuously resisted by Evangelicals as alien to Scripture and to the formularies of the Church of England. Hay Aitken, in his *Apostolical Succession considered in the light of the facts of the history of the Primitive Church* (1903), concluded that the bishops arose from the presbyterate and hence were not the successors of the Apostles. Bishops were the executive officers of the Church, commissioned to bear authority on behalf of the whole body of Christians and empowered to recognise by ordination in the name of the whole Church gifts already bestowed by God upon certain individuals.[71] The Anglo-Catholics made episcopacy the essential note of the Church, whereas the Evangelicals stressed fidelity to apostolic doctrine. Anglo-Catholics regarded ordination as the transmission of grace from the bishop to the priest, whereas Evangelicals saw the episcopal role as giving official recognition to grace already bestowed. Anglo-Catholic theory brought the Church of England into line with Western Catholicism and the Orthodox East, but the Evangelicals had little time for either and numbered among their heroes the American Congregationalist and lay evangelist D.L. Moody.[72] In one of the *Kikuyu Tracts* (1914), A.J. Tait gave a judicious summary of the Evangelical position: '... for those who regard the principles of the English Reformation as a sacred trust of English Churchmen, Episcopacy is not essential to valid ministry. On the other hand, as one expression of historic order and continuity, and as offering a necessary basis for the ultimate reunion of Christendom, the historic Episcopate must be preserved.'[73] This was as far as most Evangelicals were prepared to go.

Baptism

A fourth focus of debate, linked to Church and ministry, was provided by the sacraments. The sacrament of baptism was a longstanding bone of contention between the Evangelicals and the High Church school, including the ritualists.[74] W.H. Griffith Thomas explained the differences to an enquirer in the *Record* in August 1909, and, as usual, stated the opposing views with epigrammatic clarity: 'To the first [High Churchmen] baptism is the first implantation of spiritual life *ex opere operato*. To the latter [Evangelicals] it is "the grafting into the body of Christ's church," or the introduction of one who is already presumably alive into a sphere (the church of Christ) where, nourished by the milk of the Word and through the appointed ordinances, he grows into spiritual maturity.'[75]

The High Church position, therefore, rested on automatic baptismal regeneration. The Prayer Book declaration 'Seeing now... that this Child is by baptism regenerate...' provided justification for a viewpoint held not merely by ritualists, but by old fashioned High Churchmen of the school of Henry Phillpotts and Samuel Wilberforce. The ritualists took this traditional doctrine and restated it exuberantly in their popular manuals, often in the form of hymns to be learned by children. Thus one Yorkshire school used a hymn including this verse:

'So by this Baptismal Portal,
While our Ancient Adam dies,
Forth we come to life immortal
And a Kingdom in the skies.'[76]

In reply, the Evangelicals attacked the foundations of the High Church doctrine in Scripture and the Prayer Book. They could cite the Gorham Judgment of 1850 to prove that their interpretation of the Anglican formularies was allowable, but they sought to go beyond this and to refute the High Church case. To base the doctrine of baptism on isolated statements in the Prayer Book, claimed Barnes-Lawrence, was as unwarranted as taking the biblical reference to 'the man Christ Jesus' out of context and becoming a Socinian on the strength of it.[77] The whole principle of the liturgy was the presumption that its users were genuine Christians who meant what they said, for no liturgy could be framed on other grounds. The language of the Prayer Book was therefore that of charitable presumption – the service presumed that parents and sponsors took their vows seriously. If so, the child could expect regeneration, but this did not prove that all baptised children would be regenerated automatically.[78]

On theological grounds the debate turned on the nature of regeneration. Hay Aitken identified it with the new birth, the essential requirement for entering the Kingdom of God.[79] This was the 'great change' beloved of Evangelical devotional works, the assurance of forgiveness, salvation and peace with God. The significance for the baptismal controversy was that Evangelicals expected the new birth to be followed by a new life of holiness. 'We affirm confidently,' wrote J.C. Ryle in his delineation of Evangelical religion, 'that "fruit" is the only certain evidence of a man's spiritual condition, ' and he listed six scriptural marks of regeneration: an avoidance of habitual sin, a belief in Christ as Saviour, holiness of life, special love for other Christians, willingness to go against the opinion of the world and a scrupulous attention to the well-being of the soul.[80] These features were not apparent in the lives of many people who had been baptised, and therefore it was argued that baptism could not automatically guarantee regeneration. Hay Aitken asked 'whether men who possess none of the characteristics, and have passed through none of the spiritual experiences, which New Testament writers attribute to all members of the Church, can be part of this mystical Body of Christ, just because a certain ordinance has been performed upon them, perhaps in the most perfunctory and mechanical way.'[81]

Together with the theological and liturgical debate went a pastoral and evangelistic concern which added a sharper edge to the conflict. Evangelical Churchmen regarded the doctrine of baptismal regeneration as a spiritual sedative liable to lull the unregenerate into a false sense of security. Addressing the Plymouth Clerical and Lay Conference in 1901, the Revd Westley Bothamley, rector of St Leonard's, Exeter, claimed that ritualist teaching made it impossible to preach conversion to the baptised because they were already counted as part of the Church and truly 'in Christ'. They were taught to rely on good works as the way of salvation and to shun the doctrine of assurance as 'Methodism'.[82] Hay Aitken, as superintendent of the Church Parochial Mission Society and thus an experienced evangelist, took the same line: 'I affirm that it is becoming increasingly common to meet with people who are proof against the preaching of conversion, because they have been taught to believe that they are already regenerated.' Baptismal regeneration *ex opere operato* was a spiritual menace, a 'deprivation of the souls of the people of living truth' and a real danger to their eternal welfare.[83]

The doctrine of baptism was a crucial area of difference between the genuine Evangelicals and the so-called 'Catholic Evangelicals'. According to Dieter Voll, the mid-nineteenth century witnessed the emergence of a synthesis of the Evangelical and Oxford Movements.[84] This synthesis, 'Catholic Evangelicalism', combined parochial missions, preaching for conversion and high sacramental doctrine. It was associated with Bishop G.H. Wilkinson and the Wednesbury school of Richard Twigg, George Body and Charles Bodington, and also influenced the work of the ritualist slum priests Mackonochie, Stanton and Dolling. Stanton, curate at St Alban's, Holborn, from 1862 until 1913, held weeknight meetings with revivalist hymns and extempore prayers, while his first biographer, G.W.E. Russell, recalled that 'The constant – indeed the invariable – topics of his preaching were sin and forgiveness; the love of God towards the sinner, and the sinner's need of the cleansed heart, ' all standard Evangelical subjects, somewhat marred however by 'the guaranteed access to the Lord through the Sacrament of the Altar, and the reverent love due to the Blessed Mother of God.'[85] Addressing the ECU on 'The common creed of Catholics and Evangelicals', Russell affirmed 'If ever in my life I (an Evangelical born and bred) have heard the doctrines of sin, repentance, free grace and pardon through the Blood of Christ set forth with unflinching plainness, it has been from the pulpit of St Alban's, and by the lips of Arthur Stanton.'[86]

Some more recent studies of nineteenth century revivalism have called Voll's thesis into question, suggesting that the ritualists borrowed their techniques from Roman Catholic missioners rather than from Evangelical revivalists.[87] In its reviews of Russell's biography of Stanton and Mason's of Wilkinson, the *Record* did not claim either as Evangelicals: Wilkinson was described as a High Churchman who held to baptismal regeneration, while Stanton was dismissed as a ritualist eccentric who 'had no real point of contact with the distinctive principles of the Church of England.'[88]

Hay Aitken addressed himself to the problem of 'Catholic

Evangelicalism', appropriately, since his father had been associated with Twigg of Wednesbury.[89] He was willing to give some High Churchmen credit for sincerity and spirituality, but pointed out that their attempt to hold spiritual religion and baptismal regeneration together forced them to separate regeneration (seen as sacramental) from the experience of conversion. This separation, he claimed, was unscriptural and misleading, and still produced missions which urged people to become more religious when what they really needed was to be born again. Baptismal regeneration, according to Hay Aitken, was an impediment to spiritual High Churchmanship, forcing it to distort the biblical picture of the new birth, and tending always to suffocate true spirituality beneath the weight of *ex opere operato* dogma and sacerdotal systems.[90] High Churchmen could not evade the problem that their doctrine of baptism absolutely precluded the preaching of the full Evangelical gospel. Hay Aitken would have seen 'Catholic Evangelicalism' in Voll's sense of the phrase, therefore, as a sterile hybrid, if not a contradiction in terms.

The eucharist

In the preface to his study of *The Doctrine of Baptism*, Hay Aitken acknowledged that this rite was not the main source of contemporary controversy.[91] The debate centred on the other dominical sacrament, known variously as the Lord's Supper, the Holy Communion, the eucharist or the Mass, for it was this service which attracted the bulk of ritualist innovations; indeed, for which most of the ornaments and vestments were designed. The issue at stake was three-fold: the status of the minister, the purpose of the service and the location of the eucharistic presence of Christ.

One of the clearest statements of the extreme ritualist position on eucharistic priesthood was offered by the Revd W.J.E. Bennett, sometime vicar of St Paul's, Knightsbridge, and a leading protagonist in an earlier phase of the controversy, in his evidence to the Royal Commission of 1867. The exchange between Bennett and the commissioners was used by several Evangelical pamphleteers as a summary of ritualist opinion, and this version appeared in A.E. Barnes-Lawrence's *A Churchman and His Church* (1917):

'"Do you consider yourself a sacrificing priest?"

"Yes."
"In fact, *sacerdos*, a sacrificing priest?"
"Distinctly so."
"Then you think you offer a propitiatory sacrifice?"
"Yes, I think I do offer a propitiatory sacrifice."'[92]

Although not all Anglo-Catholics would go so far as Bennett with regard to the propitiatory nature of the eucharist, it was a feature of their theology that the Christian minister was a priest and fulfilled in some sense a sacrificial and mediatorial role. In this understanding of priesthood was to be found the basic principle of sacerdotalism.

Evangelical Churchmen flatly rejected the sacerdotal idea. James Denton Thompson, expounding moderate Evangelicalism in *Central Churchmanship* (1911), bluntly declared that 'An order of vicarious priests, that is of priests acting instead of Christ or men, in necessary mediation, is in plain contradiction to the teaching of the New Testament.'[93] In this the future bishop of Sodor and Man echoed other moderate Evangelicals on the episcopal bench – so Herbert Ryle, preaching an ordination sermon in Exeter Cathedral in September 1902, said of his ordinands, 'Theirs is no mediator's function to obscure the functions of their Divine Master. Theirs is no sacerdotal office of formalism...'[94] Among the less moderate Evangelicals, the Revd W.H.K. Soames produced a pamphlet which asked *Is Sacerdotalism Scriptural?* (1903), and concluded not only that it was not, but that it was 'the most formidable enemy of the Gospel of Jesus Christ that the world has ever seen.' For good measure, Soames rounded off his diatribe with a point by point comparison between 'an official priest' and 'a minister of the Gospel'.[95]

To some extent the argument concerned biblical interpretation and the question of scriptural support for a mediatorial priesthood. Here the Evangelicals were able to draw on the formidable scholarship of J.B. Lightfoot, whose *Dissertation on the Christian Ministry* in his commentary on *Philippians* (1868) must rank as one of the most quoted works in late nineteenth century Evangelical polemic. Lightfoot simply stated that 'The Kingdom of Christ has no sacerdotal system' and 'The sacerdotal title is never once conferred on the ministers of the Church'.[96] Griffith Thomas described this as a simple, striking and significant fact,[97] one which Anglo-Catholic theologians were hard-pressed to explain away.

Beside Evangelical indignation at the alleged introduction of unscriptural theories of the ministry, however, must be placed a deeper anger at the implications of sacerdotalism. Herbert Ryle's Exeter sermon touched on these causes of Evangelical disquiet and he spoke for all sections of the school. A mediatorial priesthood, in Evangelical eyes, derogated from the unique priesthood of Christ, obscuring, in Bishop Ryle's words, the functions of the divine Master. J.C. Ryle made the same point in his pamphlets *Have you a priest?* (1871) and *What do we owe to the Reformation?* (1877). Concentration on priestly mediation, moreover, threatened to distract the clergy from their true role of preaching the gospel. Griffith Thomas noted that while a sacerdotal caste was singularly devoid of New Testament support, there was a strong emphasis on the prophetic, preaching ministry. Such work, he claimed, was essential to the health and growth of the Church,[98] and in this he reflected the traditional Evangelical stress on preaching as a converting and edifying ordinance, and one logically prior to the sacraments.[99] Furthermore, the existence of a priestly caste seemed to undermine the position of the laity and to encourage them to leave the work of the Church to the ordained professionals.[100]

The most pernicious consequence of sacerdotalism according to the Evangelicals, however, was that it denied the priesthood of all believers by intruding a human mediator between the Christian and God. 'No subject can be more important, ' wrote the Revd Andrew Given to the *Record* in November 1902: 'the way of approach, as revealed by God, of man – sinful man – to God. This is at the bottom of all the controversy between "Evangelicals" and "Ritualists".'[101] The liberty of access to God through Jesus Christ, or, in other words, the universal priesthood possessed by all Christians, was, as Denton Thompson wrote, one of the fundamental principles of Evangelical Churchmanship.[102] Sacerdotalism blocked the way and so denied that freedom of approach, that open road to the throne of grace, which was one of the most precious blessings of the Reformation.[103] By abolishing the priesthood of all believers it threatened to make religion vicarious and second-hand, to replace spiritual communion for all with the performance of cultic functions by a few on behalf of everyone else.

In claiming to offer a propitiatory sacrifice W.J.E. Bennett was not speaking for all Anglo-Catholics. The propitiatory nature of the eucharist was a Roman Catholic doctrine; most ritualists preferred to speak in terms of a sharing in the perpetual offering of Christ, following Moberly's description of the eucharist as 'the Church's divinely ordained ceremonial method of self-identification with the perpetual offering of the atoning sacrifice of Christ.'[104] As Christ, the great high priest in heaven, offered himself to God to atone for the sins of the world, so human priests presented an earthly counterpart in the form of the Christian eucharist. Anglo-Catholic teaching varied somewhat, but common features were the God-ward nature of the sacrifice, the concept of re-presentation or sharing in the sacrifice of the Cross, and a belief that this was warranted by the Prayer Book and by the New Testament.

Insofar as ritualism proper was concerned, the doctrine of the eucharistic sacrifice lay behind several ritual practices, especially the adoption of the eastward position by the celebrant and the use of the vestments. The former was widely regarded as indicative of a sacrificial interpretation of the eucharist, and although it was declared legal by the Lincoln Judgment,[105] most Evangelicals continued to celebrate at the north end of the Communion table for that reason.[106] The vestments were still more clearly sacrificial in meaning.[107] Episcopal attempts to deny any significance to these garments provoked the *Record* to interview a selection of High Churchmen, and the results were published in May 1908 under the heading 'Why I wear the vestments'. Of the twenty-one clergymen interviewed, one replied facetiously that he had been wearing 'vestments' ever since birth for reasons of common decency, but many spoke more seriously of doctrinal continuity with the Catholic Church. Most were not interested merely in a distinctive garment for Holy Communion, and hence ritualists generally were dismissive of proposals to compromise by authorising a white vestment midway between the surplice and the chasuble. Not all went so far as Father Leeper of Devonport, who claimed to be 'saying Mass' as effectively as the bishop of Rome, but there was a consensus in favour of eucharistic vestments for doctrinal, rather than purely aesthetic reasons.[108]

As with baptism, Evangelical Churchmen responded to the Anglo-Catholic standpoint on several levels. Evangelicals rejected the biblical and liturgical evidence for the eucharistic sacrifice. On a more practical level, they deplored the implications of

Anglo-Catholic eucharistic theology which, by emphasizing the sacrifice, tended to undervalue or even to deny the importance of Communion. This was especially noticeable with the growth of the practice of non-communicating attendance, and with the development of Children's Eucharists, services to which children were taken to watch the performance of the sacrifice. As T.W. Drury complained, 'The sacrament which Christ ordained is being neglected by reason of a sacrifice which He never even named.'[109] The people were being denied the blessings of Communion, and once again it seemed that spiritual religion was being undermined and replaced by a sacerdotal system. Barnes-Lawrence told his congregation:

> 'As soon as the transition is made from the observance of the Lord's Supper as a thankful remembrance of the completed Sacrifice of Calvary to a perpetual repetition of that sacrifice by a sacerdotal priesthood, at once its whole character is altered. The meaning of the death of Christ is inevitably obscured, its gospel weakened. The earthly re-presentation of the sacrifice becomes the important thing... If the Lord's Supper is veritably a sacrifice, Christianity is changed from a spiritual religion to a series of carnal ordinances.'[110]

The third controversial aspect of Anglo-Catholic theology on the eucharist concerned the doctrine of the real presence. Some ritualists were prone to see the debate simply as a quarrel between those who affirmed a real presence (i.e. themselves) and the advocates of a Zwinglian theory of the 'real absence'. Evangelical Churchmen certainly believed in a real presence, but disagreed strongly with the Anglo-Catholics about its nature and location.

Stated in terms of sober theology, the Anglo-Catholics held to a real, objective presence of the body of Christ in or under the elements of bread and wine. The body thus present was Christ's glorified body (i.e. his post-resurrection form), and the presence was brought about by priestly consecration. As justification for this belief, Anglo-Catholics cited Christ's words, 'This is my body, ' spoken at the Last Supper. Their teaching developed from the 1860s under the influence of Littledale and Robert Wilberforce, so that by 1900 it could be summarised in an ECU Declaration which stated

> 'that in the Sacrament of the Lord's Supper the bread and wine, through the operation of the Holy Ghost, become, in

and by Consecration, according to our Lord's institution, verily and indeed the Body and Blood of Christ, and that Christ our Lord, present in the Most Holy Sacrament of the Altar under the form of Bread and Wine is to be worshipped and adored.'[111]

Evangelicals thought that this understanding of the eucharistic presence was perilously close to the Roman doctrine of transubstantiation. According to Griffith Thomas in *A Sacrament of our Redemption* (1905), it was based on a misunderstanding of the words of institution, for the full sentence was 'This is my body given for you, ' and therefore Jesus was speaking of his death.[112] Hence, Griffith Thomas argued, the elements represent not the glorified body but the body broken and blood shed upon the cross and Holy Communion is not a technique for conjuring up a special presence of Christ, but a reminder of the fact of the Atonement and a pledge to faithful Christians of the salvation that has been accomplished at Calvary. Handley Moule wrote of the elements that: 'They are our title-deeds of the peace and life we possess through the crucified Body and shed Blood of the Great Sacrifice.'[113]

Although they rejected the Anglo-Catholic view of a glorified Christ present in the elements, Evangelicals were anxious to repudiate charges of Zwinglianism. 'Where we differ, ' declared Denton Thompson, 'is not in the truth, but in its definition; not in the fact of the Lord's presence, but in its location.'[114] The Evangelical understanding was that Christ was really present to the faithful communicant, a receptionist standpoint which they shared with older High Churchmen and which had been expounded by Waterland in his *A Review of the Doctrine of the Eucharist*.[115] Anglo-Catholic theology tended towards virtualism, and in the hands of Bennett and G.A. Denison went so far as to claim that the wicked receive Christ in the elements, a clear contradiction of Article Twenty Nine.[116]

As with other issues, however, it was ritualist practice as much as Anglo-Catholic theory that infuriated Evangelical Churchmen. Ritualist manuals often stated the doctrine of the real presence in a way which Evangelicals regarded as materialistic and idolatrous; thus *St Swithun's Prayer Book*, which attracted the hostile attention of the National Church League in November 1913, included this hymn:

'O see ! within a creature's hand
The vast Creator deigns to be,
Reposing infant-like as though
On Joseph's arm or Mary's knee.'

Likewise, the *Altar Book for Children* urged the young at the Prayer of Consecration to 'Try and be very still... Jesus is now coming.'[117]

The first decades of the twentieth century witnessed a growth in the practice of reservation of the sacrament and, among extreme ritualists, the increasing use of exposition and benediction. This seemed to be a logical corollary of the doctrine of the objective real presence in the elements, as the Sheffield ritualist G.C. Ommanney observed, [118] but it was a deep affront to Protestant principles. At the height of the reservation campaign, which gathered momentum during the First World War, one thousand clergymen petitioned Convocation at its February session in 1917 against any restrictions on devotions to the blessed sacrament.[119] The Protestant Reformation Society responded by declaring reservation to be 'Inconsistent with the teaching of the New Testament, subversive of the spirit and principles of the Reformation, contrary to the clearly expressed doctrine of the Established Church, the outcome of a grossly materialistic conception and inseparable from idolatry.'[120]

At this juncture Bishop Winnington-Ingram attempted to persuade the episcopate to remove the restrictions on access to the reserved sacrament. The bishops, he said, 'might just as well have stood in Palestine in the path of fifty thousand people who thought our Lord was in a certain house, as resist what is at least the same number of people who wish to lay their burdens at His feet today.'[121] In this, however, the bishop of London provided confirmation of many Evangelical fears about the Anglo-Catholic doctrine of the real presence. There seemed to be a craving for a tangible presence of Christ in the form of a consecrated wafer to the detriment of a full grasp of the universal presence of the Holy Spirit. Devotions to the blessed sacrament could be distorted into a belief that Christ was present in the tabernacle and absent from every other area of church and life.[122] Handley Moule warned the London Clerical and Lay Evangelical Union in May 1917 that a consciousness of divine omnipresence and reliance on the indwelling Spirit were in danger of being replaced by regular visits to Jesus in the tabernacle, [123] and this was an affront to the doctrine of the Holy Spirit.[124]

Conclusion: mechanical versus spiritual religion

Underlying the often technical controversies about the rule of faith, the doctrine of justification, Church and ministry, and sacramental theology, and at the risk of seeming overly to simplify a set of highly complicated doctrinal disagreements, it might be maintained that most of the theological antipathy directed at Anglo-Catholicism by Evangelical Churchmen stemmed from the belief that ritualism represented an unspiritual system of religion. The perceived conflict between mechanical and spiritual Christianity provides a framework into which many of the specific doctrinal issues may be fitted, and reference to the Evangelical criticisms of most points of Anglo-Catholic theology will show that it was seen as basic to the controversy. This fifth aspect of the debate located anti-ritualism firmly within the matrix of Evangelical piety and spirituality, giving a popular and populist dimension to issues which could otherwise be perceived as narrowly academic.

Canon Hay Aitken elaborated the theory of two systems in *The Mechanical versus the Spiritual: Two Contrasted Conceptions of the Christian Religion*, published in 1899. As in his later work on baptism, he was prepared to give credit to many High Churchmen for genuine spirituality, but his fear was that 'Good men in all ages have proved better than their systems; but the man passes away, while the system remains, and does its own mischievous work long after the good man and his personal influence have been forgotten.'[125] The mechanical theory was that '*God has been pleased to attach the powers of the Holy Ghost to certain mechanical acts accompanied by the recital of particular formulae, so as to produce consequences of a distinctly supernatural order, whenever these mechanical conditions are complied with.*'[126] It rested on the apostolic succession, the guarantee that grace flows automatically and exclusively through episcopal channels. It implied automatic baptismal regeneration *ex opere operato*. It conferred upon a duly ordained priest, however sceptical or morally lax he might be, the power to work the miracle of the Mass, and delivered into his hands the power of the keys through the sacrament of penance. At each stage and in each rite visible actions were of primary importance, whether the bishop's imposition of hands in ordination or confirmation, the consecration of the elements or the priest's absolution in the confessional. This emphasis on externals had its natural concomitants in elaborate ceremonial for public worship and an obsession with the minutiae of ritual regulations: Evangelicals might recall the Ipswich clergyman who was summoned one afternoon to administer Holy Communion to a dying parishioner. Determined to preserve the rule of fasting communion, but lacking easy access to the reserved sacrament, he sent a colleague to scour the countryside by car in search of a church which did practice reservation, and even contemplated extending the quest as far as London.[127] Essentially it seemed that faith had been abolished and replaced by a religious system; in the case of ritualism, by a system of automatic sacramental grace, neatly summed up in the booklet *A Catholic Child*, discovered in a Lincolnshire church in 1913 by a disgusted Evangelical:

'A Catholic child am I,
And this is the reason why –
'Tis Jesus who told me I must be so,
If I'm to be saved and to Heaven would go,
And Baptism made me to be I know
  A Christian Catholic child.

'A Catholic child must make
Confessions for Jesus's sake;
For he will be happy and safe for Heaven
If only his sins can be all forgiven
So here is a sacrament, one of seven,
  For every Catholic child.

'A Catholic child will die,
His flesh in the grave will lie;
His soul will be safe if he's done his best,
If he with the sacraments has been blessed
There's nothing to fear, but a soul at rest
  For every Catholic child.'[128]

Even should the 'Catholic child' have any problems with purgatorial fire beyond the grave, these could be solved by the Church's prayers and masses for the faithful departed.

Most of the reasons for Evangelical opposition to and abhorrence of this approach to Christianity have been considered already: the scriptural evidence against Anglo-Catholic doctrine, the shaky historical foundations of the apostolic succession, the arrogant unchurching of spiritual Nonconformists, the apparent undermining of conversion and living faith. It remains only to note, therefore, that beneath the specific historical and theological arguments, at the level of fundamental doctrine and basic Christian experience, Evangelical Churchmen detested the sacerdotal, mechanical system they ascribed to the ritualists for three reasons.

The first was the antithesis between mechanical Christianity and the core Evangelical principle of justification by faith, or free access to God for each individual on account of the completed work of Christ on the cross, appropriated by faith. Handley Moule, a saint as well as a scholar, wrote of 'direct spiritual contact with the always accessible Lord, ' of 'an isolation to God, in the immediate intercourse of the regenerate soul with Him.'[129] This was the bedrock of Evangelical experience, in the last resort independent of ecclesiastical institutions, sacraments and clergy. This experience made Evangelicals resist with all their might any attempt to confine the grace of God to human channels.

Secondly, Evangelicalism laid a heavy emphasis on spiritual religion. 'Spiritual men and spiritual methods for spiritual work' was a well-tried party motto, and this meant seeking the reality of inner faith rather than worrying unduly about externals. Evangelical Churchmen were not careless about the externals of religion, but what really mattered was the disposition of the heart. Ritualism would assure a man who had been baptised and confirmed that he was 'in Christ'; the Evangelical would seek to find out if he had been born again and only then enquire about the church's rites. The story was told in Evangelical circles of the man who called on his vicar, a High Churchman, and told him of his conversion. The vicar promptly attributed this to the steady growth of the seed implanted at baptism, to which the man replied that he had never been baptised and had called in order to remedy the deficiency.

It was an Evangelical conviction that ritualism turned people away from spiritual religion by substituting a sacramental system. In doing so, moreover, the ritualists were offering another gospel, a gospel of good works which fitted in with the natural human tendency to seek self-justification before God. J.C. Ryle, always a vigorous controversialist, declared that the natural man always drifted away from the true path of spiritual religion and faith into works and idolatry. Ritualism, like Romanism, offered an ideal system for such people, and therefore was deeply dangerous.[130] V.F. Storr, the leading theologian of Liberal Evangelicalism in the years between the World Wars, held that Anglo-Catholicism substituted mechanics for dynamics, and that extreme ritualism tended towards magic.[131]

The third and final affront offered by mechanical religion to basic Evangelical principles concerned Christian holiness. Although the Evangelicals preached and taught justification by faith, they were by no means unaware of the moral demands of the Gospel. Whether traditional Calvinists like J.C. Ryle or advocates of Keswick ideas like Moule and Griffith Thomas, they paid much attention to the importance of seeking perfection. Here ritualism was at fault in Evangelical eyes because it seemed to concentrate on ceremonial rather than holy living, and to restrict religion to activities within the church building. 'So long as ritualistic worshippers can turn from matins and early communions to races and operas, and can oscillate between the confessional and the ball-room, ' wrote Ryle, 'so long the advocates of ritualism must not be surprised if we think little of the value of ritualistic worship.' Barnes-Lawrence made precisely the same point – twice – blaming fashionable ritualist churches for the moral decadence of the West End in *A Churchman to Churchmen* (1893) and again in *A Churchman and his Church* (1917).[132]

Ritualism in a Protestant Church and Nation

Evangelical antagonism to the ritualists began to move from issues of doctrine to questions of morality over the position of the Church of England and the right of Anglo-Catholics to exercise a ministry within it. The debate had its roots in theology, because contrasting interpretations of the Reformation and of the doctrinal stance of the Church were underlying causes of disagreement, but to many Churchmen these considerations were submerged beneath a sense of moral outrage that clergymen who flouted the apparent standards of Anglican practice should continue to enjoy the Church's emoluments. Before turning to the moral argument, however, some attention must be given to the issue of competing ecclesiologies.

Interpreting Anglicanism

Evangelicals venerated the Reformation, regarded the Church

of England as a Reformed Church and prided themselves on being the most faithful exponents of Reformation principles. Their veneration may be seen in tracts like J.C. Ryle's *What do we owe to the Reformation?* (1877), which listed the many benefits, spiritual, moral and material, of the religious movements of the sixteenth century. 'Whatever England is among the nations of the earth as a Christian country,' wrote Ryle, 'whatever political liberty we have, – whatever light and freedom in religion, – whatever purity and happiness there is in our homes, – whatever protection and care for the poor – we owe it to the Protestant Reformation.'[133] In *Knots Untied*, Ryle repeated the claim, developed originally in response to Tractarianism, that Evangelical principles represented the true doctrines of the Reformed Church of England. There was, therefore, an identification in the minds of many Evangelicals between the historic and authentic position of their Church and the particular doctrines emphasized by the Evangelical school. They were prepared to tolerate Broad and old-fashioned High Churchmen, but still believed that theirs was the most faithful exposition of the Anglican ideal.[134]

A sophisticated analysis of that ideal was presented by the leading Evangelical scholar and loyal Churchman, Henry Wace, in a series of essays, articles and pamphlets. Wace's Church of England was Catholic, Apostolic, Reformed and Protestant, and this four-fold description reflected the strands of teaching which had been woven together to form the national Church. One strand was the supremacy of Scripture as the Church's rule of faith, a vital principle upheld by the Reformation. A second strand was the consensus of the primitive Church, for Wace believed that the legacy of the Fathers was to be respected, albeit under the guiding eye of the Bible: 'In a word, the basis of authority in the Church of England is the Holy Scriptures; but she acknowledges that the decisions of the first four General Councils on matters of doctrine are in conformity with those Scriptures, and she therefore voluntarily accepts them as part of the law to which her children are to submit.'[135] Wace gave the Tractarians credit for their fidelity to the Fathers, but criticised them for undervaluing the Reformation and thus for veering away from the distinctive Anglican High Churchmanship of the Bull-Beveridge-Hook tradition and turning instead to Rome.[136] The Reformation was thus the crucial third strand, because it represented a return to the primitive ideal and because it reaffirmed the right of national churches to settle non-essential matters of ritual for themselves. The Church of England took advantage of this right to establish a liturgy as close as possible to primitive models in the form of the Book of Common Prayer. Wace's Church, therefore, was scriptural in doctrine, Catholic in practice and English in character. Its genesis was 'the practical result of the English mind, working on the primary truths of the Christian faith, the deep spiritual experiences of the Reformation and the special features and needs of the national character.' The liturgical expression of this Anglican Churchmanship and the measure of its Catholicity was the Prayer Book.[137]

Wace's comprehensive apologia for the Church of England did not represent in every detail the views of all Evangelicals. His attitude to the Fathers, for example, was more positive than that of many members of the school, who were suspicious of any authority other than that of Scripture. There was a consensus, however, on the position of the Church of England as part of the communion of Reformed Churches and, more significantly, a growing Evangelical appreciation of the Prayer Book.

The Book of Common Prayer had not always been popular among Evangelicals, many of whom regretted that it had not been more thoroughly reformed in the sixteenth century. There was some pressure for a Protestant revision after the Gorham Case, while Lord Ebury's Association for Promoting a Revision of the Book of Common Prayer campaigned for the same end between 1854 and 1889.[138] To Evangelicals of J.C. Ryle's generation, Anglicans who emphasized the Prayer Book were usually Tractarians, and in controversy it was essential to insist on interpreting the Prayer Book in the light of the Thirty Nine Articles.[139] Strict Evangelicals, like the Revd James Clare in Hardy's *Tess of the D'Urbervilles*, 'despised the Canons and Rubric [and] swore by the Articles', [140] for this was the safeguard against Tractarian attempts to use the liturgy to justify doctrines like baptismal regeneration.

A changing Evangelical attitude may be discerned towards the end of the nineteenth century. In contrast to the caution of his late diocesan in *Knots Untied*, T.J. Madden, one of Ryle's archdeacons, offered this undertaking when preaching to the National Protestant Church Union in May 1903:

'The bishops may accept this assurance from Evangelicals as

a whole, that we accept the Book of Common Prayer; we love its sobriety of diction, its deep spirituality of tone, its doctrinal fidelity to the Word of God.'[141]

By 1907 Canon Henry Lewis could claim that the Prayer Book backed Evangelical Anglicanism,[142] while the main contention of Denton Thompson's *Central Churchmanship* (1911) was that Evangelicals represented the authentic mainstream of Anglican thought and tradition.[143]

This realignment of Evangelical opinion was made possible by a shift in the Anglo-Catholic position with regard to the Church and its liturgy, as Tractarian reverence gave way to ritualist ridicule. In one respect there was continuity between the Oxford Movement and ritualism, in that both disparaged the Reformation and wished to separate the Church of England from continental Protestantism. Following in the footsteps of Hurrell Froude, the parish magazine of St Mary's, Dorchester, described the Reformation as 'a spiritual blight… [which] all but wiped out the religion of our Most Holy Redeemer and the Gospel of His Grace, ' while Lord Halifax declared that 'the principles of the Reformation are things to be repented of with tears and in ashes.'[144] At the time of the First World War, Anglo-Catholic clergymen were quick to link German barbarism with Protestantism and the lack of the historic episcopate. 'Made in Germany' became a term of abuse, used to denounce the Reformation.[145]

As well as this continuity of criticism, however, there was a marked contrast in attitudes to the Prayer Book and to the Church of England. Tractarians prized careful adherence to the Prayer Book and praised the Church of the Caroline divines, but ritualism had little time for either. One ritualist Order described the Book of Common Prayer as 'new and mutilated', [146] and the whole tenor of ritualist practice was towards substantial interpolation to bring the liturgy closer to that of the Sarum or Roman Missals. Ritualists believed that the Prayer Book was defective, and campaigned for a large measure of revision – initially for permission to use the 1549 liturgy and then for 'Catholic' practices to be included in the revised book under official discussion from 1906. While campaigning in Convocation, ritualists in the parishes introduced the practices of their choice almost at will. St Cuthbert's, Philbeach Gardens, held a veneration of the Cross on Good Friday; St Saviour's, Hoxton, adopted the Roman festival of Corpus Christi and from the early 1910s until 1927 conducted services entirely in Latin; benediction at St Michael's, Shoreditch, 'sounded for all the world as if one were at the Brompton Oratory, ' according to the *Daily Chronicle*.[147] The Royal Commission report of 1906 sought to separate the minority of flagrant Romanisers from the vast majority who 'honestly believe that the Ornaments Rubric covers many of the practices, and that other practices, not being expressly prohibited in the Prayer Book, are permissible.'[148] Evangelical Churchmen seldom made this distinction, and even when they did, they regarded moderate ritualism as wilful distortion of the Prayer Book, even if less offensive in its results than full-scale Romanising.

Ritualists thus attacked the Reformation and seemed to scorn the Prayer Book. Some also mocked the Church of England, treating it with open contempt, so, for example, Harry Wilson of St Augustine's, Stepney, told an ECU meeting, 'I was an Anglican once myself, ' at which the audience laughed. Anglicanism, the pride of the Tractarian *via media*, had become a joke and an embarrassment to the Romanising clergy.[149] Wace was bitterly critical of ritualism for what he regarded as its spurious Catholicity, and much of his hostility to the Prayer Book revision proposals derived from his belief that genuinely primitive practices were being replaced by medieval accretions. At the height of the Kikuyu controversy in 1913, when Bishop Weston's *Ecclesia Anglicana: for what does she stand?* attacked the twin tendencies of pan-Protestantism (represented by Kikuyu) and Modernism (represented by *Foundations*), Wace published a critique of Weston's pamphlet in the *Record*. Weston appealed to the bishops of East and West for authority in the Church, to which Wace replied by censuring the bishop for overlooking the example of Jewel and Hooker, whose appeal was to the primitive Church of the first six centuries.[150]

It may be seen that Evangelicals and Anglo-Catholics had different understandings of Anglicanism. To the Evangelicals, the Anglo-Catholic point of view was illegitimate, and represented a denial of all that the Church of England stood for as a Reformed communion. This in turn posed the question of whether it was morally right for ritualists to hold benefices in the Established Church.

Moral suspicions

The standard Evangelical answer to this question was that ritualists were at best stretching their consciences and at worst committing perjury by making the statutory declarations accepting the Prayer Book and Articles. H.E. Ryle regarded the reintroduction of transubstantiation, adoration of the Blessed Virgin and prayers for the dead into the services of the Church of England as 'the betrayal of a sacred trust', [151] while it was a regular practice of Protestant or Evangelical speakers to compare the clergyman's oath to uphold the Articles and Prayer Book with the word of a businessman upon which commerce and reputation depended. Thus Sir John Bingham, former Master Cutler of Sheffield and president of the Church Association's Northern Council, said that ritualism was 'a case of simple business morality.... A man should not be Romanising the Church of England and at the same time taking her pay.'[152] Ritualists, it was claimed, were setting an example of defying the law which bore comparison with the behaviour of the strikers of 1912 and of the suffragettes of the same period.[153]

One natural outcome of this attitude was that ritualists who took the step of seceding to Rome were always applauded for their honesty. The resignation of H.M.M. Evans, vicar of St Michael's, Shoreditch, in 1903 was treated in this light. Evans resigned when the bishop of London ruled that his doctrines of the real presence and invocation of the saints were inadmissible in the Church of England.[154] On this occasion Evangelicals were able to praise Evans and attack the ECU at the same time, because the Union suggested that Evans should have abandoned his controversial practices while retaining his private beliefs and his benefice. There was a similar response in 1910 when two Brighton incumbents, Arthur Cocks and H.F. Hinde, left their benefices after a disagreement with the bishop of Chichester.[155] The *Record* took some satisfaction in reporting an exchange of insults between G.C. Ommanney, vicar of St Matthew's, Sheffield, and a seceding curate, S.B. Thorp, which took place in August 1890. Ommanney, 'greatly disturbed' by the secession, denounced Thorp from the pulpit of St Matthew's for committing the 'most grievous sin of schism'; Thorp retorted in the *Sheffield Telegraph* that Ommanney was duplicitous for teaching the sacrifice of the Mass after subscribing the Articles.[156]

It might be thought that charges of immorality were merely Evangelical propaganda, but it would seem that there was a genuine and wider sense of grievance that clergymen were disregarding the Church's standards and the law. Hensley Henson, by no means an Evangelical, warned Lord Halifax that the ostentatious contempt for the law shown by some ritualists was giving High Churchmen a bad name and alienating the general public. The layman, wrote Henson, 'respects the law, and is really shocked that his clergyman does not.'[157] Portrayals of clerical dishonesty appeared in the popular press – for instance in Mary Cholmondeley's novel *Red Pottage* (1899) and Joseph Hocking's *The Soul of Dominic Wildthorne* (1908) – and Henson attributed the popularity of Walter Walsh's *The Secret History of the Oxford Movement* (1897) to the author's success in 'fastening on the High Church clergy the hateful accusation of religious duplicity, and so raising against them the ignorant, but essentially righteous manliness of average Englishmen.'[158] This aspect of the controversy linked ritualism with the wider debate over clerical subscription and the ethics of belief, an issue which provoked considerable discussion in the late nineteenth century as Christians sought to reconcile biblical criticism and natural science with traditional creeds and orthodoxy.[159]

Three further charges levelled against the ritualists on moral grounds may be mentioned here. The first concerned effeminacy, an accusation which perhaps arose from the close and intimate friendships of the Tractarians. By the 1890s the disapproval felt by Charles Kingsley for the 'die-away effeminacy' of Tractarianism had become abuse of ritualists as 'priests in petticoats'.[160] John Kensit, the Protestant agitator, told the Great Protestant Demonstration at the Queen's Hall in 1898 that the congregation of St Cuthbert's, Philbeach Gardens, consisted of 'very poor specimens of men (laughter).... They seemed a peculiar sort of people, very peculiar indeed.' Kensit roused the meeting to cheers when he declared: 'Dear friends, we want ministers of the gospel to be manly men.'[161] The hint of sexual aberration was taken up in popular literature, most notoriously in J.F. Bloxam's story 'The Priest and the Acolyte', published in a student magazine in December 1894, but also in Evelyn Waugh's *Brideshead Revisited* and in Mackenzie's *The Altar Steps* (1922).[162] The accusation of effeminacy clearly had propaganda value for Kensit and his colleagues; for mainstream Evangelicals it served rather to emphasize the un-Englishness of ritualism.[163]

The same might be said of the second moral charge, which related to conventual institutions. Protestant suspicion of convents had a long pedigree and the nineteenth century witnessed several attempts to secure State inspection, culminating in C.N. Newdegate's successful motion for a House of Commons Select Committee on Conventual and Monastic Institutions, which was passed in March 1870.[164] The Convent Enquiry Society was still working to the same end in the early 1900s, while the Protestant Reformation Society had an itinerant lecturer, Emma Miller, touring the West Country speaking on 'Rome's Prison Houses'.[165] Indignation at ritualist convents reached its highest pitch with the publication of *The Secret History of the Oxford Movement* in 1897, because Walter Walsh devoted a whole chapter to 'Ritualistic Sisterhoods'. This cast doubt on the financial integrity of the Orders and described in detail the humiliations inflicted on the Sisters to teach them obedience.[166] Walsh's account of the scourging of women was taken up and related with horror by a variety of Protestant orators, including the Presbyterian MP Samuel Smith and the intemperate polemicist the Revd James Mortimer Sangar.[167]

The third, and most serious moral charge, however, concerned the confessional. For Evangelicals, as has already been seen, confession was wrong theologically because it obstructed the believer's free access to God. It was also unmanly, because it abrogated personal responsibility. To these arguments, however, must be added deep suspicions about the potential abuses of the practice. The confessional, it was claimed, struck at family life by subjecting domestic affairs to the scrutiny of an outsider. Moreover it raised the spectre of lascivious clergymen interrogating women about matters of sexual morality, a prospect guaranteed to send a frisson of delighted horror down the spine of late-Victorian propriety. From the shrill polemical end of the Evangelical spectrum, James Mortimer Sangar denounced a system of religion 'that revels in the moral filth of the confessional',[168] while Prebendary Webb-Peploe, a respected Evangelical leader, called habitual confession 'filthy and degrading'.[169] No specific incident in this period aroused such a public outcry as the exposure of *The Priest in Absolution* in 1877, but there were a series of minor scandals when Anglo-Catholic clergymen attempted to impose confession as a condition for confirmation.

In 1907, for example, an East End vicar was accused of advocating confession to two teenage girls. The manual he provided for his confirmation candidates included such statements as 'I have indulged impure thoughts' and 'I have done shameful things with others', and the charges reached the correspondence columns of *The Times*.[170]

Hostility to auricular confession was not an Evangelical monopoly. Although some of the precise theological objections arose from the distinctive emphases of Evangelical religion, the moral antagonism to the practice was widespread and reflected an anti-Catholic tradition deep-rooted in the English national character. It is time to set ritualism in the context of the wider 'No Popery' strand in English society and to show how ritualism drew down upon itself generations of Protestant hatred, the fruit of an inheritance in which Evangelical Churchmen took a full share.[171]

No Popery

The Roman Catholic MP, J.F. Maguire, wrote in 1870: 'Judge the Pope by the prevailing belief of Protestant England, derived from the misrepresentations of the Press, its platform, or its pulpit, and one beholds in him a combination of temporal despot and spiritual imposter, at once the scourge of an afflicted people and the archpriest of Satan.'[172] In the mind of popular Protestantism Rome was first and foremost a political institution, seeking world domination. For Protestant pamphleteers, this made conflict between Rome and Great Britain inevitable, since Vatican tyranny could only succeed through the destruction of the British Empire. They were not surprised, therefore, when Rome supported the Boers, and Papal intrigues were detected behind the outbreak of the First World War.[173] Rome, moreover, represented a religious system which was at once superstitious, unbiblical, unscientific and irrational, so the Curia was naturally authoritarian and the enemy of liberty, science and free enquiry.[174] As a result, to many Protestants, Roman Catholicism meant despotic government, with all the apparatus of censorship and persecution of dissent represented by Index and Inquisition, combined with economic stagnation and intellectual bankruptcy. Finally, Rome was the Anti-Christ, the fountain of idolatry, whose fall was foretold in the biblical prophecies.[175]

Although this caricature of Roman Catholicism was neither

held in its entirety nor articulated explicitly by many English people in the late nineteenth and early twentieth centuries, large sections of the community accepted a substantial portion of the traditional picture. Rome's temporal claims were taken seriously and indignantly rebutted by Gladstone in *The Vatican Decrees* (1874)[176] and there was controversy over the hierarchy's attempt to stop mixed marriages through the *Ne Temere* decree.[177] The Vatican's automatic hostility to intellectual liberty was assumed and condemned by Herbert Ryle, [178] and then given new prominence by the suppression of Modernism after 1903.[179] The economic backwardness associated with Roman Catholicism seemed to be proved by examining Southern Europe, and especially by comparing Ireland with the rest of the United Kingdom. As the Home Rule issue became increasingly bitter, Unionist politicians joined Protestant orators in praising prosperous Ulster, denouncing Roman Catholicism and beating the Orange drum as loudly as possible. 'Home Rule is Rome Rule' made a powerful electioneering slogan and, until interrupted by the outbreak of war in 1914, it was a major plank in the Unionist campaign to defeat Asquith's Liberal government.[180]

At the level of instinct, anti-Catholicism resolved into a conviction that Romanism denied all that was represented by 'England' – the Protestant religion, freedom of speech, civil and religious liberty, progress, civilisation and prosperity. Romanism was alien, and hence easily linked in Protestant propaganda to effete Latins, brutal Huns or homicidal Fenians, depending on the political opportunities of the moment. This alien system, moreover, seemed to be gaining ground with the passing of Home Rule and the amendment of the Coronation declaration against Roman doctrines, and with an influx of foreign priests, monks and nuns substantial enough to be described by the *Record* in 1904 as 'The Roman Invasion'.[181]

Ritualism and anti-Catholicism

The use of 'No Popery' sentiment against ritualism was almost as old as the Oxford Movement itself, for one of the first responses to the *Tracts for the Times* had been Professor Faussett's University Sermon on *The Revival of Popery* (1838).[182] It has already been seen that Evangelical theologians of the calibre of William Goode and E.A. Litton equated Anglo-Catholic and Roman doctrine and proceeded to treat them as parts of a single dogmatic system.[183] This equation seemed to be entirely justified, since the ritualists taught many Roman doctrines, wore Roman vestments, used Roman service books and manuals of devotion and advocated reunion with the Holy See. Those who could not wait for reunion simply seceded – forty eight members of the ECU went over to Rome between 1890 and 1903.[184] As well as a trickle of individual secessions there were some more spectacular departures. In 1913 the entire Anglican Benedictine community on Caldey Island became Roman Catholic, [185] and the resignation of H.M.M. Evans in 1903 led to the departure of three hundred members of the congregation of St Michael's, Shoreditch, to the nearest Roman church, in which seventy were subsequently confirmed.[186] Evangelicals were content to accept the judgment of Hugh Benson, a seceding member of the Community of the Resurrection: 'It is this High Church teaching that is building the bridge over which Anglicans will come into the true fold.'[187]

There were two basic Evangelical interpretations of the relationship between Rome and the ritualists. The first, which made up in ingenuity for what it lacked in accuracy, was an elaborate conspiracy theory whose most articulate and successful exponent was Walter Walsh. 'The great object of the Ritualistic movement from its very birth, in 1833, ' wrote Walsh, 'was that of *Corporate* Reunion with the Church of Rome, ' and he traced the 'Romeward drift' through sixty years of Tractarian history and through the devious machinations of numerous secret societies, producing a best-seller in the process.[188] The same view was taken by Lady Wimborne in *The Ritualist Conspiracy* and by James Mortimer Sangar, who attributed the whole Oxford Movement to the Romanising plots of a 'band of deceitful schismatics'.[189] The conspiracy theory of the Oxford Movement received its most labyrinthine exposition, however, in *An Address presented to... Parliament... shewing by indubitable evidence and by revelations of the Holy Spirit, the 'treachery' and 'offence' unto God and extreme danger to our Queen, our Church, and our Country, of the Church Patronage Bill* by the Revd Thomas Berney, rector of Bracon Ash. Berney's *Address* appeared in 1895 and represented a late example of the hardy literary genre of the Jesuit plot. Relying rather more on 'revelations of the Holy Spirit' than on 'indubitable evidence', he concluded that Rome was infiltrating the Church of England with convent-born Jesuits who were directing ritualist secret societies. They were assisted by such carefully concealed co-religionists as Bishop Temple of London.[190] Ridiculous as this particular example may seem, in its more moderate form the conspiracy theory had considerable support.[191]

Walsh and his colleagues were mistaken in their analysis because they failed to take account of the sheer variety of contemporary ritualism. There were keen advocates of corporate reunion, like Lord Halifax, whose robust speech to the ECU in February 1895 urging 'Do not let us be afraid to speak plainly of the possibility, of the desirability of a union with Rome. Let us say boldly that we desire peace with Rome with all our hearts' caused particular alarm among Evangelicals and seemed to provide evidence of the Romanising aims of the Union. Many Anglo-Catholics, however, rejected Roman doctrines and most repudiated Papal infallibility.[192] The aggressive Romanisers of the Society of St Peter and St Paul were only a small element of the whole party, and it may be noted that the Society of the Holy Cross was very hostile to seceders.[193]

Those Evangelicals who were less prone to detect conspiracies honeycombing the Church were prepared to accept that most ritualists were not deliberately undermining the Church of England. They argued though that the tendency of ritualism was, albeit unwittingly, towards Rome. Archdeacon Hughes-Games cited Cardinal Vaughan's sermon 'England's Conversion', in which it was stated that 'The very doctrines stamped in the Thirty Nine Articles as fond fables and blasphemous deceits, all these are now taught from a thousand pulpits within the establishment, and are as heartily embraced by as many crowded congregations.'[194] Even when ritualists sincerely believed that offering 'Catholic' teaching and worship within the Church of England was the best antidote to Romanism,[195] it was alleged that all they were doing was cultivating a taste for the Roman system. Ultimately those reared on ritualism would desire the full 'Catholicism' which only Rome itself could offer. As Dr Barnardo told the annual conference of the Women's Protestant Union in June 1902, 'There was no third course between Bible Protestantism and unconditional surrender to the Apostate Church.'[196] The correspondent of the *Record* who proposed that the abbreviation 'EP' (i.e. eastward position) in clerical advertisements should stand for 'emasculated Popery'[197] was making the same point, that ritualism was trying to stand on a slippery slope or, to change the metaphor, to balance precariously astride the 'line of deep cleavage between the Church of England and that of Rome.'[198] The provenance of seceders proved the point to the satisfaction of Evangelicals, whatever the *Church Times* might claim about the loyalty of Anglo-Catholics. Whether deliberate or not, Evangelicals were sure that ritualism was a Trojan horse, a Roman fifth column, within the Established Church.

Undermining the Church

The equation of ritualism with Popery helps to explain the virulence of the 'Church crisis' of the late 1890s and early 1900s and the alliance between Evangelicalism and popular Protestantism. Evangelicals were as influenced by the 'No Popery' tradition as anyone else in the period – arguably more so than many, given their ideological commitment to Protestant theology. As well as contributing to the depth of emotional hostility to ritualism, however, anti-Catholicism provided another weapon for Evangelical controversialists in the form of the alleged impact of Romish (and hence unpopular) ritualism on the mission and position of the Church of England.

Where the Church was strong, claimed Evangelicals, ritualism threatened to undermine it by alienating the spiritually-minded. Barnes-Lawrence affirmed that the Church was losing 'a large number of the most spiritual, active and intelligent members' because of the reversion to pre-Reformation teaching on the part of the Anglo-Catholics.[199] A stream of reports in the Evangelical press supported this contention – thus the *Record* gave an account of a Presbyterian church in the diocese of Chester in which thirteen of the sixteen church officers were ex-Anglicans, and of a Sheffield parish where the arrival of a ritualist incumbent provoked the building of a Free Church of England by a wealthy parishioner.[200] Ritualists 'work havoc, emptying churches and filling chapels, ' claimed the Revd N.F. McNeile in May 1912.[201]

Although the Evangelicals were using the accusation of unpopularity as a weapon against ritualism, there was a genuine sense of grievance and alarm at the transformation of religion at parish level which could be brought about by an aggressive Anglo-Catholic incumbent. Compton Mackenzie, whose sympathies lay with ritualism, described in his autobiography how Sandys Wason, epitome of the 'spikes', emptied the parish church at Cury,[202] thus providing a model for Mark Lidderdale's conflict with his Cornish congregation in *The Heavenly Ladder*. A gradual process of 'levelling up' or the establishment of ritualism in a new church could proceed without much controversy, but the sudden introduction of Roman devotions into an Evangelical or moderate parish could provoke a haemorrhage into Dissent, and this worried not only Evangelical Churchmen but also the older Tractarians, who deprecated the haste and tactlessness of the ritualists.[203]

If ritualism could not hold existing congregations, it was argued, still less could it attract the unchurched masses. The nineteenth century was a great age of church extension and of evangelism, as all the main denominations sought to keep pace with the rising population and the development of new urban areas. The proclamation of the gospel was a major part of the *raison d'être* of Evangelicalism – J.C. Ryle had engraved upon his pulpit at Stradbroke the text 'Woe unto me if I preach not the Gospel' – and active evangelism was deemed essential to any well-worked Evangelical parish. The Evangelical commitment to this work may be seen especially in the careers of Hay Aitken, founder of the Church Parochial Mission Society, and of J.E. Watts-Ditchfield, who began regular Men's Services while curate at St. Peter's, Highgate Hill, in the 1890s, went on to revive the parish of St James the Less, Bethnal Green, and ended his career as first bishop of Chelmsford. Watts-Ditchfield, even more than Hay Aitken, represented the Evangelical mission to the urban working classes.[204]

The Evangelical belief that ritualism did not appeal to the masses, especially to working men, was to some extent an article of faith: a natural corollary of the claim that ritualism was un-English and alien. Having made the assertion, some sought retrospective explanations. J.C. Ryle declared in *Knots Untied* that an empty church was an inevitable consequence of the failure to preach the gospel of justification by faith, [205] while the Revd B. Herklots suggested that ritualism was incompatible with the democratic spirit of the twentieth century, besides, of course, being vulgar and foreign:

> 'The over-dressed priest has a good deal in common with the over-dressed woman. Excessive ritual can never become

really indigenous, not only because it is medieval as opposed to primitive or modern, but because it is foreign as opposed to British. It may be suitable for the national characteristics of Italy, Spain or France, but it is certainly nothing but exotic in England.'[206]

Ritualism's inability to win the working classes, especially working men, to Christianity was, however, not solely a product of imaginative Evangelical animosity. The 1902-03 survey of London church attendance confirmed the charge levelled by Protestants as diverse as John Kensit and Archdeacon Sinclair that ritualist churches attracted women and children rather than men.[207] The myth of the ritualist slum priest dies hard, but evidence shows that the most extreme churches were not to be found in the poorest urban districts. Of fifty six ritualist churches in London in 1900, J.E.B. Munson has calculated that 70% were situated in well-to-do areas and 21% in areas of mixed affluence, and even these churches drew their support from the wealthier sections of the local community. Only five churches were located in poor districts.[208] There were successful slum priests, like Arthur Stanton and Robert Dolling, and there were successful ritualist churches with working class congregations, like St Katherine's, Rotherhithe, but they were a tiny minority of the total, and they were dwarfed by the Evangelicals of Islington, Bethnal Green and South London. Jeffrey Cox's study of the borough of Lambeth has shown that there was one conspicuously successful ritualist church, St John the Divine, Kennington, in a poor district, but that the Evangelicals more than matched this with St Andrew's, Lambeth and Christ Church, North Brixton.[210] When Henry Lewis, who spent twenty years as rector of Bermondsey, living in a parish of twenty four thousand as the sole resident clergyman (even the London City Missionaries refused to live there), said that Anglo-Catholicism could not reach the common people, he spoke from experience. In Evangelical eyes that experience was reinforced by the work of the YMCA, Pocket Testament League and other evangelistic agencies during the First World War. A simple evangelical message seemed most effective in winning the troops for Christ, while Evangelical chaplains reported the unpopularity of ritualist services.[211]

As well as allegedly repelling the working classes, ritualism had a disastrous impact on relations between the Church of

England and the Protestant Nonconformists. Anti-Catholicism on the part of the Dissenters was met by episcopal exclusivity from the Anglo-Catholics. Even in its moderate form Anglo-Catholicism unchurched Protestant Nonconformists and handed them over to the uncovenanted mercies of God.[212] As for the extremists, one speaker at an ECU meeting in 1917 was reported to have said that 'No Nonconformist desires the Body and Blood of Christ... No Nonconformist has in his own body ever received more than bread and wine, and until instructed in the faith and practice of the Catholic religion he is incapable of discerning the Lord's body.'[213] According to Hay Aitken, one High Church bishop made it a rule for members of his communicants' union that they should never enter a Dissenting place of worship;[214] a story given some confirmation by the Congregationalist, the Revd Morley Wright, who related how he had once offered shelter in his church porch to a young man caught by a thunderstorm, only to be told that it was a dissenting conventicle and house of schism which he, a member of the Confraternity of the Blessed Sacrament, could not enter.[215]

It may be appreciated that such attitudes did little to promote co-operation between the Church and the Nonconformists, and this at a time when Churchmen were increasingly taking up the issue of Home Reunion. The Lambeth Conference of 1888 called for unity on the basis of the Scriptures, the Nicene Creed, the two dominical sacraments and the historic episcopate, and although the Free Church response was unenthusiastic, the quest for unity continued, fostered especially by the Grindelwald Conferences, organised by the Wesleyan Henry Lunn, and by the work of the Student Christian Movement. The SCM was highly effective in bringing Churchmen and Nonconformists together, and the Edinburgh Missionary Conference of 1910 spanned a wide range of ecclesiastical outlooks, from the Free Churches to the High Anglicans of the SPG. It was, of course, missionary co-operation which prompted the Kikuyu scheme three years after the Edinburgh Conference.[216]

Ritualism was not sympathetic to Home Reunion – significantly and symbolically, Mark Lidderdale began his incumbency at Nancepean by discontinuing the custom of joint Harvest Festivals with the Wesleyans, for 'there was not to be any running in double harness with the dissenters.'[217] As the ECU speaker of 1917 said, Nonconformists needed instruction in 'the faith and practice of the Catholic religion', and there could be no question of modifying Church teaching to accommodate Nonconformist opinion. A practical consequence of this attitude was that when Bishop Percival invited representative Free Churchmen to Holy Communion in Hereford Cathedral as part of the Coronation celebration of 1911, local ritualists responded by holding a Mass of Reparation. Frank Weston's strictures on the dangers of 'pan-Protestantism' in the aftermath of Kikuyu have already been noted.[218] Small wonder then that when the bishops of London and Chelmsford addressed the Wesleyan Conference of 1917, the Methodists showed no inclination to move towards formal links with the Establishment. One Somerset Wesleyan said that the Methodists had too much experience of suffering through trying to uphold Protestantism in the villages. The *Record* commented: 'The Church pays a heavy price for harbouring within its borders men whose sympathies are more Roman than English, and part of the cost would seem to be the refusal of Wesleyan Methodists to confer with the Church with a view to unity.'[219]

There was no single Evangelical attitude to Home Reunion. Traditionally Evangelicals had worked with Protestant Nonconformists in organisations like the Bible Society and the London City Mission, and on many essential doctrines the two groups were in agreement. By emphasizing the invisible nature of the true Church, however, Evangelicalism tended to discount organic unity,[220] and some Evangelicals continued to disapprove of Dissent, perhaps partly as self-protection against charges of lax Churchmanship. At the time of the Kikuyu controversy there was criticism of Evangelical Churchmen for their failure to support the principles of the scheme, and Dawson Walker complained that the initiative had been left to Hensley Henson, who set out the case for Kikuyu in *Quo Tendimus?* (1913) and went on to advocate the exchange of pulpits, himself preaching at the Congregationalists' City Temple in 1917.[221] Walker was one of a group of Evangelicals who did take reunion seriously, a group whose main spokesman was H.A. Wilson. As rector of Cheltenham from the end of 1915, Wilson was instrumental in establishing the Cheltenham Conference in the following year. This became an annual gathering of representative leading Evangelicals, who met to discuss a topic of contemporary interest and to produce an agreed statement, called the Cheltenham 'Findings'.

The 'Findings' of the second conference affirmed the place of Protestant Nonconformists as 'members of the Church of Christ equally with ourselves', recognised Nonconformist ministers, orders and sacraments, and applauded moves towards greater co-operation. The goal of such co-operation, declared the 'Findings', should be 'some form of federation rather than anything like organic reunion.'[222] Nonetheless, the Cheltenham statement indicated that some Evangelicals were keen to go beyond simple spiritual fellowship to co-operation on Kikuyu lines. Such aims were obstructed by the principles and behaviour of the ritualists.

Evangelicals who were not very interested in Home Reunion for positive reasons were still alarmed by the impact of ritualism on the Nonconformist attitude to the Church of England because it was held that ritualism was largely responsible for driving spiritual Nonconformists into the arms of political Dissent, and therefore for creating, or at least exacerbating, the challenge to the Establishment and the controversies over education.[223]

On disestablishment the Evangelical charge was that ritualism roused the feelings of a Protestant nation against the legal, moral and religious scandal of Romanism in the Church of England, while sapping the will of loyal Churchmen to defend an Establishment which many of them regarded as veering towards apostasy. These points were made time and again in Evangelical pamphlets of the period. Archdeacon Hughes-Games, in his published address to the Yorkshire Evangelical Union, quoted Dean Farrar: 'Disestablishment will be one of the consequences of the triumph of ritualism… There are myriads of Englishmen, and not a few even among the clergy, who will not stand a Church of England which shall have become Romish in all but name..'.[224] Both Bishop Alford and the Revd J.M. Sangar maintained that the English episcopate was helping the Liberation Society by allowing ritualism to flourish, a point to which some credence may be given when it is noted that in 1908 the Society was making propaganda use of *A Catechism for Catholics in England* which listed Baptists, Presbyterians, Congregationalists and Wesleyans under the general heading of 'false religions'.[225] In a leading article on 'Disestablishment' in February 1907, the *Record* commented: 'Up to a few years ago, when the offences of some extreme clergy began to excite fresh animosity against the Church, the cause of Disestablishment appeared to be losing ground, so far that the existence of the Liberation Society was a circumstance rather for the humorist than for the serious student of affairs.'[226] Ritualism had apparently transformed a diminishing threat into a growing menace.

This menace was especially prominent against the backdrop of the campaign for the disestablishment of the Welsh Church.[227] Welsh disestablishment became Liberal party policy in 1887, but made little Parliamentary progress until the Campbell-Bannerman administration took office in 1905. It was clearly on the Liberal agenda in the early 1900s and, following a Royal Commission to investigate the Welsh Church, two bills were put forward. The first, and more drastic, proposal was introduced in 1909, but disappeared in the political conflict over Lloyd George's budget. A new bill was brought in three years later, and although rejected by the House of Lords, was able to pass under the provisions of the 1911 Parliament Act. It received the Royal Assent in September 1914, but its implementation was delayed for the duration of the First World War, and even then there were modifications in the form of an Amending Act in 1919. Thus Welsh Church affairs played a significant part in politics from 1905 onwards, and the issue of disestablishment was never far from the minds of Churchmen.

P.M.H. Bell's study of *Disestablishment in Ireland and Wales* (1969) does not cite ritualism as a reason for Welsh hostility to the Church, but Evangelicals certainly held the ritualists responsible for at least some of the ill feeling. The *Record* noted the use made of the report of the Royal Commission on Ecclesiastical Discipline by Lloyd George, [228] and when Charles Gore defended the ritual practices at St Aidan's, Small Heath, in September 1906, a leading article headed 'The Bishop of Birmingham's Challenge' accused Gore of appearing as the champion of 'all that has created the new-born animosity against the Church which threatens her position in Wales…'[229] The threat of disestablishment provoked by ritualism was raised and reiterated throughout the period, from J.C. Ryle's warnings in *What do we owe to the Reformation?* (1877) to the fears of Sir William Joynson-Hicks that approval of the revised Prayer Book might reawaken Nonconformist hostility to 'an officially Romanized Establishment'.[230]

The second major cause of controversy between the Church

of England and the Nonconformists was education. Until 1902 the conflict raged on locally elected School Boards;[231] Balfour's Education Act abolished the Boards, but itself proved to be a fruitful source of fresh grievances because it was claimed that the Act unduly favoured Church schools. The Liberals introduced a series of education bills from 1906 onwards, which served to keep the controversy at fever pitch, and did much to embitter relations between Evangelical Anglicans and their Free Church brethren.[232]

Free Church unease at the prospect of ritualist teaching in Church schools may be traced back at least to Wesleyan opposition to Graham's factory education proposals of 1843. Even before Balfour's Act, Nonconformists were unhappy about the views being propagated by Anglo-Catholic clergymen in village schools. The Revd Morley Wright, in his address to the Church Aid and Home Missionary Society, *Home Idolatry and Home Missions* (1892), told his fellow Congregationalists of a day school in Yorkshire where the children were taught baptismal regeneration.[233] At the height of the debate over the 1902 Act, it was reported that one school in Dorchester forced children to bow to a crucifix and concluded each school day with the 'Hail Mary'.[234] Balfour's Act heightened Nonconformist anger by paying State subsidies to Church schools. Free Churchmen therefore campaigned against the 1902 Act, organised 'passive resistance' to the education rates, and lobbied the Liberal government after 1905 for new legislation. The campaign drew together a broad coalition of denominations and mobilised mass support for petitions and demonstrations. The well-known Keswick Convention preacher F.B. Meyer spoke for many who were anxious 'to protect the children from anti-Protestant instruction at the expense of the State.' Meyer cited the Royal Commission report as evidence of the opinions held by some Anglican clergymen, opinions which no Nonconformist would wish to be taught to his children. He called for the enforcement of non-denominational Bible teaching, as ordered in Board schools by the Cowper-Temple compromise.[235]

The education issue divided Evangelical loyalties. Some – a minority – were content with Cowper-Temple teaching, arguing that the Bible alone was an adequate foundation for Christianity. Most, however, agreed with Wace and Bishop E.A. Knox that the Liberal proposals would be injurious to Church schools and that they should be resisted. Both groups agreed in laying much of the blame for the dispute and its consequent bitterness at the door of the ritualists. Ritualism was a propaganda god-send to political Dissent, wrote J.N. Worsfold.[236] Watts-Ditchfield held the ECU responsible for the 1906 education bill, while Henry Wace recalled six years later the popular fears of ritualist teaching which he had encountered as he toured the country speaking on the education question.[237] Free Churchmen felt under attack, and as late as 1938 the Methodist Education Committee was justifying the retention of 121 day schools 'for defence against the propaganda of Anglo-Catholics and Romanists'.[238]

Most Evangelicals agreed that ritualism had serious consequences in terms of the Church's mission and in relation to education and disestablishment. Some were prepared to hold the ritualists responsible for a wider range of evils, and these may be mentioned briefly. As part of the National Mission in 1916, Churchmen were asked: 'What do you consider the chief causes which hold back the Church of England from being a greater spiritual force and more courageous witness than it is in the country?' Sir Edward Clarke, president of the National Church League, replied, 'The entire absence of discipline in the Church, the disregard by large numbers of the clergy of the law of the land, the Canons of the Church, and their own ordination vows, and the encouragement of this disobedience by Archbishops and Bishops.'[239] W.R. Mowll attributed neglect of Sabbath observance to ritualism,[240] while the Church Association autumn conference of 1903 heard how ritualism (admittedly the South African variety) had provoked the Boer War by upsetting the Dutch Reformed Church.[241] A.S. Lamb, chairing the spring conference of the Association in March 1900, preferred a more direct explanation – the South African War, he asserted, was a judgment on Britain's toleration of idolatry in the national Church.[242] A Protestant meeting at Ealing in the same year extended the scope of divine disapproval to include a famine in India and an influenza epidemic.[243] Those who traced the hand of God in history recalled that Calais was lost by a Roman Catholic Queen,[244] and the Revd A.G. Townshend warned in March 1909: 'If they turned their backs upon God, turned away from His Blessed Word, and rejected those principles of the Reformation which had made their country great, it would not be long until "Ichabod" was written upon their Imperial sceptre.'[245] Townshend was expressing, albeit in unusually apocalyptic language, the common Evangelical assumptions that ritualism was a distortion of the gospel, displeasing to God and therefore detrimental to the well-being of a nation whose greatness rested on loyal Protestantism, spiritual religion and consequent divine favour.

Conclusion

It is not easy to separate the causes of Evangelical hostility from the arguments which they used to persuade the general public that ritualism was a spiritual blight. How far Evangelical Churchmen genuinely believed, for example, that ritualism was a serious spur to Welsh disestablishment, is impossible to assess. Beneath the rhetoric and beneath the exploitation of political circumstances, however, lay a sincere antipathy to the churchmanship represented by ritualism. To Evangelicals it was a form of religion alien to the Bible and the Prayer Book, a spiritual poison, a false gospel. It was being propagated dishonestly within the pale of a Protestant Church by men whose aim was the reversal of the Reformation. Evangelicals believed that if Anglo-Catholicism gained the upper hand the doctrinal purity and continued establishment of the Church of England would be at risk and that their own position as a school of thought within Anglicanism might become untenable. In a sense the Church of England would have ceased to be the church of the English people; it would have become a pale copy of the alien religion of Rome. For Evangelicals ritualism was theologically erroneous from the foundations upwards. It challenged the core convictions of Evangelical religion, questioned Evangelical spirituality and threatened the mission and very existence of the Church of England. Small wonder, then, that many Evangelical Churchmen were ready for an unremitting struggle against the ritualist tide. Diversity of approach, disagreements over strategy and tactics, and an analysis of the outcomes of the controversy will form the substance of the next chapter.

Notes

1 E.N. Bennett, 'The religion of the Oxford undergraduate', *C*, November 1896, 87.

2 So G.I.T. Machin, *Victorian Studies* 25 (Bloomington, Indiana, 1982).

3 The comprehensive survey by Nigel Yates, *Anglican Ritualism in*

Victorian Britain 1830-1910 (Oxford, 1999) and W.S.F. Pickering's *Anglo-Catholicism. A Study in Religious Ambiguity* (London, 1989) are the most recent treatments. See also O. Chadwick, *The Victorian Church* (London, 1972[2]), ii, 308-19, and G. Rowell, *The Vision Glorious.Themes and Personalities of the Catholic Revival in Anglicanism* (Oxford, 1983), esp. chs 6 and 7.

4 Yates, *Anglican Ritualism*, 40-69. Compare and contrast the older interpretation offered by G.W. Herring, 'Tractarianism to ritualism: A study of some aspects of Tractarianism outside Oxford, from the time of Newman's conversion in 1845 until the first Ritual Commission in 1867', Oxford DPhil thesis, 1984.

5 Yates, *Anglican Ritualism*, 83-117, 278-94.

6 Chadwick, *Victorian Church*, 313, 316.

7 J.E.B. Munson, 'The Oxford Movement by the end of the nineteenth century', *Church History* 44 (Chicago, 1975).

8 Chadwick, *Victorian Church*, 319; *R*, 31 August 1906, 751.

9 Publication of the *Tourist's Church Guide* began privately in 1874 and was taken over by the ECU in 1878; the Union's secretary, H.W. Hill, told the Royal Commission that publication ceased when it became apparent that the *Guide* had become 'a regular directory for spies and brawlers': Yates, *Anglican Ritualism*, 70; *RCED Minutes of Evidence*, iii, 97.

10 Chadwick, *Victorian Church*, 319.

11 *R*, 13 March 1914, 255.

12 G.L. Prestige, *The Life of Charles Gore* (London, 1935), 390-94.

13 *R*, 15 February 1917, 118.

14 *R*, 22 November 1901, 1151; 21 June 1911, 593.

15 For which see Horton Davies, *Worship and Theology in England 1900-65* (Princeton, 1965), 284-90. Davies describes the situation as one of 'liturgical chaos', ibid., 287.

16 C. Mackenzie, *My Life and Times* (London, 1963-65), i, 158; ii, 65, 202, 219; iv, 31, 215; R.A. Knox, 'Tendencies of Anglicanism', *Dublin Review* 324 (London, 1918).

17 R.E. Bartlett, 'The Catholic Church', in J. Percival et al., *Church and Faith, being essays on the teaching of the Church of England* (London, 1899), 157. Compare the analysis of the London militants in Alan T.L. Wilson, 'The authority of Church and party among London Anglo-Catholics, 1880-1914, with special reference to the Church crisis of 1898-1904', Oxford DPhil thesis, 1988, esp. 43-48.

18 A.R. Vidler, *The Church in an Age of Revolution* (London, 1971), 160-62.

19 E.A. Litton, *Introduction to Dogmatic Theology on the Basis of the Thirty Nine Articles* (London, 1882, 1892), citing the one volume third edition of 1912 at xxi. On Litton, see Donald M. Lewis (ed.), *Dictionary of Evangelical Biography 1730-1860* (Oxford, 1995), ii, 690-91.

20 *R*, 18 July 1902, 687.

21 *R*, 5 May 1905, 436.

22 On the background to this section in earlier conflict between Evangelicals and Tractarians, see P. Toon, *Evangelical Theology 1833-56. A Response to Tractarianism* (London, 1979), 113-40.

23 W. Walsh, *The Secret History of the Oxford Movement* (London, 1897), citing the 1899 Popular Edition, 262; C.R. Alford, *'Stand Fast'; or, Contention for the Common Salvation against the Inroads of Ritualism a Christian Duty* (London, 1895), 5 (citing the magazine of Christ Church, Doncaster). Compare Gore's essay 'The Holy Spirit and inspiration' in Charles Gore (ed.), *Lux Mundi. A Series of Studies in the Religion of the Incarnation* (London, 1889), citing the 1895 14th edition, 249.

24 J.C. Ryle, *The Upper Room* (London, 1888), citing reprint of 1970 (Edinburgh), 19. On the case that Evangelical attitudes to the doctrine of inspiration and its corollaries had hardened during the nineteenth century, see chapter 4 below.

25 J.C. Ryle, *Knots Untied* (London, 1874), citing reprint of 1977 (Cambridge), 3.

26. W.S. Hooton and J. Stafford Wright, *The First Twenty Five Years of the BCMS* (London, 1947), 220.

27 F.D. Coggan (ed.), *Christ and the Colleges* (London, 1934), 205.

28 H.E. Ryle, *On the Church of England* (London, 1904) 39.

29 M.H. Fitzgerald, *A Memoir of Herbert Edward Ryle* (London, 1928), 156-64.

30 T. Guy Rogers (ed.), *Liberal Evangelicalism: An Interpretation by Members of the Church of England* (London, 1923), 39-45 (Rogers).

31 Ibid., 296 (E.W. Barnes), 40 (Rogers).

32 E.J. Jay, 'Anglican Evangelicalism and the nineteenth century novel', Oxford DPhil thesis, 1975, chapter 3.

33 C. Mackenzie, *The Parson's Progress* (London, 1923), 177; *R*, 15 August 1916, 497.

34 P. Toon and M. Smout, *John Charles Ryle* (Cambridge, 1976), 26.

35 Litton, *Dogmatic Theology*, 15.

36 *R*, 19 January 1906, 69.

37 H.H. Henson, *Cui Bono? An Open Letter to Lord Halifax on the Present Crisis in the Church of England* (London, 1898), 35. Compare the analysis of Evangelical biblicism as a defining characteristic of an evolving phenomenon in D.W. Bebbington, *Evangelicalism in Modern Britain. A History from the 1730s to the 1980s* (London, 1989), 12-14.

38 W.H. Griffith Thomas, *The Catholic Faith* (London, 1904), 315.

39 W. Abbott et al., *Four Foundation Truths* (London, 1895), 13.

40 Griffith Thomas, *Catholic Faith*, 318.

41 Litton, *Dogmatic Theology*, 22-5.

42 J.C. Ryle, *Knots Untied*, 256-72.

43 H.C.G. Moule, 'Tests of true religion', *Church and Faith*, 265-71.

44 W.H. Griffith Thomas, *A Sacrament of our Redemption* (London, 1905), 3-4.

45 A.E. Barnes-Lawrence, *A Churchman and his Church* (London, 1917), 8; Abbott, *Four Foundation Truths*, 16, makes explicit the accusation that the ritualists sought a rule of faith able to justify sacerdotalism.
46 J.R. Howden (ed.), *Evangelicalism by members of the FEC* (London, 1925), 265.
47 Griffith Thomas, *Catholic Faith*, section 3, chapters 4 and 5, esp. 359.
48 H.E. Ryle, *On the Church of England*, 100.
49 For Wace, see *ODCC*, 1453 and *DNB 1922-30*, 876-7. Among his publications was a four-volume *Dictionary of Christian Biography* and he was co-editor with Philip Schaff of the second series of the *Nicene and Post-Nicene Fathers* in fourteen volumes (1890-1900).
50 *R*, 20 September 1917, 630.
51 The history of the celebrated phrase is traced in Alister E. McGrath, *Iustitia Dei. A History of the Christian Doctrine of Justification* (Cambridge, 1993), ii, 1, 193. For earlier Evangelical-Tractarian debates over justification, see Toon, *Evangelical Theology*, 141-70.
52 Litton, *Dogmatic Theology*, 280. It should be noted that this is a simplified summary of two far from monolithic traditions in Western Christianity. McGrath, *Iustitia Dei*, chapters 6-8, explores variations within the main traditions.
53 Litton, *Dogmatic Theology*, 289.
54 Ibid., sections 60-66.
55 *R*, 21 November 1902, 1128.
56 J.C. Ryle, *Knots Untied*, 4, 192-205, 206-18; F.T. Woods et al., *The Creed of a Churchman* (London, 1916), 25.
57 J.C. Ryle, *Knots Untied*, 214-5; *R*, 8 November 1901, 1102.
58 *R*, 28 September 1916, 769 – thus W.J.L. Sheppard.
59 A.H.S[tanton], *Catholic Prayers for Church of England People* (London, 1897[3]), 12, 132-49, 181; C.H.H. Wright and C. Neil (eds), *A Protestant Dictionary* (London, 1904), 627.
60 *R*, 28 November 1913, 1094.
61 H.E. Ryle, *On the Church of England*, 185: echoing his formidable father's characteristic language.
62 J.C. Ryle, *Knots Untied*, 219-35.
63 Toon, *Evangelical Theology*, 171-202.
64 E. Stock, *History of the Church Missionary Society*, iv (London, 1916), 409-24; Stephen Neill, *A History of Christian Missions* (Harmondsworth, 1986[2]), 406-7; H. Maynard Smith, *Frank, Bishop of Zanzibar* (London, 1926), chapter 8. Bishop Willis gave his version of events in a letter, *R*, 5 December 1913, 1140-42.
65 Prestige, *Gore*, chapter 21; *R*, 9 April 1914, 348.
66 W. Goode, *The Divine Rule of Faith and Practice* (London, 1853[2]), i, 144.
67 Henry Wace, 'The Church', in (Various Writers), *The Church and Her Doctrine* (London, 1891), 233-309.
68 Griffith Thomas, *Catholic Faith*, 187.

69 Charles Gore, *The Church and the Ministry* (London, 1900[4]), 105; W.H.M.H. Aitken, *Apostolical Succession considered in the light of the facts of the history of the primitive Church* (London, 1903), 18.
70 Ibid., 11, 13; Barnes-Lawrence, *A Churchman and his Church*, 46.
71 Aitken, *Apostolical Succession*, 31, 33.
72 Ibid., 79.
73 A.J. Tait, *What is our deposit?* (London, 1914), 6.
74 Toon, *Evangelical Theology*, 188-95. The most celebrated incident in the controversy is described in J.C.S. Nias, *Gorham and the Bishop of Exeter* (London, 1951).
75 *R*, 27 August 1909, 865.
76 M. Wright, *Home Idolatry and Home Missions* (London, 1892), 12. Wright, a Congregationalist minister, used the alleged prevalence of Romanising in the Established Church to appeal for support for Congregationalist Home Missions.
77 A.E. Barnes-Lawrence, *A Churchman to Churchmen* (London, 1893), 49.
78 H.C.G. Moule, in R.B. Girdlestone et al, *English Church Teaching* (London, 1897), 97-111.
79 W.H.M.H. Aitken, *The Doctrine of Baptism* (London, 1901), 61.
80 J.C. Ryle, *Knots Untied*, 5, 98-101.
81 Aitken, *Doctrine of Baptism*, 27.
82 *R*, 8 November 1901, 1111.
83 Ibid.; Aitken, *Doctrine of Baptism*, 41.
84 Dieter Voll, *Catholic Evangelicalism. The Acceptance of Evangelical Traditions by the Oxford Movement during the second half of the Nineteenth Century* (Munich, 1960; E.T., London, 1963).
85 Ibid., 94, quoting G.W.E. Russell, *Arthur Stanton. A Memoir* (London, 1917), 230. Voll misattributes the statement to the Revd E.F. Russell.
86 G.W.E. Russell, *The Household of Faith* (London, 1902), 316.
87 J.H.S. Kent, *Holding the Fort* (London, 1978), 242-3.
88 *R*, 21 May 1909, 553; 21 June 1917, 434; 30 July 1909, 785 for Griffith Thomas' verdict on G.H. Wilkinson.
89 Voll, *Catholic Evangelicalism*, 51.
90 Aitken, *Doctrine of Baptism*, 32-49.
91 Ibid., v.
92 Barnes-Lawrence, *A Churchman and His Church*, 47.
93 J. Denton Thompson, *Central Churchmanship* (London, 1911), 64.
94 H.E. Ryle, *On the Church of England*, 148. Herbert Ryle defies easy classification in terms of Church parties. Yates (*Anglican Ritualism*, 176) does not include him among the 'Low Church/Evangelical' bishops appointed between 1875 and 1904; he was, however, a speaker at the Islington Clerical Conference in 1900, the year of his appointment to the see of Exeter.
95 W.H.K. Soames, *Is Sacerdotalism Scriptural?* (London, 1903), 31-2.
96 J.C. Ryle, *The Upper Room*, 324; H.C.G. Moule, *Outlines of Christian*

Doctrine (London, 1889), 223; Barnes-Lawrence, *A Churchman and his Church*, 48; F.W. Farrar, 'Christ's teaching and the primitive Church', *Church and Faith*, 63: all quoting, with varying degrees of accuracy, J.B. Lightfoot, *St Paul's Epistle to the Philippians* (London, 1868). The most celebrated passage is found in the 1879 edition at 181.

97 W.H. Griffith Thomas, *Priest or Prophet? A Question for the Day* (London, 1900), 5, 6, 8. Moberly suggested that Lightfoot's argument was unsatisfactory, ambiguous and open to misinterpretation: *Ministerial Priesthood* (London, 1897), xxxvi-ix (citing 1907 reprint of the first edition). *Ministerial Priesthood* argued extensively against Lightfoot's conclusions.

98 Griffith Thomas, *Priest or Prophet?*

99 This does not imply that all Evangelicals were great preachers – see E. Stock, *My Recollections* (London, 1909), chapter 6 and M. Barlow (ed.), *Life of William Haggar Barlow* (London, 1910), chapter 2. Some High Churchmen, like King and Liddon, were noted preachers. In the early twentieth century, however, some bishops were concerned by the ritualists' neglect of preaching, according to the Revd L. Hickin.

100 J.C. Ryle, *The Upper Room*, 329-32.

101 *R*, 28 November 1902, 1153.

102 Denton Thompson, *Central Churchmanship*, 60.

103 J.C. Ryle, *What do we owe to the Reformation?* (London, 1877), 12.

104 Moberly, *Ministerial Priesthood*, 232, note 2. This phrase is quoted, inaccurately, in P.V.M. Filleul, *Considerations regarding the Bishop of Salisbury's Recent Letter… on 'Eucharist' and 'Confession'* (London, 1899), 7.

105 P.V. Smith, 'The Archbishop's judgment', *C*, January 1891, 204-15, esp. 209-10.

106 *R*, 15 February 1907, 146.

107 Thus N. Dimock, *R*, 13 March 1908, 227; 20 March, 247, and H. Wace, *R*, 20 December 1912, 1217.

108 *R*, 15 May 1908, 441. Compare *R*, 21 June 1912, 582 and 23 December 1915, 1141 for opposition to the white vestment by Ommanney and the Alcuin Club respectively. Darwell Stone made his position clear in a paper to the 1908 Church Congress, *Official Report of the Church Congress…* 1908 (London, 1908), 75-78.

109 T.W. Drury, 'The Lord's Supper', in *Church and Faith*, 202.

110 Barnes-Lawrence, *A Churchman and his Church*, 101.

111 *R*, 22 June 1900, 611.

112 W.H. Griffith Thomas, *A Sacrament of our Redemption* (London, 1905), 82-7.

113 In Girdlestone, *English Church Teaching*, 123.

114 Denton Thompson, *Central Churchmanship*, 46.

115 Toon, *Evangelical Theology*, 195-202.

116 Griffith Thomas, *Sacrament*, 87.

117 *R*, 28 November 1913, 1094; 25 May 1900, 498.
118 *R*, 13 March 1908, 220.
119 *R*, 15 February 1917, 118.
120 Ibid., 10 May, 352.
121 Prestige, *Gore*, 392.
122 Hence Southsea schoolboys doffed their caps to churches which reserved, but not to others, because Christ was not there: *R*, 1 March 1917, 153.
123 Ibid., 31 May 1917, 390-91.
124 This was serious for those who valued the work of the Holy Spirit, as Moule did – see his *Veni Creator* (London, 1890), an examination of scriptural teaching on the Spirit.
125 W.H.M.H. Aitken, *The Mechanical versus the Spiritual. Two contrasted conceptions of the Christian religion. A word for the times.* (London, 1899), 4.
126 Ibid., 5.
127 *R*, 7 June 1912, 534. The search was unsuccessful and the clergyman was forced to celebrate without fasting and in the evening. What especially incensed Evangelicals was that the story was recounted as a plea for reservation.
128 *R*, 22 August 1913, 770.
129 Moule, 'Tests of true religion', *Church and Faith*, 271, 276.
130 J.C. Ryle, *Knots Untied*, 318; Girdlestone, *English Church Teaching*, 67.
131 G.H. Harriss, *Vernon Faithfull Storr: A Memoir* (London, 1943), 67, 69.
132 J.C. Ryle, *Knots Untied*, 234; Barnes-Lawrence, *A Churchman to Churchmen*, 110-11; *A Churchman and His Church*, 128-9. The Calvinist and Keswick traditions are considered in David Bebbington, *Holiness in Nineteenth Century England* (Carlisle, 2000) which also discusses the holiness teaching of the Anglican High Church school. An introduction to Keswick and a description of developments in the inter-war period may be found in chapter 2 of Ian M. Randall, *Evangelical Experiences. A Study in the spirituality of English Evangelicalism 1918-1939* (Carlisle, 1999).
133 J.C. Ryle, *What do we owe to the Reformation?* (London, 1877), 15.
134 J.C. Ryle, *Knots Untied*, 7; Toon, *Evangelical Theology*, 204-5.
135 R, 4 October 1901, 982 (addressing the Church Congress on 'Authority in the Church of England').
136 *R*, 5 October 1906, 882-3.
137 H. Wace, *English Religion: An Address on the Decisions of the Archbishops in regard to Incense, Lights and the Reservation of the Sacrament* (London, 1900), 12-13.
138 Toon, *Evangelical Theology*, 93; A. Bentley, 'The transformation of the Evangelical party in the Church of England in the later nineteenth century', Durham PhD thesis, 1971, chapter 3; R.C.D. Jasper, *Prayer Book Revision in England, 1800-1900* (London, 1954), 47-53, 63-7.
139 J.C. Ryle, *Knots Untied*, 48-67.

140 T. Hardy, *Tess of the D'Urbervilles* (London, 1891), citing 1974 edition, 198.
141 *R*, 8 May 1903, 443.
142 H. Lewis, 'The present condition of the Evangelicals', *Nineteenth Century and After*, 19-20 (London, August 1907), 233.
143 Denton Thompson, *Central Churchmanship*, v.
144 *R*, 20 December 1917, 879; 18 January 1907, 63.
145 *R*, 2 October 1914, 911.
146 N. Dimock, *The Crisis in the Church of England* (London, 1899), 42.
147 *R*, 21 June 1917, 433; *Speeches of Samuel Smith, Esq, MP* (London, 1898), 18-19; S.C. Carpenter, *Winnington-Ingram* (London, 1949), 170-75.
148 *R*, 26 October 1906, 941. On the Ornaments Rubric, see chapter 3 below.
149 Henson, *Cui bono?*, 37.
150 *R*, 12 December 1913, 1173. See chapter 6 below for the debate over *Foundations*.
151 H.E. Ryle, *On the Church of England*, 15.
152 *R*, 22 November 1912, 1109; *Verbatim Report of Speeches delivered at the Great Demonstration held in the Queen's Hall* (London, 1898), 5.
153 *R*, 8 March 1912, 226; 29 March 1903, 303.
154 *R*, 3 July 1903, 649.
155 *R*, 19 August 1910, 792; 26 August 1910, 801.
156 *R*, 22 August 1890, 816. Another of Ommanney's curates seceded in 1901: R, 19 April 1901, 385.
157 Henson, *Cui bono?*, 31.
158 Ibid., 32; Chadwick, *Victorian Church*, 355-6.
159 J.C. Livingston, *The Ethics of Belief* (Tallahasee, 1974), and below, chapters 4, 5 and 6.
160 E.R. Norman, *Anti-Catholicism in Victorian England* (London, 1968), 108; D. Hilliard, 'Unenglish and unmanly: Anglo-Catholicism and homosexuality', *Victorian Studies* 25 (Bloomington, 1982); Pickering, *Anglo-Catholicism*, chapter 8.
161 *Verbatim Report*, 23.
162 C. Mackenzie, *The Altar Steps* (London, 1922), 88.
163 Thus the Roman Catholic polemicist, James Britten, attacked Kensit for purveying salacious books to boost his business: *A Prominent Protestant: Mr John Kensit* (London, 1898), 3-4. See also M. Wellings, 'The first Protestant martyr of the twentieth century: the life and significance of John Kensit (1853-1902)', *SCH* 30 (Oxford, 1993), 347-58.
164 Norman, *Anti-Catholicism*, 83-4; W.L. Arnstein, *Protestant versus Catholic in mid-Victorian England. Mr Newdegate and the Nuns* (Columbia, 1982), esp. chapters 5 and 8-13.
165 *R*, 15 July 1904, 732; 22 July 1904, 768.
166 Walsh, *Secret History*, 113-40.
167 *What Ritualists teach the young: An Address... by Samuel Smith, Esq, MP*

(London, 1898); J.M. Sangar, *The Protestant Crisis* (London, 1899), 16.

168 M. Wellings, 'Anglo-Catholicism, the "crisis in the Church" and the Cavalier case of 1899', *JEH* 42 (Cambridge, 1991), 248-50.

169 Sangar, *Protestant Crisis*, 16; *R*, 25 January 1901, 120.

170 *R*, 26 April 1907, 352; 10 May 1907, 414; T, 22 April 1907, 2; 30 April 1907, 8; 8 May 1907, 5.

171 English anti-Catholicism is explored by Norman, *Anti-Catholicism*, passim, and by J.R. Wolffe, *The Protestant Crusade in Great Britain 1829-1860* (Oxford, 1991). The link between Protestantism and national character is made in Linda Colley, *Britons. Forging the Nation 1707-1837* (London, 1992), especially chapter 1.

172 Norman, *Anti-Catholicism*, 15-16.

173 *R*, 4 November 1915, 963.

174 See, for example, the article on 'Galileo' in Wright and Neil, *Protestant Dictionary*, 231-37.

175 'The Man of Sin', ibid., 386-8.

176 Norman, *Anti-Catholicism*, 80-98; H.C.G. Matthew, *Gladstone 1809-1898* (Oxford, 1999), 249; David W. Bebbington, *William Ewart Gladstone* (Grand Rapids, 1993), 228-30.

177 *R*, 17 November 1911, 1072. Leading opponents of the Decree were the Evangelical Alliance and the Revd D.H.C. Bartlett, later founder of the BCMS.

178 H.E. Ryle, *On the Church of England*, 57.

179 Vidler, *Age of Revolution*, 186-9; chapter 6 below.

180 *R*, 23 August 1912, 797; S. Salvidge, *Salvidge of Liverpool* (London, 1934), chapter 9.

181 *R*, 8 January 1904, 29, 40; 22 January 1904, 127; 29 January 1904, 151.

182 Toon, *Evangelical Theology*, 1.

183 Ibid., 86; Litton, *Dogmatic Theology*, xix.

184 Munson, 'Oxford Movement', 387.

185 *R*, 7 March 1913, 214; Prestige, *Gore*, 339-41 for the background to the secession.

186 *R*, 20 February 1903, 174; 27 February 1903, 198; Wilson, 'Church and party', 158-77.

187 *R*, 25 October 1907, 933.

188 Walsh, *Secret History*, 182; M. Wellings, 'The Oxford Movement in late nineteenth century retrospect: R.W. Church, J.H. Rigg and Walter Walsh', *SCH* 33 (Woodbridge, 1997), 501-15, esp. 511-14.

189 J.M. Sangar, *England's Privilege and Curse* (London, 1897), 8.

190 T. Berney, *An Address..* (London, 1895), 5, 8.

191 The extraordinary success of the *Secret History*, taking author, sponsors and opponents by surprise, indicates that Walsh tapped a popular vein: Wellings, 'Oxford Movement', 513-4.

192 Halifax was active in working for a better understanding between Rome and the Church of England throughout this period, especially in

the negotiations of the 1890s and in the Malines Conversations of 1921-26: J.G. Lockhart, *Charles Lindley, Viscount Halifax*, ii (London, 1936), chapters 4 and 18-22. For the 1895 manifesto, see *CT*, 15 February 1895, 181-4; *C*, March 1895, 332-6; *R*, 5 July 1901, 687.

193 Horton Davies, *Worship and Theology*, 287-8; Wilson, 'Church and party', 174-6, discusses Anglo-Catholic reactions to the Shoreditch secessions of 1903.

194 J. Hughes-Games, *The Duty of Evangelical Churchmen under Possible Eventualities* (London, 1900), 1. The sermon cited has not been traced.

195 Thus Bishop Winnington-Ingram of London, *R*, 13 October 1911, 944.

196 *R*, 20 June 1902, 590.

197 *R*, 5 April 1907, 293.

198 *RCED Report* (London, 1906), 53, referring to practices which 'lie on the Romeward side' of that line.

199 Barnes-Lawrence, *A Churchman and his Church*, 4.

200 *R*, 12 July 1907, 619; 30 June 1911, 605.

201 *R*, 17 May 1912, 465.

202 Mackenzie, *Life and Times*, iv, 11-12. Wason, former curate at St Michael's, Shoreditch, declined to follow his vicar in seceding to Rome, remaining instead to try the patience of various Anglican bishops.

203 Herring, 'Tractarianism to ritualism', chapter 13. It would, of course, be Churchmen of Evangelical sympathies who would be among the first to leave a newly ritualist church. Ritualist clergymen were often not sorry to see them go.

204 E.N. Gowing, *John Edwin Watts-Ditchfield* (London, 1926); C.E. Woods, *Memoirs and Letters of Canon Hay Aitken* (London, 1928); J.E. Watts-Ditchfield, 'Men's Services', *C*, February 1895, 255-68.

205 J.C. Ryle, *Knots Untied*, 299.

206 B. Herklots, *The Future of the Evangelical Party in the Church of England* (London, 1913), 99, 124.

207 *Verbatim Report*, 24; W. Sinclair, *The Prospects of the Principles of the Reformation in the Church of England* (London, 1893), 15; Yates, *Anglican Ritualism*, 288-90.

208 Munson, 'Oxford Movement', 391-2.

209 Chadwick, *Victorian Church*, 317.

210 J. Cox, *The English Churches in a Secular Society: Lambeth, 1870-1930* (London, 1982), 40-2.

211 Lewis, 'Evangelicals', 235; *R*, 3 August 1916, 633; 28 September 1916, 771; 28 June 1917, 454. Cox's conclusions are that activism, rather than doctrine, was the key to parochial success: *English Churches*, 42.

212 *R*, 19 October 1916, 824, citing Gore's manual for the National Mission. Compare C. Gore, *The Religion of the Church. A Manual of Membership* (London, 1916), 170-2.

213 *R*, 27 September 1917, 655.

214 *R*, 13 January 1911, 52. The implication is that the bishop was Edward King.

215 Wright, Home Idolatry, 13.

216 See R. Rouse and S. Neill (eds), *A History of the Ecumenical Movement 1517-1948* (London, 1967) for a full account of the ecumenical quest. P.V. Smith reflected on the Lambeth statement in 'The prospects of Home Reunion, *C*, January 1894, 179-92. On the SCM, see chapter 7 below, and T. Tatlow, *The Story of the Student Christian Movement* (London, 1933), especially chapters 2, 5, 9, 10, 16 and 21.

217 C. Mackenzie, *The Heavenly Ladder* (London, 1924), 2.

218 *R*, 28 July 1911, 694; F. Weston, *Ecclesia Anglicana: For what does she stand?* (London, 1913), 16-20.

219 *R*, 26 July 1917, 518, 520.

220 J.W. White, 'The Influence of North American evangelism in Great Britain between 1830 and 1914 on the origin and development of the ecumenical movement', Oxford DPhil thesis, 1963, chapter 8. The Evangelical Alliance, founded in 1846, was a federation of individual Evangelicals, not of groups and denominations.

221 *R*, 3 May 1917, 305.

222 *R*, 27 September 1917, 647.

223 The distinction between 'spiritual Nonconformity' and 'political Dissent' existed only in the minds – or polemics – of Anglicans. For the background to these issues in the mid-nineteenth century, see Timothy Larsen, *Friends of Religious Equality. Nonconformist Politics in Mid-Victorian England* (Woodbridge, 1999) and for the later period, G.I.T. Machin, *Politics and the Churches in Great Britain 1869 to 1921* (Oxford, 1987) and D.W. Bebbington, *The Nonconformist Conscience: Chapel and Politics 1870-1914* (London, 1982), especially chapters 1, 2 and 7.

224 Hughes-Games, *Duty of Evangelical Churchmen*, 8-9.

225 Alford, *'Stand fast'*, 9; J.M. Sangar, *A Curate's Protestant Speech and Subsequent Forfeiture of His Cure* (London, 1892), 18. *R*, 18 September 1908, 974.

226 *R*, 1 March 1907, 183.

227 See generally P.M.H. Bell, *Disestablishment in Ireland and Wales* (London, 1969), especially 230, 247-50 and 297-313.

228 *R*, 20 July 1906, 634.

229 *R*, 14 September 1906, 794.

230 J.C. Ryle, *What do we owe to the Reformation?*, 20; W. Joynson-Hicks, *The Prayer Book Crisis* (London, 1928), 154.

231 See, for example, J.E.B. Munson, 'The London School Board election of 1894: a study in Victorian religious controversy', *British Journal of Educational Studies* 23 (London, 1975).

232 The education controversy brought out the strong churchmanship of many Evangelicals; some accused the Nonconformists of selling out to Liberal politics or 'downgrade' theology. Wace and E.A. Knox were the

main spokesmen for those Evangelicals who clung to the old ideals of uniformity, a national Church and religious education on Church principles. They were, therefore, opposed to the nondenominational education advocated by the Dissenters, and to the nonconformity represented both by the Free Churches and by ritualism.

233 Wright, *Home Idolatry*, 11-12.

234 *R*, 1 August 1902, 730.

235 Bebbington, *Nonconformist Conscience*, 141-52; *R*, 8 February 1907, 123; John T. Smith, *Methodism and Education 1849-1902* (Oxford, 1998), 222-9.

236 *R*, 2 November 1906, 973.

237 *R*, 10 May 1907, 415; 19 April 1912, 365.

238 G. Thompson Brake, *Policy and Politics in British Methodism 1932-1982* (London, 1984), 582.

239 *R*, 5 October 1916, 785.

240 *R*, 18 May 1906, 443.

241 *R*, 20 November 1903, 1123.

242 *R*, 9 March 1900, 237.

243 *R*, 26 January 1900, 76.

244 *R*, 6 March 1903, 222.

245 *R*, 12 March 1909, 294.

CHAPTER 3

The Evangelical Response to Ritualism

'The wisdom that is from above is first pure, then peaceable' (James 3:17)

In the second volume of his monumental *History of the Church Missionary Society* Eugene Stock noted that Henry Venn, veteran honorary secretary of the CMS in the mid-nineteenth century, liked to describe the Evangelicals as a 'rope of sand', a collection of individuals united in adherence to certain fundamental principles, but not slaves to a party machine.[1] The rope of sand analogy was occasionally seen as indicative of strength,[2] but more often Evangelical Churchmen lamented their disunity in the face of the challenge of the highly organised English Church Union. The call for consolidation sounded by J.C. Ryle in *We must unite* (1868),[3] was still being repeated twenty four years later when A.J. Robinson criticised Evangelicals for behaving like 'a bag of marbles'.[4] As the twentieth century dawned Archdeacon Hughes-Games, echoing Venn's analogy, told the Yorkshire Evangelical Union:

> 'We are too like a rope of sand without cohesion, and therefore without strength. We fold our hands and do nothing… If we do not close our ranks, and stand together for the truth of the Gospel, we cannot hope to repel the steadily advancing foe… if we could only bring ourselves to act together with unanimity and decision, we should be helping to ward off the evils we deprecate, disestablishment and subsequent disruption.'[5]

Unanimity and decision, however, were not particularly visible in the Evangelical response to ritualism. Evangelicals disagreed on priorities, with some emphasizing the duty of opposing what they perceived as error and others deploring the spirit of bitterness which this produced. Even among those who were committed to the battle against ritualism there were quarrels about tactics and about the legitimacy of different methods of controversy. This disunion was symbolised and reinforced by the existence of competing Protestant societies, whose inability to unite demonstrated in institutional form the diversity of the Evangelical response to ritualism. Despite passionate calls for unity throughout the period there remained a plethora of such societies; indeed, the anti-ritualist campaign of the 1890s added to their number. G.I.T. Machin has calculated that there were at least fifty one by 1908,[6] a modest increase on the forty eight counted by the National Protestant Church Union in 1902.[7] A survey of the Evangelical response to ritualism may well begin by offering a brief analysis of these societies, before turning to the varied courses of action which they advocated and espoused.

Organising the Evangelicals

As indicators both of Evangelical disunity and of Protestant vitality the figures quoted above are somewhat misleading. It should not be thought that there were as many as fifty national Evangelical societies concerned with the ritual controversy, for some of those listed by the NPCU were local organisations like the Shrewsbury Union for the Maintenance and Encouragement of the Protestant and Evangelical Principles of the Church of England, founded in 1901.[8] Some, moreover, were non-denominational and others were primarily anti- Roman Catholic, rather than specifically engaged in the battle against ritualism. Within the loose organisation of Evangelicalism, three main groups of societies with some bearing on the ritual question may be detected.

The first group consisted of general Evangelical unions, conferences or meetings which occasionally turned their attention to aspects of the 'crisis in the Church'. Pre-eminent among these was the Islington Clerical Meeting, a gathering of Evangelicals held each January by invitation of the vicar of Islington and founded in 1827 by Daniel Wilson the elder. By 1888, when William Haggar Barlow became vicar, attendance stood at four hundred, and this figure had more than doubled by 1902.[9] In 1907 the *Record* estimated that 1250 Evangelical clergymen were present at the meeting,[10] an attendance sustained until the First World War. The Islington Meeting had a varied programme, but the ritual issue arose several times in the early twentieth century. The subject for 1900, for example, was 'The Church of England: Catholic, Apostolic, Reformed and Protestant', offering an opportunity for temperate criticism of medieval accretions by Chancellor Bernard and for a defence of Protestantism by H.E. Ryle,[11] while the 1907 meeting was entirely devoted to aspects of the report of the Royal Commission on Ecclesiastical Discipline.[12] Regional Evangelical conferences also heard papers on topics relevant to ritualism. Hughes-Games's address to the Yorkshire Evangelical Union, published as *The Duty of Evangelical Churchmen under Possible Eventualities* (1900), has already been noted. In 1905 J.H. Heywood, rector of Grasmere, spoke to the Carlisle Evangelical Union on 'The present duty of Evangelical Churchmen with regard to the widespread diffusion of Romanising practices in the National Church'[13] and the Royal Commission provided material for the Ipswich and Norwich Evangelical Clerical Society two years later.[14] From the mid-1910s the Cheltenham Conference served as an opportunity for representative Evangelicals to debate topical questions and the Cheltenham agenda included reservation (1916), Prayer Book revision (1923) and relations between Canterbury and Rome (1924).[15] None of these bodies were campaigning Protestant societies, but they acted as sources of information on current events and they helped to give some cohesion to Evangelical Churchmanship.

The second group of societies was composed of the older Protestant organisations, sometimes undenominational, which concentrated their attention primarily on Roman Catholicism. The three with the longest history were the Protestant Reformation Society, the National Club and the Protestant Alliance. The PRS was established in 1827, at the time of the agitation over Roman Catholic emancipation, and it was essentially a missionary society to Roman Catholics, producing propaganda, running mission stations and organising reply lectures to counteract Roman missions. From 1898 the clerical and general superintendent of the PRS was the Revd Dr C.H.H. Wright, a graduate of Trinity College, Dublin, and a formidable biblical scholar.[16] Although Wright and his colleagues devoted most of their resources to controversy with Rome, the PRS did give some attention to ritualism, so, for example, Walter Limbrick, the organising secretary of the Society, included 'The teachings of ritualism as stated in its own publications' in his East Anglian lecture programme in the autumn of 1903.[17] The National Club, founded in 1845, was committed to the defence of the Protestant Succession and constitution, and, although not active in polemic, offered a focus for Protestant meetings or political campaigns.[18] The Protestant Alliance, founded by Lord Shaftesbury in 1851, was an interdenominational society which saw its role as opposing the spread of Romanism in Great Britain.[19] As well as attempting to secure the enforcement of the penal statutes against the Jesuits, the Alliance also organised Protestant demonstrations which included attacks on ritualism within the Established Church.[20]

Alongside these three long-established societies were a number of more recent organisations, including the interdenominational Imperial Protestant Federation, founded by Walter Walsh in 1896 as an umbrella organisation for Protestant groups across the British Empire,[21] and the London Council of United Protestant Societies, established in 1901 in another attempt to rally the scattered forces of Protestantism.[22] Both the IPF and the London Council, which became the United Protestant Council in 1918,[23] sought to mobilise Protestant opinion on a range of issues broader than Anglican ritualism, although the ritual controversy was one of their areas of interest.

Ritualism proper was the concern of a third group, composed of a relatively small number of societies: the Church Association and its affiliates, the National Church League and the Protestant Truth Society, and these may be examined in turn.

The Church Association was founded in 1865 and initially secured considerable support from Evangelical Churchmen. By 1870 the Association had over eight thousand members, and 138 branch associations had been established.[24] Problems began to develop, however, over the policy of prosecuting extreme ritualists. In the opinion of its supporters and defenders, the Association undertook legal proceedings in order to clarify the law and to uphold the rights of aggrieved parishioners, rather than to persecute ritualists – J.C. Ryle described the Association as 'a society for the relief of perplexed bishops' because it was seeking legal decisions on controversial questions[25]- but the refusal of ritualist clergymen to obey the courts placed Evangelicals in a dilemma. Some continued to support the policy of prosecution and were ready to see contumacious ritualists sent to prison, but many regarded this policy as morally dubious and tactically unsound.[26] Between the mid-1870s and the final resolution of the

Lincoln Case in 1892 the Church Association was more effective in dividing than in uniting Evangelical Churchmen, as will be seen in more detail later. For the present, it may be noted that the Association continued to be one of the vehicles through which Evangelicals might oppose ritualism, albeit one denounced as ultra-Protestant and out of fellowship with mainstream Evangelicalism by others within the party.[27] During this period the Church Association developed a number of affiliates, creating the National Protestant League for electoral work, especially among the lower classes, in 1890,[28] co-ordinating political campaigning with Austin Taylor's Lancashire Laymen's League from 1902 onwards,[29] and absorbing the Evangelical Protestant Union, another ultra-Protestant group, in 1911.[30]

The failure of the Church Association to represent all Evangelicals was a major stimulus for the creation of the Protestant Churchmen's Alliance in 1889. A meeting held at Exeter Hall in June of that year pledged the new society to unite 'all Churchmen who desire to maintain the principles of the Reformation, the present Prayer Book and Articles, and the Act of Uniformity as their standards of doctrine and ritual, and especially, the non-sacerdotal character of the ministry of the Church of England'.[31] By April 1890 the PCA had organised in twenty five dioceses and numbered five hundred clergymen among its members. From the first it incorporated the Protestant Association and the Protestant Education Institute,[32] while in 1892 it joined with the Union of Clerical and Lay Associations (an earlier attempt to form a society acceptable to moderate Evangelicals) and became the National Protestant Church Union.[33] Advertising in the *Record* in 1904 the NPCU claimed that 'its work is mainly educational. It endeavours by means of literature, lectures, sermons, public meetings and through the press generally, to convey instruction in regard to the history and the teaching of the English Church.'[34] In this respect the NPCU was very similar to the Ladies' League for the Defence of the Reformed Faith of the Church of England, founded in 1899 by Lady Wimborne.[35] The League, later known as the Church of England League, joined the NPCU in 1906, and the new organisation, under the title of the National Church League, remained the body representing non-Church Association Protestantism for the rest of the period.[36] It may be noted that the NPCU/NCL achieved modest success in recruiting the support of non-Evangelical Protestants.

Churchmen as diverse as Archdeacon Farrar, J.J. Lias, Hastings Rashdall and the Hon and Revd W.E. Bowen appeared at its meetings;[37] it claimed to represent old High Churchmen, and proposals were even made for co-operation with the modernist Churchmen's Union. These schemes made little progress, however, partly on account of conservative Evangelical suspicion of the liberal theology of the Broad Churchmen.[38]

Among the more respectable anti-ritualist societies, two recurrent features may be detected. The first was the persistent call for unity and the second the inability of Evangelical Churchmen to combine effectively into one organisation. Each attempt to create an all-embracing Evangelical society compounded existing divisions by establishing still more committees and branches. Thus in the mid-1860s the Church Association aspired to be the focal point for Evangelical opposition to ritualism. The failure of this attempt was firmly underlined by the creation of the PCA, a point not lost on Church Association stalwarts like James Inskip and Sir Arthur Blackwood, who attacked the new society for duplicating the Association's work.[39] In the aftermath of the Lincoln Judgment some Evangelicals called for a fusion of the Church Association, the PCA and the UCLA, a scheme supported by J.C. Ryle and by Bishop Straton of Sodor and Man, but rejected by the ultra-Protestants.[40] Even the moderate NPCU failed to command the allegiance of P.V. Smith and Eugene Stock,[41] and appeals throughout the first decade of the twentieth century for Evangelicals to unite around the National Church League went unheeded;[42] indeed, Sir Edward Clarke, President of the NCL, set up a Laymen's Committee of influential figures which it was hoped would have a wider appeal than the League, and therefore succeed where it had failed.[43] When the League and the Association finally joined to form the Church Society (1950) the amalgamation was strongly opposed by moderate Evangelicals like C.M. Chavasse.[44]

While the CA and the NCL squabbled over their competing claims to speak for Evangelical anti-ritualists, much of the running in the campaign was made by a society which never entertained the idea of amalgamation with a more moderate body. The Protestant Truth Society was founded in 1889 by John Kensit, a Hoxton stationer who combined staunch Protestant principles with sound business acumen and a flair for publicity. After modest beginnings, the PTS gained considerable notoriety in the late 1890s as a result of Kensit's public protests against ritualism.[45] Although Kensit himself died after a riot at Birkenhead in 1902, whereupon his followers hailed him as 'the first Protestant martyr of the twentieth century',[46] his son kept the PTS and its band of Wickliffe [sic] Preachers in the forefront of the anti-ritual campaign well into the 1930s. Unlike the Church Association and the NCL, the Kensitites made no attempt to recruit moderate Evangelical support. Henry Lewis denounced them as ultra-Protestant fanatics,[47] and they thrived on the publicity generated by their exploits. In 1911 J.A. Kensit had to refute allegations that the PTS represented 'the Protestantism that pays', an incident recalling the criticisms levelled at his father by the Roman Catholic pamphleteer James Britten, and by *Truth* in the 1890s, and reflecting the belief that the Kensits exploited Protestant sentiment for personal gain.[48]

It is difficult to estimate the relative strengths of the different Protestant groups. In terms of influence, the NCL could command considerable support. Its presidents were, successively, W.D. Cruddas, MP, (1906-12), a partner in Armstrong Vickers and a leading benefactor of Evangelical causes, Sir Edward Clarke, KC, MP, (1912-21), a member of the Royal Commission on Ecclesiastical Discipline, and Sir William Joynson-Hicks, Bt, MP, who held a series of Cabinet offices after the First World War and was Home Secretary from 1924 to 1929.[49] The NCL could also muster a distinguished list of vice-presidents – in 1919, for example, it included the archbishop of Sydney, the bishops of Durham, Manchester, Sodor and Man, Chelmsford and Barking, the dean of Canterbury, the archdeacons of Llandaff and Stoke, Prebendary Webb-Peploe, Sir Robert Williams, MP (president of the CMS) and T.W.H. Inskip.[50] Dean Wace was chairman of the Council of the NCL for many years and was a frequent speaker at its meetings. NCL membership, moreover, was considerable. The League claimed over 120 branches by 1909[51] and a clerical membership of two thousand four years later,[52] a figure which had increased slightly by the end of the decade.[53] Against this, however, must be set constant financial problems. Joynson-Hicks, as treasurer of the League, voiced disquiet at the May Meeting of 1911, while in 1918 Clarke sent out a letter with the annual report appealing for £2000 to place the NCL on a firm footing.[54] NCL income before the First World War never exceeded £9000 per annum, which may be compared with the £370, 000 regularly achieved by the CMS, the £50, 000 of the London Jews' Society and the £20, 000 of the South American Missionary Society, one of the smaller Evangelical missions.[55]

Financially speaking, the Church Association was marginally more successful than the NCL, since its income generally reached £10, 000 per annum in the first decades of the twentieth century. Otherwise it was less influential, and certainly less able to count on the support of clerical dignitaries. J.C. Ryle was sympathetic to the Association, although he resigned his membership on his elevation to the episcopate in 1880. Archdeacon W.F. Taylor of Liverpool appeared regularly on its platforms, as did Canons Woodward and Hobson (both honorary canons of Liverpool), but the Association's main support came from a phalanx of Evangelical clerics and committed Protestant laymen.

The Protestant Truth Society claimed in 1912 to be the largest Protestant society, on the strength of its full-time staff of thirty two.[56] Its income consistently exceeded both the Church Association and the NCL – £10, 200 in 1906, £11, 300 in 1907, £15, 200 in 1911, for instance.[57] Against this, however, must be set the fact that very few Evangelical clergymen or prominent laity were seen to support the PTS. James Britten noted that the 1896-7 report only claimed thirteen ministers among the subscribers, and although he miscalculated the total by four, this still left a society with a tiny 5% of clerical subscribers. A sprinkling of titled laity and a phalanx of medical and military men added some respectability, but the PTS represented popular, rather than prestigious Protestantism, and lay enterprise rather than clerical leadership.[58] The May Meetings of the Society usually included a number of clergymen, but they were very few and were restricted to strong Protestants like J.B. Barraclough and others from the Church Association wing of the Evangelical party. The PTS gathering which received most support from Evangelicals was John Kensit's funeral in October 1902, attended by Canons Hobson and Woodward and by Prebendary F.S. Webster.[59]

It may be seen, therefore, that even in terms of organisation and structures the Evangelical response to ritualism was diverse and disunited. The disunion of the societies, represented by the different characteristics of the NCL, PTS and Church Association, was only a structural reflection of deep disagreements within Evangelicalism as to how the ritualist challenge should be met. The next sections of this chapter will explore the methods deployed by Evangelical Churchmen in this conflict and will describe the disputes which they generated inside the party.

Arguing the Evangelical Case

One aspect of the ritual controversy on which Evangelicals could unite was the need to meet the Anglo-Catholic challenge by a positive statement of Evangelical belief, or by subjecting the views of the other party to careful academic scrutiny. There was, therefore, a literary response to ritualism on the part of Evangelical Churchmen, a response which produced a considerable volume of theological and historical works, at all levels of academic attainment.

Evangelical scholarship

Some of the scholarship deployed in this period consisted merely of reprinting earlier attacks on the theology of the Tractarians, so that, for instance, Goode's *Divine Rule of Faith and Practice* appeared in a one volume abridgement in 1903.[60] There were, however, a series of new contributions to the debate and these may be noticed briefly.

It has already been observed that most of the theological issues of the ritual controversy clustered around the doctrines of the Church, the priesthood and the sacraments. The Anglo-Catholics taught that the Church was a visible divine society, secured upon the apostolic succession and the historic episcopate. They held to baptismal regeneration *ex opere operato* and they taught that the Christian minister was a priest. In the eucharist, Christ was really present in the elements and the eucharistic sacrifice was a sharing in the perpetual self-offering of Christ in heaven. Ritual practice, whether the six points of the ECU or the more elaborate ceremonial of the Romanising minority, was designed to express and reinforce these beliefs and, the ritualists claimed, both doctrine and practice were scriptural, Catholic and commanded by the Church of England. It was these claims that Evangelical Churchmen set out to refute.

The scriptural evidence for Anglo-Catholic theology was

weighed and found wanting by many Evangelical writers. The most solid works of dogmatic theology produced by Evangelicals in this period, E.A. Litton's *Introduction to Dogmatic Theology on the Basis of the Thirty Nine Articles* (1912) and H.C.G. Moule's *Outlines of Christian Doctrine* (1889) naturally included sections on Church, priesthood and sacraments in which Anglo-Catholic opinions were firmly rejected.[61] William Lefroy devoted his Donnellan lectures of 1887-8 to the subject of 'The Christian Ministry', and spent two lengthy chapters examining the arguments set out by Charles Gore in *The Church and the Ministry* (1888), coming to the conclusion that Gore's doctrine of apostolic succession was schismatical, heretical, unhistorical and unscriptural and 'has no place in Christianity'.[62] Another contribution to New Testament scholarship was made by W.H. Griffith Thomas in *A Sacrament of our Redemption* (1905), an expanded version of his degree dissertations which explored the origins of the Lord's Supper in the Gospels and Epistles. In another expanded dissertation, published in 1912 as *The Heavenly Session of our Lord*, A.J. Tait attacked the Anglo-Catholic belief that Christ makes constant propitiatory intercession before the throne of God, thereby challenging one of the chief arguments in favour of the eucharistic sacrifice.

As well as biblical scholarship, Evangelicals also deployed several patristic and liturgical experts to challenge Anglo-Catholicism. It is true that Evangelicals generally were not renowned for patristic study – J.C. Ryle, for example, remarked scornfully, 'when a man makes an idol of Fathers and Councils, and disparages the theology of the Reformation, we may be sure there is a screw loose in his theology'[63] – but nonetheless some careful work was done in this area. Nathaniel Dimock published a succession of books and articles displaying a wide knowledge of the Fathers, and after his death the NCL produced a memorial edition of his massively erudite works, comparing them favourably with those of William Goode. T.W. Drury, Moule's successor at Ridley Hall, was also a liturgical scholar of some distinction, and his monograph *Elevation in the Eucharist: its History and Rationale* (1907), prompted by his experiences as a member of the Royal Commission on Ecclesiastical Discipline, [64] drew on a wide range of sources from the primitive Church and the Western Use to the varied liturgies of the East.

One of the strengths of Anglo-Catholicism was that it possessed an historical apologetic which enabled it to claim to represent the true teaching of the Church of England. Although the extremists despised 'Anglicanism' and some regulated their services according to the rules of the Roman Congregation of Rites, most Anglo-Catholics held that they were loyal to the Anglican formularies as established at the Reformation, interpreted by the Caroline divines and restored by the Catholic revival of the nineteenth century. Percy Dearmer, the 'apostle of the English Use', claimed that the vestments and ceremonial advocated by his school were not only legal, but even commanded by the Ornaments Rubric, with its ambiguous reference to the 'second year of the reign of King Edward the Sixth'. The counterpart of Dearmer's 'British Museum Religion'[65] was the historical work of H.O. Wakeman, whose highly successful *Introduction to the History of the Church of England* (1896)[66] maintained that there was a clear distinction between the English and Continental Reformations and that Calvinist Puritanism was an alien element intruded under Edward VI and expelled in 1662. Wakeman upheld Newman's picture of the Church of England as a *via media* and he saw the Oxford Movement as the final victory of English Catholicism over the vestiges of Puritanism.[67]

The views of the Wakeman-Dearmer school did not go unchallenged by Evangelical Churchmen. Wakeman's *Introduction* was denounced by the *Record* as 'that notorious Neo-Anglican pamphlet' and attacked by Henry Wace for offering a misleading view of Anglican history.[68] Evangelicals sought to demonstrate that the Church of England was Protestant and that the *via media* idea was spurious – J.C. Ryle declared that to call the Church of England a *via media* between Rome and the Reformation was like describing the Isle of Wight as halfway between England and France.[69] In detail, the Evangelical case developed in a number of directions.

First, the liturgiologists examined the Prayer Book in its successive revisions to see whether Anglo-Catholic doctrines and practices could be justified from it. Drury's *Two Studies in the Book of Common Prayer* (1901) sought to refute the case for non-communicating attendance. Four chapters of Griffith Thomas's *A Sacrament of our Redemption* were devoted to the Prayer Book's teaching on the Lord's Supper, drawing out the doctrinal implications of the changes introduced between 1548 and 1560, and then examining the Catechism of 1604 and the final revision of

1662 before concluding that 'Our Reformers, following Scripture, placed between the churches of England and Rome a chasm with reference to the Holy Communion which is impassable except by surrender on one side.'[70] Dimock contributed to the debate in *Vox Liturgiae Anglicanae* (1897) and through a number of articles in the *Churchman*.

Arguably the most specialised and technical study concentrated on the Ornaments Rubric, introduced by the 1559 Act of Uniformity as part of the Elizabethan Settlement. The Act re-established the 1552 Prayer Book, with minor modifications, and also declared that the ornaments of the second year of the reign of Edward VI 'shall be retained and be in use... until other order shall be therein taken'.[71] The ritualists claimed that 'other order' never was taken and therefore that the vestments of 1549 were still permissable in the Church of England, an interpretation upheld by H.O. Wakeman.[72] The courts, in the Ridsdale Judgment, maintained that the Crown took 'other order' in 1566 with the publication of Archbishop Parker's *Advertisements* regulating clerical dress. Some Evangelical scholars accepted this, but some made a case for the 1559 Injunctions being the 'order' referred to in the Act. Much work was done on this subject, particularly by J.T. Tomlinson and by Joseph Nunn, both of whom produced learned works on the finer points of Elizabethan legislation and legal vocabulary.[73]

The discussion of the wording of the Prayer Book and its rubrics was amplified by a study of the opinions of the Reformers and the background of sixteenth century church history. Griffith Thomas quoted with approval Bishop Dowden's scathing attack on the use of Reformation divines by the ECU: 'It was only the very ignorant and ill-read among the clergy and laity... who could be long deceived by such scraps, torn from their context, and perverted from their original purport'.[74] Evangelical scholars buttressed their arguments with extensive catenae of quotations, or wrote specifically on the Reformers and their teaching – so Drury published *Confession and Absolution: The Teaching of the Church of England, as interpreted and illustrated by the writings of the Reformers of the Sixteenth Century* in 1903 and H.C.G. Moule edited, for his doctorate of divinity, Bishop Ridley's *A Brief Declaration of the Lord's Supper*, while in 1907 the PRS republished Cranmer's treatise on the same subject.[75] On a more popular level, J.C. Ryle asked in *Facts and Men* (1882), a much reprinted survey of Reformation history, 'Why were our Reformers burned?', demonstrating that the martyrs died for denying a real presence in the consecrated elements.[76] Later in the period Evangelicals were able to cite modern secular historical scholarship against Wakeman – thus Pollard's biographies of Henry VIII and of Cranmer were welcomed by Evangelical Churchmen,[77] and the NCL published lectures by W. Alison Phillips, professor of History at Dublin.[78] C.S. Carter produced several handbooks of church history, notably *The English Church and the Reformation* (1912), which revealed a sound grasp of primary documents and modern research.

Popular polemics

From the examples reviewed already it may be seen that Evangelicals offered an academic response to ritualism in biblical scholarship, liturgical study and church history. Evangelical Churchmen recognised, however, that learned treatises on the Ornaments Rubric or on dogmatic theology were not sufficient to refute Anglo-Catholic arguments, and so they also produced a series of more popular works, designed to place the fruits of scholarship within the reach of ordinary churchpeople and to challenge the best-selling manuals produced by the ritualists.

In January 1896 an article appeared in the *Churchman* entitled 'The need of Evangelical literature of the highest order'.[79] It covered a wide area of church life, but its author, A.C. Downer, insisted particularly that Evangelicals needed to produce shilling primers on doctrine, books that could answer the works of Sadler and Staley without running to the length or expense of Moule's *Outlines* or Lefroy's *Christian Ministry*. Downer noted the rumour that Moule, R.B. Girdlestone and Archdeacon Sinclair were working on such a book, and this duly appeared in the shape of *English Church Teaching* in 1897, albeit with T.W. Drury replacing Sinclair as the third author. The book, on the faith, life and order of the Church of England, was commissioned by the NPCU and covered the Roman and ritual controversies in considerable detail, including a conspectus of church history, an appendix on 'some texts which are frequently misinterpreted' and an 'Analytical Index, with notes on Ambiguous Words' such as absolution, images, priest, Protestant and validity of orders. *English Church Teaching* had sold fifteen thousand copies by 1903 and it remained a popular handbook for the

NPCU and NCL.[80]

Three years after the publication of *English Church Teaching* Nisbet's began to issue a series of 'Church of England Handbooks', small and inexpensive books on topical subjects. By 1901 five had been published, all under the editorial supervision of Griffith Thomas, and these were A.R. Buckland's *The Confessional in the Church of England*, Hay Aitken's *The Doctrine of Baptism*, Drury's *How we got our Prayer Book*, Moule's *The Evangelical School in the Church of England* and the anonymous volume *The Churchman's ABC*.

The next series to appear was published by John Shaw under the general title of 'Twentieth Century Papers on Great Questions of the Day'. According to his biographer, these were suggested by Samuel Garratt at the 1902 Islington Meeting and commissioned by a committee under W.H. Barlow, with Garratt as editor.[81] The papers covered higher criticism as well as ritualism and were criticised by Griffith Thomas for their brevity and cost.[82]

Despite all these attempts to produce cheap and readable Evangelical books, fears continued to be voiced that the ritualists were winning the propaganda battle. 'C.J.', writing to the *Record* in October 1908 under the heading 'Evangelicals and Literature', noted that the ritualist publications *Before the Altar* and *The Catholic Religion* had sold two hundred and ninety eight thousand and one hundred and fifty six thousand copies respectively, while Moule's *At the Holy Communion* had sold thirty seven thousand and Griffith Thomas's *The Catholic Faith* a mere ten thousand.[83] In the same year, however, a new publishing venture was launched. Plans were laid for a series of penny manuals, edited by J.C. Wright, Dawson Walker and J.E. Watts-Ditchfield, a series of shilling handbooks, edited by Griffith Thomas and some theological text books under the direction of J. Harford Battersby.[84] Nothing seems to have come of the third idea, but the 'English Church Manuals' and 'Anglican Church Handbooks', both series published by Longman's, soon began to appear. By 1911 twenty four manuals and fourteen handbooks were available, written by such representative Evangelicals as Henry Lewis, R.B. Girdlestone, Eugene Stock, Guy Warman, Drury, Tait, W.S. Hooton, G.S. Streatfeild and F.E. Spencer.[85] Neither series was directly anti-ritualist, but volumes like Sydney Carter's on *The English Church in the Seventeenth*

Century and T.A. Gurney's on *The Church of the First Three Centuries* or Moule and Drury's pamphlets on the Prayer Book provided an opportunity for positive Evangelical teaching. It may be noted that Messrs Longman's scheme was speedily copied by the Protestant publisher C.J. Thynne, who soon announced a series of penny manuals and shilling handbooks of his own, although these were reprints of Evangelical classics like Ryle's *Knots Untied*, rather than new works.[86]

As well as the series of manuals, other books sought to make the Evangelical case against ritualism at a popular level. These varied from the short but learned essays published in 1899 under the title *Church and Faith*, by contributors including Wace, C.H.H. Wright, Drury, Moule and Tomlinson to Lent Lectures like A.E. Barnes-Lawrence's *A Churchman to Churchmen* (1893). The *Record* reprinted a series of sermons on controversial topics as *The Church and Her Doctrine* in 1891, while four addresses given at St Margaret's, Westminster in 1895 appeared as *Four Foundation Truths: A Message to Churchmen of Today*. One of the most straightforward approaches to the ritual controversy was J.C. Ryle's collection of papers *The Upper Room* (1888) which set out teaching on baptism and the Lord's Supper in the form of questions and answers – twenty four on regeneration and fifty one on the Lord's Supper.[87]

Evangelicals were also ready to use didactic fiction as a teaching medium. This was a well established technique in the ritual controversy, for the novels of Mrs Warboise in the mid-nineteenth century had gone to the lengths of adding doctrinal footnotes to explain the alleged errors of Anglo-Catholicism.[88] In March 1899 the *Churchman* carried a long advertisement for the Protestant stories of Emily S. Holt, published by John Shaw. According to the publisher, 'We do not hesitate to say that anyone who possesses a thorough acquaintance with her works will not only quickly become proof against the errors of Rome, but will also be stirred to resist to the utmost any encroachments upon our Protestant liberty.'[89] Forty novels were offered for £3. Shaw's were still making this offer in 1900 when the *Record* took up the idea and appealed for donations in order to fund gift sets for deserving individuals and institutions. Between May and July 1900 over £100 was raised for this cause by a committee including Buckland, Griffith Thomas, F.S. Webster and the Revd Alfred Peache.[90] Miss Holt's works continued to be advertised at least until 1909, although her career as an author seems to have spanned the period 1870 to 1896. Miss Holt's forty eight titles were eclipsed by the ninety novels produced between 1887 and 1936 by Joseph Hocking, a United Methodist Free Churches minister. Most of Hocking's polemical works addressed the Roman controversy, but his *The Soul of Dominic Wildthorne* (1908) dealt with a ritualist clergyman, a member of the 'Community of the Incarnation', and the NCL's Church Book Room included his novels in its stock.[91] Of other novelists whose work was claimed in the Protestant interest, probably the most famous was Rider Haggard, whose *The Lady of Blossholme* (1909) was advertised by the PTS.[92] A rather different work was the Revd A.A. Isaacs' *The New Vicar* (1904), which used a series of parochial consultations between an Evangelical incumbent and his semi-ritualist flock as a setting for the demolition of the ritualist case.

Apart from literature, the main vehicle of popular Protestant education was lectures and sermons. Some series were eventually published – F.J. Chavasse's *Plain Words on Some Present Day Questions* (1898), Barnes-Lawrence's *A Churchman to Churchmen* (1893) and *A Churchman and his Church* (1917) and the lectures on the primitive church edited by Lefroy and published in 1896, but these represented a tiny proportion of the courses organised by the Protestant societies or by individual incumbents. The NPCU/NCL was especially active in this respect, both nationally and locally. Thus, for example, in the winter of 1901-2 the Hampstead and Kilburn branch arranged a course on English church history with a distinguished list of guest speakers.[93] The Lent series for 1902 in London included 'Reformation principles in their bearing upon the present dangers of the Church of England' at Christ Church, Beckenham, and 'Our Church, past and present' at St Matthias, Tulse Hill.[94] By 1905 the NPCU was able to advertise lecture courses in fifteen different churches in Manchester[95] and in 1908 the target was two hundred lectures on 'The Reformers and Martyrs: Their teaching and their testimony'.[96] In 1914 the NCL reported that one hundred and seventy two courses had been arranged, involving two hundred clergymen.[97] The Church Association also provided lecturers – the programme of the Spring conference of 1903, for example, included a lantern lecture for children entitled 'Some Famous Bonfires', which 'vividly illustrated some of the religious atrocities which took place during the Dark Ages'.[98] The Association's colporteurs and van evangelists, moreover, combined literature distribution with addressing meetings, as did Kensit's Wickliffe Preachers.

Less common didactic techniques were Protestant classes and study circles, organised by some churches and promoted by the magazine *Sunday at Home* in 1902.[99] The Church Association even produced a set of Protestant postcards adorned with pictures of Luther burning the Papal bull, Cranmer entering the Tower and other edifying historical scenes.[100]

Education

Three areas of formal education concerned Evangelical Churchmen, and these were schools, the universities and the training of the clergy. In each area the Anglo-Catholics seemed to have established themselves firmly and this period witnessed attempts by the Evangelicals to build up their own resources within the educational system.

Schools

In the sphere of middle-class schools the Anglo-Catholics benefited from the work of Nathaniel Woodard, who, from the late 1840s, established schools in various parts of England. By 1890, a year before his death, there were eleven Woodard schools, with a total of 1350 pupils. Woodard was a committed Anglo-Catholic, and ensured that his pupils received clear religious teaching, including the opportunity for confession to the school chaplain. It is hardly surprising, therefore, that members of the staff included supporters of the ECU and even of the Society of the Holy Cross.[101]

Evangelical anxiety at the work of the Woodard schools was almost as old as the schools themselves.[102] By the end of the nineteenth century the Evangelical attitude was a mixture of fear and grudging respect. P.V.M. Filleul attacked the institutions in his pamphlet *The Catholic Revival: What is it doing for England?* (1900), and Edward Darbyshire, vice-chairman of the Church Association, told the Spring conference of 1900 that 'through the Woodard schools and schools of a similar character where a good education was given at a small cost the seeds of poison had been sown into the minds of many of the young people of this land.'[103]

Darbyshire went on to criticise Evangelical apathy over education, and this too was a recurrent theme in the columns of the *Record*. J.S. Tucker complained in 1901, 'Again and again I hear of boys at the Woodard schools from Protestant homes, often the sons of clergy, ' and the same complaint was voiced by 'Magister' thirteen years later.[104]

There were a number of Evangelical schools to rival the Woodard institutions. The oldest was Trent College, founded in 1866 in conscious opposition to the Woodard schools, so that Trent's historian, M.A.J. Tarver, could note that 'The enemy was the Oxford Movement as embodied in Dr Woodard, and the schools which his influence created.'[105] By 1929, however, the atmosphere had changed somewhat:

> 'The bitterness of opposing religious factions no longer vexes the schools. The Woodard seminaries are our friends, and we play them regularly at cricket and football, nor, for many years has there been anything either in our chapel services or in the general trend of thought at Trent savouring of narrowness or bigotry.'[106]

Nonetheless, Trent was run on definite Evangelical lines: it was bought in 1892 by the Evangelical College and School Company, whose directors included Wace, Webb-Peploe, H.E. Fox and Sir Robert Lighton (hon secretary of the NPCU),[107] and the company installed John Savile Tucker as Headmaster in 1895. Tucker, an examining chaplain to Bishop Chavasse, saw Trent recover from financial crisis and expand both in numbers and facilities.[108] The Evangelical College and School Company added to its holdings in 1902 when it bought Weymouth College, founded in 1863. Under H.C. Barnes-Lawrence, brother of a noted Evangelical clergyman, Weymouth also expanded in this period and had 120 pupils by 1913.[109] Monkton Combe school, established in 1868, also passed through the hands of the company, although by 1907 it was being run by an independent Evangelical board. It claimed 150 pupils in 1913 and the Headmaster, J.W. Kearns, was a former member of Wycliffe Hall.[110] Dean Close Memorial School opened in Cheltenham in 1886 with twelve pupils. Six extensions were undertaken over the next twenty seven years and the number of pupils rose to two hundred. W.H. Flecker, the Headmaster, was a well known Evangelical and a regular speaker at the May Meetings.[111] The other main Evangelical public school was the South Eastern College at

Ramsgate, founded in 1879 and later renamed St Lawrence's College.[112] There were also a number of new foundations, for instance a girls' school at Headington, Oxford, opened in 1915.[113] The *Record* listed four girls' schools run on Evangelical principles in 1909, and this list did not include the school at Sherborne, which was certainly an Evangelical establishment.[114] The early twentieth century therefore witnessed energetic efforts in the field of public school education on the part of Evangelical Churchmen. Evangelicals were not complacent – the *Record* was still complaining in 1912 that the schools were under-funded[115] – but much work was done to build up well-equipped schools offering education in accordance with Reformation principles.

Oxbridge Pastorates

Evangelical activity in the universities focussed on the Oxford and Cambridge Pastorates, founded in 1893 and 1897 respectively. The Oxford scheme was initiated by F.J. Chavasse, then principal of Wycliffe Hall, who was anxious to place Evangelical pastoral work among undergraduates on a permanent footing and to provide an alternative to the Anglo-Catholicism of Pusey House. A trust was established under the control of the Wycliffe Hall Council, and H.H. Gibbon was appointed as the first Pastorate chaplain.[116] Concern was expressed periodically at the weakness of the Pastorate compared with Pusey House – thus E.A. Burroughs, writing in the *Churchman* in October 1911 on 'Oxford and Evangelicalism in relation to the crisis in the Church, ' painted a gloomy picture of Evangelical influence in the University and appealed for more money for the Pastorate.[117] Despite this despondency, the Pastorate maintained at least two chaplains throughout the period, and from 1922 it was formally linked to St Aldate's, then under the vigorous leadership of C.M. Chavasse.[118]

The Cambridge Pastorate followed a similar course to that of Oxford. The key figures in the foundation were John Barton, Moule, Barlow and C.J. Procter, and the first two chaplains were the Revds Philip Armitage and A.G. Dodderidge.[119] Although Cambridge had stronger Evangelical traditions than Oxford and there was no equivalent of Pusey House, Anglo-Catholic influence was still considerable. In his second report to the Ridley Hall Council (1908), A.J. Tait drew attention to the 'critical condition' of the Pastorate, continuing,

> 'There is no doubt whatever that at the present time there is a vigorous and determined endeavour to indoctrinate men with sacerdotal views. It is carried on by some of the younger dons, aided by zealous partisans amongst the junior members, as well as by visiting clergy… Just at the time when sacerdotal influence seems to be particularly aggressive, the existence of the evangelical Pastorate is threatened through lack of funds. The fund is already overdrawn to the extent of £300, and, unless fresh help is immediately obtained, some curtailment of the work is inevitable.'[120]

It would seem, however, that the Pastorate survived this financial crisis.

The idea of an Evangelical college in Oxford was raised by F.J. Chavasse before the First World War and revived in 1926. The Evangelicals held the city centre church of St Peter-le-Bailey, with its shrinking congregation, its rectory and its schools. Contributions from the Martyrs Memorial and Church of England Trust Society and gifts in memory of Bishop Chavasse, who died in March 1928, made it possible for St Peter's Hall to open in 1929, with C.M. Chavasse as Master.[121] St Peter's was the first Evangelical college not specifically devoted to the training of the clergy, and so may be seen as part of the attempt to propagate Evangelical principles within the general sphere of education.

Training the clergy

By 1890 Evangelical Churchmen controlled three institutions for clerical training. Ridley Hall, Cambridge, and Wycliffe Hall, Oxford, founded some ten years previously, catered for university graduates reading for orders, while the London College of Divinity (St John's Hall, Highbury) provided courses for those without university degrees. In addition, St Aidan's College, Birkenhead, had Evangelical traditions, although its trust deed did not commit it to any Church party.[122]

Each of these institutions sustained its work throughout this period. F.J. Chavasse steadily built up the number of ordinands at Wycliffe Hall from twelve in 1889 to thirty two in 1900.[123] Ridley Hall was larger, with an average of thirty students throughout the 1890s, and in 1905 the total in residence reached fifty one.[124] St Aidan's moved away from Evangelicalism between 1890 and 1901 following the appointment of a High Churchman as principal, but he was succeeded by A.J. Tait and the Evangelical influence was restored. Tait revived the college's fortunes and it had a full complement of fifty three students by 1908.[125] Building work was undertaken at Ridley Hall and a determined attempt was made to improve college endowments, for instance through the Peache Memorial Fund at St John's, Highbury.[126]

Despite the healthy condition of the Evangelical colleges, it was felt that more should be done to encourage Evangelical ordinands, especially those of limited means. Although scholarships and exhibitions were founded, it was thought that fees were still high, and there was no Evangelical equivalent to Mirfield and Kelham, institutions which offered a complete training, including a degree, at a reasonable cost. Evangelical Churchmen ran the risk of appealing only to the affluent ordinands and to those who could afford to take a degree before proceeding to Wycliffe or Ridley Hall.[127] It was in an endeavour to meet this need that St John's Hall, Durham, was founded. The idea of a Durham hostel was not new, [128] but the scheme came to fruition in 1909. The Hall offered Durham degrees to men who had trained at Highbury, thus enabling aspiring ordinands to avoid the expense of a separate university education.

One of the initiators of the Durham hostel was J.E. Watts-Ditchfield, and he was also the prime mover in the appeal for a Million Shilling Fund, launched with the support of the NCL in March 1911. The Fund was aimed specifically at the training of non-Oxbridge clergy and hoped to improve the facilities and reduce the fees at Durham, Highbury and St Aidan's. The appeal achieved relatively modest results, however, raising only £8000 instead of the £50, 000 initially envisaged.[129]

As well as supporting their colleges, Evangelicals made provision for the training of the clergy through a variety of ordination funds. Some, like the Elland Society, were long-established and modest in size.[130] Others were more recent: the NCL, for example, had an ordination fund which by 1915 had assisted thirty six candidates, twenty four of whom had taken orders.[131] This work was also undertaken on a somewhat larger scale by the CPAS.[132] Educational work of this kind was not directed specifically against ritualism, but rather towards the positive encouragement of Evangelical principles. It was the positive note and the absence of polemic which made the CPAS more popular and hence more effective than the confessedly Protestant societies like the NCL.

Patronage

The sometimes uneasy relationship between positive Evangelicalism and defensive or polemical Protestantism visible in the sphere of education was also apparent in the field of Church patronage. The Evangelicals were noted for their powerful patronage trusts, which controlled a considerable number of livings – in 1897 it was estimated that Simeon's Trustees held 119 advowsons, the Church Patronage Trustees 86, the Hyndman Trustees 47 and the Peache Trustees 19.[133] In the face of the ritualist challenge, moreover, Evangelicals were urged to acquire more advowsons. Both the NCL and the Church Association set up patronage committees in the early years of the twentieth century and their holdings grew steadily, so that by 1918 the Association claimed to control twenty livings. More powerful still was the CPAS, which established an advowsons committee as part of its 'Forward Movement' in 1893 and held about fifty benefices by 1917.[134] At first sight, therefore, it would seem that Evangelical Churchmen had gained effective control of a significant number of benefices and that these could be used not only to prevent the spread of ritualism, but also aggressively in the cause of Protestantism.[135]

This apparent advantage, however, was offset by other considerations. Bishops, impressed, or perhaps alarmed, by the extent of Evangelical patronage, used this as a reason for offering livings in their gift predominantly to members of other schools of thought.[136] Not all the patronage trusts, moreover, saw opposing ritualism as part of their role. It may be a significant indicator of Evangelical attitudes that the patronage of the CPAS, which adopted positive Evangelicalism and eschewed controversy, grew far more quickly than that of the Church Association or the NCL. Furthermore, the largest Evangelical trust, founded in the early nineteenth century by Charles Simeon, took no steps to increase its patronage in this period. The number of Simeon Trust livings increased by bequest or by parochial division, but the trustees deliberately refused to buy advowsons.[137] Simeon Trust incumbents were not prominent in the ritual controversy, as some Protestants complained, [138] and in 1909 the trustees were even accused of appointing a ritualist to the living of St Bede, Toxteth Park, Liverpool. 'Watchman' wrote to the *English Churchman*, the organ of the militant Protestants, that 'some holding Simeon Trust livings are a hindrance rather than a help to the Evangelical cause', while Henry Wisdom suggested that the trustees would find Simeon himself too ' "tactless" and "extreme"' to enjoy their patronage in the early twentieth century. The trustees stood by their appointment, despite the fulminations of the ultra-Protestants.[139] It may be seen, therefore, that patronage trustees were not universally committed to the priority of controversy with ritualism. They were anxious to maintain Evangelical teaching, and to that extent they assisted resistance to Anglo-Catholicism, but they were not ultra-Protestants. The attitude of the moderate trustees was summed up by E.A. Eardley Wilmot, responding on behalf of his colleagues to the criticism of 1909: the trustees, he wrote, '...claim to act... with a view to the best interests of the parishes for which they are responsible, and with a loyal attachment to Evangelical Churchmanship.'[140] Parochial needs came before the dictates of party warfare.

An attempt has now been made to describe the most positive aspects of the Evangelical response to ritualism: the active propagation of Evangelical principles through books, sermons and lectures, the development of public schools, the expansion of colleges, the creation of the Oxbridge Pastorates and the use of patronage trusts. These endeavours were only some of the measures urged on Evangelical Churchmen by those who called for a 'Forward Movement' as the best way to meet the ritualist challenge. In this respect, any attempt to strengthen the Evangelical witness could be seen as an indirect reply to ritualism, along the lines of A.J. Robinson's call for Evangelicals to 'cease fighting and to unite in work' in the aftermath of the Lincoln Judgment. Robinson, writing to the *Record*, continued, 'let us outpray and outwork those from whom we conscientiously differ. This is the best and most Christ-like way of overcoming them, ' and this call bore fruit in the expansion of the work of the CPAS under the direction of John Barton.[141]

Robinson's policy, however, was deemed inadequate by a significant number of Evangelical Churchmen. Many held that it was not enough merely to outwork the ritualists, but that an attempt should be made to curb the spread of ritual innovation in the Church of England. It was efforts made in this direction which created the most heated debate within the Evangelical party in this period.

Aggressive Evangelicalism

Alerting the public

A comparatively inoffensive controversial technique was raising public awareness of the extent of Anglican ritualism and its main features. The *Record* began a weekly column 'Lawlessness in the Church' in July 1898 and this included detailed descriptions of services at the most extreme of the London churches. The column, retitled 'The Crisis in the Church', continued until 1902, but even after this, full accounts of particularly flamboyant services appeared at regular intervals. Special reports were sent in from the provinces, describing the ritual in use at All Saints', Plymouth, Christ Church, Doncaster, St Matthew's, Sheffield, the Church of the Annunciation, Brighton and other strongholds of Anglo-Catholicism.[142] Linden Heitland published *Ritualism in Town and Country: A Volume of Evidence* in 1902, describing the services and ornaments of ninety eight churches outside London, ranging from Sheffield and Doncaster to parish churches in remote villages. A similar work was done by the Hon and Revd W.E. Bowen, who produced several books, one specially written for the information of Members of Parliament.[143] The Church Association published a *Church of England Almanack* annually from 1889, including statistics on the spread of ritualism, [144] and also extracted a 'Ritualistic Clergy List' from editions of the ECU's *Tourists' Church Guide*. The list usually included a number of mistakes, thus provoking letters from aggrieved Evangelicals like the deanery CMS secretary whom the Association accused of using altar lights.[145] The effect of these volumes in stimulating the controversy should not be under-estimated. Books like Walter Walsh's *Secret History of the Oxford Movement* (1897), which soon appeared in a cheap popular edition, and the descriptive articles in the *Record* and in the secular press did much to arouse Protestant feeling and indignation. They brought ritualism – and in its most extreme form – to the attention of the public and helped to transform the Church crisis of the late 1890s from a dispute within the Church of England into a major political issue. Publicity was a very powerful weapon, and propagandists like Walsh and Bowen had adopted a shrewd technique in choosing to broadcast selected facts about the 'Romeward drift' within the Church. They hoped to arouse latent national Protestantism and thus secure action against the ritualists.[146]

Appealing to the bishops

The single group which received the most information on the alleged enormities of ritualism was the bishops, and their information came from two main sources. The first was bewildered parishioners dismayed by the introduction of innovations into their churches or from moderate Evangelicals hoping for episcopal action. In November 1904, for example, parents from St Andrew's, Worthing, complained to the bishop of Chichester that the vicar expected their children to go to confession before he would present them for confirmation.[147] Twelve years later the inhabitants of Whiteparish in the diocese of Salisbury wrote to their bishop because a new incumbent abolished matins and introduced a choral eucharist as the principal Sunday service.[148] Complainants of this kind clearly expected redress from the bishop, and this line of policy was pursued at the beginning of the Church crisis by the *Record* and those for whom it spoke.

The second group of episcopal informants adopted a less respectful tone. They tended to demand, rather than to request action, were prone to lecture the bishops on their responsibilities and often had no connection with the parishes about which they complained. Captain Cobham, chairman of the Church Association, was particularly adept at complaints of this kind – he wrote, for instance, to the bishop of St Albans in May 1901 concerning the services at All Saints', Southend. As well as rebuking the bishop for giving diocesan funds to a church where 'idol-worship, Mary-worship and wafer-worship are now publicly performed, with a pomp and ostentation which might fill with envy the High Priest of any pagan temple, ' the Captain also enclosed for his lordship's perusal a pamphlet entitled *A Gross Scandal in the Diocese of St Alban's; Undiluted Popery and Idolatry in the Established Church under the oversight of the Bishop.*[149] The Kensits frequently wrote in similar vein and J.A. Kensit went to the extent of appealing to the London Diocesan Conference when Bishop Winnington-Ingram ignored his complaints about ritualism.[150]

Protests of the Cobham-Kensit variety were clearly designed principally for publicity. Neither the Church Association nor the PTS had much faith in the bishops; indeed, the former body brought its campaign of denunciation of the episcopate to a climax in November 1907 when a mass meeting passed a resolution 'That, in the opinion of this meeting, the official action of the bishops (with few exceptions) has been, and is now, wanting in loyalty to the Church of England, in that they have aided, abetted, defended and promoted lawless clergy bent upon Romanising the National Church.'[151] The Association produced a special souvenir programme for the meeting, the frontispiece of which depicted Britannia sternly admonishing a bishop.[152]

By 1907, however, it was not only the ultra-Protestants who were expressing dissatisfaction with episcopal action against ritualism. The *Record* began to lose patience very soon after the Kensit protests brought the ritual question to the fore in the spring of 1898. A leader on 'The bishops in council' in May likened the episcopate to 'a group of well-meaning gentlemen, desparately uncomfortable and at their wits' end to know what to do.'[153] A month later, in 'Waiting for the bishops, ' a more critical note was sounded,[154] and this was sustained for the next two decades. The *Record*'s general line was that without resorting to prosecution, the bishops had a wide range of disciplinary powers available to them. They could refuse to institute known ritualists. They could inhibit lawbreakers and so stop them officiating outside their own parishes. They could refuse to license curates or to conduct confirmations where the law was disobeyed. They could withdraw grants from diocesan funds. Sometimes these measures were used, much to the satisfaction of the Evangelical press. More often, however, bishops seemed to be inactive or even to encourage ritualism, and this seemed to justify the obloquy heaped on their heads by the ardent Protestants.

Disquiet at the perceived episcopal response to ritualism, moreover, spread beyond the ranks of partisan Evangelicalism. The report of the Royal Commission on Ecclesiastical Discipline, published in 1906, included a number of comments critical of the Church's leadership. Bishops were said to be ignorant of the condition of their own dioceses, sympathetic to the law-breakers and unduly tolerant of ritualist practices. The bishops of London and Southwark, by producing their own rules for ceremonial, had set a standard more lax than that of other dioceses and so made it more difficult for their colleagues to enforce the law.[155] In his remarks on the Report, J.J. Lias attributed much of the difficulty to the one-sided nature of episcopal appointments,[156] and certainly leading members of the bishops' bench in this period tended to come from a Tractarian or High Church background, and therefore to share many of the doctrinal views of at least the moderate ritualists.[157]

The main cause of the clash between the Protestants and the bishops was that their perceptions of the ritual issue differed sharply.[158] As was demonstrated in the previous chapter, for a whole series of reasons Evangelical Churchmen, in common with other Protestants, regarded ritualism as a serious threat to the Church of England and as a menace to be removed at all costs. The bishops, although troubled by a small minority of extremists, saw most Anglo-Catholics as hard-working clergymen loyal to the Church and therefore worthy of diocesan support and preferment. This was true not only of High Churchmen like Winnington-Ingram and E.S. Talbot, but also to some extent of Evangelical bishops like A.W. Thorold and E.H. Bickersteth. Thorold maintained cordial relations with Father Dolling, allowing him 'ampler toleration than any other clergyman in the diocese' because of his work in Portsmouth, while Bickersteth left the ritual at All Saints', Plymouth, alone until the Lambeth Opinions of 1899 compelled him to ask the vicar, G.R. Prynne, to discontinue the ceremonial use of incense.[159] F.J. Chavasse was censured by the Laymen's League when he appointed a High Churchman to an honorary canonry in 1904 and he responded by attacking 'the denunciation of devout men who, although both in doctrine and ritual they may differ from Evangelicals, are yet loyal members of the Church of England.'[160] Bishops were inclined to toleration by virtue of their position; they were acutely aware of the pastoral, financial and personal costs of controversy; and their priorities were very different from those of the Protestant stalwarts who urged decisive action against the ritualists. Although the High Church preponderance in the Southern Province throughout this period may lend some colour to Evangelical complaints that the bishops were too sympathetic to ritualism, the fact that, of the Evangelicals raised to the episcopate, only N.D.J. Straton managed not to fall foul of the Protestants at some stage in his career, would seem to indicate that Protestant expectations were somewhat unreasonable. Even E.A. Knox, who was taken to court for refusing to institute a ritualist to Sacred Trinity, Salford, could not satisfy the zealots of the Church Association.[161]

Sifting the evidence of episcopal action and attitudes, it may be suggested that no diocesan bishops, with the possible exceptions of Straton and Barnes, shared the Protestant enthusiasm of the Church Association and its allies. Most bishops, including the Evangelicals, drew a distinction between High Churchmen and disloyal Romanisers which the ultra-Protestant societies refused to recognise. In many dioceses, therefore, bishops angered the strong Protestants by failing to suppress High Church practices which, in the opinion of the episcopate, were quite innocuous. This was not the case everywhere, however, for the bishops of London, Southwark, St Albans and Chichester were consistently lenient towards extreme ritualism, as were Frere at Truro and Wakefield at Birmingham. It was in these dioceses that flagrant Romanising was allowed to develop with little hindrance, as the Royal Commission observed, and these cases lent colour to the Protestant claim that the episcopate as a whole was failing in its duty to uphold the principles of the Book of Common Prayer.

While the bishop might be the obvious initiator of action against ritualism, therefore, Protestant Evangelicals tended to regard the episcopate with a mixture of anger and contempt. The bishops, they claimed, were at best feeble and ineffective, pinning their hopes on compromise and negotiation, and at worst active supporters of the Romanising clergy. Archbishop Davidson appealed to Churchmen to 'trust the bishops'; the Church Association responded that this was like putting the Army under the command of Fenian generals. Stalwart Protestants were unlikely to appreciate the efforts of those bishops like Mandell Creighton who did conscientiously seek to achieve a settlement with recalcitrant ritualists, and who found their work undermined by extremists on both sides.[162] Those seeking firmer action to check Anglo-Catholicism therefore turned to other methods.

Protest and prosecution

Henry Miller's *A Guide to Ecclesiastical Law*, produced by the secretary of the Church Association 'for Churchwardens and parishioners', included a lengthy section on petitions, memorials and public meetings,[163] and these were techniques of protest frequently employed in this period. Public meetings followed a common pattern of set speeches proposing and seconding resolutions bearing on some aspect of the controversy and they were an opportunity for the Protestant societies to muster support both numerically through a large audience and in terms of influence by securing a platform of leading Churchmen and MPs. A large number of meetings were held, ranging from the 'Great Demonstration' organised by the Protestant Alliance in May 1898 and the Great United Protestant Demonstrations at the Albert Hall in 1899, 1900 and 1902[164] to local meetings arranged under the auspices of the NPCU/NCL or Church Association or stimulated by issues of local concern. Thus, in the winter of 1901, the NPCU held a series of public meetings in provincial centres at which a standard resolution was presented, calling for legislation to secure 'a reasonable conformity to the law of Church and realm' in the conduct of public worship.[165] The Church Association arranged a similar series in 1903 to build up support for the Church Discipline bill and again in 1906 when Kekewich's Ecclesiastical Disorders bill was before Parliament.[166] Local protests held in the period included the public meetings called in Bedford in 1903 to object to the teaching of auricular confession at St Paul's church, and the meeting of the parishioners of Whiteparish in 1916 to oppose the introduction of choral eucharist as the principal Sunday service.[167]

Petitions and memorials also appeared at regular intervals. Bishop Alford responded to the Lincoln Judgment by organising a memorial against the permissive use of the *agnus dei*, on the grounds that it might lead to eucharistic adoration. One thousand Churchmen signed the memorial and copies were sent to the archbishops and to the Queen.[168] The issue of vestments produced several petitions in the early 1900s – in June 1906 the Church Association collected one hundred and eighteen thousand signatures to a petition deploring the legalisation of vestments – and similar memorials appeared in 1908 and 1912.[169] The Association petitioned the King against lawlessness in the Church in 1913, while in the following year the NCL presented a memorial to the archbishops asking that the Communion Office be left alone by the revisers of the Prayer Book. This latter document speedily secured forty five thousand signatures, while in 1918 more than twice as many people, including nine bishops, endorsed a similar petition.[170]

Protestants dissatisfied with episcopal inaction and unconvinced by the efficacy of petitions and memorials in restraining ritualism had another option open to them and that was resort to the law. As Miller's *Guide* noted, legal proceedings could be taken under the 1840 Church Discipline Act or the 1874 Public Worship Regulation Act, or even under the Acts of Uniformity, subject to certain conditions, the best known of which was the episcopal right of veto.[171]

The policy of prosecution, pursued energetically by the Church Association from the 1860s, reached its climax in the Lincoln Case of 1888-92.[172] The prosecution of Bishop Edward King for using illegal ritual at St Peter at Gowts, Lincoln, was bitterly opposed by many influential Evangelicals. The *Record* declared that the decision to prosecute was taken 'without consultation… with any single Evangelical leader' and stated bluntly, 'Whatever else it is, it is not the work of the Evangelical party.' The newspaper was equally hostile to the prosecution of the Liverpool ritualist James Bell Cox, which began in 1885 but was still continuing five years later.[173]

Evangelical Churchmen opposed the policy of prosecution for two main reasons. One was tactical: prosecutions were highly unpopular with the general public, they created martyrs by imprisoning conscientious ritualists and they forced moderate High Churchmen to give their support to persecuted extremists. It was claimed, therefore, that prosecution was ineffective as a way of checking the growth of ritualism; all it achieved, wrote Archdeacon Sinclair in 1893, was to make ritualism popular.[174] Dean Payne Smith made the same point in the *Churchman* in February 1890: 'one prisoner shut up in Lancaster Gaol will make more ritualists than a thousand decrees of the law courts will send in the opposite direction.'[175]

The second reason for opposing prosecution was that it was unspiritual and immoral. This case was made persistently and forcefully by Samuel Garratt, himself a strong Protestant, but an equally strong opponent of 'carnal' methods of controversy. Garratt began to voice opposition to the use of legal weapons against the ritualists as early as 1872 and he maintained his position with absolute consistency until his death in March 1906. It is important to note that Garratt was by no means sympathetic to ritualism, nor did he support schemes to increase the legal comprehensiveness of the Church of England. His opposition to prosecution arose from spiritual principles, not from toleration.[176]

To some extent prosecution declined as a practical policy and as a subject of debate after 1892. Although it was not a disaster for the Protestant cause, the final verdict in the Lincoln Case was clearly a defeat for the Church Association and it was recognised as such. The Revd William Johnston wrote with satisfaction in the *Churchman*:

> 'For many years an association of able, wealthy and earnest men have appealed to the courts of law for decisions upon matters of dispute in the ritual of the church. The tide bore them awhile upon the very crest of the wave; now they find themselves deserted even by the ebb, and stranded upon the mud banks of a lone and forsaken estuary.'[177]

Moderates like P.V. Smith welcomed the Judgment; Archdeacon Taylor and Bishop Ryle regretted it; but all agreed that prosecutions should cease and that Evangelicals should henceforth eschew, in the *Record*'s words, 'a policy which has become not only useless but mischievous.'[178] Even Dr Hakes, who was still engaged in legal action against Bell Cox, decided to abandon his suit in the light of the Lincoln Judgment.[179]

It would be a mistake to believe, however, that prosecution was ruled out after 1892. It is true that the Church Association opposed further appeals to the courts until the law had been amended, but some legal action was still undertaken. There were a succession of faculty cases, in which aggrieved Protestants sought to secure the removal of illegal ornaments from Anglo-Catholic churches. One case, involving the Church of the Annunciation, Brighton, and in which the plaintiff was supported by the Church Association, lasted from 1899 until 1903 and resulted in a somewhat hollow victory for the Protestants. There were similar, albeit briefer, faculty suits at Woolwich in 1900 and Shirebrook in 1905-06.[180]

Renewed resort to prosecution for the use of illegal ritual was also raised as a possibility. Towards the end of 1900 it was rumoured that a case would be brought against a number of London ritualists and this eventually led to a prosecution initiated by Colonel Alfred Porcelli and vetoed by Bishop Creighton.[181] It is significant that with the growing extremism of a minority of ritualists, Evangelical opinion began to swing back towards prosecution as a viable option. In January 1900 the *Record* expressed itself willing to see ritualists who flouted the Lambeth Opinions on incense and lights brought before the courts,[182] an attitude which provoked opposition from moderates like P.V. Smith and Sir John Kennaway, but support from other correspondents like 'J.H.', who wrote at the end of March: 'nothing but compulsion will prevail against ritualism.'[183] Although Henry Wace continued to oppose prosecution, by 1907 A.E. Barnes-Lawrence was criticising the bishops for not using their legal powers against the extremists, and Sir Edward Clarke was sympathetic to the repeated attempts to prosecute the incumbent of Thorpe, all of which were vetoed by Bishops Ryle and Talbot of Winchester.[184] In reporting the Thorpe case between 1910 and 1913, and a similar case at Potters Bar in 1914, the *Record* reserved its criticism for the bishops and did not attack the plaintiffs.[185] Even the *Churchman* was ready to contemplate prosecution over the issue of reservation in 1917.[186] No ritual prosecutions initiated by the laity took place in this period, since the few cases brought under the Public Worship Regulation Act were vetoed by the bishops, but this does not mean that all Evangelicals had abandoned prosecution as a weapon against ritualism; indeed, the debate over the morality and utility of legal action continued until at least the 1920s, with the protagonists on both sides repeating the arguments voiced in the last quarter of the nineteenth century.

Parliamentary pressure

It has already been noted that the Church Association abandoned legal action under the Public Worship Regulation Act after 1892. This should not be taken to denote a new moderation on the part of the Association, however, but rather to indicate that the ultra-Protestants were dissatisfied with the existing condition of the law. From 1892, and especially from 1898, when the 'Crisis in the Church' began to attract wider public attention, the Association devoted a large part of its resources to political campaigning, hoping to secure changes which would render prosecution more effective and less unpopular. To this end, a series of bills were introduced in the House of Commons, mostly seeking to abolish the episcopal veto and to substitute deprivation for imprisonment as the penalty for contumacy.

The political campaign was launched at a meeting held in October 1892 at the National Club, and it formed part of a wider 'Scheme of Future Policy'. The Association hoped to build up the work of the National Protestant League, to secure the election of Protestant MPs and to unite them into a Protestant Parliamentary Party.[187] It may be asked how far these objectives were achieved and how influential Protestantism was in political affairs.

The Church Association certainly constructed an impressive political organisation, which was at its height in the early years of the twentieth century. By 1900 the Association had seven full-time parliamentary agents, each responsible for a region of the country, [188] and two years later it was reported that a Protestant organisation existed in 225 out of the 443 constituencies in England and Wales.[189] Protestant electoral rolls were compiled, listing electors who were pledged not to promise their vote until candidates' views on Protestant questions had been ascertained. The Association was active in all the General Elections of the period from 1900 to 1918 and also campaigned in by-elections. Major appeals for funds were issued in 1900, 1903 and 1905 to meet the cost of this work.[190]

The effectiveness of the Association's political activity is difficult to gauge. Henry Miller claimed great successes for his 'Protestantism before Politics' campaign, and, for instance, produced a detailed analysis after the General Election of 1900 affirming that 294 MPs were pledged to support the Church Discipline bill and that in almost ninety contested constituencies the Protestant candidate had been successful.[191] The Protestant influence was acknowledged by a number of politicians and contributed to several by-election results, so that when E.A. Villiers defeated Gerald Loder, a newly appointed Lord of the Treasury, in the Brighton by-election of 1905, the victorious Liberal 'attributed his capture of Brighton very largely to the unanimous support of the Protestants – many of them not Liberals.'[192] By-election evidence, however, was far from conclusive. Victories at Elland and Southport in 1899 were offset by defeats at Osgoldcross and East St Pancras in the same year. In the General Election of 1900 Kensit failed to secure election for Brighton and Benjamin Nicholson was defeated in Kent, although Protestantism dominated the representation of Liverpool and even achieved the removal of Walter Long, the Minister for Agriculture, who refused to support the Church Discipline bill.[193] The High Churchman Canon MacColl told Lord Salisbury that the Church Association and Laymen's League were 'a negligible quantity in the electorate, '[194] but politically Protestantism was far from negligible. It was able to bring disciplinary legislation before the Commons annually until 1908 and again in 1911, to muster a delegation of one hundred MPs to lobby the archbishop of Canterbury and to compel Balfour to set up the Royal Commission of 1904-06 after his opposition to the 1903 bill had produced a vote of censure from his own constituency party and rumours of a backbench rebellion.[195]

Protestantism was influential, but the Church Association never succeeded in changing the law with respect to ritualism. The 1903 bill was the only one to gain a second reading and even it ran out of parliamentary time.[196] To some extent, Protestant issues went the way of general ecclesiastical legislation in this period and were crowded out of a busy parliamentary timetable. Protestantism, moreover, could not win the wholehearted support of either of the main political parties. The Liberals were happier using ritualism against the Established Church than seeking to settle the controversy and strident Protestantism could alienate their Irish Roman Catholic allies. The Unionists numbered High Churchmen as well as Evangelicals among their supporters and were not anxious to endorse a Protestant crusade. Both parties were non-confessional bodies, seeking pragmatic solutions to political problems.[197] Between 1898 and 1904 the Protestants were able to bring considerable pressure to bear on the Government (although even at the height of the Church crisis, Imperial issues made a greater impression on the electorate),[198] but their influence began to decline once Balfour appointed the Royal Commission. Austin Taylor, son of J.C. Ryle's archdeacon of Liverpool, MP for East Toxteth and leader of the Laymen's League, wanted a Select Committee; Balfour, on Archbishop Davidson's advice, chose a Commission instead, and by opposing the Commission outright Taylor lost the opportunity to influence its composition.[199] Most MPs accepted the Commission as a sensible measure and thereby inaugurated two years of painstaking work, followed by two decades of debate arising from the 1906 report. While the commissioners were at work and the Convocations were debating their recommendations, popular Protestant fervour declined. By 1918, Church Association canvassers found that when they questioned parliamentary candidates on ritualism and Prayer Book revision 'many expressed ignorance on the subjects at issue.'[200] With the exception of Liverpool, where the presence of a large Irish community maintained religious tensions into the 1930s, Protestantism ceased to be an issue in politics as the attention of an expanding working class electorate increasingly focussed on social concerns. As one Labour MP said during the 1928 debate on Prayer Book revision, 'The working man is not interested in the Prayer Book, but in the rent book.'[201] Mobilising voters for the Protestant cause thus became increasingly difficult.

Protestantism before politics was not a campaign which all Evangelicals were eager to endorse, and at times it proved as controversial as the policy of prosecution. Canon Garratt continued his opposition to 'carnal' weapons, observing that deprivation was no better than imprisonment – 'To deprive a man and his family of home and food, however ecclesiastical it may look as compared with imprisonment, is as carnal a weapon for punishing wrong doctrine or ritual... [the Church Discipline bill] is not God's method and will not have His blessing.'[202] Other Evangelicals pointed out that the Church Association policy meant supporting Liberal candidates who were also pledged to Home Rule, to disestablishment and to education measures harmful to Church schools. This issue was raised by A.W. Gough and Dean Lefroy early in 1904 and continued to appear periodically until 1910.[203] Robert Douglas censured the Association for co-operation with 'unbelievers, secularists, Home Rulers and "Little Englanders"' in April 1905, [204] while W.J.L. Sheppard called its policy 'suicidal' after the Eye by-election of 1906, when a disestablishing Liberal opposed to Church schools narrowly defeated a Conservative Churchman reluctant to abolish the episcopal veto.[205] After the Dulwich election of the same year, A.E. McAdam attacked the Association for supporting a Liberal merely because of 'the side-issue of what they call "Protestantism before politics".'[206] In October 1906 Lady Wimborne wrote to the *Record* commending the Liberal party for its Protestant stance, thereby adding fuel to the political controversy. J.J. Beddow supported her, but the majority of correspondents attacked the Liberals and their Protestant allies. G.F. Chambers described the Church Association's MPs as 'the servile followers of Sir Henry Campbell Bannerman, ' and declared:

> 'they have done nothing – absolutely nothing – to promote the Protestant cause... What they have done has been to advance the Reign of Terror in Ireland, to advance disestablishment in Wales, and to promote the destruction of

> religion as a factor in the public elementary (and all other) schools in England.'

Miller replied with a scornful reference to those 'who prefer to put their politics before their Protestantism.'[207] It may be seen, therefore, that not all Evangelicals made ritualism their first concern when deciding their political allegiance, and education, disestablishment and Home Rule made political decisions very difficult for Evangelical Churchmen in the decade before the First World War.

Direct action

The most notorious Evangelical response to ritualism was the public protest at ritualist services perpetrated by the Kensits and their imitators.[208] John Kensit began his campaign by objecting at Mandell Creighton's confirmation as bishop of London in January 1897, because the bishop-elect had worn a mitre while bishop of Peterborough. He continued with protests at St Ethelburga's, Bishopsgate, a year later, but achieved greater publicity when he interrupted the veneration of the Cross at St Cuthbert's, Philbeach Gardens, on Good Friday. As the congregation were going to kiss the crucifix, Kensit seized it and said: 'In the name of God, I denounce this idolatry in the Church of England; God help me.'[209] These protests continued, so that in 1900 the Kensitites appeared, for example, at Christ Church, Belper, St Matthew's, Sheffield, and Christ Church, Doncaster, while in 1911 J.A. Kensit emulated his father by disrupting the veneration of the Cross at Holy Trinity, Hoxton.[210] As well as protesting at ordinary services, the Kensitites also objected at the ordination of ritualist deacons to the priesthood and to the confirmation of the election of Winnington-Ingram as bishop of London in 1901.[211] There were some more bizarre incidents too, like the visit paid by 'Kensit and Co., Removers of Illegal Ornaments' to the church at Womersley in Yorkshire, which ended with the churchwardens and police pursuing the Kensitites (carrying images and crucifixes) across the countryside.[212] This publicity-conscious exploit was repeated in 1912 when two Wickliffe Preachers removed an image of the Virgin and Child from St Matthew's, Sheffield, and presented it to a somewhat bemused archbishop of York.[213] A year later one of their colleagues, in a rare act of iconoclasm, visited the same church and smashed the image.[214] As well as the regular protests of the Kensitites, there were a few other examples of direct action against the ritualists, like that of the Revd R.J. Fillingham, vicar of Hexton, who disturbed the service at Kettlebaston church in the spring of 1900 by shouting, at the elevation of the host: 'This is all idolatry. Protestants, leave this House of Baal!'[215]

Protests of this kind were discountenanced by most Evangelical Churchmen. When Liverpool Protestants tried to interrupt an Anglo-Catholic speaker at a meeting in 1904 Bishop Chavasse told them that 'You make the good name of Protestantism to stink in the land.'[216] In the previous year, the violent demonstrations in ritualist churches in the city provoked a letter to the *Record* from five NPCU members, headed by Canon Robson of Birkenhead, in which the protests were roundly condemned as 'injurious to Protestantism, injurious to the Church of England, and a dishonour to the name of our Lord Jesus Christ.'[217] A leading article in the *Record* on 'The case of St Ethelburga' in January 1898 spoke of 'the most injudicious methods and the repulsively rude language of Mr KENSIT and his friends, ' and, a few weeks later, the newspaper suggested that 'repeated acts of disorder can only help the cause attacked, and bring discredit upon Protestant work.'[218]

Although the *Record* never endorsed the Kensit campaign and most Evangelicals continued to stand aloof from the PTS, a growing feeling did emerge that the Kensitites' protests were less reprehensible than the ritualist services which they disrupted. Canons Bell and Fleming and the Revd Trevor Fielder soon made this point in Spring 1898, [219] and the *Record* itself gradually moved to a similar position, so that by 1901, when the Kensits protested at Winnington-Ingram's confirmation, the newspaper blamed the authorities, not the protesters, for the subsequent riot.[220] Likewise, in 1912 a leader on 'The ritual trouble' came very close to supporting the protest at the consecration of St Silas the Martyr, Kentish Town, on the grounds that drastic action was needed to curb ritualism in the diocese of London.[221]

Conclusion

It is difficult to avoid the conclusion that the Protestant campaign failed to achieve its objectives. Ritualism continued to develop in this period, as noted in the previous chapter, although the most extreme churches remained concentrated in a few dioceses. Attempts to curb Anglo-Catholicism, whether by episcopal persuasion, legislation or mob violence proved unsuccessful. Some bishops complained that Protestant pressure made the extremists more intransigent and less open to advice from their fathers-in-God – as Davidson wrote to Balfour, the bishops had 'to look helplessly on while ignorant fanatics bring into court the very men whom they... are trying to guide into sounder paths,'[222] but the archbishop's comment should not be taken entirely at face value. Most of the bishops were only prepared to act against the most extreme of the ritualist 'spikes', and the latter were not receptive to episcopal admonition, regardless of Protestant agitation. Men like Wason of Cury, H.M.M. Evans of Shoreditch and Harry Wilson of Stepney were determined to retain their 'Catholic' privileges whatever the bishops might advise and only legal action could dislodge them.[223] Protestant pressure could not make them more committed than they were already, although it could compel the bishops to take notice of a situation which they might have preferred to ignore. The key problem for Protestantism was legal and political, as well as ecclesiastical. To curb ritualism required decisive legal action against the extremists. The bishops were unwilling to take such action, partly on principle and partly because of its cost. The bishops would not act and, because of the episcopal veto, other Churchmen were also precluded from prosecution. This situation was clearly grasped by the Church Association, which responded by attempting to change the law, an attempt which failed, leaving Evangelical Churchmen dependent as before on an episcopate collectively reluctant to prosecute and individually often sympathetic to Anglo-Catholicism. The result was a climate in which moderate ritualism flourished and in which a minority could introduce full Roman rites with comparative impunity.[224]

Coming to Terms with Ritualism

Evangelicals could react to this state of affairs in one of three different ways. One was to concentrate on short term campaigning against Anglo-Catholicism, supporting memorials against the vestments, objecting to the introduction of choral eucharist as the principal Sunday service or promoting the work of the NCL as a positive statement of Evangelical beliefs. A second and more drastic option for dedicated Protestants, and one discussed at intervals in these years, was secession from the Church of England.

Secession

Tractarianism and ritualism had provoked a number of Evangelical secessions earlier in the nineteenth century, as had the disputes over the doctrine of baptism which lay behind the 'Western schism' of the 1810s and the departure of some fifty clergymen from the Established Church in the early 1830s. Several London Evangelicals were described as 'nearly seceding' in 1843, and, some thirty years later, Capel Molyneux, incumbent of St Paul's, Onslow Square, urged Evangelicals to leave the Church as a result of the Bennett Judgment (1872).[225] Few heeded the call, and this pattern was repeated after the final resolution of the Lincoln Case in 1892. On 5 August the *Record* published two letters advocating secession, one from Charles Stirling, vicar of New Malden, who called for disestablishment to save the Reformation, and one from the Hon and Revd E.V. Bligh.[226] The response to this appeal was entirely hostile. J.C. Ryle, writing under his usual pseudonym of 'A Northern Churchman', declared:

> 'Secession is not necessary. So long as the Articles and Prayer Book are not altered we occupy an impregnable position. We have an open Bible and our pulpits are free... Above all, secession would be cowardly. To launch the longboat and forsake the ship because she has carried away her masts and lost her rudder and is at present helpless – to leave an innocent body of passengers to the charge of a mutinous and unfaithful crew... would be an unworthy and disastrous mistake...'

W.F. Taylor wrote in more prosaic terms that secession 'would but hand over positions of influence and usefulness to others who would probably not be sorry if we took that step.'[227] The debate continued, but in the end only Stirling and the Revd N.R. Toke left the Church of England.[228]

Secession as a potential duty was raised again in the early 1900s, particularly in connection with the legalisation of the vestments. Some toyed with the idea of using the threat of secession as a weapon against ritualism, but generally the Evangelical leadership spoke out clearly against abandoning the Church – thus F.J. Chavasse, in his Charge of 1909, quoted his predecessor's words from 1890: 'I charge my brethren not to listen for a moment to those who counsel secession.'[229] The only Evangelical to secede publicly in this period was J.J. Beddow, vicar of Drypool, Hull, who resigned his living in 1914 and became pastor of an independent chapel at Lewes.[230] An article advocating secession appeared in the *Hibbert Journal* in 1910, signed by 'An Evangelical Layman' and claiming that 'Our efforts to uphold the reformed Catholic religion have failed, ' but it was described as 'folly and madness' by the *Churchman* and seems to have had little effect.[231] Evangelicals remained in the Church partly, no doubt, through inertia and self-interest, but partly also because they could claim that they were the truest representatives of the principles of the Reformation. As J.C. Ryle never tired of proclaiming, while the Prayer Book and Articles remained unaltered and while the pulpits were free, Evangelicals could in good conscience stay in the Church, and they had a duty to do so. An Evangelical secession would only leave the Church in the hands of the ritualists and perhaps thereby provoke the calamity of disestablishment by a Protestant nation.

While opposing wholesale secession, some Evangelicals were prepared to support activities contrary at least to the spirit of the Act of Uniformity. Evangelical laymen were encouraged to attend Dissenting chapels rather than ritualist churches,[232] and independent Evangelical chapels were built at Lightbowne, near Manchester, and at Dorchester in Oxfordshire, the latter being funded by the Church Association.[233] One of the functions of Kensit's Wickliffe Preachers, moreover, was to take the gospel message into ritualist parishes. Independent Protestant action of this kind was not common; generally speaking, the clergy clung to the Church while the Evangelical laity moved parishes or turned to Dissent.

Toleration

The third possible response to the fact that ritualism was well-established and growing within the Church of England was an attempt to agree on a plan of comprehension. Many Evangelicals regarded prosecution as undesirable and saw no hope of driving ritualism out of the Church, so they sought instead to find a way of bringing moderate ritualism within the bounds of the law and the rubrics, partly to end the state of liturgical anarchy and partly to separate the moderates from the extremist minority. A series of plans were put forward from the late 1880s and these may be considered briefly.

The first scheme was proposed in the summer of 1889 by J.J.S. Perowne, dean of Peterborough. Perowne suggested that the Ornaments Rubric should be taken in its natural sense as defining the legal maximum of ritual, but that this should be permissive only. In other words, surplice, hood and stole or scarf would be compulsory and other vestments optional.[234] In the same year a body calling itself 'Churchmen in Council' proposed seeking a definitive ruling on the Ornaments Rubric from a reformed Convocation.[235] Another attempt to set limits to Anglican comprehensiveness was made in 1903 when Henry Wace read a paper to the Bristol Church Congress on 'Variations in the National Church in aspects of doctrine'. Wace urged that the limits of Catholicity should be the teaching and approved practice of the first six hundred years of Christianity and he launched an 'Appeal to the first Six Centuries' which resulted in a memorial to the archbishops.[236] Proposals for a distinctive white vestment for Holy Communion were approved by the largely Evangelical York House of Bishops in 1908, and schemes for the permissive use of vestments were drawn up by P.V. Smith in 1906 and by G.E. Ford in 1909.[237] Finally, J.E. Watts-Ditchfield used his presidential Address to the Church Congress of 1920 to issue the so-called 'Chelmsford Eirenicon', urging 'whole-hearted inclusion' of Anglo-Catholicism within the Church of England on the basis of toleration of diversity and obedience to duly reformed Church courts.[238]

The comprehension schemes had a number of features in common. They all recognised, implicitly or explicitly, that ritualism could only be controlled by expanding the limits of Anglican toleration, so that at least some ritualist practices would receive the sanction of law. Even Wace, whose 'Appeal' was basically a conservative and semi-polemical measure designed to divide the High Church party by invoking Catholicity against the Medievalists, acknowledged that Evangelicals might have to tolerate practices which they did not like once the principle of the first six centuries had been accepted.[239] The other schemes all allowed some form of vestments, albeit in Ford's case with a declaratory rubric renouncing any doctrinal significance for them. This acceptance of greater elasticity linked the schemes to the 1906 Royal Commission Report and to the process of Prayer Book revision, as did the motive behind the proposals, which was to restore order to the Church by setting a standard of ritual which all could accept and which could then be enforced. A recognition of the problem of authority – the ritualist rejection of the Judicial Committee of the Privy Council as the final court of appeal – may be detected behind Perowne's reliance on Convocation and the Chelmsford proposals for canon law revision, a reform of the ecclesiastical courts and the creation of diocesan synods.[240] Both Perowne and Watts-Ditchfield were seeking to produce a settlement acceptable to High Churchmen and not open to rejection as Erastian.

In many ways the Prayer Book revision proposals also were attempts to keep Anglo-Catholicism within the Anglican fold without endorsing ritual anarchy, and the fate of Prayer Book revision was shared by the Evangelical schemes for comprehension. Each scheme was subjected to the same criticism – that it could only satisfy the ritualists at the cost of alienating the Evangelicals, and that the ritualists would only be satisfied by a return to Rome. Canon Bell attacked Perowne's plan for giving legislative sanction to erroneous teaching, a point echoed by J.C. Ryle, writing as 'An Old Soldier'.[241] Evangelicals, declared the *Record*, could not tolerate the Mass vestments: 'We will not because we cannot, ' and this case was still being argued thirty years later against the Chelmsford eirenicon of 1920.[242] Conservative and Protestant Evangelicals from Ryle to Wace emphasised that there was a doctrinal gulf between Anglo-Catholicism and Protestantism which could not be bridged. Proposals for white vestments were beside the mark, because the ritualists would only be satisfied by the full medieval or Roman garments. It was the 'Mass that mattered', both to them and to their opponents, and this made comprehension on agreed terms impossible. A form of armed neutrality or *de facto* toleration was the most that could be achieved.

Some development and alteration in Evangelical attitudes may be detected between the late 1880s and the 1920s. It is true that there was a strong Protestant element within the party and that this persisted throughout the period. It appeared in bitter opposition to Perowne's scheme in 1889. In its most extreme form it stood against Wace's 'Appeal to the first Six Centuries', pointing to the fall of the sub-apostolic Church from scriptural purity and producing a counter-declaration signed by 110 clergymen representing the Protestant ultras: W.F. Taylor, Samuel

Garratt, W.R. Mowll, F.C. Burrough, C.T. Porter, J.C. Wilcox, the 'chaplain to the Kensit Crusade', and other stalwarts of the Church Association.[243] It voiced regular criticisms of any proposals to tolerate the vestments or even the eastward position, and it was deeply suspicious of any co-operation with the Anglo-Catholics, keeping a particularly close eye on joint meetings between the CMS and the SPG.[244]

Beside this Protestant group, however, there developed a body of Evangelicals who were much more tolerant of ritual diversity. In the 1890s they were represented by Perowne, P.V. Smith, Eugene Stock and a few others, but in the early twentieth century their numbers increased. They were not necessarily sympathetic to elaborate ceremonial, but they held that the ritual controversy had reached stalemate and that toleration was desirable to end the conflict. Watts-Ditchfield spoke for this group in 1920 when he wrote that seventy years of controversy had paralysed the Church and crippled its mission, so that 'we are now drifting fast to disaster and dragging the Nation with us.'[245] The message was the same as Perowne's in 1889, but whereas then the dean could count on little Evangelical support,[246] by 1920 the bishop of Chelmsford was backed by a significant section of Evangelical opinion. One reason for this change was the influence of ritualism upon the Evangelicals themselves, seen in the development of 'Liberal Evangelicalism' or 'Central Churchmanship'.[247]

Liberal Evangelicalism

'Liberal Evangelical' was a term frequently used but seldom defined in the early 1900s. Clerical advertisements in the *Record* employed it regularly – it appeared 149 times in 1900, for example, 158 times in 1901 and 145 times in 1902. In 1904 a correspondence on 'Liberal Evangelicalism' was published and the contributors concerned themselves entirely with questions of ritual. A 'Liberal Evangelical', it was suggested, was one who wore a stole, intoned the service and took the eastward position.[248] Clearly some Evangelicals at least were 'levelling up' in their conduct of public worship, and it may be asked what prompted this.

To some extent this process was a matter of obedience to the law and to the rubrics. Some Evangelicals were anxious to observe the letter of the Prayer Book's requirements, partly in order to strengthen their position against the ritualists. Thus 'An Attached Evangelical', writing to the *Record* in March 1903 urged his brethren that, while resisting pressure to take the eastward position, they should be scrupulous in holding daily services and celebrating Holy Communion on saints' days. Canon Fleming began to preach in a surplice after the Ridsdale Judgment of 1877 because he believed that practice to be the most faithful to the rubrics. In these ways Evangelicals hoped to avoid the common ritualist charge, voiced in evidence before the Royal Commission, that they too disregarded the letter of the law.[249]

Legal pressure and rubrical scrupulosity, however, were less influential than custom and taste. The prevailing fashion in church architecture was medieval, and the Gothic style was even used for Liverpool cathedral, begun under an Evangelical bishop in 1903. Gothic churches were designed for ceremonial and it is significant that most of the leading ecclesiastical architects of the day were High Churchmen.[250] There was also a move towards 'brighter' services, marked by music and colour and designed to be attractive to the unchurched masses. As several younger Evangelicals pointed out, Evangelicalism had no modern ritual of its own, so incumbents looking for change and dissatisfied with the traditional preaching service were prone to drift into the practices of the Anglo-Catholics for want of an alternative. E.C. Dewick, J.R. Darbyshire and Bernard Herklots contributed articles to the *Churchman* in 1913 on the need for a distinctive Evangelical ritual, recommending, for instance, celebrating the eucharist facing the people from the west side of the table and beginning the service by kneeling to pray rather than standing for the entry of choir and clergy[251] – but these ideas were never thoroughly expounded and could not rival the completeness of Dearmer's *Parson's Handbook*. As Darbyshire complained, 'some features of old-fashioned Evangelicalism were unnecessarily and unhappily sacrificed for the substitution of a poor and worthless imitation of some "High Church" innovations.'[252] Long before this, in November 1901, J.T. Inskip observed that Evangelicals had, in all innocence and considerable ignorance, adopted such ritualist practices as processional hymns and facing the holy table for the ascription before the sermon.[253]

The preferences of congregations and patrons also had a role to play. In 1900 the Evangelical E.A.B. Sanders was appointed vicar of Edmonton, a living in the gift of the dean and chapter of St Paul's. It was claimed that Sanders had to undertake not to hold evening communion and to adopt the eastward position, and he was criticised for this by 'A Disgusted Layman', who complained to the *Record* that 'many laymen... have as little faith in the Evangelical clergy sticking to their principles as they have strong confidence that the ritualists will adhere to theirs.'[254]

This process of levelling up should not be exaggerated. Most of the practices introduced in the early 1900s, even when judged according to the standards of the 'Centigrade Ritualometer' published in the *Rock* twenty years earlier,[255] were fairly inoffensive. Preaching in a surplice was widespread by 1900, so that the retention of the black gown was cause for comment in clerical obituaries.[256] Surpliced choirs were not uncommon in Evangelical churches, nor were crosses and flower vases, and all these points were below the thermometer's 'danger' level of 1882.[257] The eastward position, which the *Rock* placed well up the scale of ritualist practices, had been declared doctrinally indifferent by Church and State in 1892 and so, it could be argued, Evangelicals were free to adopt it. This was the main point of controversy between the Protestants and the liberals and was a regular subject of debate in the Evangelical press. E.S. Woods, a leading Liberal Evangelical, began wearing the eucharistic vestments in the late 1920s, but this was highly unusual.[258]

'Liberal Evangelicalism' in the ritual sense produced two mutually antagonistic responses. The Protestants reacted with anger and anguish to what they interpreted as a betrayal of Evangelical principles. Several complaints may be found in the papers of the Simeon Trust – for instance, a letter of 1894 from Major General Davidson, writing on behalf of the seatholders of Christ Church, Clifton, to object to the introduction of monotoning the responses, 'to the great offence of many of the older and attached Evangelical members.'[259] The *Record*'s correspondence of 1904 denounced Liberal Evangelicalism as timid, and Bishop Ingham spoke in 1918 of those 'weak-kneed' Evangelicals who took the eastward position.[260] The Protestant belief that levelling up was an unacceptable compromise with error was set out by F.C. Burrough in September 1904:

> 'We are living in a time when our beloved Church lies in the greatest danger of disruption through betrayal from within.

> Romish doctrine and practice are rife within her borders.. Most carefully and insidiously the doctrines of the Reformation are – by preaching, symbol and practice – being undermined. On this account and at such a time I claim that a true hearted man who honours himself with the name of "Evangelical" cannot afford to be so "broad-minded" or "liberal" as to trifle with the symbols or the practices of the enemy.'[261]

The practical expression of this attitude was the Holdfast Union, whose members were pledged to eschew 'crosses &c., eastward (sacrificing) position, *Hymns Ancient and Modern* and sung prayers' and to support 'evening Communions, the teacher's preaching gown and full-length surplice, scarf, not Romish stole.'[262] In its most extreme form it was represented by Evangelicals like James Neil, who denounced musical services as unscriptural, unreal, selfish, sensuous, worldly, uncongregational, unprotestant, doing evil that good might come and injurious to the ministry, or the Kensitite J.C. Wilcox, who deliberately reintroduced the black gown as late as 1900.[263]

On the other side were those who regarded the ritual dispute as an unimportant squabble over inessentials. Opposition to stoles, surpliced choirs and the eastward position was seen as adherence to shibboleths, a clinging to 'the letter which killeth' and a form of 'black gown ritualism' just as unspiritual as the ceremonialism of the sacerdotalists.[264] Pleas for liberty were uttered at regular intervals: in 1904, over the definition of 'Liberal Evangelicalism', in 1910 by Guy Warman at the Southport Conference, and by T.Guy Rogers in 1913 and 1917.[265] Rogers and Warman were not in favour of levelling up, but they were anxious to emphasise that the differences between Evangelicals and Anglo-Catholics were doctrinal, rather than ceremonial, and that the ritual expression of doctrine might change – for instance, through the legalisation of the once abhorrent eastward position. Evangelicalism, they claimed, should concentrate on spiritual teaching and avoid an obsession with the externals of ritual.[266]

Ritualism, therefore, exercised some influence within the Evangelical party itself. Few Evangelical churches were able to avoid the general effect of the Gothic revival and the move towards more musical services. The extent to which Evangelicals adopted the trappings of moderate ritual varied considerably, from surplices to vestments and from crosses to altar lights,[267] and this created scope for conflict within the party. It was no coincidence that the first tensions in the CMS in the twentieth century were prompted by Protestant suspicions about levelling up, and these were still present as the backdrop to the wider liberal-conservative debates of the late 1910s.[268]

In his defence of the 'Chelmsford eirenicon' of 1920 Watts-Ditchfield wrote that the ritual controversy had diverted Evangelical attention away from soul-saving to fighting the Anglo-Catholics.[269] Although this might be debated, it was certainly the case that the controversy influenced Evangelical attitudes to many other issues, sometimes to the detriment of the best interests of the Church. There was, for example, a consistent Protestant opposition to the creation of new bishoprics, on the grounds that the episcopate should show that it could suppress ritualism before its size might be increased.[270] Any Church reform proposals designed to augment episcopal power were resisted by the ultra-Protestants, because they believed that such power would be used to benefit Anglo-Catholics.[271] The Church Association opposed the Enabling Act of 1919, fearing that the National Assembly would be more sympathetic to ritualism than the House of Commons.[272] Only a minority of Evangelicals opposed Church reform for Protestant reasons; many supported the proposals and others had different reasons for opposition, but the ultras managed to ensure that the ritual controversy always formed part of the background to the debate.

Conclusion

The Evangelical response to the development of ritualism in the Church of England was many-sided, and it covered a wide range of activities. These may be reduced, however, to two broad categories. There were the relatively uncontroversial schemes: for better Evangelical organisation, for more effective education, for academic and popular literature to set out the Protestant case, for active use of the resources of patronage and for general improvements in the working of Evangelical agencies like the CPAS. Anne Bentley has described these steps as a positive policy, whereby Evangelical Churchmen sought to make the most of their existing strengths in terms of spirituality and commitment to parochial ministry.[273] This could co-exist with an avoidance of controversy, other than perhaps on the field of literature, and some Evangelicals believed that it was a sufficient response to ritualism.

Most members of the Evangelical school, however, did not agree. They regarded ritualism as doctrinally false, pastorally dangerous and as an alien intrusion into the Anglican fold. They therefore wanted something done to prevent its expansion and to check at least the most flagrant of the Romanising clergy. Sure in their opposition, but uncertain as to strategy, Evangelical Churchmen tried a variety of methods to curb the ritualists, from petitions to parliamentary campaigns. No single scheme commanded the support of the whole party and some led to strong internal disagreements.

Only two agencies could have stopped the rise of ritualism in this period: the bishops and the courts. The bishops lacked the will to take decisive action and some were more sympathetic to Anglo-Catholicism than to Evangelicalism. Few were prepared to alienate a large and well-organised body of hard working clergy and influential laity merely to enforce a standard of uniformity which many Churchmen believed was too narrow for the twentieth century. The episcopal veto, moreover, blocked access to the courts and 'Protestantism before Politics' was never quite strong enough to pass another Church Discipline bill. Parliamentary pressure could only produce a Royal Commission, and, while it largely vindicated Evangelical complaints, the 1906 Report left action once again in the hands of the bishops. By this stage, some Evangelicals were inclined to agree with the episcopate that ritualism must be granted a measure of toleration and legal comprehension as a step towards ending liturgical anarchy in the Church. This belief produced a series of schemes to redefine Anglican uniformity and the series culminated in the revised Prayer Book of 1927-8.

Insofar as they tried to suppress ritualism, therefore, Evangelicals had to confess failure. As the period unfolded, moreover, they gradually moved from attack to defence, from speaking of expelling Anglo-Catholicism to fighting for the preservation of the *status quo* through the long process of Prayer Book revision. Anglo-Catholicism seemed triumphant by the 1920s, not only in the form of the great Congresses and the exuberant Romanising of the Society of St Peter and St Paul, but more subtly through its influence on worship throughout the Church of

England, an influence which had spread even within the boundaries of Evangelicalism.[274] The process of levelling up was placing a strain on the fragile unity of the Evangelical party, but it was not the only cause of disquiet. Alongside issues of ritual, other questions had arisen to perplex Evangelical Churchmen and to add to the tensions within their ranks. It will be the task of the next two chapters to explore those controversial questions and to analyse their role in the fragmentation of Anglican Evangelicalism in the early twentieth century.

Notes

1 E. Stock, *The History of the Church Missionary Society*, ii, (London, 1899), 652. The analogy may be traced to a rueful comment by George Whitefield: J.W. Etheridge, *The Life of the Revd Adam Clarke* (London, 1858[2]), 166.

2 E.R. Garratt, *Life and Personal Recollections of Samuel Garratt* (London, 1908), 96-8.

3 A. Bentley, 'The transformation of the Evangelical party in the Church of England in the later nineteenth century', Durham PhD thesis, 1971, 172.

4 *R*, 12 August 1892, 824.

5 J. Hughes-Games, *The Duty of Evangelical Churchmen under Possible Eventualities: A Paper read before the Yorkshire Evangelical Union, June 7th, 1900* (London, 1900), 13-15.

6 G.I.T. Machin, 'The last Victorian anti-ritualist campaign, 1895-1906', *Victorian Studies* 25 (Bloomington, 1982), 282.

7 *R*, 2 May 1902, 406.

8 *R*, 7 June 1901, 573.

9 M. Barlow (ed.), *Life of William Haggar Barlow* (London, 1910), chapter 11; *R*, 17 January 1902, 61.

10 *R*, 18 January 1907, 49.

11 *R*, 12 January 1900, 40, 42.

12 *R*, 18 January 1907, 57-68.

13 *R*, 22 September 1905, 859.

14 *R*, 12 April 1907, 304.

15 *R*, 6 July 1916, 546; 'Cheltenham conference papers', *C*, July 1923, 189-242; 'The Cheltenham conference', *C*, July 1924, 193-254.

16 The roots of the PRS are explored by John Wolffe in *The Protestant Crusade in Great Britain 1829-1860* (Oxford, 1991), 34-62. On Dr Wright, see J. Silvester, *A Champion of the Faith: A Memoir of the Revd C.H.H. Wright* (London, 1917), especially chapter 10.

17 *R*, 18 December 1903, 1231.

18 *R*, 6 February 1903, 137. Wolffe, *Protestant Crusade*, 210-20, traces the

history of the Club.

19 Ibid., 250-4; *R*, 24 April 1903, 398.

20 For example, the Great Protestant Demonstration of May 1898, of which a *Verbatim Report* was published.

21 *R*, 31 August 1900, 830 (advertisement listing affiliates); *Who was who 1897-1915* (London, 1920), 543-4.

22 *R*, 22 March, 1901, 305 (listing officers).

23 *R*, 25 June 1918, 470.

24 Bentley, 'Transformation', 124-5; James C. Whisenant, 'Anti-ritualism and the division of the Evangelical party in the second half of the nineteenth century', Vanderbilt PhD thesis, 1998, 82-90.

25 Bentley, 'Transformation', 134.

26 Ibid., 133-4, 145-59; 'Church Association', in C.H.H. Wright and Charles Neil (eds), *A Protestant Dictionary* (London, 1904), 108-10. Whisenant, 'Anti-ritualism', 97-101, 160- 68, 297-308 and 364-430 plots Evangelical reactions to the policy of prosecution from the 1860s to the 1890s, drawing general conclusions on 430-37.

27 H. Lewis, 'The present condition of the Evangelicals', *Nineteenth Century and After 19-20* (London, August 1907), 232.

28 P.J. Waller, *Democracy and Sectarianism: A Political and Social History of Liverpool, 1868-1939* (Liverpool, 1981), 117.

29 *R*, 10 October 1902, 941.

30 *R*, 17 March 1911, 250.

31 Bentley, 'Transformation', 192-4.

32 G.I.T. Machin, *Politics and the Churches in Great Britain, 1869-1921* (Oxford, 1987), 179.

33 Bentley, 'Transformation', 188, 194.

34 *R*, 8 January 1904, 43.

35 Machin, *Politics*, 241-2.

36 *R*, 9 May 1906, 374.

37 *R*, 27 September 1901, 926; F.W. Farrar, *Protestantism: Its Peril and Its Duty* (London, 1893).

38 W.A. Cunningham Craig, 'Liberals and Evangelicals – a plea for co-operation', *MC*, (London) August 1911, 263-70; W.J. Sommerville, 'Co-operation of Evangelicals and Liberals – a reply', ibid., September 1911, 335-40, with comments in the NCL's *Church Gazette* (London), October 1911, 231-2, and *C*, November 1911, 807-08. See alsoW.R. Inge, 'The relations of Liberal and Evangelical Churchmanship', *C*, February 1912, 89-99, with editorial and other reactions, ibid., March 1912, 162-3. An earlier attempt at Liberal-Evangelical co-operation produced a set of resolutions against reservation, habitual confession and a localised real presence agreed at a 'Conference of Churchmen' convened by H.E. Ryle, J. Llewelyn Davies, Webb-Peploe and Sir John Kennaway in 1899. In the late 1920s the NCL provided legal advice to the Modernist Bishop Barnes in his conflicts with the Birmingham rit-

ualists, for which see E.J.W. Barnes, *Ahead of his Age* (London, 1979), 226-32, 236-85, especially 230 and 239.

39 *R*, 28 June 1889, 641.

40 *R*, 19 August 1892, 850.

41 *R*, 21 June 1889, 613; E. Stock, *My Recollections* (London, 1909), 180-1.

42 *R*, 20 November 1908, 1243.

43 *R*, 16 February 1912, 171-2.

44 S. Gummer, *The Chavasse Twins* (London, 1963), 209. Compare Wolffe, *Protestant Crusade*, 292, on the early nineteenth century Protestant societies' 'incapacity… to speak with a united voice.'

45 M. Wellings, 'The first Protestant martyr of the twentieth century: the life and significance of John Kensit (1853-1902)', *SCH* 30 (Oxford, 1993), 347-58; Machin, 'Anti-ritualist campaign', 285-7; James Britten, *A Prominent Protestant (Mr John Kensit)* (London, 1898).

46 Wellings, 'First Protestant martyr', 347-8; *CM*, November 1902; Waller, *Democracy and Sectarianism*, 192.

47 Lewis, 'Present condition', 232.

48 *R*, 20 October 1911, 978; Britten, *Prominent Protestant*, 6-7; Wellings, 'First Protestant martyr', 355-6.

49 H.A. Taylor, *Jix, Viscount Brentford* (London, 1933), 70.

50 *C*, August 1919 (cover).

51 *R*, 18 June 1909, 655.

52 *R*, 30 May 1913, 502.

53 *C*, August 1919 (cover).

54 *R*, 12 May 1911, 451; 12 September 1918, 550.

55 See the May Meeting reports in the *Record*.

56 *R*, 1 March 1912, 223.

57 *R*, 25 May 1906, 467; 24 May 1907, 457; 26 May 1911, 512. This may be compared with the very modest total of £355 5/3 in 1896-7, before Kensit's most dramatic public protests: PTS *Report for the year 1896-7* (London, n.d.), 19.

58 Britten, *Prominent Protestant*, 9. The PTS *Report* for 1896-7, 14-19, lists seventeen clergy, seven titled laity, four doctors and twelve military or naval officers among the 338 named subscribers. Of the thirteen vice-presidents listed in *CM*, November 1902, 345, all are lay.

59 *R*, 17 October 1902, 990.

60 *R*, 9 October 1903, 969.

61 E.A. Litton, *Introduction to Dogmatic Theology on the Basis of theThirty Nine Articles* (London, 1912[3]), sections 76-100; H.C.G. Moule, *Outlines of Christian Doctrine* (London, 1889), chapters 9-11.

62 W. Lefroy, *The Christian Ministry: Its Origin, Constitution, Nature, and Work* (London, 1890), 416.

63 J.C. Ryle, *Facts and Men: Being Pages from English Church History between 1553 and 1683 with a Preface for the Times* (London, 1882), 222. The comment refers to Archbishop Laud.

64 T.W. Drury, *Elevation in the Eucharist: Its History and Rationale* (Cambridge, 1907), vii.
65 Horton Davies, *Worship and Theology in England: The Ecumenical Century, 1900-65* (Princeton, 1965), 285-7, describes Dearmer's school.
66 It had reached a sixth edition by 1899.
67 H.O. Wakeman, *An Introduction to the History of the Church of England from the Earliest Times to the Present Day* (London, 1896), 385-8, 492.
68 *R*, 13 October 1899, 982; H. Wace, *The Evangelical Pastorate for Undergraduates at Oxford..* (Oxford, 1898), 9-10.
69 A.E. Barnes-Lawrence, *A Churchman and his Church* (London, 1917), 108.
70 W.H. Griffith Thomas, *A Sacrament of our Redemption* (London, 1905), 113.
71 W.H. Griffith Thomas, *The Catholic Faith* (London, 1904), 434.
72 Wakeman, *Introduction*, 482-3. Some ritualists went further and claimed that Edward's second year was 1548, when all the vestments were compulsory.
73 See, for example, J. Nunn, 'The report of the five bishops on vestments', *C*, April 1908, 212-9; May 1908, 285-91; June 1908, 347-57.
74 Griffith Thomas, *A Sacrament of our Redemption*, 113.
75 *R*, 4 October 1907, 850.
76 Ryle, *Facts and Men*, chapter 1. The book was retitled *Light from Old Times* in 1891, when a chapter was added on Wycliffe, and it featured regularly in C.J. Thynne's catalogue.
77 *C*, November 1902, 81.
78 W. Alison Phillips, 'The study of the Reformation', *C*, October 1925, 261.
79 A.C. Downer, 'The need of Evangelical literature of the highest order', *C*, January 1896, 201-07.
80 *R*, 28 August 1903, 833.
81 Garratt, *Samuel Garratt*, chapter 8.
82 *R*, 13 March 1903, 266.
83 *R*, 2 October 1908, 1022.
84 *R*, 17 January 1908, 42.
85 See J. Denton Thompson, *Central Churchmanship* (London, 1911).
86 *R*, 24 January 1908, 91.
87 J.C. Ryle, *The Upper Room: Being a Few Truths for the Times* (London, 1888), chapters 18 and 20.
88 E. Jay, 'Anglican Evangelicalism and the nineteenth century novel', Oxford DPhil thesis, 1975, chapter 3.
89 *C*, March 1899 (cover).
90 *R*, 13 July 1900, 674; 18 May 1900, 469.
91 On Joseph Hocking, see Roger Thorne, 'Hocking family' in John A. Vickers (ed.), *A Dictionary of Methodism in Britain and Ireland* (Peterborough, 2000), 160, and James Britten, *'The Scarlet Woman'; or,*

the methods of a Protestant Novelist (London, 1906) and *A School for Slander; or, 'The Soul of Dominic Wildthorne'* (London, 1909); *C*, October 1927, 327 (NCL advertisement).

92 *R*, 3 December 1909, 1245.

93 *R*, 27 September 1901, 926.

94 *R*, 10 January 1902, 22.

95 *R*, 3 March 1905, 207.

96 *R*, 24 January 1908, 77.

97 *R*, 15 May 1914, 496.

98 *R*, 6 March 1903, 223.

99 *R*, 19 October 1906, 912; 19 September 1902, 873.

100 *R*, 3 May 1901, 467.

101 On the Woodard schools, see B. Heeney, *Mission to the Middle Classes:The Woodard Schools 1848-91* (London, 1969), especially 39, 53 and 64. A criticism of the schools may be found in P.V.M. Filleul, *The Catholic Revival: What is it doing for England ?* (London, 1900), 10-11.

102 Heeney, *Mission to the Middle Classes*, 78.

103 *R*, 16 March 1900, 262.

104 *R*, 11 January 1901, 59; 24 April 1914, 393.

105 M.A.J. Tarver, *Trent College 1868-1927* (London, 1929), 4.

106 Ibid., 8.

107 See the Company's *Report* for 1907.

108 *R*, 16 May 1913, 454.

109 *R*, 25 July 1913, 701.

110 *R*, 17 October 1913, 969.

111 *R*, 18 July 1913, 688. See also Charles Williams, *Flecker of Dean Close* (London, 1946), chapter 4.

112 G.R. Balleine, *A History of the Evangelical Party in the Church of England* (London, 1908), 275-6.

113 *R*, 30 September 1915, 855.

114 *R*, 1 October 1909, 990; 30 May 1902, 537.

115 *R*, 18 October 1912, 994.

116 G.I.F. Thomson, *The Oxford Pastorate: The First Half-Century* (London, 1946), 20-24.

117 E.A. Burroughs, 'Oxford and Evangelicalism in relation to the crisis in the Church', *C*, October 1911, 755-65.

118 Thomson, *Oxford Pastorate*, 95. The history of the Oxford Pastorate is the subject of a forthcoming study by Mark Smith.

119 F.W.B. Bullock, *The History of Ridley Hall, Cambridge*, i (Cambridge, 1941), 296.

120 F.W.B. Bullock, *The History of Ridley Hall, Cambridge*, ii (Cambridge, 1953), 25.

121 Gummer, *Chavasse Twins*, chapter 9. See also the detailed account of the involvement of Percy Warrington and the Martyrs' Memorial Trust in W.A. Evershed, 'Party and patronage in the Church of England 1800-

1945', Oxford DPhil thesis, 1985, chapter 6.

122 For Ridley Hall, see Bullock, *Ridley Hall*. For St Aidan's, see F.B. Heiser, *The Story of St Aidan's College, Birkenhead, 1847-1947* (Chester, 1947).

123 J.B. Lancelot, *Francis James Chavasse* (Oxford, 1929), 108.

124 Bullock, *Ridley Hall*, i, 332, 431.

125 Heiser, *St Aidan's*, 51-6.

126 *R*, 17 January 1902, 53.

127 *R*, 9 July 1909, 733. Watts-Ditchfield spoke of the accusation that 'Evangelicals are wedded to a class ministry with a money qualification.'

128 *R*, 27 October 1905, 1000.

129 *R*, 3 March 1911:207; E.N. Gowing, *John Edwin Watts-Ditchfield, First Bishop of Chelmsford* (London, 1926), 95-6.

130 T.A. Stowell, 'The Elland Clerical Society', *C*, May 1896, 417-26.

131 *R*, 13 May 1915, 447.

132 *R*, 16 May 1913, 461.

133 W. Sinclair, 'Church reform: methods of preferment', *C*, November 1897, 94.

134 *C*, March 1918, 12 (advertisement); July 1893, 558; R, 31 May 1917, 394.

135 The aggressive use of patronage by the Martyrs' Memorial Trust is described by Evershed, 'Party and patronage', chapter 6.

136 S.C. Carpenter, *Winnington-Ingram* (London, 1949), 214.

137 W.D. Balda, 'Spheres of influence: Simeon's Trust and its implications for Evangelical patronage', Cambridge PhD thesis, 1981, 126.

138 *R*, 18 October 1901, 1039.

139 *English Churchman*, 12 August 1909, 508; 26 August, 540; 23 September, 604. Details and press cuttings may be found in the SimeonTrust papers, CUL Add. MSS 8293, box 2 (Liverpool diocese).

140 *English Churchman*, 19 August 1909, 524.

141 *R*, 12 August 1892, 824; Bentley, 'Transformation', 490-8; C.E. Barton, *John Barton: A Memoir* (London, 1910), chapter 8.

142 *R*, 29 November 1901, 1166 (Doncaster); 19 April 1901, 386 (Sheffield); 5 April 1907, 285 (Plymouth and Brighton).

143 Machin, *Politics*, 235.

144 *R*, 25 October 1889, 1060.

145 *R*, 25 January 1901, 119.

146 Machin, *Politics*, 234-6. An account of benediction at St Michael's, Shoreditch, in 1898 was published in the *Daily Chronicle* and cited by Samuel Smith in the House of Commons; *Speeches of Samuel Smith, Esq, MP, June 16th and 21st 1898* (London, 1898), appendix. On the interaction between Protestant polemic and anti-ritual protests, see M. Wellings, 'The Oxford Movement in late nineteenth century retrospect: R.W. Church, J.H. Rigg and Walter Walsh', *SCH* 33 (Woodbridge, 1997), 511-14.

147 *R*, 25 November 1904, 1183.

148 *R*, 2 November 1916, 865.
149 *R*, 24 May 1901, 522.
150 *R*, 26 May 1911, 512. As early as September 1893 Kensit developed his distinctive signature, 'Yours for the Truth', *CM*, September 1893, 259.
151 *R*, 29 November 1907, 1054.
152 *R*, 8 November 1907, 985.
153 *R*, 13 May 1898, 465.
154 *R*, 3 June 1898, 540.
155 J.J. Lias, 'The report of the Ritual Commission', *Twentieth Century Quarterly* (London), August 1906, 18-9.
156 Ibid., 18.
157 Carpenter, *Winnington-Ingram*, 195-201. N. Yates, *Anglican Ritualism in Victorian Britain 1830-1910* (Oxford, 1999), 172-94, discusses the composition of the episcopal bench and the consequences for the Church's response to ritualism.
158 Compare Davidson's description of ritualism as 'a mere speck' in the range of episcopal concerns with Joynson-Hicks' assessment that 'clerical anarchy and lawlessness' was 'one of the gravest dangers to the future stability of the Church of England', *RCED Minutes of Evidence*, ii, 372 and iii, 294.
159 C.H. Simpkinson, *The Life and Work of Bishop Thorold* (London, 1896), 362; F.K. Aglionby, *Life of Edward Henry Bickersteth* (London, 1907), 175-6; A.C. Kelway, *George Rundle Prynne* (London, 1905), 174-81.
160 *R*, 12 February 1904, 182.
161 *R*, 10 April 1908, 322; E.A. Knox, *Reminiscences of an Octogenarian* (London, 1935), 302-03, 320-1; *English Churchman*, 16 September 1909, 587.
162 *R*, 3 May 1907, 393; L. Creighton, *Life and Letters of Mandell Creighton* (London, 1904), ii, 285-315, 367-8; M. Wellings, 'Anglo-Catholicism, the "crisis in the Church" and the Cavalier case of 1899', *JEH* 42 (Cambridge, 1999), 253-5; Alan T.L. Wilson, 'The authority of Church and party among London Anglo-Catholics 1880-1914, with special reference of the Church crisis of 1898-1904', Oxford DPhil thesis, 1988, chapter 3.
163 H. Miller, *A Guide to Ecclesiastical Law. For Churchwardens and Parishioners* (London, 1912[10]), 87-8, 97-101.
164 *Verbatim Report of Speeches delivered at the Great Demonstration.. May 3rd 1898* (London, 1898); *R*, 5 January 1900, 2; 7 February 1902, 126.
165 *R*, 7 December 1901, 1190.
166 *R*, 27 February 1903, 198; 14 December 1906, 1129.
167 *R*, 29 May 1903, 535; 2 November 1916, 865.
168 *R*, 25 November 1892, 1205; 9 December, 1248.
169 *R*, 8 June 1906, 504; 10 April 1908, 322; 23 February 1912, 183.
170 *R*, 18 April 1913, 342; 3 April 1914, 317-8, 410; G.K.A. Bell, *Randall Davidson* (London, 1935), ii, 1326.

171 Miller, *Ecclesiastical Law*, 67-75.

172 James Bentley, *Ritualism and Politics in Victorian Britain. The attempt to legislate for belief* (Oxford, 1978), 97-120; Yates, *Anglican Ritualism*, 245-76.

173 Ibid., 269-73; Bentley, 'Transformation', 192, 169; Ian D. Farley, *J.C. Ryle. First Bishop of Liverpool* (Carlisle, 2000), 205-35.

174 W. Sinclair, *The Prospects of the Principles of the Reformation in the Church of England* (London, 1893), 11.

175 R. Payne Smith, 'Prosecutions for ritual observances', *C*, February 1890, 226.

176 Garratt, *Samuel Garratt*, 87-100.

177 W. Johnston, 'The Lincoln Judgment', *C*, October 1892, 9.

178 *R*, 12 August 1892, 821-2; 26 August 1892, 873; P.V. Smith, 'The Lincoln Judgment', *C*, September 1892, 645.

179 *R*, 30 September 1892, 982.

180 *R*, 14 March 1902, 245; 5 January 1900, 2; 15 December 1905, 1186.

181 *R*, 7 December 1900, 1166.

182 *R*, 5 January 1900, 1.

183 *R*, 2 February 1900, 106; 16 February 1900, 163; 13 March 1900, 283.

184 *R*, 18 January 1907, 67; 23 December 1910, 1554; 14 July 1911, 650; 20 October 1911, 966; 3 January 1913, 8; 16 May 1913, 457.

185 *R*, 2 January 1914, 1; 13 February 1914, 151.

186 *C*, July 1917, 389.

187 *Church Association. Scheme of Future Policy presented by the Council and approved by the Conference held at the National Club on October 25th, 1892* (London, 1892), 4.

188 *R*, 16 March 1900, 254.

189 *R*, 25 June 1902, 625.

190 *R*, 27 July 1900, 709; 23 October 1903, 1036; 30 June 1905, 628.

191 *R*, 26 October 1900, 1022-3.

192 J.E.B. Munson, 'The Oxford Movement by the end of the nineteenth century', *Church History* 44 (Chicago, 1975).

193 Machin, *Politics*, 246-9; *R*, 6 July 1900, 642; 27 July 1900, 710.

194 Machin, *Politics*, 247.

195 *R*, 13 March 1903, 246; 17 April 1903, 366.

196 *R*, 14 August 1903, 783.

197 Machin, *Politics*, 110.

198 Ibid., 247.

199 Waller, *Democracy and Sectarianism*, 210, 513; Bell, *Davidson*, i, 454. *RCED Minutes*, iv, 1, lists Commission members and their record of attendance at the 118 sittings. Among the most assiduous was the Evangelical T.W. Drury.

200 Waller, *Democracy and Sectarianism*, 281.

201 Machin, *Politics*, 11.

202 *R*, 17 April 1903, 385.

203 *R*, 15 January 1904, 81.
204 *R*, 20 April 1905, 376.
205 *R*, 20 April 1906, 340.
206 *R*, 18 May, 453.
207 *R*, 12 October 1906, 898; 23 November 1906, 1044; 14 December 1906, 1113.
208 Wellings, 'First Protestant martyr'; J.C. Wilcox, *John Kensit, Reformer and Martyr. A Popular Life* (London, 1903); Machin, 'Anti-ritualist campaign', 286.
209 *R*, 1 January 1897, 1, 20; 27 January 1897, 77, 89; *CM*, April 1897, 107-8; Wilson, 'Church and party', 50-1, 61.
210 *R*, 19 January 1900, 68; 2 February 1900, 100; 13 February 1900, 171; 21 April 1911, 361.
211 *R*, 4 March 1904, 254; 19 April 1901, 387.
212 *R*, 16 March 1900, 243.
213 *R*, 26 January 1912, 84.
214 *R*, 31 January 1913, 100.
215 *R*, 30 March 1900, 295.
216 Lancelot, *Chavasse*, 162.
217 *R*, 27 November 1903, 1146.
218 *R*, 28 January 1898, 89; 18 February 1898, 149.
219 *R*, 15 February 1898, 189; 22 April 1898, 380; 29 April 1898, 395.
220 *R*, 19 April 1901, 393.
221 *R*, 1 November 1912, 1033.
222 Munson, 'Oxford movement', p 385. Cf. episcopal comments to the Royal Commission of 1904-6, *RCED Minutes*, ii, 341-73 (Davidson); *R*, 9 November 1906, 988.
223 Wilson, 'Church and party' and note 162 above on Creighton's struggle with Harry Wilson; Carpenter, *Winnington-Ingram*, 193, describes the Shoreditch prosecution of 1903.
224 Ibid., 170-75, for an account of St Saviour's, Hoxton, where the Latin Missal was used in the 1910s and early 1920s.
225 On earlier secessions, see W.J.C. Ervine, 'Doctrine and diplomacy: some aspects of the life and thought of the Anglican Evangelical clergy, 1797-1837', Cambridge PhD thesis, 1979, 71, 104; P. Toon, *Evangelical Theology 1833-1856. A Response to Tractarianism* (London, 1979), 76-7; Bentley, 'Transformation', 130; Grayson Carter, *Anglican Evangelicals. Protestant Secessions from the Via Media, c. 1800-1850* (Oxford, 2001).
226 *R*, 5 August 1892, 801.
227 *R*, 12 August 1892, 822; 26 August 1892, 873.
228 *R*, 16 September 1892, 944; 21 October 1892, 1077.
229 *R*, 26 March 1909, 328.
230 *R*, 16 January 1914, 46; 20 February 1914, 171; 3 February 1916, 108.
231 An Evangelical Layman, 'Divorçons', *Hibbert Journal*, (London, 1909-

10), 330-39; *C*, February 1910, 82.
232 J.G. Gregory, *Idolatry, Ancient and Modern* (London, 1891), 15.
233 *R*, 23 March 1900, 268; 10 October 1902, 946.
234 *R*, 26 July 1889, 735.
235 C.H. Minchin, 'Churchmen in council', *C*, October 1890, 18-25.
236 The text of Wace's appeal may be found in H. Wace and F. Meyrick, *An Appeal from the New to the True Catholics;or, The Faith and Practice of the first Six Centuries* (London, 1904), 43-53.
237 *R*, 29 May 1908, 509-10; 5 January 1906, 5; 28 May 1909, 381.
238 *Official Report of the Church Congress, Southend on Sea, October 1920* (London, 1920), 35-6.
239 Wace and Meyrick, *An Appeal*, 52.
240 *R*, 26 July 1889, 735; *1920 Church Congress*, 35-6.
241 *R*, 9 August 1889, 784; 23 August 1889, 832.
242 *R*, 13 September 1889, 901; 4 November 1920, 878.
243 The opposition was set out in *The Case against the proposed Appeal to the first Six Centuries* (London, 1905). See also Garratt, *Samuel Garratt*, chapter 9.
244 *R*, 4 April 1902, 312; 9 April 1903, 363; 1 July 1915, 607.
245 *R*, 11 November 1920, 897.
246 Thus Chancellor Dibdin's analysis, *R*, 8 November 1889, 1098.
247 A term derived from Denton Thompson's book of that title, published in 1911.
248 *R*, 19 August 1904, 839; 26 August 1904, 858.
249 *R*, 20 March 1903, 278; A.R.M. Finlayson, *Life of Canon Fleming* (London, 1909), 142-8; *RCED Minutes*, i, 65-74, records complaints against Evangelical churches and clergy from Athelstan Riley.
250 On ecclesiastical architecture, see P.F. Anson, *Fashions in Church Furnishings 1840-1940* (London, 1960[2]) and N. Yates, *Buildings, Faith and Worship. The Liturgical Arrangement of Anglican Churches 1600-1900* (Oxford, 2000[2]), chapters 7 and 8.
251 E.C. Dewick, 'Evangelicals and the problem of ritualism', *C*, January 1913, 8-17; J.R. Darbyshire, 'Evangelicals and the problem of ritualism', *C*, March 1913, 178-84; B. Herklots, 'Evangelicals and the problem of ritualism', *C*, May 1913, 352-9.
252 Darbyshire, 'Evangelicals and ritualism', 184.
253 *R*, 29 November 1901, 1184.
254 *R*, 10 August 1900, 765; 21 September 1900, 985-6.
255 Reprinted in Bentley, 'Transformation', appendix B.
256 *R*, 4 September 1908, 912, on Canon Woodward.
257 See, for example, J.N. Morris, 'Religion and urban change in Victorian England: a case study of the borough of Croydon, 1840-1914', Oxford DPhil thesis, 1986, 97-102.
258 O. Tomkins, *The Life of Edward Woods* (London, 1957), 81-2.
259 Trustees' Minute Book, 1894-1905, 13 (Autumn 1894).

260 *R*, 26 August 1904, 858; 2 May 1918, 298.

261 *R*, 9 September 1904, 899.

262 *R*, 13 March 1900, 284.

263 J. Neil, *Musical Service; Is it right?* (London, 1903^2), 16; *R*, 14 December 1900, 1201.

264 *R*, 2 September 1904, 879; Simpkinson, *Thorold*, 360.

265 *R*, 17 June 1910, 596; 11 July 1913, 664; 12 July 1917, 489.

266 *R*, 11 July 1913, 664.

267 According to J.S. Peart Binns, C. Lisle Carr introduced altar lights while vicar of Sheffield: A. Dunstan and J.S. Peart Binns, *Cornish Bishop* (London, 1977), 66.

268 G.W. Bromiley, *Daniel Henry Charles Bartlett: A Memoir* (Burnham on Sea, 1959), 22-3.

269 *R*, 11 November 1920, 897.

270 *R*, 14 August 1903, 783, among other examples.

271 *R*, 11 April 1913, 326.

272 See, for instance, the four *Church Association Enabling Bill Leaflets* (London, 1919).

273 Bentley, 'Transformation', chapters 9 and 10.

274 Yates, *Anglican Ritualism*, 303-14 and 351-64, describes the period from 1920 to 1950 as one of 'triumph' for Anglo-Catholicism.

CHAPTER 4

Evangelical Churchmen and Higher Criticism

'All Scripture is given by inspiration of God.' (2 Timothy 3:16)

Towards the end of 1902 the correspondence columns of the *Record* were given over to a debate on the topic 'Is controversy justifiable?', which revealed wide differences of opinion on the value and validity of the battle against ritualism. On 12 December a letter appeared from G.S. Streatfeild praising the work of the NPCU, but suggesting that speeches on the Roman and ritual controversies were 'little more than the flogging of a dead horse', since 'the fact, surely, is that the stress and strain of religious controversy, for our younger men, do not lie with Rome or her imitators. The centre of the struggle has shifted. For every *one* who is now asking "What is Truth?" as between Rome and the Reformed churches, a *hundred* are asking "What is Truth?" as between science and the essentials of the Christian faith, between the Higher Criticism and traditional interpretation, as between Labour and Capital, between the rich and the poor, between nationalization of wealth and private enterprise.'[1] Ritualism was not the sole issue perplexing Evangelical Churchmen in this period, and among those listed by Streatfeild, questions posed by higher criticism were particularly difficult and divisive. The purpose of this chapter is to explore the Evangelical response to higher criticism, and although it will concentrate mainly on the Old Testament, which was the focus of most debate in this period, some observations about New Testament criticism may be made first by way of introduction to the new approaches to biblical interpretation.

Comforting Conclusions: The Results of New Testament Criticism

There was relatively little concern in Evangelical circles about New Testament criticism in the late nineteenth century, and this may be attributed to the broadly conservative position held by the leading English New Testament scholars. In the middle of the century the New Testament seemed to be under attack from the demythologising of Strauss and particularly from the literary analysis of F.C. Baur and the Tübingen school, which allowed only four of the epistles to be Pauline and which dated the Fourth Gospel well into the second Christian century. Baur's theory that Catholic Christianity emerged as a synthesis from a conflict between Peter and Paul was subjected to a thorough investigation by J.B. Lightfoot, and the English theological world was convinced that Lightfoot had provided a conclusive refutation of the German ideas.[2] A.C. Headlam expressed the comfortable consensus when he wrote that 'to the English mind, the writings of Bishop Lightfoot proved, as conclusively as any facts in history can be proved, the genuineness of those writings usually classed as the Apostolic Fathers, and, as a necessary result of this, the complete overthrow of those theories of the development of Christianity which were associated with the Tübingen school, and their followers and representatives.'[3]

Radical New Testament criticism was not totally destroyed by Lightfoot, for the Dutch scholar Van Manen continued to challenge the authenticity of the Pauline epistles, while Paul Schmiedel published some provocative articles on the Gospels in the *Encyclopaedia Biblica* (1899-1903), suggesting that the New Testament contains very few reliable sayings of Jesus. The period also witnessed controversy over Harnack's *What is Christianity?* (1901) and Schweitzer's *Quest of the Historical Jesus* (1910), while F.C. Burkitt's paper on 'The limits of biblical criticism' at the 1908 Church Congress produced an angry response from conservative Churchmen.[4] Radical conclusions, however, tended to be theological rather than textual and scholars like Van Manen were clearly untypical of the general trend of research. In other words, liberal Protestantism might produce startling theological interpretations of the life of Christ, but these were generally based on fairly conservative conclusions with regard to the accuracy of the Gospel records. Thus an editorial note in the *Churchman* in April 1911 could claim that the higher criticism of the New Testament had achieved its purpose, because scientific methods, employed by scholars like Sanday and Harnack, had confirmed traditional solutions to the Synoptic Problem.[5]

Evangelical Churchmen of all shades of opinion welcomed and shared the conservative consensus on New Testament scholarship. G.T. Manley, writing in the conservative symposium *Evangelicalism by members of the FEC* (1925), reviewed the state of New Testament criticism and affirmed that traditional views were well supported by the scholars.[6] V.F. Storr agreed, commenting in *Liberal Evangelicalism* (1923): 'it is satisfactory to note that the general tendency of this criticism is in a conservative direction.'[7] Edward Woods was still more positive and claimed in 1910 that 'It is not too much to say that as far as the Gospels are concerned the battle of criticism in its main issue has been fought and won, and the Gospels are now admitted, by impartial critics, to be substantially true.'[8] Debate might continue about the authorship of 2 Peter, but the authenticity and reliability of the New Testament seemed to have been confirmed by critical scholarship.

The chief significance of this was that it made critical methodology respectable and useful to conservative Churchmen. Charles Gore drew attention to the consequences of this in *Lux Mundi*, published in the same year as Lightfoot's *Essays on 'Supernatural Religion'*, when he observed that the methods which had been used to defend the New Testament could not be excluded from the study of the Old.[9] Criticism could not be dismissed as illegitimate, therefore, without damaging the defence of the New Testament, and, moreover, the results of New Testament criticism could be used to encourage the timid to welcome further Old Testament study too. Conservative Evangelicals frequently used the demise of the Tübingen school as a caution to critics, but in so doing, they had to admit the propriety of the critical methods which had refuted Baur's theories.[10] The very success of criticism in confirming conservative conclusions on the New Testament therefore made it impossible to rule out the application of similar techniques to the Old, where results were less acceptable to traditionalists and where significant differences of opinion appeared within the Evangelical party. Before considering this debate, however, an account must be given of the development of Old Testament criticism during the nineteenth century.

Old Testament Criticism from Astruc to Wellhausen

According to the Evangelical F.E. Spencer's *A Short Introduction to the Old Testament*, published in 1912, higher criticism was that branch of biblical scholarship which concerned itself with the analysis of the contents, authorship and date of the canonical books, being distinguished, therefore, from lower criticism which concentrated solely on textual questions. Spencer attributed the term 'higher criticism' to J.G. Eichhorn, whose *Einleitung ins Alte Testament*, the first Old Testament 'Introduction', appeared between 1780 and 1783, establishing the leading role of German scholars in the development of Old Testament studies.[11]

Two significant questions dominated Old Testament scholarship in the nineteenth century. The first concerned the literary structure and composition of the canonical books, especially of the Pentateuch. Astruc in the eighteenth century had identified two sources in the book of Genesis and had labelled them J and E, referring to their characteristic use of the divine names Jehovah and Elohim. Eichhorn incorporated Astruc's documentary hypothesis into his *Einleitung* and this division was a mainstay of Old Testament criticism for the next century and beyond. The literary analysis of the Pentateuch was taken further in the early nineteenth century by a succession of German scholars – W.M.L. de Wette, Wilhelm Gesenius, C.P.W. Gramberg, J.F.L. George and Hermann Hupfeld. By the 1860s a critical consensus had emerged with regard to the composition of the Pentateuch since scholars agreed that there was a basic source, or *Grundschrift* (Astruc's E), which had been amplified by a second source, J. Although there was some disagreement about the unity of E, the dominant opinion was that it was the earliest element of the Pentateuch.[12]

This theory was demolished in the third quarter of the nineteenth century by K.H. Graf, Abraham Kuenen and Julius Wellhausen. They divided the *Grundschrift* into an early historical section, E, and a much later legal section, P, so called because it was believed to derive from a priestly school. The new hypothesis, put forward by Graf in 1865, received its most thoroughgoing expression in Wellhausen's *History of Israel* (1878), in which the Greifswald professor advocated a four-source theory of the composition of the Hexateuch (Pentateuch and Joshua): J, E, D (the Deuteronomic writer, responsible only for Deuteronomy) and P. Wellhausen's hypothesis was supported by a wealth of literary scholarship and textual analysis and it included a sophisticated understanding of the development of the basic documents, by which J and E were subjected to editing and adjustment before their incorporation into the Hexateuch. As John Rogerson has pointed out, Wellhausen's combined source JE was really a weaving together of the third redaction of both documents, so a complicated literary history preceded the final form of the canonical books.[13]

The Graf-Wellhausen hypothesis drew some of its academic strength from its linking of literary analysis with Israelite history, and thus to a solution to the second basic question posed by Old Testament study, the historicity of the biblical books. The key to Wellhausen's theory was its identification of the three main literary sources (JE, D and P) with three stages of development in Israelite religion. Wellhausen began by contrasting the picture presented by the Pentateuchal legislation with the reality of religious life described or assumed by the historical books and the prophets. From this observation he drew the conclusion that much of the Pentateuch was an idealization of Israelite religion, an attempt to attribute to Moses a system which only arose in the years following the return from the Exile. In his historical and literary analysis Wellhausen concentrated on the evolution of the priesthood and sanctuary, placing a particular emphasis on the book of Deuteronomy and the Josian reforms of 621 BC (2 Kgs 22). He argued that the law book found in the Temple during the reign of Josiah was Deuteronomy, that it was a recent composition perhaps written specifically to support the reforms, and that the centralisation of the cult on the Jerusalem Temple, far from being a return to a Mosaic ideal, was in fact an innovation. Wellhausen therefore claimed that there were three broad stages of development in Israelite religion. The first was marked by a multiplicity of local shrines and no formal priesthood (corresponding to the JE source). The second, accomplished by Josiah with the help of the pseudo-Mosaic Deuteronomy, led to the suppression of local shrines and the concentration on Jerusalem as the focus of the cult. The third stage was the post-Exilic flowering of priestly religion, represented by the ritualistic details of the Priestly Code (P), and associated with the school of Ezekiel.[14]

The Graf-Wellhausen answer to the two fundamental questions of Old Testament study, therefore, was that the Pentateuch (or rather, the Hexateuch), was a composite production, made up of four main strands as well as numerous special sources and editorial alterations, and that it was thoroughly unhistorical. The Old Testament presents a picture of a Mosaic revelation followed by national apostasy; on Wellhausen's theory, as his disciple Duhm wrote, 'At one stroke the Mosaic period is wiped out.'[15] The Law became a late development, evolving as the Israelites rose from primitive religion to ethical monotheism under the influence of the eighth century prophets. Those parts of the Old Testament which purported to recount Mosaic religion were unhistorical (Wellhausen was particularly scornful of the veracity of the books of Chronicles), while chance references within the reliable historical books were ascribed to interpolation by later Deuteronomic editors. The Patriarchal narratives were myths, compiled thousands of years later and with little, if any, historical content; Abraham, for example, was 'a free creation of unconscious art', according to Wellhausen.[16]

The main conclusions of higher criticism in the late nineteenth century concerned the Pentateuch, but other parts of the Old Testament also fell victim to the critical scalpel. The book of Isaiah was divided into at least two sections, with the second being ascribed to the period of the Exile. Zechariah also became a composite work and Daniel was reassigned to the era of the Maccabees.[17] Much debate raged around the date and authorship of the Psalms: Reuss and Kuenen refused to allow any to David, while Delitzsch maintained that forty four of the seventy three ascribed to him were genuine.[18] Furthermore, Old Testament scholarship continued to develop after Wellhausen, and at the turn of the century it began to consider the origins of Israelite religion and its debt to the myths of the great Near Eastern civilisations. The early years of the twentieth century thus witnessed the 'Bibel – Babel' controversy in German academic circles, as the extent of Babylonian influence in the Old Testament was fiercely debated.[19]

Higher Criticism in England: Resistance and Acceptance

Critical study flourished in Germany, where, even in the first half of the nineteenth century, there were seventeen Protestant theology faculties capable of serious Old Testament teaching, besides German-speaking faculties in Switzerland and elsewhere.[20] The German academic system was geared to promote research and this bore fruit in the development of increasingly sophisticated literary criticism.

The situation in England was very different. Although there was a gradual increase in the number of universities in the course of the century, biblical studies bore no comparison in volume and erudition with the flourishing work of German scholars.[21] English theologians, moreover, were slow to accept the conclusions of much European scholarship. It is a significant indication of the conservatism of the English academic world that the theological translation libraries, which provided translations of European theology for the English market, concentrated almost exclusively on works attacking the higher critics.[22] Even those who did not share the views of Edward Tatham, sometime rector of Lincoln College, Oxford, who wished 'all Jarman critics at the bottom of the Jarman ocean,'[23] imbibed the scholarly conservatism of Hengstenberg and Hävernick rather than the works of De Wette and the radical critics. English theologians who were deemed to have embraced the more controversial German theories were bitterly attacked, as may be seen from the reactions to Milman's *The History of the Jews* (1829-30), to Samuel Davidson's edition of T.H. Horne's *Introduction* (1856), to *Essays and Reviews* (1860) and to the works of Bishop Colenso (1862-79).[24]

It is possible to detect a change in the climate of scholarly opinion in the second half of the nineteenth century. Dean Stanley's *Lectures on the History of the Jewish Church* (1863-76) combined an acceptance of some critical methods with conservative conclusions, and drew on the work of the German critic Heinrich Ewald. J.B. Mozley's lectures of the 1870s also revealed a degree of sympathy for critical questions, and Mozley's pupils of that period included several members of the later *Lux Mundi* school. Although T. and T. Clark's Foreign Theological Library continued to produce translations only of conservative works, Williams and Norgate's Theological Translation Fund Library turned to volumes by Ewald and by the radical Dutch scholar Abraham Kuenen.[25]

The crucial period of transition in the academic world stretched from 1880 until 1891, and was marked by a succession of important developments. The first of these was the publication of two books, *The Old Testament in the Jewish Church* (1881) and *The Prophets of Israel* (1882), both by William Robertson Smith. Robertson Smith was a member of the Free Church of Scotland, a professor at the Free Church College, Aberdeen, until he lost his chair for his espousal of critical opinions, and a follower of Wellhausen, whose *Prolegomena* he translated into English. More significantly, Robertson Smith was a man of acknowledged orthodoxy with a strong evangelical faith. His lectures and books did much to counter the assumption that support for higher criticism automatically implied heterodox or infidel opinions.[26] Then 1882-3 brought the accession of two critical scholars to the Hebrew chairs at Oxford and Cambridge, when A.F. Kirkpatrick became Regius professor at Cambridge and S.R. Driver succeeded the ultra-conservative E.B. Pusey at Oxford. Driver was a cautious, reverent and orthodox scholar, who made a powerful case for the broad acceptance of Wellhausen's critical theories in a series of books and articles culminating in his *Introduction to the Literature of the Old Testament* (1891), a standard work which reached a fifth edition by 1894 and a ninth in 1913. Two other key figures in the universities were H.E. Ryle, Hulsean professor at Cambridge from 1887 until 1901, and William Sanday, who occupied the Dean Ireland and Lady Margaret chairs at Oxford between 1882 and 1919. As well as their university influence, these scholars were particularly adept at reconciling Anglican orthodoxy with higher criticism.[27] This task was assisted by the publication of *Lux Mundi* in 1889. In that volume, Charles Gore and the younger generation of Anglo-Catholics declared their support for critical approaches to the Old Testament. They were prepared, wrote Gore, to recognise the idealization of history in parts of the Old Testament, and they called for greater openness to critical debate.[28]

These changes made higher criticism a topic of considerable controversy in most of the main English denominations during the 1880s. The 'battle of the standpoints' raged in the periodical press; Spurgeon fulminated against the 'downgrade' theology of the Baptist Union; R.F. Horton's *Inspiration and the Bible* (1888) divided the Congregationalists; and the Presbyterians refused to offer a chair at their English college to George Adam Smith.[29] As for the Established Church, in December 1891 thirty eight Churchmen sent a 'Declaration on the Truth of Holy Scripture' to the *Times*, affirming a very conservative position and even seeming to deprecate the value of reason if deployed against traditional beliefs.[30] On one level the controversy was fierce, but brief. Whereas Alfred Cave could claim as late as 1880 that 99% of English biblical scholars held to the Mosaic authorship of the Pentateuch[31] and Herbert Ryle feared 'a stake in the market-place'on account of his opinions, [32] by 1890 the new scholarship had triumphed in the universities and the heavyweight periodicals. The battle, claimed G.A. Smith, had been fought and won: 'Modern criticism has won its war against the Traditional Theories. It only remains to fix the amount of the indemnity.'[33]

This judgment of a contemporary higher critic has been endorsed by modern scholars, who agree that the methods and assumptions of the critics, if not Wellhausen's conclusions in their entirety, were triumphant by 1900.[34] Beyond the academic world, however, the position was far less clear-cut. The younger generation of clergy were increasingly accommodating themselves to some form of higher criticism, but there were still influential advocates of traditional beliefs, and conservatism remained deep-seated among the laity. Evangelicals, in particular, showed no signs of accepting that the battle over higher criticism had ended. Indeed, Evangelical Churchmen, in common with their fellows in other denominations, continued the campaign well into the twentieth century, with serious consequences for the unity of their school of thought.

Evangelical Awareness of Higher Criticism

In 1901 the Islington Clerical Meeting addressed the subject of 'The old century and the new: experiences of the past and lessons for the future.' During general discussion the Revd G. Harford Battersby called for openness to the new critical methods and warned his fellow Evangelicals against setting up 'Protestant Popes' and relegating 'to a limbo of unblessed heresy all who cannot pronounce the old shibboleths of the older doctrine of inspiration.'[35] The response to this appeal was slight, but later in the same year a lively debate was provoked by G.S. Streatfeild's paper 'Questions that must be faced; or, Evangelicalism and modern thought, ' given to the Southport Conference on 22 May. The correspondence in the *Record* continued, albeit with a break, into 1902, and although the main emphasis was on evolution, issues of biblical criticism were raised, especially with regard to the early chapters of Genesis. Streatfeild sought to defend sober and reverent criticism and to suggest that it could not harm the foundations of the faith, but his reference to Genesis 3 as a 'sacred allegory'[36] provoked angry refutations from Trevor Fielder and A.A. Isaacs, asking where the allegorising would end.[37] It is noteworthy that the *Record*'s leading article which closed the first phase of the correspondence in September 1901 thought it necessary to defend Streatfeild's claim to be a loyal Evangelical and Streatfeild himself feared that he was regarded with suspicion by most of his clerical brethren.[38]

A second controversy broke out in 1911 when W.T. Pilter used an Islington Meeting address on 'Recent criticism of the Old Testament' to attack the Wellhausen theory as pseudo-rationalistic, 'unsound in reason and untrue in fact' and based on an 'almost puerile' literary analysis of the Pentateuch. Pilter seemed to pledge Evangelical Churchmen to the entire trustworthiness of biblical history, and he was followed by a paper from Henry Wace defending the substantial accuracy of the Bible in the context of proposals to Convocation that the question committing candidates for the diaconate to 'unfeignedly believe all the Canonical Scriptures of the Old and New Testament' should be amended.[39] Even before the papers were published, a letter appeared in the *Record* from H.L.C. de Candole, vicar of Holy Trinity, Cambridge, and J.R. Darbyshire, vice-principal of Ridley Hall, appealing to the Reformation principles of 'liberty of thought and the right of unfettered study of the Bible.' They continued, 'without associating ourselves with any particular school of biblical criticism we wish to protest against the idea that a particular attitude towards these questions is to be made a test of Evangelical Churchmanship.'[40] The subsequent correspondence revealed deep differences of opinion. The Liberal Evangelicals H.E.H. Probyn, E.C. Dewick, H.A. Wilson, F.B. Macnutt and C.F. Russell supported the Candole-Darbyshire position, as did Guy Warman and Dawson Walker in their editorial notes for the *Churchman*.[41] A.R. Whately, moreover, criticised the conservatives for failing to 'comprehend the standpoint and the needs of the typical thoughtful Evangelical of the younger generation.'[42] For the conservatives, Edward Miller, rector of Wrabness, declared that 'the conservative position in Biblical Criticism ... is ... the very foundation and sheet-anchor of Evangelical Churchmanship, '[43] a point echoed by F.C. Burrough, G.H. Hewitt, C.F. Harford and F.S. Webster; Webster referred to the liberals as 'weaker brethren' who should be treated gently and urged to keep their doubts to themselves.[44] A.W. Sutton, speaking for the conservative laity, considered that 'there is no halting-place between the non-acceptance of the Old Testament Scriptures which our Lord Himself endorsed and the denial of the Godhead of Jesus of Nazareth,'[45] while E.G. Bowring asked whether there was any difference between the Liberal Evangelicals and Broad Churchmen.[46] By the time that Sir John Kennaway, the veteran president of the CMS, urged that the correspondence be closed,[47] it had become very clear that the Evangelical school included a vociferous group pressing for toleration and resentful of the conservatism of the traditionalists, as well as a strong conservative element for whom higher criticism was subversive of essential Evangelical doctrines. Although an open breach was avoided in 1911, the issues were not resolved and they were to emerge again later in the decade in the committee room of the CMS.

A complicated matrix of factors influenced Evangelical responses to higher criticism. Among the most important were acquaintance with critical theories, judgments about their provenance, the perception of consequences, the balance of scholarship and the weight of doctrinal presuppositions. These elements may be examined in turn.

Some Evangelicals proved receptive to higher criticism and found the critical case convincing. This was particularly true of the younger generation of Evangelicals, those passing through university in the 1880s and 1890s, because at this time the theology faculties were increasingly falling into the hands of the critics. With Driver, Cheyne, Sanday, Ottley and Cooke at Oxford, Ryle, Kirkpatrick, Kennett and Burkitt at Cambridge and Nairne at King's College, London, advocates of critical opinions were in most of the key positions.[48] There were a few conservatives, like H.C.G. Moule at Cambridge and Stanley Leathes in London, but they were outnumbered. There was no English equivalent of the strong conservative Princeton school in the USA, and many younger Evangelicals felt that the traditional beliefs were academically untenable. In the biography of Theodore Woods, a student at Cambridge between 1892 and 1897, Moule's ability to help his pupils is called into question:

'As a teacher ... [he] was weakest as a guide through the

intellectual difficulties which were then besetting younger men at Cambridge, especially in connection with the Higher Criticism of the Old Testament. Intensely conservative in mind and outlook, he shrank from and never mastered the new learning; and some of his pupils remember their wonder at his reluctance to make definite mental decisions on many of the important issues which were occupying thoughtful men in the university.'[49]

Evangelical converts to higher criticism, however, and those like G.S. Streatfeild, who were eager to make their clerical brethren come to terms with modern thought, complained long and loud about the failure of many in the party to address themselves to the questions being asked by thoughtful believers.[50] H.E.H. Probyn, writing in the *Record* in August 1907, cited a colleague who told him that 'he was convinced that Higher Criticism was a device of the Evil One, '[51] while another Evangelical vicar said of the new critics: 'I do not read their books myself, but I do my duty in warning my people against them.'[52] This persistent obscurantist trend within Evangelicalism derived from several sources.

First, there was an unintellectual element in Evangelical religion, one which emphasized faith at the expense of reason. Sydney Smith sneered at the early adherents of the eighteenth century Revival as a 'nest of consecrated cobblers, ' and the charge of anti-intellectualism was frequently repeated.[53] A more sympathetic observer, L.E. Elliott-Binns, wrote: 'Evangelicals had never been conspicuous for depth or originality of thought, being prone to attach greater value to the instinctive and emotional than to the products of the reason... Zeal and a spotless orthodoxy were prized above intellectual ability or theological research; the latter, indeed, might often arouse their suspicions.'[54] The Keswick influence might be cited here as an example of an Evangelical activity concentrating on the devotional side of Christianity and tending to neglect intellectual problems, so that the *Record*'s report of the Convention of 1908 noted approvingly that Keswick was too busy using the Bible to worry about issues of higher criticism.[55] Second, the busyness of Evangelical Churchmen – Bebbington's hallmark of 'activism' – might also detract from scholarship. Higher criticism was seen as a donnish preserve and one for which the parochial clergy had no time. 'Vigilans' ruefully described the successful Evangelical incumbent in these terms:

> '[He] was active, wiry, always on his feet, always on the doorsteps of his parish; fluent, extempore, unctuous in his pulpit; ready with "Gospel" phraseology, and with a Bible constantly under his arm. I am not finding fault. But this man never read, in the wide and serious meaning of the term. He "had no time". "Duty" did not allow of "study". I have heard him say ... that he regarded all the writers of the Scriptures as verbally, mechanically inspired, "as, in fact, *automata* in the hands of God." A member of his congregation remonstrated with him for similar utterances in the pulpit. His reply was "It is a good working theory;" and he had no other answer. This man despised, by neglecting, general learning... But he constantly spoke of his large church, his great congregation, the blessed work he was enabled to do. His promotion was rapid.'[57]

Those who were too busy to keep abreast of modern scholarship were prone to discount higher criticism as a mere fad, so that one contributor to a correspondence in the *Record* headed 'They don't read' advised young Evangelicals to read Pearson on the Creed and Moule on Romans, rather than Driver on the Pentateuch, because higher criticism was 'really only a passing phase'.[58] Even those who did take critical views more seriously were liable to encourage this attitude by suggesting that the new criticism was one in a succession of temporary attacks on the Bible and was doomed to failure in the fullness of time.[59] It may be seen that this scarcely encouraged awareness of higher criticism, and indeed Evangelicals continued to produce a stream of sermons and devotional volumes with little or no reference to critical questions. F.S. Webster's *Jonah* (1906) mentioned higher criticism only to reject it,[60] while W.H. Griffith Thomas contributed three volumes on Genesis to a series published by the Religious Tract Society which specifically ignored the problems raised by modern scholarship.[61]

Provenance: Reverence or Rationalism?

Reluctance to take the trouble to examine higher criticism seriously often derived from instinctive suspicions about the provenance of the new theories, grounded in previous experience of the sources of critical opinions. The provocative views of Strauss and Baur had alarmed conservative Churchmen, and insofar as German scholarship reached England in the mid-nineteenth century, it had taken the form of the attacks of Hengstenberg's 'Confessionalist' school upon the alleged unorthodoxy of the radical higher critics. Many English critical works in this earlier period, moreover, originated from mavericks like Colenso or outright infidels like F.W. Newman.[62] Before higher criticism could gain a hearing from Evangelical Churchmen on the level of scholarship, therefore, it had to overcome its associations with rationalism and infidelity. Some Evangelicals continued to use the provenance of critical theories as a reason for paying no attention to them – thus the ultra-conservative newspaper *Word and Work* carried an article in April 1892 which traced the pedigree of higher criticism from nineteenth century German rationalism through Colenso and Davidson to S.R. Driver, also apparently 'a German rationalist.' 'Higher criticism is rationalism; and rationalism is bald infidelity, ' declared *Word and Work.* [63] William Marle, writing in the *Record* in the same month, called it 'this hybrid child of German rationalism and English unfaithfulness,'[64] but such extreme reactions were rare among Evangelical scholars. C.A. Heurtley spoke for many when he declared that 'all truth is of God and must be accepted as such', even if it requires a modification of received opinions.[65] Bishop Perowne underlined this point in his *Charge* of 1895: 'We may leave God to take care of His own truth. It does not need and cannot be made stronger by our timid fences and feeble props.'[66] In any case, as the American conservative journal the *Bibliotheca Sacra* observed in an article on 'The philosophy and theology of the leading Old Testament critics', there was no real proof that heterodox beliefs marred biblical scholarship.[67] Moreover, by the 1890s there was a strong school of 'reverent criticism', composed of men like Driver, Kirkpatrick and H.E. Ryle. Most Evangelicals were willing to recognise the genuineness of their faith, so G.C.M. Douglas, writing in the conservative collection *Lex Mosaica* (1894) noted: 'I am happy to know that so many of the critics in England are believers.'[68] 'Reverent criticism' still drew the fire of some conservative writers,[69] and allusions to rationalism or to German influence were used against the critics, but this was mostly done as a supplement to, rather than a replacement for, a reply or refutation on academic grounds. Even A.H. Carter, who ascribed higher criticism to Satanic machinations, appealed to archaeology in support of his conservative opinions.[70]

Consequences: Devastation or Liberation?

When Evangelicals did explore higher criticism, they often began and sometimes ended with its perceived consequences, and these were frequently seen as antagonistic to Christian faith, or, more precisely, as antagonistic to Scripture. In January 1892, for instance, the *Record* opened its discussion on criticism under the tendentious heading 'The attack on the Bible', [71] and many of the specific points made against the critics stemmed from a reaction to the challenge posed by critical conclusions to the accepted place of the Bible in the Evangelical scheme of Christianity.

David Bebbington has identified 'biblicism' as one of the enduring characteristics of evangelicalism.[72] Evangelical religion was Bible-based and a love of Scripture was one of the central features of Evangelical piety. Christians in the Evangelical tradition had an emotional attachment to Holy Writ amounting almost to bibliolatry – indeed, J.C. Ryle wrote, 'Let us not fear being idolaters of this blessed book. Men may easily make an idol of the church, of ministers, of sacraments, or of intellect. Men cannot make an idol of the Word.'[73]

Higher criticism seemed to undermine the foundations of scriptural Christianity by depriving Evangelicals of the Bible. In *On What Authority?* (1922), E.A. Knox challenged the radical critics with a question posed by ordinary believers:

> '"You have robbed us of the prophecies which we traced from the Fall to the last page of Malachi, you have cast the trail of pseudonymous literature on the ceremonial law and on the marvellous appeals of Deuteronomy, you have removed some Messianic prophecies, altered the significance of others; you have turned loose an army of redactors and revisers too often alleged to be re-writing or re-editing books in their own private interests; the Bible which God used to bring us to Christ is so much altered by your re-editing, re-dating, re-translating, that the old book is almost gone. What have you to give us in exchange?"'[74]

The critics, it was claimed, robbed people of the Bible in two ways. First, they made it a book which only scholars could understand and appreciate. J.J. Lias referred to the new clericalism of the critics, meaning their creation of a new priestly caste with exclusive access to the truths of Christianity.[75] Second, and more seriously, the critics allegedly destroyed the reader's faith in the truthfulness of Scripture. Henry Wace told the Liverpool Diocesan Conference in 1901, 'When he heard of these criticisms, the average man simply concluded that the Bible at least in its plain meaning, was not to be fully trusted... If they could not read their Bible without feeling that there was a legend there, a myth here and an inaccurate representation there, plain men would feel their belief shaken.'[76]

From this loss of understanding and confidence in Scripture, there flowed a series of further consequences, each fatal to traditional Evangelical religion. Scriptural exposition was the mainstay of Evangelical preaching, so that Eugene Stock, recalling the preachers of Islington in his youth, remembered their style of working through the Bible verse by verse.[77] With the advent of higher criticism, preaching of this kind became very difficult, because a literal interpretation or rigid adherence to textual details, especially of the Old Testament, was no longer easy to sustain. Some Churchmen stopped preaching on controversial Old Testament passages altogether, and a number of articles appeared to help perplexed Evangelicals through the minefield of Old Testament exegesis.[78]

Expository preaching arose from the conviction that Scripture was God's living word to humanity. This belief also undergirded the Evangelical use of the Bible in the devotional life and as a means of conversion. Regular Bible study was one of the mainsprings of Evangelical piety, and the twin emphasis on the Bible both as a converting and an edifying medium helps to explain the commitment of Evangelical Churchmen to the Bible Society, the Scripture Gift Mission, the Bible and Prayer Union and other organisations designed to circulate the Scriptures or ensure their daily devotional use.[79]

Under the impact of higher criticism, however, many Evangelicals held that Bible reading would decline, because no-one would see any need to read a discredited book, even if they could understand the results of criticism well enough to know which parts of the Scriptures were still endorsed by modern scholarship.[80] For some, criticism would provide a useful excuse to abandon Christianity altogether, an implication noted by E.H. Hopkins in a letter to the *Record* in 1892 and observed by J.J. Lias in the *Churchman* seven years later, when he recalled a working man whose sons had deserted the faith because, they said, the Bible was '"all a make-up"'.[81]

As for evangelism, conservative Evangelicals were very anxious about the influence of critical theories on apologetics and missionary work. The testimony of the *Record*'s 1892 correspondence was unanimously that shaking the Bible's authority would have a disastrous impact on home missions of all kinds. Wilson Carlile wrote that if Church Army officers taught that Jonah was a myth, 'we believe it would greatly hinder our work, especially amongst the ignorant classes.'[82] T.S. Treanor, chaplain to the Missions to Seamen, agreed: if they were told that Christ was mistaken about the Old Testament, 'missionary work among sailors is at an end.'[83] Lukyn Williams said the same of Jewish missions, while a youthful Guy Warman, writing as a London Sunday School teacher, accused the critics of leading the city's street arabs into 'infidelity and ruin'.[84] Some years later, J.E. Watts-Ditchfield, vicar of St James-the-Less, Bethnal Green, which had a large congregation of working-class men, reacted angrily to the advocacy of higher criticism at the 1908 Church Congress: 'Working as I do among working men, and having to deal directly and indirectly with thousands of them, I unhesitatingly say that a paper like the one read at this Congress the other day by Professor BURKITT will cause me more difficulty in my ministerial work than all the writings of Mr BLATCHFORD.' The *Record* quoted these words in a leading article and continued: 'The many unwise statements of the Higher Criticism are destroying the influence of the Bible upon those who are unable to appreciate those niceties of scholarship in which Professors delight.'[85] It was not for nothing that the Rationalist Press produced a cheap edition of the *Encyclopaedia Biblica*.[86]

As well as crippling home missions, it was claimed that higher criticism also provided a useful weapon for the enemies of Christianity overseas. This began with the use of critical theories by Moslem and Hindu controversialists to discredit the Bible, so that W. Salter Price, vicar of Wingfield, recalled a debate with a Brahmin who cited Christian scholars against the authority of Scripture,[87] while C.H. Waller complained that missionaries had to 'refute the teaching of our own universities'[88] and W. St Clair Tisdall drew attention to the problem in a paper to the 1907 Church Congress.[89] The situation became more serious when critical views spread to the missionary societies, a subject of increasing concern among conservative Evangelicals in the early twentieth century. The Bible League traced the spread of higher criticism in the mission field[90] and H.E. Fox devoted his pamphlet *Rationalism or the Gospel?* (1912) to a description of the enervating effects of critical opinion on Christian outreach.[91] As will be seen later, anxiety about the toleration of higher criticism within the CMS was a major cause of the schism within the Society in the 1920s.[92]

The uncertainty generated by higher criticism was also blamed for the declining number of ordinands in the late nineteenth century. George Ensor described a student destined for the ministry who encountered higher criticism and became a Socinian instead,[93] while G.S. Brewer, writing on 'The dearth of candidates for holy orders' in the *Churchman* for October 1905, made the unsettlement provoked by biblical criticism one of the two major causes of the problem, the other being ritual lawlessness.[94]

The controversies over ritualism and higher criticism met in the Evangelical emphasis on the primacy of Scripture. Traditionally, as has already been seen, Evangelicals relied on Scripture as their weapon against Roman and Anglo-Catholics, emphasizing its place as the rule of faith. This case, elaborated in Goode's *The Divine Rule of Faith and Practice*, was still being advocated with vigour at the end of the century. J.C. Ryle insisted 'The only question we ought to ask is this, "Is it written in the Bible? What saith the Lord?"'[95] The Protestant Reformation Society in its reply lectures and other challenges to Roman Catholicism depended on the Bible as its weapon,[96] and W.R. Mowll was ready to trust the free circulation of the Bible as the best antidote to ritualism, telling the Church Association May Meeting of 1902:

> 'Let the book as they had it now in all its simplicity be taught to the children, and they could leave the Word of God to do its own work.. Their one hope rested in letting the Word of God be known by the people on the right hand and the left. The ritualists and Romanists would never make much headway so long as that book was read.'[97]

Higher criticism clearly threatened to destroy this potent weapon by reducing the Bible to a confusing mixture of myths, fables and pious fabrications. Moreover, by shaking the reliability of Holy Writ, the critics were said to prompt those seeking certainty in religion to turn instead to sacerdotalism, either of the Anglican or the Roman variety. E.H. Hopkins predicted this drift towards High Churchmanship in the *Record* for 1892 and he was not alone in linking sacerdotalism and criticism.[98] E.A. Knox wrote of *Lux Mundi*: 'To Evangelicals it seemed no new thing that opponents of the Reformation should seek to undermine the authority of Scripture,'[99] and the synthesis of ritualism and rationalism in the person of Charles Gore helps to explain the virulence of the opposition to his appointment as bishop of Worcester in 1901.[100]

Two other aspects of the Evangelical world-view threatened by higher criticism may be mentioned. The first was a deep interest in the interpretation of prophecy, regarded by some as the key to the future. Evangelical Churchmen differed in their approach to the biblical prophecies, since some adopted a futurist or dispensationalist outlook, holding that the age of prophetic fulfilment would not dawn until the Second Advent. Many, however, adhered to the historicist position and they keenly read the signs of the times in the light of the detailed visions of Daniel, Ezekiel and Revelation. The Liberal Evangelical Elliott-Binns commented scornfully on prophetic interpretation as 'a cult which provided so useful an occupation... for retired army officers in our inland watering-places,' and suggested that it had declined due to the development of the crossword puzzle,[101] but scholars of the calibre of C.H.H. Wright also devoted much attention to the finer points of Daniel.[102] An Evangelical tradition stretching back at least to E.B. Elliott's *Horae Apocalypticae* valued the prophecies, and therefore relied on the precise text of Scripture, for each reference and turn of phrase could be of deep significance. The critics, however, struck at the prophetic school both by their textual iconoclasm and by reinterpreting the prophets as champions of social righteousness and ethical monotheism rather than as foretellers of the future.[103]

Finally, Evangelical Churchmen linked fidelity to Scripture with morality and national prosperity. One legacy of the Reformation and of deep-rooted Protestant nationalism was the assumption that a Bible-based religion was the source of divine favour and national greatness. Lady Wimborne, addressing the May Meeting of the Ladies' League in 1903, after referring to the Bible as 'our one infallible guide', went on to claim that 'some vital cause... invariably connects Protestantism and prosperity,'[104] while the United Protestant Council called Scripture 'the granite pillar on which social righteousness, liberty, peace and true prosperity must ever rest.'[105] This equation of the Bible and national success was explained partly in terms of a reward for fidelity to 'God's Word Written' and partly as a consequence of the free and democratic principles which a Bible-reading laity would naturally develop. According to Evangelicals, nations which neglected the Bible were doomed to decline – thus the earl of Harrowby, presiding at the Trent College Speech Day in 1871, attributed the result of the recent Franco-Prussian war to the fact that every German soldier had a Bible in his knapsack, while the French troops read 'books you cannot name'.[106]

Thus as higher criticism spread, conservative Evangelicals claimed to see the disturbing signs of a moral collapse. H.E. Fox drew attention to a decline in Sabbath observance in *Rationalism or the Gospel?*, [107] while fiction was used to convey a similar message, so *Word and Work* carried a serial story, 'James Wylie; or, a tale of conscience, ' about a hypocritical liberal Nonconformist minister and his spendthrift wife.[108] Conservative propaganda reached new heights, however, with the outbreak of the First World War, when the Bible League in particular plotted the steady decline of Germany from endorsement of higher criticism via militarism to a policy of atrocities inevitable in a nation whose allegiance was given to Nietzsche rather than to Christ. German biblical criticism was likened to poison gas and Britain was urged to reject German ideas as it would repel an invasion of German troops.[109] Germany's apparent decline into barbarism was seen as a salutary lesson of what would happen to a nation that turned away from the Word of God.

Faced by this conservative antipathy to the alleged consequences of higher criticism, Evangelicals sympathetic to the critical outlook had to produce an apologia emphasizing the beneficial results of modern scholarship. They were able to point out a number of advantages which could be derived from critical conclusions, beginning with the success of higher criticism in reconciling orthodox Christianity with the best results of modern thought, thus ensuring that educated people did not reject the faith as exploded by the advance of knowledge. Herbert Ryle's biographer put the matter thus: 'The new learning could afford a firm foundation for Christian belief to which the old theory of verbal inspiration, irretrievably shattered by the advance of human knowledge, could never make good its claims again.'[110] Progressive revelation allowed the critic to explain the bizarre miracles and the science of the Old Testament as the poetic memories of a primitive nation falsely interpreted by the traditionalists as historical facts. The Hebrews, wrote V.F. Storr, were 'a simple and undeveloped race. They had little or no knowledge of science, their ideas of God were often crude, their religion admitted of the presence of much superstition…; they were like children, whose intelligence has not been fully trained. Is it surprising, then, that in their sacred literature we should find records of strange and marvellous phenomena?'[111] By separating the fact of revelation from its form, therefore, most of the scientific and historical problems posed to the thoughtful Christian could be removed. Storr, Elliott-Binns and Edward Woods, among others, made much of this gain from critical scholarship.[112] Whereas Leslie Stephen had abandoned Christianity in the 1860s because he was unable to reconcile science, religion and his conscience, by the 1890s higher criticism had solved the dilemma of conscientious clergymen who could only proclaim as true a faith which could be combined with modern thought.[113]

Progressive revelation also offered a solution to the moral problems raised by the Old Testament. Despite attempts to justify the bloodthirsty sections of the Hebrew Scriptures, some Christians in the Victorian era were disturbed by the unedifying catalogue of massacres, often apparently commanded by God. The commendation of Jael for treacherously killing Sisera, the slaughter of the Canaanites and the loss of divine favour by Saul when he spared Agag seemed difficult to accept as the will of a God of love.[114] Progressive revelation dealt with the perplexity by ascribing those parts of the Old Testament which were deemed to be sub-Christian to the primitive understanding of the Hebrew nation and its 'many imperfect notions about God'.[115]

By explaining Old Testament science, justifying its historical mistakes and excusing its un-Christian morality, higher criticism not only strengthened the faith but also offered a potent weapon against infidelity. Secularist propaganda made much use of the apparent contradictions between the Bible and modern science, and there was a long tradition of attacking discrepancies in the text or mocking morally questionable stories.[116] Armed with critical scholarship, however, Christians could destroy the secularist case. As H.E. Ryle wrote in 1909: 'The assaults of the atheist and the infidel, based on contradictions, on defective morality, on historical blunders or imperfect science, are met and repelled by modern criticism.'[117]

The other main benefit of higher criticism, according to the liberals, was that it brought the Bible to life in a new way. It achieved this by explaining difficulties, by arousing interest in the historical background to the biblical narrative and by transforming Scripture from a collection of atomised proof-texts into a living volume describing God's revelation through the spiritual pilgrimage of real people. The Bible lost its infallibility, but gained a deeper human interest. Furthermore, by changing the emphasis of the prophetical books from future prediction to present social comment, the Old Testament acquired a new relevance to the political and economic conditions of the day. This social dimension of Christianity reflected the Liberal Evangelical interest in a this-worldly kingdom of God, and some of the roots of that doctrine derived from a new perspective on the Old Testament.[118] According to Edward Woods, biblical criticism would have 'as it percolates down from the scholar to the plain person the result of bringing the Bible again into common use, as the indispensable *vade mecum* of every strong, true Christian life.'[119]

The Contribution of Scholarship

The debate on higher criticism, however, could not rest at the level of perceived consequences. Liberal Evangelicals were eager to press the academic case for the new theories, and conservatives, too, were prepared to engage in debate on the merits of competing scholarship. Any reluctance on the part of the traditionalists to enter the scholarly arena with the higher critics, moreover, was outweighed by assumptions about the unity of truth, confidence in scientific methodology and the internal logic of Evangelical principles.

The nineteenth century witnessed the development of scientific history, combining scrupulous attention to detail with a great confidence in the potential of the scientific method for discovering objective truth. The search for facts, the study of origins and the questioning of received opinions were increasingly accepted in academic circles,[120] and Evangelical Churchmen could only reject the scientific study of Scripture if they were willing to accept the charge of obscurantism, a point made by opponents of the 1891 'Declaration on the Truth of Holy Scripture'.[121] Evangelicalism, moreover, had long stressed the right of private judgment and the importance of an open Bible, two principles much to the fore during the ritual controversy.[122] It might be argued, therefore, that Evangelicals could hardly avoid scholarly study of the Bible. An authoritative book must be allowed to speak for itself, and so in some ways the foundation principles of Evangelicalism laid the movement open to scientific biblical criticism. Leslie Stephen, writing in 1895, said that 'Protestantism in one aspect is simply rationalism still running about with the shell on its head. This gives no doubt one secret of the decay of the Evangelical party. The Protestant demand for a rational basis of faith widened among men of any intellectual force into an inquiry about the authority of the Bible or of Christianity.'[123] Another former Evangelical, John Henry Newman, made a similar point in his *Lectures on the Prophetical Office of the Church.*[124]

Evangelicals, therefore, had to listen to the critics; they could not ignore critical questions altogether or reject the results merely because the consequences were unpalatable – as Wace told the Newcastle Church Congress of 1900: 'They must be prepared to accept truth, whatever its consequences.'[125] This commitment to truth formed the background for a debate within Evangelicalism on the academic merits of the new critical theories.

The liberals had little need to promote their side of the scholarly debate, since it was being done very effectively by the theology faculties and through Church Congress papers and theological translation fund libraries. The Liberal Evangelical contribution to this cause could not be described as extensive, and it consisted mainly of attempts to popularise higher criticism through the manuals of the AEGM and the Student Christian Movement. Edward Woods, V.F. Storr and H.B. Gooding contributed pamphlets or chapters to this end, while Elliott-Binns produced a commentary on *The Book of Exodus* in the series 'The Revised Version for the Use of Schools'. This took the accepted critical position of four sources, with the latest being dated to

300-500 BC, and the introduction recommended works by Driver and McNeile for further reading.[126] A more solid piece of scholarship was John Battersby Harford's *Since Wellhausen: A Brief Survey of Recent Pentateuchal Criticism*. Published in 1926, this volume consisted of articles written for the *Expositor* in the previous year defending the central tenets of the Graf-Wellhausen hypothesis against a variety of critics ranging from the conservative James Orr to the radicals Eerdmans and Dahse. Harford displayed a firm grasp of historical and textual criticism and concluded that the attempts to shake Wellhausen had been unsuccessful.[127]

To some extent the conservative Evangelicals also relied on non-Evangelical or non-Anglican scholars for their arguments against the higher critics. Among the most regular contributors to the *Churchman* on biblical questions were J.J. Lias, Stanley Leathes and H.M. Wiener. Leathes was almost certainly not an Evangelical; Wiener was a Jew; and Lias' ecclesiastical pedigree included membership of the ECU until 1871 and an acknowledgment of an intellectual debt to Maurice and Kingsley, as well as Lightfoot, Westcott and Hort.[128] The Scottish conservatives Orr, Robertson and Baxter also provided ammunition for the battle, as did the American periodicals the *Bibliotheca Sacra* and the *Princeton Theological Review*.[129] Nonetheless, Evangelical Churchmen could field a number of conservative scholars, with Henry Wace, W.H. Griffith Thomas, Robert Sinker, F.E. Spencer, C.H. Waller and R.B. Girdlestone contributing the most to the debate.

The first element in the conservative attack on higher criticism was to assert that critical methods and conclusions were vitiated by false presuppositions. This linked up with the old charge of rationalism and infidelity, and could lead to a simple theological syllogism: understanding of the Bible requires spiritual discernment, and higher criticism is irreverent, so it is small wonder that it comes to false conclusions. J.C. Ryle voiced this charge in *Is all Scripture Inspired?* (1891), when he likened the irreverent critical approach to Scripture to 'a man botanising on his mother's grave.'[130] The call for spiritual perception was also made by Griffith Thomas in *The Catholic Faith*,[131] and by Trevor Fielder, who warned in his *The Truth of the Bible* that 'unsanctified erudition is among the devil's best tools.'[132]

Critical irreverence was deemed to be demonstrated particularly by a suspicious attitude towards the Old Testament's view of itself. Spencer wrote of the 'unnatural historical scepticism' of the critical method,[133] and this charge enabled the conservatives to claim that the critics failed to give due weight to the testimony of Judaism and of Christianity to the historical reliability of the Scriptures. In a leading article on 'The problem of the day' in January 1892, the *Record* warned against a hasty adherence to new theories at the cost of ignoring the witness of generations of believers,[134] while Griffith Thomas asked, 'Is the testimony of nineteen centuries of Christian history and experience of no account in this question?' and 'Does the New Criticism readily agree with the Historical Position of the Jewish nation as seen throughout the centuries?'[135] The issue was partly one of the reliability of internal evidence, so Spencer devoted one section of his *Did Moses write the Pentateuch after all?* to an examination of literary traditions, seeking to prove their trustworthiness,[136] but it also developed into an argument about presumption. The conservatives began by assuming that Scripture was true until proved false, whereas the critics apparently took almost the opposite position. The consensus of the centuries should be respected, claimed Wace; Scripture was 'in possession' and it was for the critics to prove their case beyond a shadow of doubt; otherwise the traditional view should be upheld.[137]

The scepticism of the higher critics was generally ascribed by their opponents to an unjustified and unscientific prejudice against miracles or any manifestations of the supernatural. Such a starting point was bound to make them highly suspicious of the Old Testament narratives, but it was a presupposition which robbed them of any claim to academic impartiality. Wace drew attention to the 'great philosophical bias' of the German scholars and others made the same point.[138] F.E. Spencer went so far as to assert that the whole superstructure of higher criticism rested on two false principles:

> 'that "the history of all ancient nations, without exception, is lost in its beginning in the cloudland of myths and legends… and, in its later historical stage, is the resultant of natural and intelligible forces influenced in no special manner, either from above or from beneath" and, following the teaching of science, that "the history of Israel is an evolution from the embryonic and atomic, without any influence from without".'

The historico-critical method, wrote Spencer, was designed 'for the express purpose of destroying the evidence that Israel is an exception to a scientific law of development, which is assumed to be without exception.'[139] Such a method could hardly claim to be truly scientific. Moreover, as Girdlestone observed, traditional Christian faith resting on the Incarnation, could have no quarrel with the concept of miracle: 'The Bible is unique because redemption is unique. We do not expect that the events which led up to the manifestation of the *logos* would be on a par with those which we read in the daily paper.'[140]

To the conservatives, therefore, criticism began with a false view of Israelite history. What Scripture presents as revelation, Wellhausen ascribed to evolution, and any form of divine activity was ruled out of court. This presupposition was not only invalid in Christian terms, but it also led to poor scholarship, because judgments were made purely on the basis of assumptions about miracles. Griffith Thomas noted Driver's reluctance to allow Genesis 49 to be genuine and ascribed this to an *a priori* dislike of predictive prophecy.[141] In his *A Short Introduction to the Old Testament* (1912), Spencer attacked the critical conclusions on Isaiah for their *a priori* origins: 'De Wette's maxim, *omne vaticinium post eventum* (every prophecy after the event) is demonstrably false, though it enters largely into the critical treatment of the Hebrew prophets, and is often the somewhat concealed, but decisive element in critical decisions.'[142] This fatal flaw, claimed the conservatives, applied not only to the most radical German critics, but also to the moderate English scholars, who had taken over the false presuppositions when they gave their allegiance to the historico-critical method. As conservative writers never tired of pointing out, 'reverent criticism' was in reality a vain attempt to reconcile Christian orthodoxy with pseudo-scholarly techniques alien to the faith. Griffith Thomas, answering the question, 'Can purely naturalistic premisses be accepted without coming to purely naturalistic conclusions?', cited the warning offered by the Princeton professor, W.H. Green: 'They who have themselves been thoroughly grounded in the Christian faith may, by a happy inconsistency, hold fast their old convictions, while admitting principles, methods and conclusions that are logically at war with them. But who can be surprised if others shall with stricter logic carry what has been thus commended to them to its legitimate conclusion?',[143] while James Orr alerted readers of the *Churchman* to the fact that Driver was atypically moderate as a higher critic, because he failed to apply his own principles with full rigour.[144]

Conservative scholars did not rest entirely upon the issue of presuppositions. They proceeded to attack higher criticism on methodological grounds and on specific conclusions. One frequently repeated charge was that the critics were far too confident about the capabilities of their literary techniques to determine historical questions. The *Record* censured the fourth volume of the *Encyclopaedia Biblica*, published in 1903, for 'rather too much of the "I am Sir Oracle" style',[145] and a series of reviews in 1901 accused the critics of advancing their theories as if they were as certain as the propositions of Euclid.[146] The critics were prone to speak and write of 'assured results' and this provoked their opponents to voice doubts as to whether the degree of certainty and precision claimed by the liberal school was really attainable. Both Henry Wace and Robert Sinker questioned the reliability of a method which claimed to be able to assign verses and even half-verses of ancient documents to specific sources, suggesting that the division was far too precise to be trustworthy.[147]

A ploy frequently used in controversy, moreover, was to consider the application of higher critical methods to other fields of literature, in an endeavour to demonstrate their weaknesses. Wolff's analysis of Homer was used as an example of ingenious, but entirely mistaken, theorising,[148] and various conservatives challenged the critics to use their methods to dissect modern composite works.[149] As an alternative, some writers speculated on future higher critical analysis of Milton and Tennyson, two authors whose stylistic variety might encourage speculation about the presence of more than one authorial hand.[150]

Another aspect of unjustified critical self-confidence, in the opinion of conservative scholars, was the refusal of the dominant school to take seriously the points raised by its opponents. The *Record*, in its review of Orr's *The Problem of the Old Testament*, complained of a 'conspiracy of silence' against conservative works,[151] and J.J. Lias in particular accused the critics of assuming a monopoly of scholarship and of adopting a dismissive and contemptuous attitude towards other theories. Referring to the critics, Lias wrote, 'one would think they might be willing to admit that their theory was still at least *sub judice*. But no. The oracle has spoken and in no dubious tone. "Scholars are agreed." If anyone does not agree, he is not a scholar.'[152] Lias likened this to the Roman Catholic method of ignoring opponents,[153] while F.E. Spencer described it as 'intellectual terrorism', with its implication that 'anyone daring to differ from the new light in the present must be a fool.'[154] This accusation was not merely due to conservative pique, for some of the higher critics were prone to treat conservative opinions with amused contempt, or merely to ignore them as unworthy of a reply. W.H. Bennett and W.F. Adeney, in their *Biblical Introduction* (1899) dismissed *Lex Mosaica* as 'a very useful and interesting study... [which]... affords no real evidence against the Grafian theory, '[155] while Charles Raven recalled his astonishment that 'anyone with sufficient education to pass the Little-go should still believe in the talking serpent or Jonah's whale or Balaam's ass.'[156] Wace complained in 1905 that the booklist prepared for the Central Society for Sacred Study by Professor Driver omitted conservative works,[157] and the same point was made about the set books for the Durham BD in 1908.[158]

The refusal to give conservative scholarship a fair hearing fuelled the accusation that higher criticism was academically disreputable. In his contribution to *Lex Mosaica*, J.J. Lias lampooned the critical approach thus:

> 'Take every difficulty in a compendious and artless narrative, and magnify it as much as you can. Reject all attempts at explaining it. Insist on the conclusion being drawn that we have in it evidence of the use of two or more irreconcilable sources of information. Meet every difficulty in the way of your own theory by representing any passage which obstinately refuses to fit in with the theory as a "gloss" or the "addition of a later editor" or of a scribe who was desirous of bringing the history into conformity with the religious ideas prevalent in his own time. Overwhelm your opponents with indignation if *they* venture to represent any passage as a gloss or the later addition of a copyist. And then your induction is complete, your conclusions unassailable. If you cannot prove them, you can at least challenge anybody to disprove them, for if any credible witness appears, he is at once ordered out of court at the request of the counsel for the prosecution.'[159]

Lias clearly expressed the opinion of many conservatives that glosses and copyists were a useful device invented for the removal of awkward pieces of evidence. The same could be said, wrote F.E. Spencer, of that convenient, but shadowy character, the Deuteronomic editor, to whom could be attributed all references to Mosaic institutions in the historical books.[160] Some were prepared to press the charge further and to accuse the higher critics of deliberately suppressing evidence. The contributors to *Lex Mosaica* certainly held Wellhausen to be guilty of this,[161] and George Ensor accused Driver of misusing an inscription and Herbert Ryle of misleading the public by failing to explain the incomplete nature of Hebrew genealogies.[162] Behind these criticisms lay the conservative belief that the critics manipulated literary analysis in the interests of preconceived theories about the historicity of the Old Testament and the evolution of the religion of Israel.

Conservative scholars were quite prepared to enter the arena of philological and literary debate and to try to refute the critics on their own ground. In 1894 fourteen conservatives produced the massive symposium *Lex Mosaica; or, the Law of Moses and the Higher Criticism* and this tome set out to prove 'that the traditional view of the Old Testament books and the orthodox view of the Old Testament Dispensation, do correspond with the historical records and with the writings of the prophets; that the Law of Moses is presupposed throughout the history, and the influence of the books of Moses is implied in the books of the prophets.'[163] In other words, *Lex Mosaica* challenged the basic conclusion of the Wellhausen school that the Law was later than the prophets, a challenge sustained through over 600 pages of detailed analysis, including Girdlestone's defence of Joshua, Sinker on the Josian reforms (with a consideration of Hebrew archaisms in Deuteronomy) and F.E. Spencer on Ezekiel and the Priestly Code. Each essay sought to demonstrate on the basis of literary and historical evidence that the views of the critics were unfounded. A similar aim lay behind Spencer's *Did Moses write the Pentateuch after all?* (1892) and his *Short Introduction to the Old Testament* (1912), as well as Girdlestone's *The Foundations of the Bible* (1891) and parts of his *Doctor Doctorum* (1892). The *Churchman* published many articles on points of Old Testament criticism from Prebendary F.T. Bassett's 'The Old Testament and the Critics' in August 1890 through E. Flecker's 'Chapters 1 and 2 of the Polychrome Isaiah' in January 1900 to H.M. Wiener's theories on the text of the Old Testament, H.A. Redpath's eight part refutation of Driver's commentary on Genesis and J.J. Lias on

'The authorship of the Pentateuch', a series which began in December 1895 and concluded in August 1902 after thirty one articles, mostly dealing with detailed literary questions.

Although he gained a reputation as a leading spokesman of the conservative school, Henry Wace wrote little on the minutiae of literary criticism. His role was to promote the broad conclusions of traditional scholarship and he fulfilled this through regular contributions published in the *Churchman* and the *Record*. In 1903 Wace gave a series of lectures to the clergy of the diocese of Norwich, by invitation of Bishop Sheepshanks, and these were subsequently published as *The Bible and Modern Investigation*. In his lectures Wace built up a careful case for the substantial historicity of the Old Testament, citing Driver, and using Strack and Dillmann against Wellhausen.[164]

In his Norwich lectures Wace also drew on the conclusions of archaeology, [165] and in this he was typical of contemporary conservative writers, for perhaps the most frequently repeated conservative response to higher criticism was the appeal to the monuments as a convincing refutation of the arid speculations of literary criticism.[166] This was a period of substantial archaeological discovery in the Near East, since from 1890 Flinders Petrie was working in the Holy Land under the auspices of the Palestine Exploration Fund, and a large quantity of Babylonian, Assyrian and Egyptian material was excavated. The Tell el-Amarna letters, found in Egypt in 1887, and a series of inscriptions uncovered in the 1880s and 1890s did much to throw light on a period of history formerly known only from the biblical records.[167] In some respects, archaeology seemed to provide solid evidence against the critics. It demonstrated the antiquity of writing, thus showing that a Mosaic Pentateuch was not impossible, as some critics had claimed. By expanding knowledge of Ancient Egypt it enabled conservatives to trace the influence of the Exodus in books supposedly written thousands of years later. The monuments, moreover, confirmed some of the historical details of the Old Testament, for example, the 'War of the Kings' described in Genesis 14.[168] So it was that F.E. Spencer, in his *Short Introduction to the Old Testament*, placed a particular emphasis on archaeology,[169] while the *Record*, commenting on discoveries in Egypt in 1906, declared:

> 'The spade is the bugbear of "advanced critics". It has a very awkward habit of turning up the remains of people who

ought really to keep out of the way of those wholly imaginary writers of the Bible... The British School of Archaeology in Egypt ... is in a fair way to demonstrate that several historical impossibilities actually happened.'[170]

There is some truth in L.E. Elliott-Binns' claim that the conservative use of archaeology was undiscriminating and ill-informed.[171] For some it was no doubt a convenient excuse for avoiding the challenge of higher criticism and their comprehension of the issues may have merely extended to a vague idea that Sayce, Hommel and other archaeologists opposed the conclusions of the Wellhausen school. This does not apply, however, to all conservative writers. The *Churchman* carried reviews of the works of Hommel, Sayce, Naville and Pinches, among others.[172] W.T. Pilter, whose conservative paper at the Islington meeting stirred up a controversy in 1911, was sufficiently acquainted with scholarship to write a book on *The Law of Hammurabi and Moses* (1907), review T.G. Pinches' work on Assyriology and translate König's *The Bible and Babylon* from the German in 1905.[173] If some Evangelicals exploited archaeology as a reason for dismissing higher criticism, others regarded it as a testimony to the general accuracy of the Old Testament. Thus when the Liberal Evangelical M. Linton Smith challenged the conservative attempt to find external testimony to support every detail of the Old Testament, Wace replied in the *Record* that archaeology was a supplementary witness reinforcing the received reliability of the canonical books.[174]

In the opinion of the conservatives archaeology was only one of the disciplines neglected by literary critics, with the result that their conclusions were flawed and incomplete. Writing as a trained lawyer, H.M. Wiener attacked those who sought to analyse the legal codes of the Pentateuch without a degree of expertise in ancient legislation.[175] Likewise, George Ensor's refutation of H.E. Ryle's *Early Narratives of Genesis* made much of Ryle's ignorance of Assyriology, geology and astronomy.[176] Some conservatives even accused the critics of forgetting that the Bible was an Eastern book and that it should be handled accordingly.[177] The general point was that literary criticism was only one aspect of Old Testament study and that it needed to be balanced by other disciplines. Lawyers, secular historians, scientists and archaeologists should all be heard, especially when their conclusions in their own spheres of expertise conflicted with the judgment of the higher critics.

There was no single Evangelical response to higher criticism at an academic level. Broadly speaking, the party might be divided into a liberal section which accepted Driver's conclusions and a conservative section which did not, but this would be an over-simplification. There were conservatives who rejected biblical criticism altogether, whatever its conclusions, and more who paid no attention to it. Most conservatives, however, accepted the right and duty of criticism, but dissented from the Wellhausen theories, regarding them as extreme and unproven. These nuances in the Evangelical position will be considered further below.

Doctrinal Presuppositions

Scholarly debate on higher criticism could not be conducted in a doctrinal vacuum. All shades of Evangelical opinion were aware of the need to reconcile their particular conclusions with fundamental Christian doctrines, particularly those of biblical inspiration and Christology. The relationship between doctrine and scholarship was a complicated one and the role played by each element varied according to the standpoint of the particular Evangelicals concerned.

Biblical inspiration

With regard to inspiration and its corollaries, it may be suggested that the Evangelical position with regard to biblical criticism developed and became more rigid in the course of the nineteenth century. In this period it was often asserted that the most conservative Evangelicals were merely echoing the opinions of their forebears in the faith, so J.C. Ryle could claim that:

> 'The spiritual reformers of the last century taught constantly *the sufficiency and supremacy of Holy Scripture*. The Bible, whole and unmutilated, was their sole rule of faith and practice.They accepted all its statements without question or dispute. They knew nothing of any part of Scripture being uninspired. They never allowed that man has any "verifying faculty" within him, by which Scripture statements may be weighed, rejected or received. They never flinched from asserting that there can be no error in the Word of God; and that when we cannot understand or reconcile some parts of

its contents, the fault is in the interpreter and not in the text.'[178] Conservative Evangelicals were naturally content to claim descent from the leaders of the eighteenth century Revival, and Liberal Evangelical writers were ready to allow the appeal. In *The Development of English Theology in the Nineteenth Century, 1800-60* (1913), V.F. Storr presented a general picture of a narrow and static system gradually adjusting to new ideas. Part of this process was the demolition of the old Evangelical doctrine of Scripture under the impact of biblical criticism.[179]

More recent research, however, has discovered that Evangelicalism in the early nineteenth century was not unsympathetic to the new techniques of studying the Bible. Charles Simeon admitted the possibility of errors in Scripture, 'inexactnesses in references to philosophical and scientific matters', and Daniel Wilson welcomed and used the textual studies of Marsh and Michaelis.[180] The most comprehensive work on this subject produced by an Evangelical scholar in the period, T.H. Horne's *Introduction to the Critical Study and Knowledge of the Holy Scriptures* (1818), advanced a theory of progressive revelation and allowed contradictions within the Gospels.[181] This outlook was not unchallenged within Evangelicalism – Ryle was reported as having commented, 'I never thought old Daniel Wilson of Calcutta sound about inspiration'[182] – but its existence refutes the claim that the Simeonites were hostile to critical study.

Two developments may account for the hardening of the Evangelical doctrine of Scripture during the nineteenth century. As has already been seen, the rise of the Oxford Movement drove Evangelicals to reassert the supremacy of Scripture as the rule of faith. While Evangelicals were appealing to the supremacy, sufficiency and perspicuity of Scripture against the Tractarians, they were unlikely to welcome suggestions that the accepted doctrines of inspiration and authority needed radical revision.

The second development was the spread of hostile biblical criticism and of liberal theology. In the light of *Essays and Reviews* Evangelical Churchmen set their faces against radical criticism and defined a doctrine of inspiration more rigid than that of their forebears.[183] Thus C.H. Waller, an undergraduate at Oxford during the controversy over *Essays and Reviews*, later acknowledged his debt to J.W. Burgon for expounding a conservative view of Scripture and declared: '...before I left the university, I had reached a position which I have held ever since, and hold (thank God) to this day, that every known syllable of Scripture has the authority of the Word of God.'[184]

In this context of stricter doctrines of inspiration, the conservative Evangelicals collided with the theories of the Wellhausen school in three main respects: the uniqueness of the Bible, the question of revelation and the concept of verbal inspiration, or rather, with its presumed consequences.

Evangelical Churchmen of conservative views were thoroughly persuaded of the uniqueness of Scripture. J.C. Ryle made the first of the propositions that he set out to prove in *Is all Scripture Inspired?* the fact that the Bible is 'utterly unlike all other books that were ever written'. Ryle went on to deprecate comparisons between the inspired Word of God and other works of religious or secular literature. To set the Bible alongside the Koran or the Book of Mormon, wrote Ryle, was like comparing Skiddaw with a mole-hill or the Koh-i-Noor diamond with a bit of glass. As for literary comparisons, 'to talk of the inspiration of the Bible, as only differing *in degree* from that of such writings as the works of Homer, Plato, Shakespeare, Dante and Milton is simply a piece of blasphemous folly ...'[185] The critical method of treating the Bible like any other book was, therefore, highly suspect, for there was, in Joseph Parker's words, 'None like it.'[186]

Closely linked to the uniqueness of Scripture was the question of revelation. As has already been seen, some critical scholars treated the history of Israel as no different in kind from that of other nations, and this could become an assumption that the Old Testament was the product of evolutionary change without any need for divine intervention. Conservative opposition to this presupposition has already been noted and discussed, and it may merely be observed here that Griffith Thomas reduced the whole debate to one of revelation versus evolution as the source of the Old Testament.[187]

The third subject of dispute concerned verbal inspiration. This issue has been confused by problems of terminology, particularly the use of phrases like 'general superintendence', 'plenary inspiration' and 'mechanical dictation' without adequate definition. Further confusion has been caused, moreover, by the Liberal Evangelical tendency to attribute views to the conservatives which the latter never held,[188] a tendency which the unguarded language of some conservative writers did little to discourage.

For the sake of clarity, it may be stated that conservative Evangelicals did not hold a doctrine of mechanical dictation and that several took pains to repudiate it. Commenting on the theory that the biblical writers were mere pens used by the Holy Spirit, J.C. Ryle wrote:

> 'I do not admit for a moment that they were mere machines holding pens, and, like type setters in a printing office, did not always understand what they were doing. I abhor the "mechanical" theory of inspiration. I dislike the idea that men like Moses and St Paul were no better than organ pipes, employed by the Holy Ghost, or ignorant secretaries or amanuenses who wrote by dictation what they did not understand.'[189]

Recalling his ordination in 1858 some fifty years later, Canon Henry Sutton claimed that the Evangelicals of that period had indeed adhered to mechanical dictation,[190] but it is possible that he was mistaken, or that he misrepresented the general outlook of the Evangelical school. Certainly C.A. Heurtley rejected such a theory in his university sermon *The Inspiration of Holy Scripture*,[191] preached in 1857 and published in 1861, while Ryle's repudiation in the 1870s was clear and firm.[192] By the earlier years of the twentieth century H.E. Fox could even suggest that mechanical dictation was a term 'probably coined for controversial purposes' since 'such a view is not held, and probably never has been held, by any writer of credit.'[193]

The doctrine commonly held by conservative Evangelicals was one of concursive inspiration,[194] a theory which recognised the freedom and individuality of the human writers of Scripture, but maintained that God exercised an overall control on the products of their pens. Hence J.C. Ryle's statement,

> 'I believe that in some marvellous manner the Holy Ghost made use of the reason, the memory, the intellect, the style of thought, and the peculiar mental temperament of each writer of the Scriptures ... there is both a Divine and a human element in the Bible, and ... while the men who wrote it were really and truly men, the book that they wrote and handed down to us is really and truly the Word of God.'[195]

A comparison was sometimes drawn between the union of divine control and human freedom in Scripture, the written

Word, and the union of two natures in the Person of Christ, the Word made flesh. Both were a mystery, but both were essential aspects of Christian truth.[196]

Evangelicals were happy to confess that the process of inspiration was beyond their understanding. The implications of inspiration, however, were clear, and these led to conflict with higher criticism. H.E. Fox wrote of 'a Divine control which secures the inspired utterances from error,'[197] thus illustrating the standard conservative assumption that inspiration was inextricably linked to factual accuracy. J.C. Ryle simply assumed this when he attacked the German higher critics for reducing Genesis to 'a collection of interesting fables' and thereby seeming 'boldly [to] deny the inspiration of large portions of the Old Testament.'[198] An inspired book, for the conservatives, had to be a book free from errors, particularly errors in facts open to independent confirmation. This was both a consequence of its nature as the Word of God and a necessity for faith, for as T.W. Gilbert pointed out in his analysis of Evangelical attitudes towards inspiration, the conservatives regarded a Bible which was mistaken on verifiable matters of fact as utterly unreliable on unverifiable matters of religious truth.[199] Harold Smith described this position as 'All or None' in the *Churchman* for 1924 and criticised its narrowness.[200]

Although perceived as narrow by some Evangelicals, the conservative commitment to some form of verbal accuracy, be it infallible original autographs or a reliable English Bible, was a logical deduction from their doctrine of revelation. Ryle stated this principle in *Is all Scripture inspired?* when he stressed the need for a trustworthy account of God's Word, [201] while Griffith Thomas linked the issues of inspiration, revelation and accuracy firmly together in a reply to a questioner in the *Record* in April 1913. After defending plenary inspiration against the charge of copyists' errors (by appealing to the autographs), he continued, 'The possibility of the authority of the Bible, and therefore of its inspiration, lies in the fact of our need of an objective standard of truth from God.'[202] In *The Catholic Faith* he went further and insisted that since revelation must be in words, the very words of Scripture must be reliable.[203] This was the burden also of T.C. Hammond's essay 'The fiat of authority' in the conservative volume *Evangelicalism by members of the FEC* (1925). Hammond argued from the existence of a personal God to the probability of revelation, with the requirement that such a revelation should be communicated in language comprehensible to rational beings. 'Inspiration of utterance' was therefore needed to ensure that God's message reached its destination intact, for 'An inspired man who could not give utterance to his inspiration would be as little use to humanity as St Paul was when he was "caught up into the third heaven and heard unspeakable words which it is not lawful for man to utter"'. God's ideas were communicated through inspired men in the form of inspired words; thus, when the men died, the ideas lived on in the words of Scripture.[204]

These interpretations of inspiration and revelation were not easy to reconcile with the conclusions of the dominant school of higher criticism. By the 1920s conservative scholars like T.C. Hammond were quite prepared to accept the presence of fiction and parable within the Old Testament, but only on condition that passages so described were clearly intended to be taken thus by their authors: 'Fiction and parable it may be admitted can teach Divine truth, but they must teach it in the form of fiction and parable, and must not be obtruded on the mind masquerading as facts.'[205] Clearly an inevitable antagonism existed between a theory of verbal inspiration relying on scriptural accuracy and a critical hypothesis which regarded large sections of the Pentateuch as a blend of pious fraud and pure invention.

For the conservatives this was a good reason for the rejection of the results of higher criticism; for those persuaded of the truth of the critical theories it was a spur to modify their doctrine of inspiration, and this was done in two main ways.

The first step was to reject the conservative assumption that inspiration automatically implied factual accuracy in every sphere and on all subjects. The younger Anglo-Catholics led the way with Gore's essay on inspiration in *Lux Mundi*, admitting the possibility that the Old Testament included idealized history.[206] In the early twentieth century the divorce of inspiration from factual accuracy was a commonplace of Liberal Evangelical theology, expressed by Elliott-Binns in his commentary on *The Book of Exodus* (1924) and by Edward Woods in *Modern Discipleship and what it means* (1910). In a series of books and pamphlets, V.F. Storr took up the question of revelation, claiming that God only revealed those things which humanity could not discover for itself. Science and history, therefore, were not proper subjects for revelation and thus we should not expect Scripture to be an infallible guide on these matters. The significant message of the Bible was moral and spiritual; this was the proper province of inspiration and here the words of Scripture were to be heeded. '*The inspiration,*' wrote Storr, '*lies in the nature of the spiritual message contained in the books.* We believe the Bible to have come from God, because of the moral and religious truth it teaches.'[208]

The Liberal Evangelicals maintained that the Word of God was spiritual treasure in earthen vessels, divine truth mediated through the thought-forms of the ancient world. Flaws in the vessel could not harm the precious contents, so, in the words of H.E. Ryle, 'the determination of... literary problems fails to affect the fundamental relation of the Christian believer to the written word.' The Bible's truth consisted 'in the message it bore to your spirit, ' not in 'some cherished point of criticism, some favourite authorship, some traditional date of composition.'[209] Literary criticism could not touch the essentials of Scripture, because the spiritual message of the Bible to the individual believer was not open to historical investigation. Storr quoted on a number of occasions Coleridge's maxim that the Bible is inspired because it 'finds me'; the expression of a subjective theory of revelation immune to harm from higher criticism.[210]

The second element of the Liberal Evangelical apologia for higher criticism was an emphasis on the human side of the Bible. Fed perhaps by the doctrine of immanence and the theory of evolution, the concept of God working with free human agents seemed theologically superior to the perceived conservative view of mechanical dictation which the liberals persisted in misrepresenting throughout this period. The liberals could claim that they were giving due recognition to the human element in the Bible and that to do so meant allowing for the possibility of error. 'These biblical writers were human beings, ' wrote Storr. 'They were not infallible; and with our increased knowledge today we find ourselves greatly in advance of their intellectual level.'[211]

For the Liberal Evangelicals, therefore, inspiration was concerned with the Bible's moral and spiritual message, and this could, indeed did, exist alongside historical inaccuracies, primitive science and the mythology of an ancient people. Higher criticism could be welcomed as an aid to understanding the background of the Bible without posing any threat to its fundamental value or religious teaching.

Between the liberals and the ultra-conservatives was a third group of Evangelical Churchmen, corresponding to those who were receptive to some aspects of higher criticism but hostile to the full Wellhausen system. On the issue of inspiration they were caught between two fundamental principles. On the one hand, they refused to invoke inspiration in order to close critical questions, so C.H.H. Wright affirmed that 'Theological prepossessions ought not... to be permitted to stand in the way of historical investigation.'[212] Scholarship could not be ignored in such a cavalier fashion. On the other hand, however, this group was not prepared to adopt the liberal solution of divorcing inspiration from historical truth. Henry Wace was the chief spokesman of this outlook, and the constant refrain of his addresses on biblical criticism was that the key issue was the basic truthfulness of Scripture. The European critics, Wace told the Church Congress of 1900, maintained 'that... the narrative of the history of Jewish religion as taught in the Pentateuch and the historical books was a mistaken one,'[213] and this was important because inspiration was incompatible with substantial inaccuracy. For Wace, a book which included major misrepresentations of facts could not be inspired and he saw this as the main difference between his beliefs and those of the leading English critics.[214]

The solution for conservative scholarship was to defend the 'substantial accuracy' of Scripture. T.W. Gilbert described this position at the Cheltenham Conference of 1925 and distinguished it from 'conservative Evangelicalism', which he identified with a commitment to inerrancy. According to Gilbert, Evangelicals of this central type were prepared to accept progressive revelation and a full human contribution to the record of God's dealings with humankind, including the possibility of inaccuracies in minor detail, some idealization of history and the use of myths to convey spiritual truth. The record, however, was basically accurate and not a late fabrication by a priestly clique.[215] Gilbert's analysis of 1925 may have given more ground to the critics than Wace would have been prepared to allow, but many conservative scholars in the early years of the century had certainly abandoned verbal inerrancy, if for no other reason than necessity once the presence of copyists' mistakes was acknowledged.[216]

The debate on inspiration was not primarily concerned with the technique of producing inspired books, despite the oft-repeated gibes at 'dictation' in the works of the Liberal Evangelicals. It has been seen that the liberal portrayal of conservative opinion often descended to caricature, for even conservatives as staunch as J.C. Ryle, H.E. Fox and C.H. Waller affirmed a full human contribution to the making of Scripture. The crucial issue was the result of inspiration. Ryle and those whose views he represented held that inspiration guaranteed factual accuracy in all respects. The liberals, from Perowne to Storr, narrowed the range of inspiration to spiritual truth contained within the earthen vessels of Israelite history. Wace and the moderate conservatives upheld the substantial accuracy of the Old Testament, rejecting the mere moral truth of the liberal outlook and using their biblical scholarship to satisfy themselves that the Scriptures were indeed broadly reliable as historical documents. Evangelicals readily agreed on their ignorance of the mode of inspiration; it was the interpretation of its consequences that produced very different reactions to the results of higher criticism.

Christology

The second area of doctrine affected by higher criticism was Christology. In essence the problem was very simple: according to the New Testament records, Christ endorsed the traditional view of the Hebrew Scriptures. How could this endorsement be reconciled with the conclusions of critical scholarship and what were the implications of higher criticism for an understanding of the Person of Christ?

Three broad arguments were put forward by the critics and the Liberal Evangelicals to explain Christ's apparent disagreement with Wellhausen. The first was that he had no interest in literary questions. His mission on earth was to reveal God to humanity, wrote V.F. Storr, and to give men and women power to live as children of God.[217] His references to the Old Testament had no bearing on this mission and therefore could not be taken as evidence of divine revelation with regard to the authorship of the Hebrew Scriptures.

This position could be developed into two other arguments. It might be maintained that Christ accommodated himself to the beliefs of his contemporaries. If he were to communicate with them at all, he had to adopt their language and basic world-view, including the traditional ascription of the Law to Moses and the Psalms to David, since 'in all His teaching He had to move on ground which was common to Himself and His hearers.'[218] On this understanding, Christ was aware of the flaws in the Jewish understanding of the Old Testament, but deliberately chose not to contradict them. As Perowne suggested, 'if error there was, it was not one He thought it necessary to correct, it was not one that touched religion.'[219]

The other, related, argument was the doctrine of the kenosis, so called because of the reference to Christ's 'humiliation' or 'emptying' (*ekenosen*) in Philippians 2. This theory held that the Incarnation of necessity involved the imposition of limitations on Christ, and these included a loss of divine omniscience, so that Christ as man shared the beliefs of his contemporaries, including their understanding of the Old Testament. H.E. Ryle, preaching on 'The Old Testament and Modern Criticism' in July 1889, declared of Christ:

> 'He took upon Himself all the limitations of our manhood, both in body and in mind. In His moral and spiritual vision, He, in His sinless purity, possessed a power of perfect insight ... But to His intellectual powers in His humanity there seem to have been assigned the natural barriers of the time in which He lived.'[220]

V.F. Storr made the same point more strongly, asserting: 'He had no more knowledge than the Jews of His day.'[221] Storr maintained that to ascribe omniscience to the human nature of Christ was 'gross unorthodoxy' and that if he was fully acquainted with the conclusions of modern science and literary criticism then 'He was not true man,'[222] an argument echoed by E.W. Barnes in his contribution to *Liberal Evangelicalism* where he attacked the conservative standpoint as Apollinarian and 'fundamentally heretical'.[223] The true humanity of Christ required that he should share the mistaken beliefs of first century Judaism about the date and authorship of the Old Testament.

Before turning to the conservative reply to the kenosis and its allied theories, it is worth noting that the appeal to Christology against hostile biblical criticism was a standard weapon of traditional scholarship and an accepted principle of nineteenth century Evangelical apologetics. Recalling his conversion in the late 1860s, H.C.G. Moule stated:

> 'When my Lord Christ became a living and unutterably necessary Reality to me, I remember that one of my first sensations of profound relief was: HE absolutely trusted the Bible, and, though there are in it things inexplicable and intricate that have puzzled me so much, I am going, not in a blind sense, but reverently, to trust the book because of Him.'[224]

C.A. Heurtley appealed to the testimony of Christ and the Apostles in *The Inspiration of Holy Scripture* (1861),[225] as did Harrington Lees nearly fifty years later in *The Joy of Bible Study* (1909).[226] Indeed, it is noticeable that despite the rise of critical theories and of the doctrine of the kenosis, conservative Evangelicals were still prepared to use Christ's authority as the final and decisive argument against the conclusions of the higher critics. Bishop Perry, opening a correspondence on 'A great question' (i.e. Christ and the Old Testament) in the *Record* in April 1890, regarded Christ's reference to Psalm 110 as absolutely conclusive proof of its Davidic authorship,[227] while a whole series of conservative writers appealed to Christ's endorsement of the Mosaic origins of the Pentateuch.[228] This would seem to suggest that conservative scholars were unimpressed by the kenosis theory and it may be asked what arguments they deployed against it.

The conservatives began by refuting the suggestions that Christ took no interest in literary issues or that he accommodated himself to mistaken contemporary beliefs. It was easy to demonstrate that he quoted the Old Testament frequently and regarded it as authoritative, and that he used its authority in controversy with his opponents – the significance of Psalm 110 in this context was that Christ's whole case depended on the precise point of its Davidic authorship.[229] The accommodation theory was subjected to careful scrutiny by Girdlestone in *Doctor Doctorum* (1892) and pronounced unsatisfactory.[230] It was morally dubious (as V.F. Storr recognised[231]), because it implied that Christ condoned falsehood, concealed truth and exploited the ignorance of the Pharisees to win an argument based on premisses he knew to be mistaken. Moreover, the character of Christ portrayed in the New Testament was not one likely to refrain from correcting contemporary mistakes, especially on vital questions of truth.[232]

Having cast grave doubts on the idea of accommodation, the

conservatives turned to the kenosis theory proper. The textual evidence for the doctrine was examined and found wanting – Girdlestone's conclusion after a comparison of classical and Septuagint Greek nuances was that 'when the Lord took human nature He impoverished and restricted Himself not in respect to His personality, or essential attributes as Word, but in respect to His glory, that is, to the exhibition of those attributes amongst men.' In other words, Philippians 2:7, 8 could not be used to prove that Christ as human lacked the divine knowledge of the Godhead. Furthermore, Girdlestone continued, Christ could not 'unknow' as God Incarnate what he had known before the Incarnation. He could not divest himself of knowledge, although he could refrain from using that knowledge, so 'He might teach less than He knew, but He could not teach contrary to what He knew.'[233]

Two supplementary points were made against the kenosis theory. The first was that Christ did not teach on his own authority, but claimed instead that God the Father was the source of his utterances.[234] The second point was that the Gospels record teaching about Moses and the prophets after the resurrection when the limitations of Incarnation (and kenosis) would have been removed.

There were some differences of understanding within conservative Christology. Bishop Perry placed great emphasis on the baptism of Christ and on the role of the Holy Spirit in guiding his words, an emphasis which Talbot Greaves regarded as dangerously close to derogating from Christ's Godhead.[235] Some, like C.H.H. Wright, were ready to speak of a voluntary, but real limitation and to give full weight to the New Testament passages which suggested a degree of ignorance,[236] while others thought this an unnecessary concession. Some insisted on the omniscience proper to the second Person of the Trinity, but others thought it foolish that the boy Jesus should know Chinese while his mother was teaching him to speak Aramaic.[237] All agreed, however, that Christ's words were infallible, whether protected by innate Godhead or indwelling Spirit. It was possible, moreover, to accept that his knowledge was veiled on some subjects, without conceding that he could err in positive teaching; indeed, his reticence with regard to the Second Advent implied that he only taught what he knew to be true.[238]

There were also some differences of opinion over the propriety of the Christological appeal. In the era of *Lux Mundi* perhaps it was natural that discussion should rapidly move from higher criticism to Christology, and for some Evangelicals Christ was the unanswerable response to the critics and thus the weapon of first resort in controversy. Others, however, counselled caution. Henry Wace, when eventually induced to enter the correspondence in the *Record* in 1892, complained of the tendency to jump from uncertain critical hypotheses to deep theological speculation:

> 'One or two professors in our universities have suddenly surrendered important traditional beliefs respecting the Old Testament to an extreme school of German critics, and we are forthwith called upon to apologise for our Lord's assumed ignorance on such points and to discuss the relations which we may conceive in the abstract to have existed between His Divine and human consciousness!'[239]

E.A. Knox also warned against 'too hasty recourse to our Lord's Divinity for solution of all Old Testament problems.'[240] Knox believed that some conservatives were trying to prove too much, whereas Wace's interest, as ever, was in collecting testimony to the general accuracy of Scripture. He was prepared to use Christ's words to this end, but regarded a more specific appeal as difficult to sustain.[241] Griffith Thomas tried to assign limits in *Old Testament Criticism and New Testament Christianity* (1905):

> 'Let us be clear ... as to what we mean in making this appeal [to Christ]. We do not for an instant intend thereby to close all possible criticism of the Old Testament. There are numbers of questions quite untouched by anything our Lord said, and there is, consequently, ample scope for sober, necessary, and valuable criticism. But what we do say is, that anything in the Old Testament stated by our Lord as a fact, or implied as a fact, is, or ought to be, thereby closed for those who hold Christ to be infallible ... *Dominus locutus est;causa finita est.* The Lord has spoken; the matter is closed.'[242]

Unfortunately, as the history of the CMS in the 1910s and 1920s demonstrated, the role of Christ in Old Testament criticism was neither as clear nor as easily settled as Griffith Thomas hoped, and the Christological controversy continued to cause major divisions within the Evangelical school for several decades.

The relationship between higher criticism and the doctrines of inspiration and Christology had two central features. On the one hand, doctrine provided an answer to the critics, so that conservative Evangelicals could and did invoke the inspiration of Scripture or the authority of Christ against the critical theories. Revelation required verbal reliability. The divinity of Christ guaranteed the truth of his utterances and hence undergirded the traditional view of the Old Testament. On the other hand, however, criticism challenged doctrinal certainties, for, as J.J.S. Perowne wrote in 1890:

> 'We have been told that the Bible must be free from every flaw of imperfection, and we find it is not so. We have been told that the Bible must be in accordance with the discoveries of science, and we find science says one thing and the Bible another. We have been told that discrepancies ought not to exist, and we find they do exist.'[243]

Christian believers could respond in one of two different ways. Some clung to traditional beliefs and rejected the new theories – hence J.C. Ryle's claim that the German critics were denying inspiration and D.H.C. Bartlett's Christological case against Liberal Evangelicalism in the CMS.[244] In an extreme form, this could lead to the attribution of anti-Christian motives to the critics, as in A.H. Carter's *God's Word Supreme* (1914), which saw the attempt to challenge Christ's infallibility as 'a prime movement on the part of Satan to destroy the force and efficacy of the Word of God' and as a 'dastardly attack upon the foundations of the Christian faith.'[245] Such an attitude naturally made for bitter hostility between conservative and liberal Evangelicals.

The alternative course of action was to modify doctrine to take account of criticism, and this was done by the liberal Evangelicals from H.E. Ryle and J.J.S. Perowne to V.F. Storr and the AEGM. Lest it be thought that there was a complete polarisation within the Evangelical school it must be emphasized that opinions lay along a broad spectrum and that each individual succeeded in reconciling his own doctrinal tenets with his convictions on critical scholarship. Tensions only arose when one section of the party attacked the synthesis of another, either as academically disreputable or as beyond the pale of orthodox Evangelicalism.

Conclusion

In their response to higher criticism, therefore, Evangelical

Churchmen wrestled with several apparently conflicting principles. The doctrines of inspiration and revelation, a traditionally high Christology and a deep reverence for Scripture encouraged conservatism, as did the perceived consequences of higher criticism across a range of issues from preaching and prophecy to overseas missions and national morality. On the other hand, private judgment and a commitment to truth seemed to demand an openness to scholarly criticism. The attempt to balance these different considerations underlay the variety of Evangelical reactions to the issues raised by the higher critics.

Contrary to the simplistic division of the party into two sections, a small group favourable to the Wellhausen theories and a larger one clinging to an antiquated doctrine of verbal inspiration, it is possible to identify at least three broad schools of opinion with respect to higher criticism.

The first consisted of those who reacted to the critical challenge by reasserting a traditional doctrine of inspiration or by an appeal to the authority of Christ. This group held the views which had developed in the mid nineteenth century within Evangelicalism and its case was stated by J.C. Ryle in *Is all Scripture inspired?* (1891), a revised edition of one chapter of his *Old Paths* (1877) with a section added to deal with higher criticism. The *Record*'s correspondence of 1892 on 'Old Testament criticism' also saw this group well represented.

The second section comprised those Evangelicals who accepted the conclusions of the Wellhausen school. With the important exception of H.E. Ryle, whose Evangelicalism was open to question, little trace of such a group can be found in the early 1890s, although V.F. Storr contributed to the 1892 debate, suggesting that the literary history of the Old Testament was of little importance to Christian faith, since the latter was about a relationship with the living Christ.[246] By 1911, however, when the conservative attack on the critics at the Islington Meeting provoked a flurry of letters, there was a distinct 'Liberal Evangelical' group ready to defend the right of Evangelicals to adopt the prevailing critical theories.

Between these two groups was an amorphous collection of Evangelical Churchmen who were opposed to Wellhausen but ready to accept some form of higher criticism. The degree of acceptance varied. Some were wholeheartedly in favour of full and free investigation, but as a result of such enquiry believed that the Wellhausen position was academically unsound. One such Evangelical was J.J.S. Perowne, who wrote two articles for the *Contemporary Review* in 1888 supporting criticism, but challenging the late date assigned to the Pentateuch. Perowne was happy to accept a Hexateuch and regarded the theory of its composite nature as 'unassailable'; he simply disagreed with the denial of the Mosaic origin of the books.[247] Perowne was fairly liberal for the 1890s – E.A. Knox thought him not quite sound on Genesis 1,[248] although his views of the Hexateuch were very similar to those set out by C.H.H. Wright in his *An Introduction to the Old Testament* (1890).[249] According to J.W. Bardsley, this was Bishop Ellicott's 'rectified traditional view', arguing for a Mosaic compilation from earlier documents.[250] By 1901, when the lengthy correspondence on 'Evangelicalism and modern thought' appeared in the *Record*, it was being emphasized that acceptance of the composite nature of the Pentateuch need not imply agreement with other and more radical conclusions,[251] a point endorsed by a leading article in December 1904 which regarded the composite theory as quite compatible with Evangelical orthodoxy.[252]

Other Evangelicals of the 1890s, while paying lip-service to the need for scholarship, held more conservative opinions. Thus Robert Sinker accepted the composite theory in principle, but not in detail,[253] and both he and R.B. Girdlestone asserted the key role of Moses as originator of the Pentateuch.[254] F.T. Bassett, writing in the *Churchman* in August 1890, was more conservative still, rejecting the J-E division of Genesis altogether.[255]

This central group of Evangelicals therefore agreed on the importance of scholarship, but differed in their conclusions. Some were close to the liberals – Perowne's doctrine of inspiration certainly was on the liberal end of the Evangelical spectrum – while others, although using scholarship against the radical critics, were also prepared to invoke a conservative Christology as their last line of defence. Perhaps the crucial division came between those who felt compelled by their critical conclusions to modify their doctrines of inspiration and the Person of Christ, and those who began from inspiration and Christology and saw no reason to move from a traditional position. Scholarship, doctrine and the practical consequences of higher criticism found a place in the response of each Evangelical to the new theories, even if the relative importance of each factor differed according to the individual. The potential for variety was considerable, and this helps to explain why attempts to define the boundaries of acceptability with regard to attitudes to the critical hypotheses were futile, and ultimately proved fatal to the unity of the Evangelical school of thought.

Notes

1 *R*, 12 December 1902, 1180.

2 S. Neill, *The Interpretation of the New Testament 1861-1961* (Oxford, 1964), chapters 1 and 2; Horton Harris, *The Tübingen School* (Leicester, 1990[2]).

3 A.C. Headlam, 'English theology', *Theologisch Tijdschrift* (Leiden, 1917), 147. R. Morgan, '*Non Angli sed Angeli*: some Anglican reactions to German Gospel criticism', in S. Sykes and D. Holmes (eds), *New Studies in Theology*, i (London, 1980), 8, dissents from Headlam and Neill's assessment of the effectiveness of Lightfoot's reply to Baur.

4 *R*, 9 October 1908, 1070; 30 October 1908, 1154, 1172; P.W. Schmiedel, 'Gospels', in T.K. Cheyne and J. Sutherland Black (eds), *Encyclopaedia Biblica*, ii (London, 1901), columns 1761-1898, especially column 1881.

5 *C*, April 1911, 246.

6 J.R. Howden (ed.), *Evangelicalism by members of the FEC* (London, 1925), 151-2.

7 T.G. Rogers (ed.), *Liberal Evangelicalism: An Interpretation by members of the Church of England* (London, 1923), 92.

8 E.S. Woods, *Modern Discipleship and what it means* (London, 1910), 67n.

9 C. Gore (ed.), *Lux Mundi: A Series of Studies in the Religion of the Incarnation* (London, 1889), citing the twelth edition (1891), xvii-xviii.

10 H. Wace, *The Bible and Modern Investigation* (London, 1903), 9.

11 F.E. Spencer, *A Short Introduction to the Old Testament* (London, 1912), 7-8.

12 J. Rogerson, *Old Testament Criticism in the Nineteenth Century:England and Germany* (London, 1984), Part One; R. Sinker, *'Higher Criticism':What is it and where does it lead us?* (London, 1899), 37.

13 Rogerson, *Old Testament Criticism*, 265.

14 Ibid., chapter 19; R.E. Clements, *A Century of Old Testament Study* (Guildford, 1983[2]), chapter 2; J.J.S. Perowne, 'The age of the Pentateuch', *Contemporary Review* (London), January 1888, 129-44; February 1888, 242-61.

15 Sinker, *Higher Criticism*, 96.

16 J. Wellhausen, *Prolegomena to the History of Israel*, translated by J.S. Black and A. Menzies (Edinburgh, 1885), 320.

17 Rogerson, *Old Testament Criticism*, Part One.

18 C.H.H. Wright, *An Introduction to the Old Testament* (London, 1890), 177-9, 223, 157; L.E. Elliott-Binns, *English Thought 1860-1900: The*

Theological Aspect (London, 1956), 143-4.

19 Ibid., 149; Clements, *Century of OT Study*, 14.

20 Rogerson, *Old Testament Criticism*, 138.

21 See ibid., Part Two, for English O.T. scholarship 1800-80.

22 Ibid., 176. Chapter 12 discusses the level of awareness of German scholarship in England before 1859.

23 *C*, July 1890, 556.

24 Rogerson, *Old Testament Criticism*, 184, 197-9, 209-19, 220-37.

25 Ibid., 245-7, 248.

26 Ibid., 275-9; *ODCC*, 1284; W.B. Glover, *Evangelical Nonconformists and the Higher Criticism in the Nineteenth Century* (London, 1954), 117-28; John Sutherland Black and George Chrystal, *The Life of William Robertson Smith* (London, 1912), chapters 5-10.

27 Glover, *Evangelical Nonconformists*, 116-7; Rogerson, *Old Testament Criticism*, 273-5; A.M.G. Stephenson, *The Rise and Decline of English Modernism* (London, 1984), 32-5.

28 C. Gore, 'The Holy Spirit and inspiration' in Gore, *Lux Mundi*, 259.

29 Glover, *Evangelical Nonconformists*, 163-85, 199-204. Spurgeon lamented in 1889 that 'scarcely a denomination is free from the enemies of the truth', *The Sword and the Trowel* (London), December 1889, 663.

30 *T*, 18 December 1891, 5; *Word and Work* (London), 25 December 1891, 117.

31 Glover, *Evangelical Nonconformists*, 36.

32 M.H. Fitzgerald, *A Memoir of Herbert Edward Ryle* (London, 1928), 98.

33 G.A. Smith, *Modern Criticism and the Preaching of the Old Testament* (London, 1901), 72.

34 Glover, *Evangelical Nonconformists*, 283-6; Rogerson, *Old Testament Criticism*, chapter 20.

35 *R*, 18 January 1901, 92.

36 *R*, 7 June 1901, 588.

37 *R*, 14 June 1901, 598.

38 *R*, 6 September 1901, 868-9, 871-2.

39 *R*, 13 January 1911, 46-48, 50-51.

40 *R*, 13 January 1911, 39.

41 *C*, February 1911, 82; March 1911, 165.

42 *R*, 17 February 1911, 162.

43 *R*, 3 February 1911, 117.

44 *R*, 17 February 1911, 162.

45 *R*, 3 March 1911, 221.

46 *R*, 3 March 1911, 222.

47 *R*, 24 March, 282.

48 A comprehensive list of the holders of university chairs is to be found in F.W.B. Bullock, *A History of Training for the ministry of the Church of England in England and Wales, 1875-1974* (London, 1976), 6-7, 32-5, 62-3, 65-6, 91-4.

49 E.S. Woods and F.B. Macnutt, *Theodore, Bishop of Winchester* (London, 1933), 30-1.
50 *R*, 6 September 1901, 872.
51 *R*, 9 August 1907, 694.
52 *R*, 6 February 1903, 136.
53 [Sydney Smith], 'Strictures on two critiques in the *Edinburgh Review*, on the subject of Methodism and Missions..', *Edinburgh Review* 14 (Edinburgh, 1809), 40.
54 Elliott-Binns, *English Thought 1860-1900*, 313. See also D. Rosman, *Evangelicals and Culture* (London, 1984), especially chapter 9, on Evangelicalism and intellectual pursuits in the early nineteenth century.
55 *R*, 31 July 1908, 795.
56 D.W. Bebbington, *Evangelicalism in Modern Britain. A History from the 1730s to the 1980s* (London, 1989), 3, 10-12.
57 *R*, 6 December 1901, 1198.
58 *R*, 16 February 1906, 156.
59 W.H. Griffith Thomas, *Old Testament Criticism and New Testament Christianity* (Stirling, 1905), 32; B. Herklots, *The Future of the Evangelical Party in the Church of England* (London, 1913), 114-16.
60 F.S. Webster, *Jonah: Patriot and Revivalist* (London, 1906), 9-17.
61 See the cover to Griffith Thomas, *Genesis: A Devotional Commentary*, i, (London, 1907).
62 Rogerson, *Old Testament Criticism*, 251, 192, 220-37.
63 *Word and Work*, 8 April 1892, 423.
64 *R*, 8 April 1892, 377.
65 *R*, 8 January 1892, 30, and cf. C.A. Heurtley, *Wholesome Words* (London, 1896), 203-12.
66 J.J.S. Perowne, *A Charge delivered by the... Lord Bishop of Worcester at his Primary Visitation..* (London, 1895), 17.
67 Albert C. Knudson, 'The philosophy and theology of the leading Old Testament critics', *Bibliotheca Sacra* (Andover), 1912, 1-21.
68 R. Valpy French (ed.), *Lex Mosaica; or, the Law of Moses and the Higher Criticism* (London, 1894), 77. Cf. R.B. Girdlestone, *Doctor Doctorum* (London, 1892), 157.
69 Hence W.S. Hooton's attack on 'reverent' criticism in his 'What is reverence?', *C*, September 1919, 483-90, and C.H. Waller's suggestion that Driver was technically apostate under 9 William 3, c. 35 – the burden of his *Moses and the Prophets* (London, 1907).
70 A.H. Carter, *God's Word Supreme* (London, 1914), 99, 112, 120.
71 *R*, 8 January 1892, 25.
72 Bebbington, *Evangelicalism*, 3, 12-14; cf. chapter 2, above.
73 J.C. Ryle, *Is all Scripture inspired? An Attempt to answer the question* (London, 1891), 73.
74 E.A. Knox, *On What Authority?* (London, 1922), 224-5.

75 *R*, 3 March 1911, 222.
76 *R*, 1 November 1901, 1079.
77 E. Stock, *My Recollections* (London, 1909), 69.
78 J. Whale, *One Church, One Lord* (London, 1979), 124; C.C. Waller, 'The limits of Old Testament exegesis', *C*, February 1902, 254; H.A. Redpath, 'The preaching and teaching of the Old Testament', *C*, April 1907, 214; P.V. Smith, 'The first three chapters of Genesis', C, October 1925, 299.
79 Three presidents of the Scripture Gift Mission in the early twentieth century were the Evangelicals Handley Moule, H.W. Webb-Peploe and John Taylor-Smith – see E.L. Langston, *Bishop Taylor-Smith* (London, 1939), chapter 6; the Bible and Prayer Union was founded by Thomas Richardson, vicar of St Benet's, Mile End, in 1876, and had enrolled 310, 000 members by 1892 – *R*, 15 January 1892, 81.
80 Elliott-Binns, *English Thought 1860-1900*, 191.
81 *R*, 15 January 1892, 72; J.J. Lias, 'The witness of the historical Scriptures to the accuracy of the Pentateuch (2)', *C*, September 1899, 622.
82 *R*, 8 January 1892, 33.
83 *R*, 15 January 1892, 73.
84 *R*, 5 February 1892, 162.
85 *R*, 16 October 1908, 1092.
86 R. Lloyd, The Church of England, 1900-65 (London, 1966), 93.
87 *R*, 8 January 1892, 32.
88 C.H. Waller, *Moses and the Prophets* (London, 1907), 278.
89 *R*, 18 October 1907, 925.
90 Bible League Council Minutes, 5 May, 1909.
91 H.E. Fox, *Rationalism or the Gospel?* (London, 1912).
92 See below, chapter 7.
93 G. Ensor, *Bishop Ryle and Genesis* (London, 1904), 26.
94 G.S. Brewer, 'The dearth of candidates for holy orders', *C*, October 1905, 695-6.
95 J.C. Ryle, *Knots Untied* (London, 1874), 3, 84.
96 e.g., *R*, 21 September 1906, 810.
97 *R*, 9 May 1902, 457.
98 *R*, 15 January 1892, 72.
99 E.A. Knox, *Reminiscences of an Octogenarian* (London, 1935), 125.
100 G.L. Prestige, *The Life of Charles Gore* (London, 1935), chapter 13; cf. *R*, 9 May 1902, 455.
101 Elliott-Binns, *English Thought 1860-1900*, 189.
102 See his two volumes *Daniel and His Prophecies* (London, 1906) and *Daniel and Its Critics* (London, 1906), which combine thorough textual scholarship with a traditional historicist interpretation of the prophecies.
103 Cf. A.F. Kirkpatrick's AEGM pamphlet *Old Testament Prophecy* (London, 1924).

104 *R*, 15 May 1903, 479.
105 *R*, 25 April 1918, 272.
106 M.A.J. Tarver, *Trent College, 1868-1927* (London, 1929), 7-8.
107 Fox, *Rationalism or the Gospel?*, 20.
108 *Word and Work*, January-June 1892.
109 *R*, 20 May 1915, 478; 9 December 1915, 1107.
110 Fitzgerald, *H.E. Ryle*, 77.
111 V.F. Storr, *The Inspiration of the Bible* (Winchester, 1908), 23.
112 Elliott-Binns, *English Thought 1860-1900*, 185; Woods, *Modern Discipleship*, 169-70.
113 O. Chadwick, 'The Established Church under attack', in A. Symondson (ed.), *The Victorian Crisis of Faith* (London, 1970), 96-100.
114 H.R. Murphy, 'The ethical revolt against Christian orthodoxy in early Victorian England', *American Historical Review* 50 (Washington, 1955), 800-17.
115 Storr, *Inspiration of the Bible*, 21.
116 See E. Royle, *Victorian Infidels* (London, 1974) and E. Royle (ed.), *The Infidel Tradition from Paine to Bradlaugh* (London, 1976) for an account of secularism and infidelity in this period.
117 Fitzgerald, *H.E. Ryle*, 212-3.
118 Woods and Macnutt, *Theodore, Bishop of Winchester*, chapters 5 and 8.
119 In Rogers, *Liberal Evangelicalism*, 245.
120 Elliott-Binns, *English Thought 1860-1900*, 93-8; H.D. McDonald, *Theories of Revelation: An Historical Study 1860-1960* (London, 1963), 83-4.
121 R, 8 January 1892, 31.
122 P. Toon, *Evangelical Theology 1833-1856. A Response to Tractarianism* (London, 1979), 204-5, argues that Goode exaggerated the place of private judgment in his response to Tractarian teaching.
123 L. Stephen, *Life of Sir James Fitzjames Stephen* (London, 1895), 309.
124 J.H. Newman, *Lectures on the Prophetical Office of the Church* (London, 1837), 34-6, and cf. *Apologia pro Vita Sua* (London, 1864), citing 1865 edition, 68.
125 *R*, 28 September 1900, 903.
126 L.E. Elliott-Binns, *The Book of Exodus* (Cambridge, 1924), 3-5.
127 J.B. Harford, *Since Wellhausen: A Brief Survey of Recent Pentateuchal Criticism* (London, 1926), 144.
128 *R*, 7 December 1916, 961.
129 *R*, 30 March 1906, 275.
130 J.C. Ryle, *Is all Scripture inspired?* (London, 1891), 71.
131 W.H. Griffith Thomas, *The Catholic Faith* (London, 1904), 339.
132 T. Fielder, *The Truth of the Bible* (London, 1912), 103.
133 Spencer, *Short Introduction*, 30.
134 *R*, 8 January 1892, 38.
135 Griffith Thomas, *Old Testament Criticism*, 5-6.
136 F.E. Spencer, *Did Moses write the Pentateuch after all?* (London, 1892),

168-77.

137 *R*, 17 November 1911, 1069; 8 December 1911, 1169.
138 Wace, *Bible and Modern Investigation*, 47.
139 F.E. Spencer, *Present Day Problems* (London, 1904), 141-4.
140 Girdlestone, *Doctor Doctorum*, 176.
141 W.H. Griffith Thomas, *Genesis: A Devotional Commentary*, iii (1908), 166-9.
142 Spencer, *Short Introduction*, 109n.
143 Griffith Thomas, *Old Testament Criticism*, 22.
144 J. Orr, 'Cambridge biblical essays', *C*, April 1910, 247-55.
145 *R*, 10 July 1903, 685.
146 *R*, 22 February 1901, 213; 22 March 1901, 309.
147 Wace, *Bible and Modern Investigation*, 28-9; Sinker, *Higher Criticism*, 83.
148 Spencer, *Moses*, 288.
149 Sinker, *Higher Criticism*, 99-100.
150 *R*, 12 February 1892, 186. The same technique was applied, to withering effect, by a Churchman of very different stamp: R.A. Knox, *Essays in Satire* (London, 1928), chapters 5, 7, 8.
151 *R*, 11 May 1906, 416.
152 J.J. Lias, 'The authorship of the Pentateuch', *C*, November 1895, 128.
153 Lias, 'Witness of the historical Scriptures', 625.
154 Spencer, *Moses*, 4.
155 W.H. Bennett and W.F. Adeney, *Biblical Introduction* (London, 1899), 39.
156 C.E. Raven, *A Wanderer's Way* (London, 1928), 43, misquoted in O.R. Barclay, *Whatever happened to the Jesus Lane Lot?* (Leicester, 1977), 95.
157 *R*, 3 November 1905, 1023.
158 *R*, 4 September 1908, 911.
159 French, *Lex Mosaica*, 275.
160 Spencer, *Moses*, 180-1.
161 French, *Lex Mosaica*, 334, 360.
162 Ensor, *Bishop Ryle's Genesis*, 127.
163 French, *Lex Mosaica*, 612.
164 Wace, *Bible and Modern Investigation*, 23-6, 34-45.
165 Ibid., 49-58.
166 This appeal extended beyond conservative Evangelicals in the Church of England to a broader conservative and fundamentalist constituency, for instance in the publications of the Bible League and the Wesley Bible Union.
167 Elliott-Binns, *English Thought 1860-1900*, 99-104.
168 Wace, *Bible and Modern Investigation*, 56-7, 53.
169 Spencer, *Short Introduction*, v.
170 *R*, 8 June 1906, 501.
171 Elliott-Binns, *English Thought 1860-1900*, 147.
172 *C*, May 1894, 440 (Sayce); July 1898, 555 (Hommel); W.T. Pilter, 'Assyriology and the early records of the book of Genesis', *C*, May

1903, 436-44 (Pinches); January 1905, 218 (Sayce); March 1914, 234 (Naville).

173 *C*, September 1905, 661-2; May 1903, 436-44.

174 M. Linton Smith, 'Spade and Bible', *C*, October 1911, 749-55; November 1911, 819-27; *R*, 17 November 1911, 1069.

175 H.M. Wiener, 'Some results of modern criticism of the Old Testament (1)', *C*, January 1908, 16.

176 Ensor, *Bishop Ryle's Genesis*, 16, 98.

177 G.E. White, 'Deuteronomy in eastern light', *C*, November 1909, 825.

178 J.C. Ryle, *The Christian Leaders of the last century; or, England a Hundred Years ago* (London, 1869), 26, quoted in H.D. McDonald, *Ideas of Revelation:An Historical Study 1700-1860* (London, 1959), 212.

179 V.F. Storr, *The Development of English Theology in the Nineteenth Century, 1800-60* (London, 1913), 73.

180 A. Pollard, 'Anglican Evangelical views of the Bible 1800-50', *C*, July-September 1960, 169, 171; Bebbington, *Evangelicalism*, 86-91.

181 W.J.C. Ervine, 'Doctrine and diplomacy: some aspects of the life and thought of the Anglican Evangelical clergy 1797-1837', Cambridge PhD thesis, 1979, 133-37.

182 Ibid., 319.

183 A. Bentley, 'The transformation of the Evangelical party in the Church of England in the later nineteenth century', Durham PhD thesis, 1971, chapter 3. Note the attack on *Essays and Reviews* by C.A. Heurtley in *The Inspiration of Holy Scripture. Constancy in Prayer.. Two Sermons preached before the University of Oxford* (Oxford, 1861), 6-7n, 29n.

184 C.H. Waller, *The Authoritative Inspiration of Holy Scripture* (London, 1887), 10. For Burgon, see McDonald, *Theories of Revelation*, 284-5.

185 Ryle, *Is all Scripture inspired?*, 10, 22-3.

186 McDonald, *Theories of Revelation*, 204.

187 *R*, 17 January 1908, 45.

188 eg., V.F. Storr, *The Bible: What it is and what it is not* (London, 1924), 4; Woods, *Modern Discipleship*, 168.

189 Ryle, *Is all Scripture inspired?*, 37.

190 *R*, 1 January 1909, 4.

191 Heurtley, *Inspiration of Holy Scripture*, 19-22.

192 Ryle's *Is all Scripture inspired?*, with its emphatic rejection of mechanical dictation, was a reprint of the chapter on inspiration from his *Old Paths* of 1877.

193 Fox, *Our Lord and His Bible*, 64n. Compare J.I. Packer, *'Fundamentalism' and the Word of God* (London, 1958), citing 1982 edition, 78-9, and contrast the confident ascription of belief in verbal dictation to the Evangelicals in J.W. Walmsley, 'The history of the Evangelical party in the Church of England, 1906-28', Hull PhD thesis, 1980, 130.

194 Packer, *'Fundamentalism'*, 80.

195 Ryle, *Is all Scripture inspired?*, 37.

196 *R*, 2 August 1901, 774-5; E.A. Litton, *An Introduction to Dogmatic Theology* (London, 1882, 1892), citing third edition (1912), 20.
197 Fox, *Our Lord and His Bible*, 64n.
198 Ryle, *Is all Scripture inspired?*, 62-3.
199 T.W. Gilbert, 'The inspiration of Holy Scripture', *C*, July 1925, 221.
200 H. Smith, 'All or none?', *C*, April 1924, 139-45.
201 Ryle, *Is all Scripture inspired?*, 6, 44.
202 *R*, 25 April 1913, 385.
203 Griffith Thomas, *The Catholic Faith*, 329.
204 Howden, *Evangelicalism*, 156-206, 164-5.
205 Ibid., 178.
206 Gore, *Lux Mundi*, 260.
207 Elliott-Binns, *Exodus*, 8; Woods, *Modern Discipleship*, 167-70.
208 Storr, *Inspiration of the Bible*, 14.
209 H.E. Ryle, *On Holy Scripture and Criticism* (London, 1904), 81, 148.
210 Storr, *Inspiration of the Bible*, 15;also *Inspiration* (London, 1924), 8.
211 Storr, *Inspiration of the Bible*, 16.
212 Wright, *Introduction to the Old Testament*, 76.
213 *R*, 28 September 1900, 903.
214 *R*, 20 October 1905, 975.
215 Gilbert, 'Inspiration of Holy Scripture', 220-27.
216 R.B. Girdlestone, *The Building Up of the Old Testament* (London, 1912), 305.
217 Storr, *Inspiration of the Bible*, 29-30.
218 Ibid., 30; also V.F. Storr, *Jesus Christ and the Old Testament* (London, 1924), 9.
219 J.J.S. Perowne, 'The inspiration of the Bible and modern criticism', *Expository Times* (Edinburgh), December 1890, 56.
220 H.E. Ryle, *On Holy Scripture*, 184.
221 Storr, *Jesus Christ*, 11.
222 Ibid., 11.
223 E.W. Barnes, in Rogers, *Liberal Evangelicalism*, 297.
224 J.B. Harford and F.C. Macdonald, *H.C.G. Moule, Bishop of Durham. A Biography* (London, 1923), 138.
225 Heurtley, *Inspiration of Holy Scripture*, 6.
226 H.C. Lees, *The Joy of Bible Study* (London, 1909), chapter 14.
227 *R*, 25 April 1890, 392.
228 e.g., Waller, *Moses and the Prophets*, 100.
229 e.g., Fox, *Our Lord and His Bible*, 46-8.
230 Girdlestone, *Doctor Doctorum*, 146-55.
231 Storr, *Jesus Christ*, 211.
232 Girdlestone, *Doctor Doctorum*, 151.
233 Ibid., 29, 39 52.
234 Fox, *Our Lord and His Bible*, 88-9.
235 *R*, 25 April 1890, 392; 2 May 1890, 424.

236 Wright, *Daniel and Its Critics*, xii-iii.
237 *R*, 2 May 1890, 424.
238 *R*, 2 August 1901, 774.
239 *R*, 29 January 1892, 125.
240 Knox, *On What Authority?*, 133.
241 Wace, *Bible and Modern Investigation*, 64.
242 Griffith Thomas, *Old Testament Criticism*, 24-5, 27.
243 Perowne, 'Inspiration of the Bible', 57.
244 Ryle, *Is all Scripture inspired?*, 62-3; G.W. Bromiley, *Daniel Henry Charles Bartlett: A Memoir* (Burnham on Sea, 1959), 46.
245 Carter, *God's Word Supreme*, 99.
246 *R*, 29 January 1892, 128-9.
247 Perowne, 'Age of the Pentateuch'; compare the cautious advocacy of moderate biblical criticism in another conservative denomination by the Wesleyan W.T. Davison, *BW*, 26 March 1891, 351.
248 Knox, *Reminiscences*, 176.
249 Wright, *Introduction to the Old Testament*, 78-84.
250 J.W. Bardsley, 'Inspiration', *C*, October 1894, 18.
251 *R*, 28 June 1901, 662.
252 *R*, 2 December 1904, 1213.
253 Sinker, *Higher Criticism*, 139.
254 R.B. Girdlestone, *The Foundations of the Bible* (London, 1891^2), 193.
255 F.T. Bassett, 'The Old Testament and the critics', *C*, August 1890, 574.

CHAPTER 5

The Challenge of Darwinism

'In the beginning God created the heavens and the earth.' (Genesis 1:1)

One of the more bizarre contributions to the ritual controversy was a paper read to the Mid-Devon Clerical and Lay Association in June 1902 by the Revd J.D.W. Warden, rector of Wembworthy. Warden's paper was entitled 'The influence of the evolution theory in modern ritualism', and it compared *The Origin of Species* with the *Tracts for the Times*, accusing both of materialism, before concluding that 'Probably the two stood or fell together.'[1] This analysis was unique in this period – no other Evangelical Churchman linked Darwin and ritualism in this way – but at a time when Evangelicals were concentrating on the ritual controversy, they were also being urged to face the questions posed by modern science. Of these, the most pressing derived from Darwinian biology, and this chapter concerns the Evangelical response to that challenge.

Darwinism and Evolution

Darwinism was and remains a protean term, used to describe not only the theories directly attributable to Charles Darwin himself, but also other scientific developments connected with the idea of evolution. As will be seen later, however, in discussing the Evangelical response to the challenge of biological and geological science it is important not to equate Darwinism with evolution, so it is necessary to establish from the outset what Darwin's theory actually was and to identify its main features. This is not to guarantee, of course, that nineteenth century Evangelicals were always aware of the differences between Darwinism and other theories or that their use of terminology was scientifically precise.

Charles Darwin did not produce the first theory of evolution.

Evolutionary hypotheses had been advocated in the late eighteenth century by Lamarck, as well as by Erasmus Darwin in his *Zoonomia* (1794-96), and they were also expounded in the best-selling but controversial volume *Vestiges of the Natural History of Creation*, published in 1844.[2] Darwin's contribution was to take a theory generally dismissed by leading scientists and to establish it as an accepted working hypothesis, supported by a wealth of evidence and closely argued deduction. He accomplished this by supplying a mechanism to explain the process of evolution and this mechanism was the principle of natural selection.[3]

Working as a naturalist in the 1830s and 1840s, Darwin observed the slight variations existing among species. Combining this with Malthusian ideas about competition for survival, he suggested that those organisms which possessed variations which assisted survival in their particular environment would be most likely to live and breed. Competition favoured certain adaptations and heredity would ensure their transmission to the next generation. A succession of tiny variations, each beneficial for survival under particular conditions, could account for the development of different species from a small number of primitive life-forms. In place of the fixity of species, therefore, Darwin advocated transmutation through random variation guided by the process of natural selection.[4] This theory was set out, first in a paper to the Linnaean Society in 1858 and then in 1859 in *The Origin of Species*. Twelve years later, Darwin made explicit what had been implicit in his earlier work when *The Descent of Man* argued the case for human evolution.[5]

Writing in 1924, in the AEGM pamphlet *Evolution and the Christian Faith*, J.M. Wilson declared that Darwinism 'at once met with all but universal acceptance among naturalists as a working hypothesis.'[6] This, however, was not an entirely accurate statement. Darwinism, or evolution by natural selection, was subjected to a strong and sustained criticism by the scientific establishment, most notably by the anatomist Richard Owen and the paleontologist Louis Agassiz. Debates continued at the British Association for the Advancement of Science throughout the 1860s and, as will be seen later, respectable scientific opinion could be cited against the Darwinian hypothesis well into the twentieth century. It would be fair to say that by the 1870s most leading biologists were also evolutionists, although by no means all also accepted natural selection.

Indeed, a whole series of scientific challenges to Darwinism were produced in this period, ranging from Kelvin's work on the age of the earth, which drastically reduced the time available for Darwin's slow evolutionary process to take place, to Mivart and Wallace's attack on the principle of natural selection as an adequate explanation for evolution. It must be emphasized that natural selection was the distinguishing feature of Darwinian biology and that this feature was questioned or rejected by many scientists who nonetheless embraced some form of evolution.[7]

During the last third of the nineteenth century, evolution became one of the leading principles not only of biology but also of the other sciences. It was invoked to explain the development of the inorganic world, of society and of religion. In the hands of Herbert Spencer, evolution became the foundation of a whole world-view, expounded in his *System of Synthetic Philosophy*, which occupied six thousand octavo pages and thirty six years of work.[8] When V.F. Storr gave a course of lectures in the philosophy of religion at Cambridge in 1904-05, he observed that 'Evolution or Development is the key-word which unlocks the mind of the present age.'[9] By 1926, J.A. Fleming could begin his *Evolution and Revelation* by assuming that 'The system of thought and ideas with regard to the origin and mode of production of the things we see around us, commonly called the doctrine of evolution, has obtained such wide acceptance that not to agree with it is now frequently considered to be a mark of imperfect education.'[10] Informed opinion in Britain accepted evolution wholeheartedly and regarded the Scopes trial in Tennessee in 1925 with blank incomprehension.[11]

The Acceptance of Evolution by the Church

This general acceptance of evolution extended to large sections of the Christian Church. Evolution and natural selection raised various problems for Christian apologists and for ordinary believers: questions concerning the reconciliation of Genesis with science, of random variation with providence and design and of human evolution with the traditional doctrines of creation, fall and redemption. Some of these questions were not new – the development of geology from the 1820s, for example, had caused difficulties for the orthodox upholders of the Mosaic cosmogony[12] - but Darwinism gave a further impetus to the challenge to reconcile science and Christianity. What is noteworthy is that many Christian leaders quickly assimilated evolution, albeit not always in its Darwinian form.

Most of the earliest favourable reactions to *The Origin of Species* came, not unexpectedly, from Broad Churchmen, for whom the Mosaic cosmogony was already shaken by the geologists and who were able to adjust evolution to fit their ideas of God working through natural law. Baden Powell, a leading liberal, welcomed Darwin's work with enthusiasm as 'masterly' in his contribution to *Essays and Reviews*, adding a reference to the *Origin of Species* at the proof stage of the work.[13] F.J.A. Hort wrote eagerly to Westcott in March 1860 that *The Origin of Species* was 'unanswerable',[14] while Charles Kingsley wrote to F.D. Maurice three years later that 'Darwin is conquering everywhere and rushing in like a flood by the mere force of truth and fact.'[15] It was the Broad Churchman F.W. Farrar who proposed that Darwin's funeral should take place in Westminster Abbey,[16] and in 1884, two years later, Frederick Temple endorsed evolution in his Bampton lectures, *The Relations between Science and Religion*. Temple was not a thoroughgoing Darwinian, since he subordinated natural selection to a power of development inherent in created matter, but he argued powerfully for the acceptance of evolution both at Oxford in 1884 and at the Lambeth Conference of 1888.[17]

By the late 1880s High Churchmen too were writing sympathetically about evolution. In the first years of Darwinism Pusey viewed the new theories with suspicion, although R.W. Church regarded *The Origin of Species* as a great improvement on the unscientific *Vestiges* of 1844.[18] Liddon, preaching at St Paul's Cathedral shortly after Darwin's death, said that although his works were formerly 'largely regarded by religious men as containing a theory necessarily hostile to fundamental truths of religion... a closer study has greatly modified any such impression.[19] Alongside this cautious welcome must be set the enthusiastic Darwinism of Aubrey Moore, expressed in several books and articles, including his contribution to *Lux Mundi*. Moore used evolution to underpin the doctrine of divine immanence, and in this he was followed by Charles Gore and by J.R. Illingworth.[20]

When F.R. Tennant reflected on 'The influence of Darwinism

upon theology' in the *Quarterly Review* for 1909, he felt able to write 'The truth that the world, including man, is a product of gradual evolution – however it may stand with Darwin's account of the process, is nowadays received practically without exception amongst Churchmen equipped with any knowledge of modern theology...'[21] Indeed, John Kent has suggested that the accommodation was too easy and too rapid, and that it took place without an adequate solution being found to the theological problems posed by evolution.[22]

Two important qualifications should be made to this picture, however. The first is that the acceptance of evolution by Bampton lecturers and Oxbridge Fellows did not automatically ensure the spread of a similar attitude among the clergy at large and among the laity. Aubrey Moore called evolution 'an established doctrine' in 1888, but, over thirty years later, the reaction of correspondents in the *Church Times* to E.W. Barnes's 'Monkey Sermon' to the British Association suggested otherwise.[23] Due weight should be given to Tennant's admission that it was those acquainted with modern theology who were likely to be evolutionists.

The second qualification concerns the attitude of Evangelicals. Broad Churchmen and High Churchmen of the *Lux Mundi* school adopted a form of evolution in the late nineteenth century, but was this also true of the Evangelicals?

Evangelical Responses to Evolution

The response of evangelicals, both Anglican and Free Church, to Darwinism and to evolution has been the subject of recent investigation by D.N. Livingstone. Ellegård's survey of the reception of Darwin's theories between 1859 and 1872 indicated that the 'Low Church' press remained consistently hostile to evolution throughout that period.[24] Livingstone, however, has examined a number of leading evangelicals, both in Britain and North America, and has reached the conclusion that many were favourable to evolutionary theories, particularly in the last quarter of the nineteenth century. Asa Gray, G.F. Wright and James Dana represented Christian Darwinism in the United States; McCosh and Warfield introduced evolution to the impeccably orthodox faculty at Princeton, and among the Scottish theologians, Iverach and Orr assimilated some aspects of modern science.[25] Livingstone has sought to show that the tradition of an outright evangelical hostility to evolution is an invention of fundamentalist historiography dating from the 1920s and that in the preceding decades the leaders of evangelical thought were open to at least some of the insights of Darwinism.[26] Livingstone's analysis is multi-denominational and international, and it concentrates almost exclusively on a theological and scientific élite. It may be asked how far his conclusions extend to Evangelicals in the Church of England, and whether they were as receptive to evolution by the 1890s as his study would seem to suggest.

In the mid-nineteenth century Evangelical opinion varied somewhat, but generally opposed both evolution and Darwinism. There was a pattern of Evangelical hostility to science when it seemed to threaten revelation, and this was sustained throughout the period, from suspicion of the fledgling British Association in the 1830s through to an attempt to censure the Tract Committee of the SPCK for publishing T.G. Bonney's *A Manual of Geology* in the 1870s.[27] In the Bonney controversy the *Record* denounced 'books which adopt as if proved to be infallible the stammering and even blundering babblings of undeveloped science.'[28] On the specific issue of evolution, the *Christian Observer*, usually the mouthpiece of scholarly and moderate Evangelicalism, published a scathing article entitled 'Darwin on the origin of species' in August 1860. After attacking Darwin's work as 'conjecture throughout', the reviewer concluded 'we can only express our regret that a man, evidently possessed of much patience and perseverence, and no inconsiderable powers of investigation, should have prostituted his talents to so bad a purpose, and have entitled himself, not to the gratitude, but to the reprobation, of the whole Christian world.'[29] T.R. Birks maintained a similar tone of vigorous criticism, describing *The Origin of Species* as 'an experiment how far the passive credulity of some readers will extend.'[30] J.H. Pratt, the archdeacon of Calcutta, in the seventh (1872) edition of his much reprinted treatise *Scripture and Science not at Variance*, also rejected Darwinism, declaring that it was 'a disgrace to Science.'[31] It is hardly surprising, therefore, that the burial of Darwin in Westminster Abbey was received with less than enthusiasm by the Evangelical press. The *Record* made little comment at first, merely announcing the fact of the death and burial of 'the celebrated naturalist, and author of *The Origin of Species*.' Later, however, the paper relaxed its respect for the dead sufficiently to claim in a leading article that Darwin's theories 'have done more than perhaps anything else in the world to promote the cause of unbelief in our generation, ' and to deprecate his burial beside Newton and Herschell.[32]

Not all Evangelicals were as virulently opposed to Darwinism as these examples might suggest. H.B. Tristram, canon of Durham and a respected ornithologist, read Darwin's paper in the Linnaean Society's *Proceedings* of 1858 and was much impressed. Although Tristram later revised his opinions, he still wrote sympathetically about 'the development theory so ably set forth by Mr Darwin' in the *Contemporary Review* for 1866.[33] Likewise, Charles Cardale Babington, who succeeded Darwin's teacher Henslow as professor of Botany at Cambridge in 1861 and who corresponded with Darwin, combined natural science and support for the British Association from its inception with a firm Evangelical faith which included membership of the Council of Ridley Hall.[34] Sir George Stokes was another Evangelical scientist who, while disagreeing with aspects of Darwin's theories, was still ready to accept a form of evolution.[35] Evangelical Churchmen between 1860 and 1890 therefore seem generally to have opposed Darwinism, and many also demonstrated bitter hostility to all forms of evolution. Some, however, were prepared to welcome aspects of evolutionary theory, albeit with modifications to the pure Darwinian model.

The spectrum of opinion on Darwinism and evolution was revealed by a long running controversy in the *Record* in 1901-02. The controversy was provoked by a paper entitled 'Questions that must be faced; or, Evangelicalism and modern thought,' delivered at the Southport Conference in May 1901, and subsequently published in two parts in the *Record*.[36] The paper was given by G.S. Streatfeild, vicar of Christ Church, Hampstead, and it included a wide-ranging criticism of Evangelicalism for its failure to address the issues perplexing contemporary society. Of these, science was a major concern. Streatfeild himself supported evolution, paid tribute to the works of Moore, Illingworth and Henry Drummond and castigated his fellow Evangelicals for ignoring the whole subject: 'Evangelical theology, so far as I know, contains not a hint at the change which has come over the world of thought... Evolution and the Divine Immanence might never have been heard of so far as they are accepted, I might almost say recognised, by our leading Evangelical writers..'[37]

If Evangelicals had been ignoring evolution before May 1901, Streatfeild's challenge stirred them into action. Letters to the *Record* for the rest of the year and into 1902 set out a variety of attitudes, ranging from outright hostility to general acceptance of the evolutionary hypothesis. The correspondence revealed not only diversity of opinion, but also most of the issues involved in the Darwinian controversies: the theological questions posed by the new science, the practical implications of taking evolution into the Christian world-view, the debate within science about the validity of Darwinism and the reluctance of some Christians to face up to doctrinal restatement. In the remainder of this chapter, these themes will be explored in an attempt to explain the Evangelical response to Darwinism and evolution in the late nineteenth and early twentieth centuries.

Ignoring the issues?

A preliminary point which may be made is that a review of the Evangelical Anglican literature on evolution does much to bear out Streatfeild's criticism that Evangelical Churchmen were simply not addressing the issues. As has already been seen, in the period immediately following the publication of *The Origin of Species*, T.R. Birks devoted several books to the subject of evolution and Archdeacon Pratt modified his work on science and Scripture to take account of Darwinism. Later in the century, however, treatments of evolution from an Evangelical perspective are difficult to find, at least so far as Anglicans are concerned. Birks, who died in 1883, is the only Anglican Evangelical mentioned in James Moore's *The Post Darwinian Controversies* (1979)[38] and Livingstone concentrates on Scottish and American evangelicals like Orr and Warfield. Of the major works of dogmatic theology produced by Evangelical Churchmen in this period, E.A. Litton's *Introduction to Dogmatic Theology* (1882, 1892) dismissed evolution in three pages, before going on to devote sixty pages to a review of the Pelagian controversy,[39] while the treatment afforded by R.B. Girdlestone in *Old Testament Theology and Modern Ideas* (1909) was so meagre that even the *Record*'s reviewer drew attention to its inadequacy.[40] W.H. Griffith Thomas was equally cursory in *The Catholic Faith*

(1904),[41] and it was only H.C.G. Moule's *Outlines of Christian Doctrine* (1889) which gave space to some of the issues raised by evolution.[42] Although evolution featured in Stokes' Gifford lectures of 1891 and 1893, there was no detailed theological discussion to compare with Orr's *God's Image in Man* (1905) and *Sin as a Problem of Today* (1910), and no enthusiastic advocate of evolution like Asa Gray in the United States or Henry Drummond in Scotland. Nor was there much theological reflection on evolution and divine immanence, with the possible exception of V.F. Storr's *Development and Divine Purpose* (1906). Apart from a few books and some AEGM pamphlets,[43] Evangelical expressions of opinion were largely limited to sections of general works, articles and commentaries on Genesis.

The main exception to this neglect was the work of the Victoria Institute. The Institute was founded in 1865 and its first aim was 'to investigate fully and impartially the most important questions of Philosophy and Science, but more especially those that bear upon the great truths revealed in Holy Scripture; with the view of reconciling any apparent discrepancy between Christianity and Science.'[44] Although it was not an exclusively evangelical society, Evangelical Churchmen played a leading role in the Institute. Shaftesbury was its first president and he was succeeded in 1885 by Sir George Stokes, who held the office until his death in 1903. Wace, Girdlestone, A.I. McCaul and G.F. Whidborne were all on the Council of the Institute for many years, and the membership numbered such Evangelical stalwarts as Hay Aitken, H.E. Fox, Samuel Garratt, Canon Tristram, Sir John Kennaway and Prebendary Webb-Peploe.[45] The Victoria Institute received, discussed and published papers on a wide variety of scientific subjects, and a proportion of these were on aspects of the debate over evolution. The Institute, moreover, had some claim to be taken seriously by scientists, since its membership in the 1890s stood at 1400, including 150 members of learned societies.[46]

The aim of the Victoria Institute – the removal of 'any apparent discrepancy' between Christianity and science – effectively captured the mood of the Evangelical Anglican response to evolution. Unlike Asa Gray and Aubrey Moore, they did not welcome the new theories. A few Evangelical Churchmen were excited by the doctrine of immanence, but most of those who wrote on the issue of evolution did so defensively, seeking to limit the impact of science on the traditional formulation of the faith either by reconciling differences or by raising doubts about scientific conclusions. This essentially defensive approach may explain why Evangelical comments on evolution are usually to be found only when apologetically essential or where science could be used to support accepted orthodox opinions. Evangelical theology was not creative in this period; it tended only to respond to challenges and then only when absolutely necessary. There was some truth, therefore, in Streatfeild's complaint that Evangelicals had little to say about evolution.

The debate over design

The Evangelical response to Darwinism, in common with that of other Churchmen, was partly determined by theological and ideological considerations. As with higher criticism, there were a number of factors which disposed Evangelicals to treat the new scientific theories with caution or hostility, and these may be reviewed briefly.

Perhaps the most significant theological challenge posed by Darwinian evolution was the conflict between natural selection and a Christian teleology. It has already been seen that Darwin made natural selection the central feature of his hypothesis, and this seemed to make chance the governing factor of the universe. At a stroke, Darwin abolished the adaptations upon which Paley had based his argument from design, for to the Darwinian, they were simply evidence of natural selection at work. Ends and purposes also seemed at risk from a process guided by random variations.[47]

It has been claimed that the challenge to design was the feature of Darwinism which attracted the most hostility from theologians. James Orr, writing on 'Darwinism past and present' in the *Churchman* for March 1909, stated that the fundamental objection to Darwin was that he abandoned the principle of intelligent design and explained nature without teleology: he '*invokes fortuity to do the work of mind.*'[48] Other theologians made the same point. Archdeacon Pratt criticised it as unbiblical[49] and T.R. Birks called it an attempt to exclude God from his universe.[50] Ellegård has suggested that the initial controversy over evolution died down in the late 1860s partly because it became possible to accept evolution while rejecting natural selection. Although Paley's argument from design was demolished, a new teleology was produced, combining Lamarckian theories of inherent powers of development with a doctrine of divine immanence tracing the hand of God at work in the evolutionary process.[51]

Design, with its implications for natural theology, did not, however, feature prominently in Evangelical reactions to Darwinism. Those scholars like James Moore and Don Cupitt who have assumed that teleology was the main problem and that the consequences of evolution for biblical interpretation and authority were comparatively unimportant have overlooked the priorities of a substantial body of Anglican Churchmen.[52] As noted above, Birks and Pratt did mention design, although, significantly, the latter justified teleology from Genesis rather than from natural theology, but Evangelical disquiet over evolution concentrated largely on biblical issues. The *Record* correspondence of 1901-02, for example, made very few references to teleology, but a great many to the interpretation of the book of Genesis. Attention must now be given, therefore, to the implications of evolution for the understanding of Scripture.

The challenge to Scripture

For many Evangelicals, the main objection to evolution was that it was held to contradict the plain teaching of the Bible. The previous chapter discussed the place of Scripture in Evangelical theology and piety at some length and there is no need to repeat that survey, but it may be emphasized again that any theory which seemed to oppose Scripture would be regarded with considerable hostility. Some Evangelicals saw evolution in this light and two main areas of dispute may be identified.

The first issue was the narrative of the creation in Genesis chapters 1 and 2. Genesis seemed to teach creation in six days and at a period only about six thousand years from the nineteenth century – in 4004 BC, for those who accepted Ussher's chronology based on the biblical genealogies. Darwin, following the geologists, placed the beginning of life millions of years earlier, partly to take account of the fossil records and partly to allow time for evolution by a process of tiny cumulative variations. Genesis taught the special creation of species, each 'according to its kind', and at least implied that species were fixed. Darwin's whole theory rested on transmutation. There were, moreover, differences between Genesis and the geologists regarding the order in which the various forms of life appeared on earth.

Set out in this way, there was a clear conflict between Darwin and Genesis. In fact, few Evangelicals upheld six day creation and Ussher's chronology exactly as stated above, and, as will be seen later, various techniques were employed to reconcile Genesis and geology. Nonetheless, many Victorians believed that Darwin was somehow opposed to Genesis – the youthful G.M. Trevelyan, for example, discovered at the age of thirteen in 1889 'that Darwin had disproved the early chapters of the Bible', and forthwith abandoned Christianity.[53] Faced with the same challenge, Evangelicals were more likely to follow the advice of A.H. Carter in *God's Word Supreme* (1914): 'When we come across statements in the Book that seem to be at variance with Modern Science, it is our duty to accept the statements of the Inspired Word of God.'[54] Despite the harmonisations and the reassurances of the evolutionists, the conviction remained that Darwinism had been effective 'in loosening the faith of thousands in the revealed Word of GOD, '[55] and therefore that it was to be resisted. As with higher criticism, moreover, Christology was invoked to support Genesis by a lot of conservative writers,[56] and Horace Noel told readers of the *Record* in June 1894 that 'The question is ultimately between Christ and Darwin.'[57]

More controversial even than the order of creation was the evolutionary theory of the origin of the human race. Again, two issues were raised. The first involved the disagreement between Genesis, which stated that God directly created Adam and Eve in his own image, and Darwin, who suggested that the human race evolved slowly from a species of ape. J.H. Pratt called Darwin's theory 'contrary to reason, ... degrading to man, and... offensive as regards Divine revelation.'[58] The Darwinian view clearly challenged the uniqueness of the human race and contradicted the Genesis narrative. It was also a claim which many found offensive, so that Darwinism was lampooned as linking humankind to monkeys.

A second and more serious theological point than human dignity was the origin of sin and the doctrine of the fall. G.J. Romanes noted that Adam, the fall and the origin of evil, 'all taken together as Christian dogmas, are undoubtedly hard hit by the scientific proof of evolution, ' and he continued, 'and, as constituting the logical basis of the whole plan, they certainly do appear at first sight necessarily to involve in their destruction the entire superstructure.'[59] The traditional doctrine of sin was that humankind was created perfect, chose to disobey God and as a consequence fell from perfection. The fall was regarded as an historical event, involving a real couple, Adam and Eve, who were the progenitors of the whole human race. The historicity of the fall was held to be essential to the reality of redemption by the new Adam, Jesus Christ. Evolution, on the other hand, replaced the fall by an ascent from animal instinct to moral consciousness. According to the evolutionists, humans gradually acquired ethical characteristics and only then did a fall become possible. Evolutionists spoke of a 'fall upwards' and interpreted sin as the vestiges of instincts once necessary, but now inappropriate to human beings.

The most comprehensive attack on Darwinism and the doctrine of the fall from an evangelical standpoint came from the Scottish Free Churchman James Orr, and his conclusions will bear quotation:

> 'Sin, as Scripture and experience represent it, is irreconcilable ... with an evolutionary theory which, like Darwin's, pictures man as having arisen, bodily and mentally, by slow gradations from the animal, and as subsisting through uncounted milleniums in a state of semi-brutishness and savagery. Sin implies relation to God, but here there is no knowledge of God, or possibility of right relation to Him. Sin implies the possibility of sinless development; here such possibility is precluded. Sin implies voluntary departure from rectitude; here it is made a necessity. Sin implies possession of enough knowledge of moral law to enable the moral being to act rightly. Here the glimmer of light in reason and conscience, if present at all, is of the faintest. Sin postulates freedom; here man is a slave to animal impulse and passion from the first.'[60]

Sir George Stokes added that if humankind had evolved, sin became a natural part of its development and God would have to be held responsible for it.[61]

The doctrine of sin was a central component of the Evangelical system of theology. Handley Moule wrote in his *Outlines of Christian Doctrine* that 'It has been said that every heresy shows some subtle connexion with inadequate views of the "exceeding sinfulness of sin".'[62] Evangelical dogmatics emphasized sin.

Evangelical preaching, moreover, set out the 'Three R's' of ruin, redemption and regeneration. Holiness teaching, whether that of Keswick or of J.C. Ryle's Puritan Calvinism, stressed the fallenness of human nature. It may be seen, therefore, how disturbing it was for Evangelical Churchmen when E.W. Barnes told the British Association, meeting at Cardiff in 1920, that Christian thinkers 'find it necessary to abandon the doctrine of the Fall and arguments deduced from it by theologians from St Paul onward.'[63] Not all 'Christian thinkers' agreed with Canon Barnes, but many Evangelicals were ready to accept that his interpretation of the consequences of evolution was accurate and therefore that evolution undermined orthodox Christianity and the whole plan of salvation.

Evolution was thus alleged to conflict with the biblical view of creation, of human nature and of the fall. It is important to note that by no means all Evangelicals accepted the allegation, but insofar as it was accepted, it was a powerful reason to dissuade Evangelical Churchmen from adopting evolutionary theories.

A further twist was added to the biblical argument, moreover, by the debate over higher criticism which raged in the closing decades of the nineteenth century. Wellhausen and the radical critics suggested that Genesis 1 dated from the period of the Exile and that the Mosaic cosmogony was essentially an Assyro-Babylonian document purged of polytheistic elements. Conservative scholars like Henry Wace and F.E. Spencer used the scientific accuracy of Genesis to defend its antiquity and to cast doubt on the theories of the critics.[64] By challenging Genesis, therefore, Darwinism became involved in the wider conflict around the nature and authority of the Bible.

Evolution and miracles

Besides a perceived incompatibility with Scripture, evolution had other consequences or associations liable to provoke Evangelical antipathy. One was an implied hostility to miracles, both in Darwin's methods and his conclusions. According to the *Christian Observer*, Darwin's 'transparent object was to cast God out of His own Creation',[65] and there seemed to be a danger that, by providing an entirely naturalistic explanation for the origins of life, evolution would render God superfluous and divine intervention in the world impossible. A natural order governed by rigid laws could not permit the miraculous and so seemed to rule out not only creation, but also the incarnation and the resurrection.[66] It is significant that apologists seeking to defend creation often began from the life of Christ, arguing that his birth, deeds and resurrection, well attested by the early Church, destroyed the *a priori* objection to miracles and therefore made a miraculous creation at least a possibility.[67]

From the issue of miracles it was only a short step to the claim that evolution implied or fostered atheism and unbelief. This charge could be justified to some extent from the anti-Christian position of leading evolutionists like Tyndall and Huxley and from the use made of Darwinism by Blatchford and the secularists.[68] Horace Noel wrote to the *Record* in 1882: 'It is true enough that a Darwinite need not be an atheist, but it is quite certain that he lends a helping hand to atheists.'[69] Some Evangelicals went further and equated evolution with philosophical materialism. T.R. Birks' hostility to evolutionary science was fuelled by his belief that it was the foundation upon which Herbert Spencer built his system of philosophy, denounced by Birks as 'a modern revival of pagan Fetichism'.[70] The Revd Gerard Smith, addressing a Clerical and Lay Association meeting at Derby in 1880, announced that evolution 'leads to practical atheism', because of its materialist implications.[71] Many Evangelicals were ready to assume or assert a necessary connection between Darwinism, determinism and atheism. At best, they claimed, evolution offered polemical weapons for people to use against Scripture and Christianity and at worst it implied a materialist philosophy destructive both of religion and of moral responsibility. So it was that some Evangelicals held that Darwinism threatened to undermine the very fabric of society.[72]

A more moderate analysis of the influence of evolution maintained that the real danger was posed by the purely naturalistic world-view which left people unaware of a spiritual dimension to life. George Nickson, bishop of Jarrow, addressed the Islington Meeting of 1914 on 'Sin: a fact in human experience'. The bishop attributed the weak sense of sin in the contemporary world partly to a scientific outlook which had abolished a personal, transcendent God.[73] J.A. Fleming made a similar point about the spiritual consequences of Darwinism in *Evolution or Creation?* (1933), writing:

'If ... [evolution] is employed as a substitute for ... Divine

> Creative Power, and, in short, has characteristics of Deity attributed to it, which is very commonly done, then it is atheistic in tendency and unlimitedly pernicious. Its adoption in human thought weakens or destroys the God-consciousness latent in every human soul, and with it that of the serious consequences of a disparity or disagreement between the Divine and the human will which is the source of sin and that latent desire for an agreement which is the starting-point for a thirst after righteousness and spiritual life.'[74]

Likewise, Samuel Smith, in his review of Drummond's *The Ascent of Man*, affirmed 'men will not "deny themselves, take up their cross and follow Christ, " for an Intelligence scarcely separable from nature.'[75] The sense of incompatibility between evolution and Christian faith was set out most bluntly by Trevor Fielder in the *Record*'s correspondence of 1901-02. Fielder, an ultra-conservative, responded to G.S. Streatfeild's advocacy of evolution by asking if this teaching was 'blessed ... to the salvation of souls.'[76] Fielder and Smith, like Fleming, detected an anti-spiritual tendency in the theory of evolution.

Viewed from an Evangelical perspective, therefore, evolution had many undesirable features. It seemed to contradict the teaching of Scripture on creation and the fall, and so to challenge the gospel of sin and salvation which Evangelicals made it their duty to proclaim. It destroyed traditional natural theology and created a world free of miracles. As a consequence of this, moreover, it seemed to abolish God altogether, or to make him a remote figure, unable to act in human life. Evolution, it was claimed, assisted the enemies of the faith and made for a climate of opinion in which spiritual realities were often neglected.

Confronting the issues

Evolution could not be rejected, however, merely because of its perceived consequences for Christian life and belief. Unlike higher criticism, which was predominantly an academic subject of little interest to the churchgoing public, the theory of evolution was widely disseminated – even the lengthy *Origin of Species* had sold 100,000 copies by 1900.[77] It has already been seen that evolution was applied as a general principle to explain matters far beyond the confines of biology. Streatfeild raised the question of Evangelicalism and modern thought in 1901 largely because of his own pastoral experience in dealing with people perplexed by the issue of science and religion.[78] An Evangelical response was a pastoral and apologetic necessity in the face of the dominant movement in contemporary thought. Evangelicals, moreover, were impelled to consider evolution for at least two other ideological reasons, in addition to the apologetic weakness of obscurantism.

First, the Evangelical doctrine of Scripture required that the Bible should be true. The debate on higher criticism revealed differences of opinion as to the extent of biblical truth, but moderate and conservative Evangelicals – those most likely to be suspicious of evolution – maintained that there was a broad correlation between inspiration and accuracy. Robert Payne Smith, dean of Canterbury, made this point repeatedly in his works on science and revelation. In a lecture published by the Christian Evidence Society he affirmed:

> 'Whatever is mixed up with revelation, owing to the manner in which God has been pleased to bestow it, must, at least, be true. It would be impossible for us to accept the authority of the Bible upon those points in which we cannot judge of its truth, if in those points in which we are competent judges we found it erroneous. The teachings, therefore, of science and revelation must be compared ...'[79]

Some years later, Payne Smith wrote in the introduction to his commentary on Genesis: 'We could not believe a book to be inspired which was incapable of being shown to be in accordance with truth.'[80] E.A. Tindall echoed this in the *Record* in August 1901: 'it is difficult to perceive how the Bible can speak with its wonderful force of spiritual utterance if it contains any inaccuracy of scientific or historical statement.'[81] The defence of inspiration therefore required Evangelicals to address the question of evolution, if only to prove the truth of Scripture.

The second reason for Evangelicals to take notice of evolution was the belief, which they held in common with other Christians, that science and religion were in harmony, because both were aspects of God's truth. The unity of truth demanded a reconciliation of apparent contradictions, and, since science came from God, its conclusions could not be dismissed without due consideration. This may be compared with the Evangelical response to higher criticism, which was also guided by certain basic principles about methodology and truth which ruled out unthinking rejection.

The harmony of science and religion was fundamental to the aims of the Victoria Institute, as has already been observed. Sir George Stokes, president of the Institute and a past president of the Royal Society, set out the principle of harmony in his presidential address of 1883: 'Those who believe that a revelation has been made from God to man, and who believe also that the system of nature and the laws which govern it are His work, must accept as an axiom that there can be no real antagonism between the two; that accordingly any apparent antagonism must be due to a mistake, either on the one side or the other.'[82] This axiom may be found elsewhere in Stokes' works, and it echoed J.H. Pratt's belief that 'it is *impossible* that Scripture can, when rightly interpreted, be at variance with the works of the Divine hand.'[83] J. Russell Howden, a leading conservative Evangelical of the 1920s, drew the inevitable conclusion that 'whatever is true in other sciences theology must find room for.'[84]

It may be seen, therefore, that Evangelical Churchmen had to take evolution seriously. Their doctrines of inspiration and creation compelled them to compare the discoveries of science with the teaching of Scripture, for there could be no separation between scientific and theological truth. Self-conscious or deliberate obscurantism was not an option, so if evolution was to be rejected, it would have to be on scientific grounds; otherwise, some form of accommodation would have to be found between the new science and Evangelical convictions.

Evangelical Critiques of Evolution

Evangelicals believed that there was no conflict between revelation correctly interpreted and true science. One solution to apparent conflict, therefore, was to show that the scientific conclusions opposed to the faith were inaccurate or misleading. This approach may be detected in a series of criticisms levelled at evolution from 1859 onwards.

Methodology

The first criticism was methodological and it took several forms. Some attacked Darwin for departing from the hallowed principles of Baconian science by indulging in deduction from hypotheses rather than adhering to induction based on a full survey of all the evidence. This complaint was voiced by Charles Hodge, the Princeton theologian, and supported by the geologist J.W. Dawson and by T.R. Birks.[85] For Birks and for the *Christian Observer*, Darwin's main offence against induction was his neglect of the biblical testimony to the origin of species.[86] Archdeacon Pratt noted a contrast between the hasty and speculative conclusions of nineteenth century scientists and the solid, careful induction of Sir Isaac Newton.[87] Seventy years after Darwin, J.A. Fleming used modern physics to illustrate the limitations of deductive science. Confidence in science's ability to explain the world, wrote Fleming, had been shaken by the unexpected discovery of X-rays and Quantum theory, and the new physics counselled caution with regard to hypotheses formerly taken to be established facts.[88]

Closely linked to this criticism about methodology was the allegation that Darwin's theories were mere speculation devoid of proof. Sometimes this was simply asserted, so, for example, the *Christian Observer* accused Darwin of using imagination as a substitute for evidence.[89] Other writers drew attention to the absence of modern examples of transmutation or to the lack of intermediate forms in the geological strata.[90] This problem of 'missing links' was generally admitted to be a weakness of the Darwinian position, especially since Darwin had predicted in 1859 that such links would be discovered by further geological research.

Although it was sometimes used as an excuse for dismissing evolution, lack of evidence was not merely a debating point made by conservative polemicists. Sir George Stokes, speaking as an eminent physicist, said that the acceptance of Darwinism was '...puzzling to an outsider, especially one accustomed to the severe demands for evidence that are required in the physical sciences.'[91]

Darwin's mechanisms of variation, gradual change and natural selection also came under attack. Variations, as Fleming observed, could regress as well as progress, and therefore need not be cumulative in the direction of transmutation. Mendel's study of genetics, moreover, taken up at the beginning of the twentieth century by De Vries and Bateson, showed that what was passed on from generation to generation was not small variations, but large unit characters, and that this inheritance followed a fixed ratio. Critics also noted that some variations only fulfilled the criterion of utility at a certain stage in their development – the giraffe's neck, for instance, was beneficial at six feet in length, but of no apparent value at only two feet.[92] Meanwhile, physicists reduced the time available for gradual evolution to take place by calculating the age of the earth to be significantly less than the hundreds of millions of years required by Darwin.[93]

Another criticism was the failure of evolution to account for the origin of life itself. Some scientists advanced a theory of spontaneous generation, but this remained simply an hypothesis, and, as such, could easily be dismissed by the critics.[94]

Human evolution

Many of the points raised against evolution generally were also made against the evolution of the human race. Russell Howden, T.B. Bishop and H.C.G. Moule, among others, drew attention to the lack of evidence of human evolution from apes.[95] Every apparent 'missing link' was examined and declared to be inadequate to bridge the gap between man and monkey. J.W. Bardsley, addressing the Victoria Institute on 'The origin of man', cited the duke of Argyll's observation that human development ran counter to the principles of natural selection, for a slow evolution would result in a deprivation of speed and other abilities before intelligence grew to remedy the loss. Evolution was also deemed unable to account for human rationality and spiritual awareness: 'Between man and the brutes, ' said Archdeacon Bardsley, 'there is a great gulf fixed.'[96] Attempts to cross the gulf by claiming that primitive peoples were ape-like were refuted through reference to anthropology and archaeology. The geologists were recruited to show that humankind was at most ten thousand years old and the archaeologists to indicate that, far from evolving out of primitive barbarism, early humans had built major civilisations which in some cases had subsequently degenerated.[97]

By the early twentieth century almost every aspect of Darwin's original theory had been subjected to scientific criticism. Many biologists no longer adhered to the principle of gradual evolution by random variation, controlled by natural selection. Ideas of rapid mutation, involving a much shorter time-scale and leaving no fossil records, were advocated in some quarters, and other scientists replaced random change by 'directionism', a power of development somehow inherent in the organism. It was admitted that geology had not produced the confirmation of evolution which Darwin had expected in 1859, that the genealogy of the human race was still uncertain and that science could not yet account for the origin of life.

Evangelical Churchmen were thus able to find many arguments against Darwinian evolution. Even if mediated to the public at several removes, most of the evidence came originally from the work of reputable scientists and included genuine criticisms of the Darwinian theories. Experts like Stokes and Fleming used their scientific prowess to question aspects of Darwinism, and their conclusions, along with those of biologists like Mendel, Cope, De Vries and Bateson were used by theologians and apologists.[98] This use, however, was not uniform, but fell into two main categories. Some Evangelicals were content to cast doubt on Darwinism and to use the conclusions of science to justify the claim that not merely Darwinism, but also evolution in general was no more than a 'working hypothesis'. Samuel Garratt and G.F. Whidborne took this position in 1901, as did other conservative Evangelicals. Reacting to the notorious 'Monkey Sermon' of 1920, W. St Clair Tisdall wrote a leading article for the *Record* headed 'Canon Barnes again' in which 'the thoughtful Christian' was portrayed as one 'always ready to learn whatever science *proves*', but suspicious of unproven assertions.[99] This conservative attitude, however, could easily imply that a 'theory' was something which no one needed to take seriously, and this assumption was roundly condemned by Streatfeild.[100] He represented those Evangelicals who began to move towards a reconciliation with science, based on a modified theory of evolution. If for some Evangelicals, therefore, scientific uncertainty was sufficient reason to ignore evolution altogether, for others it provided an opportunity for accommodation with a scientific outlook from which some theological problems had been removed. The next section of this discussion will examine the various attempts made by Evangelical Churchmen to harmonise their beliefs with the latest conclusions of modern science. Not all of the attempts were successful; some were mutually incompatible, but they did represent an endeavour to come to terms with some form of evolution.

Attempts at Accommodation

Design

On the general question of design and teleology a number of positions could be taken. Aubrey Moore and the enthusiastic Darwinians attributed the whole process of evolution to God and claimed that the doctrine of immanence allowed them to see the Creator working through natural laws. Evolution was the method of secondary creation and the divine purpose could be detected behind it.[101]

Some Evangelicals were persuaded by Moore's Darwinian 'new teleology'. Edward Woods, considering the challenge of modern thought in *Modern Discipleship and what it means* (1910), took a favourable view of orthodox evolution and affirmed that 'if man developed from a jellyfish and the world developed from a nebula, the demand for a creator is not thereby diminished, but intensified.'[102] Others, however, found the principle of natural selection a major obstruction to design. As has already been seen, scientists in this period increasingly questioned the reliance on natural selection as the mechanism behind evolution, and a popular alternative was the suggestion that organisms possessed a power of development which guided their development. The theory bore some affinity to the ideas of Lamarck; it was promoted in the late 1860s by St George Mivart, and it soon acquired a scientific following. Fleming wrote in the 1920s of 'the broad conclusion… that in all these manifestations of life there is some guiding power, which has been called *Directivity*.'[103]

Directivity had obvious attractions for teleologists. It made the evolutionary process purposeful and, moreover, made it plausible to claim that the natural world displayed the working of a creative Mind. James Orr took up directivity with enthusiasm and expounded it at some length in his *God's Image in Man and its Defacement in the Light of Modern Denials* (1905). Orr's objection to Darwinism was its rejection of purpose and mind, so the new biology enabled him to adopt many of the conclusions of evolution without abandoning a teleological view of the universe. Blind chance and evolution by natural selection were abhorrent to Orr, but evolution as the outworking of design was 'not only not inconceivable, but may even commend itself as a higher and more worthy conception of the Divine working than the older hypothesis.'[104] Among Evangelical Churchmen, Sir

George Stokes produced a theory of 'directionism' which claimed to see a non-material force guiding the operation of natural laws,[105] and Stokes' ideas, incorporated in his Gifford lectures, were welcomed by orthodox divines like R.B. Girdlestone.[106] Evolution in a non-Darwinian sense, based on a definition which restricted it to 'a power working from within', was also given favourable consideration by the Victoria Institute.[107]

The most comprehensive Evangelical attempt to produce a teleology in the light of evolutionary science was V.F. Storr's *Development and Divine Purpose* (1906). Storr accepted the destruction of Paley's natural theology and affirmed 'We are compelled by scientific evidence to believe that all organisms have arisen by progressive modification from a common stock.'[108] He also faced the challenge of natural selection, and, while acknowledging that Darwin regarded it as fatal to design, argued that the whole concept of useful and progressive variation was really teleological. Unlike Orr, Storr found the neo-Lamarckian theory of directivity attractive, but unconvincing, preferring to base his teleology on the intelligibility of nature (hence implying its emanation from a rational Mind), on the harmony of the natural world and on the existence of the human race as an obvious 'end' of the process of development.[109] Storr recognised limitations and objections to his argument, but believed that it was possible at least to contend that 'what we call design in man has in God a real counterpart, inasmuch as the results achieved both by God and man are achieved through the operation of conscious intelligence.'[110] Although Storr was the only Evangelical Churchman to write a whole book on teleology in this period, *Development and Divine Purpose* was probably less influential than the works of James Orr. The *Record* described Storr's volume as 'too abstruse for the ordinary reader'[111] and it was the Scottish theologian whose books were usually recommended to the Evangelical public.

It was possible, therefore, to combine evolution and teleology. Some Evangelicals followed the Darwinian theory, but more welcomed the neo-Lamarckian concept of directivity, perhaps because this option seemed closer to a traditional picture of purposive control by a personal God than Moore's identification of God with the process of natural selection. Immanence could make God a vague and misty figure; directivity could be personified and equated with the Creator's guiding hand.

Divine intervention

The inability of evolution to account for life in its entirety allowed conservative Churchmen to invoke divine intervention to bridge the gaps in the evolutionary process. The so-called 'God of the gaps' argument was used by Liddon in his tribute to the recently deceased Darwin in 1882 and it was also taken up by the Evangelicals.[112] Sir George Stokes deemed evolution insufficient to explain the huge variations between species – for instance, between oysters and the human race – and therefore maintained that creative power must have been exerted at various points in history to bring new species into being.[113] The most common gaps identified were those between organic and inorganic matter and between animals and humankind. It was a commonplace of Evangelical apologetic that evolution could not explain how life began, and the point was also frequently urged that the rational and spiritual faculties of the human race required a special divine intervention.[114] As well as preserving the principle of miraculous creation, this also helped to safeguard the uniqueness of human nature made in the image of God. Biological support for this approach, combining creation and evolution, came from those scientists like A.R. Wallace who regarded natural selection as unable to account for human life, and from those who espoused a theory of evolution by rapid mutation. On the latter theory, the sudden large changes could be attributed to God.

Evangelical scientists and theologians often adopted a compromise which accepted a form of evolution, while leaving scope for direct creative action. Stokes held that 'the commencement of life upon the earth required the exertion of a power above the ordinary laws of nature' and that, although evolution might operate 'to a certain extent', divine intervention was needed too, especially for the creation of human beings.[115] Fleming took the same view, claiming that evolution might operate in some ways, but could not produce life, mind or humanity.[116] In a review of 1906 the *Record* commented 'evolution deals only with phenomena, and not with origins; and whatever truth there may be in evolution as a law of physical development, it can have absolutely no bearing on the spiritual and intellectual part of man.'[117] Even G.S. Streatfeild seemed to align himself with A.R. Wallace and to repudiate Darwinism.[118] The point made by Aubrey Moore that 'In nature everything must be His

[God's] work or nothing'[119] was not really addressed, and only V.F. Storr drew attention to the potential danger of a case based on a 'God of the gaps', writing that:

> 'Theologians have often pointed in triumph to the failure of science to bridge the gulf between the inorganic and the organic, or between the unconscious and the conscious. They have argued that the existence of gaps in our interpretation of the process of evolution is proof that special interpositions of Divine activity occurred at the points where the gaps exist. The foolishness of such a procedure is obvious, for if one day the gulfs should be bridged, the theologians are instantly defeated in their contention. An activity is no less Divine because it is continuous ... Intermittancy of operation is no proof of specially Divine power.'[120]

Science and Scripture

It has already been noted that for Evangelicals, even if not for other Churchmen, the major obstacle presented by Darwinism was its apparent challenge to the Bible. Given their commitment to truth and their doctrinal and experiential reliance on Scripture, Evangelicals had to find a way of reconciling the Bible with modern science. There was no single solution to this problem; indeed, at least three broad positions may be identified.

Harmonisation

The first, and most traditional position, was occupied by those who sought to demonstrate a complete harmony between the teaching of Scripture and the discoveries of science. This school existed long before the publication of *The Origin of Species*, for geologists in the early nineteenth century had, by suggesting that the earth was very ancient, already called some aspects of the Mosaic cosmogony into question. Churchmen had already begun, therefore, to produce schemes of harmonisation. As seen above, the main problems confronting the harmonisers were the order and time scale of creation, the origins of the human race and the historicity of the fall. On creation, three different attempts were made to reconcile Genesis and geology, and each could be extended to meet the challenge of evolution.

Faced with the apparent contrast between six day creation and a world which developed over thousands, or even millions, of years, some Evangelicals resorted to an interpretation which divided Genesis 1:1 from the rest of the chapter.[121] On this theory, expounded by J.H. Pratt in *Scripture and Science not at Variance* and by Henry Moule in several papers, the original creation took place at 'a period utterly illimitable by us' and then, after 'countless ages', the earth became desolate.[122] This desolation, occurring some seven thousand years ago, was the prelude to a restoration by God, in the course of a creative week, in preparation for the appearance of the human race. As Moule wrote in his *Scripture interpreted on Scripture Principles* (1874), 'Between the first and second verses, then, of this Divine record of the creation and early history of the earth, revelation leaves a great white page, on which, if it had been good for man, might have been written the records now to be found only in the rocks.'[123] This idea was not confined to Evangelical Churchmen, for it was ascribed by Pratt to Chalmers, Buckland and Sedgwick, [124] and it was supported by Pusey.[125] Its advantages were that it took the word 'day' in Genesis literally, while leaving full scope for geology – or for evolution – in the time which elapsed between creation and the arrival of humankind.

The theory suffered, however, from a number of drawbacks. It failed to account for the continuity of some forms of life over many thousands of years, since it suggested a total re-creation in about 5000 BC. As J.J.S. Perowne pointed out in a review of Pusey's *Daniel the Prophet* moreover, the whole attempt to interpose a large period of time between Genesis 1:1 and 1:2 was highly dubious exegesis. Perowne was scathing about the Hebrew scholarship behind this attempt and dismissed it as a case of special pleading.[126] Although popular in the mid-nineteenth century, it would be fair to say that, with a few exceptions, this theory had been abandoned by 1900.[127]

A second theory gave a figurative meaning to the creative days of Genesis and claimed that they represented periods of undefined length. Those who accepted this so-called 'day-age' or 'period-day' theory went on to compare the record of creation in Genesis with the appearance of different forms of life shown by fossils. Russell Howden, in *The Old Paths in the Light of Modern Thought* (1921), produced a table labelled 'Genesis and Geology' to demonstrate the close correspondence between the order of creation and the evidence of the geological strata,[128] and in this he was following the work of evangelical geologists like J.W. Dawson.

The day-age theory fitted evolution better than the gap theory outlined earlier. The latter was vague about original creation, practically ignored geology and then invoked a literal week of special divine intervention to prepare the world for humankind. The former, on the other hand, could minimise direct divine action and so adjust to the view of God working through evolution and natural law. Dean Payne Smith set out an elaborate scheme of harmonisation in his commentary on Genesis, beginning with the creation of chemical and mechanical laws which then operated to bring the earth into being. Payne Smith used direct creation at various stages in the process, but left much of the development to the outworking of the laws of nature.[129] It may be seen how this sort of interpretation could be held alongside a form of directed evolution whereby natural processes were occasionally supplemented by creative acts. The apparent agreement between the days of Genesis and the periods of geology and the scope for comparing the biblical picture of development with evolution made the day-age theory very popular among those attempting a harmonisation of Genesis and modern science.

The third possibility was that the days of creation represented visions given to Moses of successive stages in the creative process.[130] This view was not widely held, and many commentators on science and Scripture did not allude to it at all.[131]

After the apparent conflict between science and the biblical account of the world's creation, the second major problem for the harmonisers was the origin of the human race. Geology and biology seemed to suggest that humankind was the product of physical evolution and that the race was far more ancient than the biblical records implied. One possible response to this situation was to claim that humanoid beings existed before Adam, perhaps as stages in the evolutionary process, but that they lacked the spiritual faculties which marked Adam as a man made in the image of God.[132] J.A. Fleming sought to distinguish between 'rational man' and 'spiritual man', and speculated about the existence of rational, but unspiritual, pre-Adamites.[133] A. Rendle Short, in *The Bible and Modern Research* (1931), also supported the pre-Adamite theory.[134] Again, it may be seen that this was a method both of reconciling Genesis and science and of preserving an element of special creation in the origins of humanity. It was not supported by all evangelicals: James Orr, for instance, was highly suspicious of the whole concept of physical evolution when applied to human beings, because he held that mind and brain were a unity and so that it was illogical to combine a specially created mind with an evolved brain – 'You could not put a human mind into a simian brain.'[135] T.B. Bishop cited Genesis 1:27 against the pre-Adamite theory, and other evangelicals agreed that it was unscriptural, but it appealed to some.

Those who rejected pre-Adamism dealt with the antiquity of the race in other ways, usually by combining scientific criticism and biblical interpretation. Thus science was used to show that humanity was not as ancient as some evolutionists maintained, while the genealogies in Genesis were pronounced to be incomplete, thus lengthening the biblical chronology.[137] In this way, a close approximation could be achieved between the biblical and scientific dates for the creation of humankind.

With regard to the fall, harmonisation was comparatively straightforward once the issue of human origins had been settled. Given a spiritual nature, whether linked to a specially created mind or bestowed on a pre-Adamite humanoid, a fall in the traditional sense became possible. It has already been seen that plenty of scientists could be cited to support an intervention to bridge the gap between animals and human beings, and this created the conditions required for a fall from a special status. Writers like Payne Smith who devoted much space to geology saw no need to justify the fall at such length, for once the biblical account of creation had been firmly established, the doctrine of the fall followed automatically.[138]

Schemes of harmonisation were not welcomed by all Evangelicals. Aubrey Moore wrote in 1888 that 'We cannot sympathise with those "reconcilers" who would read between the lines of the Mosaic history a meaning which, if it had been stated in plain words, would have put an infinitely greater strain on the faith of those for whom it was written than even its verbal accuracy would put on ours in the present day,'[139] and some Evangelicals shared his opinion. The anti-evolutionist Horace Noel wrote to the *Record* in 1894 that evolution could only be reconciled with Scripture by treating Genesis 1 and 2 in the same way that Newman had treated the Thirty Nine Articles;[140] other Evangelicals agreed, but instead of rejecting evolution, used science as one argument for adopting a new view of Scripture.

The Appeal To Higher Criticism

For men like V.F. Storr and Herbert Ryle, higher criticism offered a solution to the questions raised by modern science. Ryle wrote and preached frequently on higher criticism, especially with reference to Genesis,[141] and his consistent position was that the book should not be regarded as scientifically accurate in any sense. In *The Early Narratives of Genesis* (1892), he wrote that Genesis 1 'is not... upon any literal interpretation, scientifically accurate', and he criticised the harmonisers for special pleading.[142] The day-age theory he regarded as forcing an unnatural interpretation onto the text in the interests of preserving a link between Genesis and science.[143] Twenty years later, he wrote in a commentary on Genesis that the creation story was a 'simple, concrete, and unscientific narrative' and that 'the Hebrew cosmogony is devoid of scientific value.'[144] Attempts to read modern scientific theories, like the nebular hypothesis of the formation of the world, into Genesis were dismissed as 'an expedient not to be entertained by any scholarly interpreter.'[145] For Ryle,

> 'The supreme value of the book of Genesis has always consisted in its religious message. Its influence has not resulted from perfection of scientific or historical accuracy, but from its power of presenting, through the medium of the people's traditions and folk-lore, the essential truths of the Revelation of the God of Israel ... It was neither infallible nor perfect. But it was part of that inspired witness by which throughout the ages the Spirit of God has spoken to the spiritual nature of man with a voice adapted to his understanding.'[146]

The accounts of the creation and fall, according to Ryle, were Semitic legends, probably derived from Assyro-Babylonian sources and purified by the removal of polytheism.

V.F. Storr followed Ryle's lead. Genesis 1 was 'an allegory or magnificent parable', teaching spiritual truth, but not science.[147] The fall was also an allegory, explaining the nature of sin.[148] Storr wrote of the biblical writers: 'We call them inspired just because they were able to turn all this material of tradition and primitive folk-lore to such spiritual uses... Our faith does not depend on the accuracy of these statements about what was "in the beginning." It does depend on the truth of the character and purpose of God set forth in these writings.'[148]

The Liberal Evangelicals of the AEGM took the same view as

Storr, their most lucid theologian,[149] but there were echoes of this approach too in E.A. Knox's charge of 1916, published as *The Glad Tidings of Reconciliation*. Bishop Knox called for a new understanding of the Bible as 'the record of a revelation', not protected from 'all possibility of errancy as to facts.'[150]

The Middle Ground

E.A. Knox was not a Liberal Evangelical, but nor was he a supporter of ultra-conservatism in biblical scholarship. His position illustrates the fact that between the harmonisers and the liberals was a broad spectrum of Evangelical opinion working to reconcile Christianity with the insights of science. Some of the beliefs of this third group may now be considered.

Unlike the harmonisers, moderate Evangelicals did not attempt to establish a detailed comparison between Genesis and modern science. W.H. Griffith Thomas called the biblical cosmogony a 'simple popular account of creation from the religious standpoint, '[151] while Handley Moule likened Genesis 1-3 to the last chapters of Revelation: truth, but taught partly through 'hieroglyphic signs'.[152] J.J.S. Perowne wrote a series of 'Notes on Genesis' for the *Expositor* in 1890 and 1891, in which he was at pains to disclaim any harmonising intentions. Having made this clear in the first article, he repeated the disclaimer a month later: 'I am not concerned to make out any harmony between the first chapter of Genesis and the discoveries of modern science. I have no sympathy with the impatience which insists on settling questions of this kind.' Just in case readers had failed to take the point, Perowne added a footnote to his next article re-iterating his misgivings about the day-age theory.[153]

Alongside this reaction to harmonisation may be placed the conviction that the Bible is not a scientific textbook. In *The Building Up of the Old Testament* (1912), R.B. Girdlestone complained that 'In modern times the pendulum has been swinging between those who expect a complete cosmogony in a page and those who disregard that page because it is not couched in the expressions reached by modern scientific research.'[154]

Many of this central group went on, however, to affirm that although the Bible does not teach science, yet neither does it contradict science. This view was held by C.H. Waller and J.C. Ryle, and by basically conservative writers like Griffith Thomas. Bishop Ryle maintained in *Is all Scripture inspired?* (1891) that 'it never flatly contradicts science, ' and Griffith Thomas echoed this in his commentary on Genesis.[155] Perowne appended to his articles in the *Expositor* letters from several leading scientists giving their opinions on Genesis and one, Sir George Stokes, was prepared to defend a 'general accordance' between Genesis and science.[156] It may be noted that there was a difference between Ryle, Waller and Griffith Thomas, who were contending for inerrancy and claiming that no scientific errors could be proved, and Perowne and Stokes, who rejected 'slavish literalism',[157] but held that the order of creation in Genesis was remarkably similar to that revealed by science. While both groups agreed that the Bible was 'substantially accurate', they differed over their interpretation of that phrase.

Behind the claim of substantial accuracy or general trustworthiness was a belief that the scriptural account of the creation and the fall rested on historical facts. Griffith Thomas categorically rejected the idea that Genesis 3 was a myth – he regarded the verses as 'pictorial records of actual fact.'[158] Handley Moule agreed, affirming that the early chapters of Genesis were 'records of fact – not parables or mere imaginative poems.'[159] The language might be symbolic, but the events recounted actually took place. Herbert Ryle's theory of Semitic folk-lore was not acceptable to this section of the Evangelical school.

It may be seen, therefore, that the attempt to reconcile Evangelical Christianity and evolution produced three broad groups of Churchmen. The most conservative sought a detailed harmonisation of science and Scripture, while the most liberal denied any scientific accuracy to the Bible. Between these extremes a spectrum of Evangelicals contended for the general trustworthiness of Scripture and for the historicity of the early chapters of Genesis.

Conclusion

Evolution in general and Darwinism in particular posed a series of challenges to all Christians in the late nineteenth century. Traditional doctrines had to be reformulated in the light of modern science, and that process of revision was unsettling and controversial. Controversy was reduced and accommodation made more straightforward when some scientists modified Darwinian biology, replacing it by a system more amenable to divine guidance and intervention. The diversity of evolutionary thought – Darwinians, neo-Darwinians, neo-Lamarckians and so on – made it possible for most Churchmen to find a scheme which was theologically acceptable, and for those who could not to appeal to the scientific confusion as a reason for ignoring all of the contending parties.

Theologians seem to have agreed that teleology and design were the main victims of Darwinism, but this was not the case among Evangelical Churchmen, for whom the reliability of Scripture and the doctrine of the fall were perceived to be the targets of the new biology. With a very few exceptions, Evangelical Anglicans did not welcome evolution. It was regarded as a threat requiring an answer, rather than as an opportunity to develop a modified theology of incarnation and immanence. Often it was ignored or dismissed as a mere theory, and this attitude persisted into the first decades of the twentieth century.

Apologetic necessity and conviction about the unity of truth compelled some Evangelicals to face the questions posed by evolution, and when they did so, the response was very similar to that provoked by higher criticism. Some continued to oppose all forms of evolution, partly on scriptural grounds and partly because of the evidence marshalled against it by scientists. Some accepted the new theories, even in their Darwinian form, and used the insights of higher criticism to deal with the apparent conflict between science and Scripture. Between the ultra-conservatives and the liberals was a diverse central group represented by scientists like Sir George Stokes and J.A. Fleming and biblical scholars like Bishops Perowne and Moule. They were able to weave together creation and evolution, science and Scripture. They held to a Bible which was substantially accurate and based on historical truth, but yet not written in the language of modern science. They were prepared to come to terms with evolution in the sense of development and sometimes to accept a degree of transmutation, but they rejected, theologically and scientifically, the derivation of all life, including humankind, from simple protoplasm. They wished to preserve a place for miracles and for special creation, and in 'directionism' some of them found an opportunity to do so.

As events like E.W. Barnes' sermon to the British Association in 1920 demonstrated, when biology was used to question perceived orthodoxy, a hostile response could be expected, but accommodation with evolution was not an Evangelical priority in this period. The attention paid to it was far less than that devoted to higher criticism and bore no comparison to the energy expended on the ritual controversy. This apparent lack of concern for the issues dominating modern thought was a major spur to the development of Liberal Evangelicalism, and this will be explored in the next two chapters.

Notes

1 *R*, 13 June 1902, 587.

2 The definitive biography of Darwin is Adrian Desmond and James Moore, *Darwin* (London, 1991). See also James R. Moore, *The Post-Darwinian Controversies (1870-1900)* (Cambridge, 1979), 142-3; R.M. Young, 'The impact of Darwin on conventional thought', in A. Symondson (ed.), *The Victorian Crisis of Faith* (London, 1970), 14.

3 I.B. Cohen, *Revolution in Science* (London, 1985), 291; I.G. Barbour, *Issues in Science and Religion* (London, 1966), 85.

4 Ibid., 84-86; D.N. Livingstone, *Darwin's Forgotten Defenders: The Encounter between Evangelical Theology and Evolutionary Thought* (Edinburgh, 1987), 36-8.

5 Desmond and Moore, *Darwin*, chapters 32 and 38; A. Ellegård, *Darwin and the General Reader. The Reception of Darwin's Theory of Evolution in the British Periodical Press, 1859-72* (Goteborg, 1958), 293-6.

6 J.M. Wilson, *Evolution and the Christian Faith: A Study in Outline* (London, 1924), 9.

7 Desmond and Moore, *Darwin*, chapters 37 and 38; Ellegård, *Darwin and the General Reader*, chapter 4 describes debates at the British Association; Livingstone, *Darwin's Forgotten Defenders*, 57-60 gives an outline of the career of Agassiz; Moore, *Post-Darwinian Controversies*, part 2, explains the post-Darwinian debates within biology.

8 Ibid., 153-73.

9 V.F. Storr, *Development and Divine Purpose* (London, 1906), 210.

10 J.A. Fleming, *Evolution and Revelation: A Vindication of the Divine Origin of the Bible* (London, 1926), 5.

11 G.M. Marsden, 'Fundamentalism as an American phenomenon, a comparison with English Evangelicalism', *Church History*, 46 (Chicago, 1977), 217; G.M. Marsden, *Fundamentalism and American Culture. The Shaping of Twentieth Century Evangelicalism 1870-1925* (New York, 1980), 184-88, describes the Scopes trial.

12 Barbour, *Science and Religion*, 82-3; C.C. Gillispie, *Genesis and Geology* (Cambridge, Ma, 1951); M. Ruse, 'The relationship between science and religion in Britain, 1830-70', *Church History*, 44 (Chicago, 1975), 505-22.

13 Baden Powell, 'On the study of the evidences of Christianity', *Essays and Reviews* (London, 1860), 139; Ruse, 'Science and religion', 520; Desmond and Moore, *Darwin*, 500.

14 A.F. Hort, *Life and Letters of F.J.A. Hort* (London, 1896), i, 414.

15 *Charles Kingsley. His Letters and Memories of his Life. Edited by his Wife* (London, 1877), ii, 171.

16 Reginald Farrar, *The Life of Frederic William Farrar* (London, 1904), 109. Farrar continued to defend the immutability of species: ibid., 108.

17 Peter Hinchliff, *Frederick Temple, Archbishop of Canterbury. A Life* (Oxford, 1998), chapter 7, especially 185-8, 191; Moore, *Post-Darwinian Controversies*, 221; A.M.G. Stephenson, *The Rise and Decline of English Modernism* (London, 1984), 36-38.

18 Mary C. Church (ed.), *Life and Letters of Dean Church* (London, 1895), 154.

19 *Sunday at Home*, 17 June 1882, 379.

20 Moore, *Post-Darwinian Controversies*, 259-68; A.L. Moore, *Darwinism and the Christian Faith* (London, 1888); C. Gore (ed.), *Lux Mundi* (London, 1889), especially chapters 2 and 5; C. Gore, 'The theory of evolution and the Christian doctrine of the fall', reported in *Expository Times* (Edinburgh), April 1897, 292-5.

21 F.R. Tennant, 'The influence of Darwinism upon theology', *Quarterly Review* (London), October 1909, 420.

22 J.H.S. Kent, *From Darwin to Blatchford. The Role of Darwinism in Christian Apologetic, 1875-1910* (London, 1966), especially 37.

23 Moore, *Darwinism*, 1; K.W. Clements, *Lovers of Discord: Twentieth Century Theological Controversies in England* (London, 1988), 131-2; E.J.W. Barnes, *Ahead of His Age:Bishop Barnes of Birmingham* (London, 1979), 125-30.

24 Ellegård, *Darwin and the General Reader*, appendix II, analyses press opinion.

25 Livingstone, *Darwin's Forgotten Defenders*, 60-76 (Gray, Wright and Dana), 106-22 (McCosh and Warfield), 138-43 (Iverach and Orr).

26 Ibid., 170-73.

27 J.B. Morrell and Arnold Thackray, *Gentlemen of Science: Early Years of the British Association for the Advancement of Science* (Oxford, 1981), 234; A. Bentley, 'The transformation of the Evangelical party in the Church of England in the later nineteenth century, Durham PhD thesis, 1971, 115.

28 Ibid., 115; *R*, 2 February 1877 (n.p.).

29 'Darwin on the origin of species', *Christian Observer* (London), August 1860, 565, 574.

30 T.R. Birks, *Modern Physical Fatalism and the Doctrine of Evolution* (London, 1882^{2}), 293.

31 J.H. Pratt, *Scripture and Science not at Variance; with remarks on the Historical Character, Plenary Inspiration, and Surpassing Importance, of the Earlier Chapters of Genesis* (London, 1872^{7}), 200. Pratt (1809?-71) was a

Fellow of the Royal Society and Third Wrangler – *DNB*, xvi, 294. *Scripture and Science* was first published in 1856.

32 *R*, 21 April 1882, 89; 28 April 1882, 117; 5 May 1882, 167.

33 Cohen, *Revolution in Science*, 289-90; *DNB Twentieth Century 1901-11*, 536; H.B. Tristram, 'Recent geographical and historical progress in zoology', *Contemporary Review*, 2 (London, 1866), 119.

34 A.M. Babington (ed.), *Memorials, Journal and Botanical Correspondence of Charles Cardale Babington* (Cambridge, 1897), xix, xxix, lviii-lxii, 355-6.

35 Sir George Stokes, *Natural Theology* (London, 1891, 1893); D.B. Wilson, 'A physicist's alternative to materialism: the religious thought of George Gabriel Stokes', *Victorian Studies*, 28 (Bloomington, 1984); *DNB Twentieth Century 1901-11*, 421-4.

36 *R*, 7 June 1901, 588-9; 14 June 1901, 610.

37 *R*, 14 June 1901, 610.

38 Moore, *Post-Darwinian Controversies*, 201.

39 E.A. Litton, *Introduction to Dogmatic Theology on the Basis of the Thirty Nine Articles* (London, 1882, 1892), citing the one volume third edition (1912), 108-10.

40 *R*, 28 May 1909, 577.

41 W.H. Griffith Thomas, *The Catholic Faith* (London, 1904), 65.

42 H.C.G. Moule, *Outlines of Christian Doctrine* (London, 1889), 152-70.

43 See Wilson, *Evolution*; E.W. Barnes, *Religion and Science* (London, 1924) and J.G. Adami, *The Unity of Faith and Science* (London, 1924).

44 *Objects of the Victoria Institute* (London, n.d.), 1.

45 See the *TVI* for the 1880s and 1890s.

46 *TVI* 31 (1899), with a list of members and associates appended.

47 Storr, *Development and Divive Purpose*, chapter 2.

48 J. Orr, 'Darwinism past and present', *C*, March 1909, 175.

49 Pratt, *Scripture and Science*, 251.

50 Birks, *Modern Physical Fatalism*, 310.

51 Ellegård, *Darwin and the General Reader*, 17, 59-61.

52 Moore, *Post-Darwinian Controversies*, 219; D. Cupitt, 'Darwinism and English religious thought', *Theology*, 78 (London, 1975), 125-7.

53 G.M. Trevelyan, *An Autobiography and other essays* (London, 1949), 23.

54 A.H. Carter, *God's Word Supreme* (London, 1914), 75.

55 *R*, 5 May 1882, 167.

56 T. Fielder, *The Truth of the Bible* (London, 1912), 55; H.E. Fox, *Our Lord and His Bible* (London, 1905), 32.

57 *R*, 29 June 1894, 641.

58 Pratt, *Scripture and Science*, 205.

59 J. Orr, *Sin as a Problem of Today* (London, 1910), 129n.

60 Ibid., 163-4.

61 Stokes, *Natural Theology*, ii, 177.

62 Moule, *Outlines*, 172.

63 *R*, 2 September 1920, 685.

64 H. Wace, *The Bible and Modern Investigation* (London, 1903), 60; F.E. Spencer, *Did Moses write the Pentateuch after all?* (London, 1892), 100. A.J. Tait, *Lecture Outlines on the Thirty Nine Articles* (London, 1910), 79, uses the nature of the Genesis cosmogony as a proof of inspiration.
65 *Christian Observer*, August 1860, 570.
66 Young, 'Impact of Darwin', 21.
67 J.A. Fleming, *Evolution or Creation?* (London, 1933), 104-07.
68 Kent, *Darwin to Blatchford*, 28-30.
69 *R*, 3 November 1882, 845.
70 T.R. Birks, *The Scripture Doctrine of Creation, with reference to Religious Nihilism and Modern Theories of Development* (London, 1872), 192.
71 G. Smith, *Successive Creation or Progressive Evolution. A Paper read at the Annual Meeting of the Church of England Clerical and Lay Association, held in Derby, June 8th, 1880* (London, 1880), 11.
72 Ellegård, *Darwin and the General Reader*, 101.
73 *R*, 16 January 1914, 60.
74 Fleming, *Evolution or Creation?*, 113.
75 S. Smith, *'The Ascent of Man' by Professor Henry Drummond. A Review* (London, 1894), 7.
76 *R*, 4 April 1902, 322.
77 Young, 'Impact of Darwin', 16.
78 *R*, 6 September 1901, 868-9, 871-2.
79 R. Payne Smith, *Science and Revelation. A Lecture delivered in connection with the Christian Evidence Society, April 28, 1871* (London, 1871), 36.
80 R. Payne Smith, *The First Book of Moses, called Genesis* (London, 1885), 52.
81 *R*, 30 August 1901, 850.
82 Sir George Stokes, 'On the absence of real opposition between science and revelation', *TVI* 17 (1883), 10.
83 Pratt, *Scripture and Science*, 6.
84 J.R. Howden, *The Old Paths in the Light of Modern Thought* (London, 1921), 2.
85 Moore, *Post-Darwinian Controversies*, 204.
86 *Christian Observer*, August 1860, 563; Birks, *Scripture Doctrine of Creation*, 223-32.
87 Pratt, *Scripture and Science*, 276.
88 Fleming, *Evolution or Creation?*, 98-101.
89 *Christian Observer*, August 1860, 561.
90 Litton, *Dogmatic Theology*, 110; Howden, *Old Paths*, 46.
91 Stokes, 'Science and revelation', 200.
92 Fleming, *Evolution or Creation?*, 33-4.
93. J. Orr, *God's Image in Man and its Defacement in the Light of Modern Denials* (London, 1905), 105.
94 T.B. Bishop, *Evolution Criticised* (London, 1918), 329.
95 Howden, *Old Paths*, 39; Bishop, *Evolution Criticised*, 20-59; Moule,

Outlines, 154.

96 J.W. Bardsley, 'The origin of man', *TVI* 17 (1883), 271-2.

97 Howden, *Old Paths*, 53, 56; Orr, *God's Image*, 165-75.

98 See especially Bishop, *Evolution Criticised*.

99 Griffith Thomas, *Catholic Faith*, 66; *R*, 21 June 1901, 636; 5 July 1901, 685-6; 9 September 1920, 708.

100 *R*, 31 January 1902, 119.

101 Moore, *Post-Darwinian Controversies*, 259-69.

102 E.S. Woods, *Modern Discipleship and what it means* (London, 1910), 157.

103 Fleming, *Evolution and Revelation*, 17-18.

104 Orr, *God's Image*, 96.

105 Stokes, *Natural Theology*, ii, 47-8.

106 R.B. Girdlestone, *Old Testament Theology and Modern Ideas* (London, 1909), 47, 54.

107 J.J. Lias, 'Modifications in the idea of God, produced by modern thought and scientific discovery', *TVI* 34 (1902), 58.

108 Storr, *Development and Divine Purpose*, 38.

109 Ibid., 81, 93, 89, 129-30.

110 Ibid., 208.

111 *R*, 12 April 1906, 310.

112 *Sunday at Home*, 17 June 1882, 380.

113 Wilson, 'George Gabriel Stokes', 89; Stokes, *Natural Theology*, i, 43.

114 Fleming, *Evolution or Creation?*, 63-80; W.H. Griffith Thomas, *Genesis: A Devotional Commentary* (London, 1907), 37.

115 Stokes, *Natural Theology*, i, 41-4; ii, 148.

116 Fleming, *Evolution or Creation?*, 8, 63.

117 *R*, 12 October 1906, 894.

118 *R*, 26 July 1901, 751.

119 Aubrey Moore, 'The Christian doctrine of God', in Gore, *Lux Mundi*, 74-5.

120 Storr, *Development and Divine Purpose*, 122.

121 This technique was adopted by Henry Melvill in the 1830s: J. Whale, *One Church, One Lord* (London, 1979), 112.

122 H. Moule, *Scripture interpreted on Scripture Principles* (London, 1874), 12, 13; H. Moule, *More than one Universal Deluge recorded in the Scriptures* (London, 1869); Pratt, *Scripture and Science*, 37-51.

123 Moule, *Scripture interpreted*, 15.

124 Pratt, *Scripture and Science*, 38.

125 J.J.S. Perowne, 'Dr Pusey on Daniel the Prophet', *Contemporary Review*, 1 (London, 1866), 117.

126 Ibid., 118-9.

127 One exception was the Revd Owen Bulkeley in *Scripture and Science not at variance in the statements of Genesis 1* (Ryde, 1903), a pamphlet acknowledging a debt to J.H. Pratt.

128 Howden, *Old Paths*, 94.

129 Payne Smith, *Genesis*, 50-51, 55.

130 D.N. Livingstone, 'Preadamites: the history of an idea from heresy to orthodoxy', *Scottish Journal of Theology*, 40 (Edinburgh, 1987), 41.

131 Pratt, *Scripture and Science*, 37, allows only two options.

132 See Livingstone, 'Pre-Adamites', passim, for an account of the theory.

133 Fleming, *Evolution and Revelation*, 25.

134 A. Rendle Short, *The Bible and Modern Research* (London, 1931), 56-7.

135 Orr, *God's Image*, 152-3.

136 Bishop, *Evolution Criticised*, 158. Modern creationists regard the theory as unscriptural: see N.M. de S. Cameron, *Evolution and the Authority of the Bible* (Exeter, 1983), chapter 5.

137 Bardsley, 'Origin of man', 261-5; G. Ensor, *Bishop Ryle and Genesis* (London, 1904), chapter 11.

138 Payne Smith, *Genesis*, 92-102.

139 Moore, *Darwinism*, 30.

140 *R*, 6 July 1894, 665.

141 See, for example, his *On Holy Scripture and Criticism* (London, 1904) and *Physical Science and the first chapter of Genesis* (London, 1896).

142 H.E. Ryle, *The Early Narratives of Genesis* (London, 1892), 7.

143 Ibid., 25.

144 H.E. Ryle, *The Book of Genesis in the Revised Version* (Cambridge, 1914), 1, 10.

145 Ibid., 3.

146 Ibid., xlvi-vii.

147 V.F. Storr, *The Inspiration of the Bible* (Winchester, 1908), 16-7.

148 V.F. Storr, *Inspiration* (London, 1924), 14.

149 See note 43 above.

150 E.A. Knox, *The Glad Tidings of Reconciliation* (London, 1916), 9.

151 Griffith Thomas, *Genesis*, 19.

152 J.B. Harford and F.C. Macdonald, *H.C.G. Moule, bishop of Durham: A Biography* (London, 1923), 176.

153 J.J.S. Perowne, 'Notes on Genesis', *Expositor* (London), October 1890, 241; November 1890, 325; December 1890, 431.

154 R.B. Girdlestone, *The Building Up of the Old Testament* (London, 1912), 117.

155 J.C. Ryle, *Is all Scripture Inspired?* (London, 1891) 52; Griffith Thomas, *Genesis*, 21-6; C.H. Waller, *The Authoritative Inspiration of Holy Scripture* (London, 1887), 70-84.

156 J.J.S. Perowne, 'Genesis and science', *Expositor* (London), January 1891, 47.

157 Ibid., p 47.

158 Griffith Thomas, *Genesis*, 48.

159 Harford and Macdonald, *H.C.G. Moule*, 176.

CHAPTER 6

Evangelicals and Liberal Theology

'Contend for the faith which was once delivered unto the saints.' (Jude 3)

From the publication of *Lux Mundi* in 1889 to the Girton Conference of Modern Churchmen in 1921 the Church of England was convulsed by a series of theological controversies, all of which involved what might loosely be defined as 'liberalism', in the sense that they stemmed from attempts to restate Christian doctrine in terms more acceptable to contemporary science, philosophy, ethics or history, sometimes at the expense of the hallowed conclusions of creeds and councils.[1] Churchmen who were content with the traditional formulations of Christian belief organised protests, signed petitions, penned open letters and demanded episcopal action against those who were deemed to have betrayed the faith by their concessions to modern thought, while the liberals attacked what they regarded as obscurantism and equipped themselves with an organisation, the Churchmen's Union for the Advancement of Liberal Religious Thought, founded in 1898, and with a journal, the *Modern Churchman*, established in 1911.[2] At the same time as this general conflict over the limits of orthodoxy was taking place, a body of 'Liberal Evangelicals' was developing, beginning with the Group Brotherhood in the early years of the twentieth century and becoming the Anglican Evangelical Group Movement in 1923. The purpose of this chapter is to examine the part played by Evangelical Churchmen in the general controversies over liberal theology, both within and beyond the boundaries of the Church of England, and then to look at the thought of Liberal Evangelicalism to see how it differed both from the traditional viewpoint of the Evangelical school and from the radical outlook represented by the Churchmen's Union. Since it is concerned with the detailed description and analysis of a series of incidents, the chapter is somewhat episodic in structure, but nonetheless, attempts are made to draw general conclusions about the loyalty of Evangelicals to the teaching of the historic creeds. The history of the AEGM and the narrative of the divisions provoked within the school by Liberal Evangelicalism will form the subject-matter of the next chapter.

The Momerie Affair, 1889-91

The focus of theological debate in the late 1880s was biblical criticism, expressed particularly in the reactions to *Lux Mundi* (1889) and to S.R. Driver's *Introduction to the Literature of the Old Testament* (1891). Before the publication of *Lux Mundi*, however, some Evangelical Churchmen were involved in a minor skirmish with liberal theology in the person of the professor of Logic and Metaphysics at King's College, London, the Revd A.W. Momerie. The 'Momerie affair' was comparatively insignificant, but it serves to introduce the conflicts of the period and, more important, it demonstrated the unflinching orthodoxy of Henry Wace, principal of King's College and later opponent of all forms of doctrinal liberalism.

Alfred Williams Momerie (1848-1900) was raised in the 'ultra-orthodox' atmosphere of Calvinist Congregationalism. While training for the ministry at New College and at the University of Edinburgh he abandoned his parents' creed and, after proceeding to Cambridge, was ordained into the Church of England, choosing the Established Church partly for reasons of ambition and partly because it offered a freer atmosphere for enquiry than the Dissenting denominations.[3] He was appointed to the chair of Logic and Metaphysics at King's College, London in 1880, three years before Wace became principal,[4] and, as Morning Preacher at the Foundling Hospital from 1884, succeeded in attracting large congregations to hear his sermons, which were not only eloquent but also critical of conventional orthodoxy. Momerie recalled 'one old lady of the Evangelical school' whose face grew longer and longer as his sermon proceeded and he commented, 'I do not suppose I could have made a sermon to suit her even if a year had been allowed me to do it in.'[5]

Early in 1889 Momerie published some of his discourses as *'Inspiration' and other sermons delivered in the chapel of the Foundling Hospital*. The volume was not likely to appeal to the orthodox: it included a sermon on 'The inaccuracies of the Bible' (which were described as 'innumerable'), emphasized the contradictory characters of God presented in Scripture, attacked justification by faith as 'injurious to morality' and declared that 'the Christianity of Christendom *is not* the Christianity of Christ.'[6] The *Record* criticised the tone of Momerie's book, drawing attention to its 'dogmatic self-sufficiency' and 'flippant sarcasm',[7] while Wace wrote to ask for an explanation. The principal was anxious to avoid a repetition of the F.D. Maurice controversy and proposed that Momerie should retain his chair, but that it should be transferred from the theological department to the department of General Literature and Science, so that ordinands would no longer be obliged to attend Momerie's lectures. This arrangement was accepted by the professor, endorsed by Bishop Temple of London and approved by the Council of King's College in July 1889.[8]

Some eighteen months later Momerie again came into conflict with Wace. The occasion was an interview, published in *Wit and Wisdom* and then taken up by the *Pall Mall Gazette*, which printed extracts under the headline 'A Sequel to *Lux Mundi*: Outspoken Declaration by Dr Momerie'. Among other comments, Momerie was alleged to have claimed that 'Huxley in science or Freeman in history are far more inspired' than Scripture and that 'I consider that *In Memoriam* is in advance of St John's Gospel.'[9] Wace again sought an explanation; Momerie did not reply, and the College Council wrote formally, demanding an answer.[10] In February 1891 Momerie sent an apology for the tone of the interview, but defended its substance as no more extreme than that of his published works.[11] He followed this up with an article on 'Theology at King's College' in the *Contemporary Review* for April 1891, in which he used his experiences over '*Inspiration*' to illustrate the thesis that 'Change and progress are hateful to the truly clerical mind. Stagnation is the ecclesiastical ideal.'[12] The *Record* dismissed this article as more evidence of Momerie's liking for self-advertisement,[13] but the *Guardian* was more critical of the professor, denouncing his books as a blend of bad theology and bad taste and regretting his continued employment at King's College.[14]

That employment was brought to an end in June 1891 after a further act of provocation by Momerie. On 25 May he delivered an 'Oration' at Prince's Hall, Piccadilly, on 'The Corruption of the Church'.[15] According to the *Times*, 'the principal doctrines which he assailed were those of original sin, the atonement, predestination and the Holy Trinity. Each of these he characterized as nonsense.'[16] Reports also appeared in other daily newspapers, as well as in the ecclesiastical press. On 12 June Wace informed the Council of King's College that he would be proposing Momerie's dismissal, 'on the ground that it is inconsistent with the principles and character of the College that such opinions... should be propagated by any person occupying one of its chairs.'[17] After consultation with Temple, the Council resolved on 26 June that the chair be declared vacant.[18]

The Momerie affair was not a major ecclesiastical conflict. The professor's opinions were extreme and he expressed them with scant regard for tact, thereby uniting Churchmen as diverse as Dean Gregory, Frederick Temple and Henry Wace in opposition to his continued association with King's College. His dismissal was welcomed not only by the *Guardian* and the *Record*, but also by the Nonconformist *British Weekly*.[19] The more significant debates which followed the Momerie affair displayed less agreement between the Church parties, however, and it is to these that attention must now be given.

Lux Mundi, 1889

It has already been noted that the *Pall Mall Gazette* used *Lux Mundi* as a standard with which to compare the views of Professor Momerie, but the former was vastly more important, both as a contribution to theology and as a source of controversy in the Church. The volume was published in November 1889, with the subtitle 'a series of studies in the religion of the incarnation' and the aim of seeking 'to attempt to put the Catholic faith into its right relation to modern intellectual and moral problems.'[20] The significance of *Lux Mundi* for contemporaries was that it represented a frank acceptance of modern thought on the part of the younger Anglo-Catholics. Aubrey Moore and J.R. Illingworth welcomed the theory of evolution, while Charles Gore, the editor of the collection, showed a willingness to assimilate Old Testament criticism in his essay on 'The Holy Spirit and inspiration'. Gore described the early chapters of Genesis as myths, acknowledged the presence of idealized history in the Old Testament and dealt with the traditional appeal to Christology by maintaining that 'He [Christ] willed so to restrain the beams of Deity as to observe the limits of the science of His age, and He puts Himself in the same relation to its historical knowledge.'[21] At a time when 'the battle of the standpoints' was raging and when questions of criticism were eagerly debated in press and pulpit, this statement from the centre of Tractarian orthodoxy was both influential and controversial.[22]

The High Church response to *Lux Mundi* was not uniform, as correspondence in the *Church Times* indicated.[23] The Council of the English Church Union was urged to censure the book, but refused to do so, much to the disgust of the conservatives.[24] Opposition to it was led by Canon Liddon and Archdeacon Denison. Liddon described Gore's essay as 'a thunderbolt out of a clear sky' and continued, 'Not only could Dr Pusey never have written these pages: it would have been difficult to have written anything more opposed to his convictions.'[25] In a series of sermons Liddon asserted the value of the Old Testament and the importance of Christ's witness to it, while Denison tried unsuccessfully to secure the appointment of a committee of Convocation to investigate the alleged errors of *Lux Mundi*. The controversy continued throughout 1890: the May issue of the *Review of Reviews* gave a full summary of the essays and the *Pall Mall Gazette* mischievously suggested that the authors could have produced a best-seller if only they had cast their work in the form of a novel like *Robert Elsmere*.[26] Gore added further prefaces to explain and justify his Christology, prompting the Evangelical Canon Tristram to tell the Hull Church Congress that higher critical theories changed as rapidly as *Lux Mundi*'s prefaces,[27] and corrected his essay to remove the implication that he believed Christ to have been fallible. Meanwhile the general debate on higher criticism continued, so that reactions to *Lux Mundi* became entangled with wider arguments on the study of the Old Testament.

The initial reaction of the Evangelical press to *Lux Mundi* was one of sympathetic disagreement. The *Record*'s review called the book 'a volume of thoughtful and well-written essays' and said that it would be of 'deep interest' to 'all thoughtful readers'. Aubrey Moore's essay on 'The Christian doctrine of God' was singled out for particular praise, and the reviewer also welcomed Talbot's essay on 'The preparation in history for Christ'. Lock's essay on the Church, Paget's on the sacraments and Lyttelton's on the atonement were described as careful, reverent and devout, although taking a different standpoint from that of Evangelical Churchmen. The real criticism was reserved for Scott Holland on 'Faith' and Gore on inspiration, in each case on account of their attitude to the Bible and acceptance of modern criticism. According to the *Record*, Scott Holland was far too ready to put modern science above Scripture, a tendency apparently visible in Gore's essay too, and also clear in Illingworth's espousal of evolution. The review concluded, 'We rise from reading them [the essays] with a fuller conviction than ever that, while there is much spiritual truth that Evangelicals and ritualists hold in common, the line of demarcation which divides them is not after all a slight one, and that, far beyond all the dispute about externals, they are separated by widely different views of Revelation and of the access of man to God.'[28]

The *Churchman* did not review *Lux Mundi*, although it did publish an extensive extract from a criticism by Stanley Leathes in the *Theological Monthly* which concentrated exclusively on Gore's opinions.[29] The *Rock*, on the other hand, produced three review articles. Like the *Record* it welcomed Moore's essay. Unlike its contemporary, however, the *Rock* was unimpressed by Lock and Paget, describing the latter's work as 'vague, dreamy, poetic [and] misty', while welcoming Lyttelton on the atonement as the most sound and spiritual part of the whole book.[30] There was little comment on Scott Holland, but a whole article was devoted to Gore's essay. 'We fancy, ' wrote the *Rock* on 6 December 1889, 'the most drastic critic in the old *Essays and Reviews* would have been satisfied with Mr GORE'S concessions... Has it come to this, then, that Ritualism and Agnosticism are going to clasp hands, just as Romanism and Infidelity did before the French Revolution?'[31] Some months later the *Rock* accused Gore's 'Neo-Ritualists' of trying to infiltrate modern thought by adopting the conclusions of destructive criticism.[32]

By this stage the *Rock* had abandoned its earlier judgment that *Lux Mundi* would be 'read for a season, and chattered over, as is usual with clever books and then... dismissed from recollection.'[33] Between December 1889 and May 1890 the issue had changed from a minor disagreement to a major controversy, and attention had narrowed from the whole book to Gore's essay on inspiration.[34] The same process may be traced in the *Record*, which devoted a leading article to 'The new *Essays and Reviews*' in March 1890. The article, with its telling headline, focussed entirely on Gore's ideas and tried to draw parallels with those of Jowett, Wilson and Williams.[35] Thus Evangelical Churchmen were moving from a broadly sympathetic response to a volume of High Church essays to a hostile response to a perceived attack on the Old Testament.

After the first reviews, therefore, *Lux Mundi* became the starting point for a more general consideration of Old Testament criticism and its implications. On 4 April a leading article in the *Record* on 'A great question' began a debate on the kenosis theory and the relevance of Christ's teaching on the Old Testament and this continued for several months.[36] The Islington Meeting of 1891 took as one of its subjects 'The testimony of Christ to Holy Scripture', and both appointed speakers defended the conservative position. T.T. Perowne offered a careful presentation of the traditional case, while C.H. Waller argued that the pre-existent Christ was a witness to the events of the Old Testament. Waller exclaimed, '... that the Son of God Himself should be mistaken about scenes in which He was the chief actor, as His converse with Moses at Sinai, or about persons with whom He Himself spoke, as Jonah or Daniel – this is thought to be true divinity! this is genuine theological learning! this may be put forth under the vain-glorious title of *Lux Mundi* – light to the world!'[37] In June 1890 Robert Payne Smith, dean of Canterbury, attacked the book in his presidential address to the South Eastern Clerical and Lay Association, taking it to support Wellhausen's theory of the composition of the Pentateuch.[38]

More weighty academic replies to Gore's essay from Evangelical Churchmen are difficult to find. Owen Chadwick has identified Bishops Hervey, Ellicott and Ryle as representatives of an Evangelical response to *Lux Mundi*, [39] but of the three, only J.C. Ryle should be classed as an Evangelical Churchman[40] and his Charges of 1890 and 1893, while defending Genesis and attacking the kenosis theory, made no specific references to Gore or to *Lux Mundi*.[41] Essays in *The Church and Her Doctrine* (1891) by C.H. Waller and H.C.G. Moule also criticised kenotic Christology, and R.B. Girdlestone examined the problem at length in *Doctor Doctorum* (1892), but by this time Driver's *Introduction* and Gore's Bampton lectures had developed the critical position beyond that stated in *Lux Mundi*. The most that can be said is that the essay on inspiration contributed to the pressure exerted by critical scholarship in general, which then led to the production of books attacking higher criticism from the mid-1890s.

Evangelicals gave cautious support to the Denison-Liddon campaign, although they had considerable misgivings about the archdeacon's proposals for synodical action. Liddon's sermons were warmly received and a sympathetic leading article in the *Record* after his death noted his agreement with the Evangelical position on inspiration.[42] Evangelicals were not numerous in Convocation, where Denison's request for a committee of enquiry was debated in February 1891, but Archdeacons Kaye and Perowne, while voicing disquiet about *Lux Mundi*, nonetheless opposed the motion.[43] Evangelical caution over co-operation with High Churchmen also surfaced with regard to a 'Declaration on the truth of Holy Scripture' which was published in December 1891. The 'Declaration' began with a correspondence between Denison and the Evangelicals J.W. Marshall and H.W. Webb-Peploe, leaders of the London Clerical and Lay Union, about a petition.[44] In the course of the negotiations, Denison sent the Evangelical leaders a lengthy document, which was eventually signed by thirty eight clergymen, including Berdmore Compton, Dean Gregory, Canon Carter and Archdeacon Wagner for the High Churchmen and Webb-Peploe, Marshall, Payne Smith and Archdeacon Clarke for the Evangelicals.[45] The *Record* was unenthusiastic about the 'Declaration';[46] other Evangelicals criticised it, either for exalting the authority of the Church or for deprecating reason, and Marshall had to write a letter of explanation.[47] This was not the first time that attempts to produce an alliance between Evangelicals and High Churchmen had created divisions within the Evangelical party, and it was not the last.

Accounts of the *Lux Mundi* controversy have generally concentrated on the relationship between Gore and Liddon, representing the tension between modern Anglo-Catholicism and older Tractarian orthodoxy. It may be seen that Evangelical Churchmen supported Liddon's reaction to *Lux Mundi*, particularly when the issue was simplified into a debate over Christology and Old Testament criticism. Essays on God or the atonement initially received with sympathy were forgotten and attention concentrated on 'The Holy Spirit and inspiration'.[48] Thirteen years after *Lux Mundi*, when the Church Association attempted to prevent Gore's appointment as bishop of Worcester, extracts from his controversial essay were produced as evidence of his unfitness to be a bishop, and Gore, who 'in his own person... combined the Neologian and the Sacerdotalist extremes',[49] was still being attacked for his opinions on the Old Testament in 1916.[50] By this time, ironically, Gore was regarded by many moderate Churchmen as a bastion of orthodoxy, a role which developed in the early 1900s in a series of debates on the creeds and in his response to R.J. Campbell and the 'New Theology'. These issues, and the part played in them by Evangelical Churchmen, form the next sections of this chapter.

The New Theology, 1907

The 'New Theology' was not a controversial issue within the Church of England, since it was confined to the Protestant Nonconformist denominations, primarily to Congregationalism, but Churchmen expressed opinions on the subject and their analysis of the issues fed internal Anglican conflicts.

New Theology was associated particularly with R.J. Campbell (1867-1956) who, at the time of the controversy, was minister at the City Temple, one of the leading Congregationalist churches in London. Campbell was of Free Church stock, educated in Ulster and then at Oxford in the early 1890s, where he was much influenced by Gore and Paget. Misgivings about some aspects of Anglo-Catholicism, especially its apparent leaning towards Rome, kept him from taking Anglican orders and instead he became pastor of the Union Street Congregational chapel, Brighton, in 1895. His achievements there led to his appointment to succeed Joseph Parker at the City Temple in 1903.[51]

The main theme of Campbell's theology was the doctrine of divine immanence, which he soon developed into an assertion of an essential identity between the human and the divine. A theological address on this subject to a ministers' meeting in 1906 was noticed by the press and in January 1907 Campbell was interviewed by a Special Correspondent of the *Daily Mail*.[52] He told the reporter that 'We believe that there is... no real distinction between humanity and Deity... We reject wholly the common interpretation of the Atonement... We believe that Jesus is and was divine, but so are we. His mission was to make us realise our divinity and our oneness with God.'[53] Orthodox Nonconformists like Robertson Nicoll and P.T. Forsyth led the attack on Campbell, who responded by producing a summary of his beliefs under the title *The New Theology*, published in March 1907. The controversy continued, developing into a debate on Christology in the early 1910s, until Campbell withdrew his book, resigned from the City Temple and entered the Church of England as an orthodox High Churchman in 1916.[54]

Evangelical Churchmen were not deeply involved in the arguments over the New Theology. The *Record* commented briefly on the growing notoriety of R.J. Campbell at the end of 1906 and beginning of 1907, but this was really little more than the observation of an interested outsider.[55] A leading article on 'The passion for heresy' suggested that Campbell was merely a fresh sensation for the popular press, like a new music hall artiste or a trunk mystery.[56] *The New Theology* received a scathing review at the end of March, beginning: 'There is no sign that Mr Campbell has been a careful student of Holy Scripture; no evidence that he has tried to grapple with the literature of any part of his subject; nothing to show that he has read any master of Christian theology, that he has ever weighed the work of a reputable apologist; that he has ever admitted the possibility of there being anything worth attention in the writing of those to whom the Creed is precious... Mr Campbell lives with other authorities, and not with many of these.'[57] Several publicity-conscious Evangelical clergymen took the opportunity to preach sermons on the 'Old Theology', reaffirming points denied by Campbell. The Church Association, with typical forthrightness, called the New Theology 'devil doctrine',[58] and Canon Girdlestone wrote a paper for the *Churchman* on 'Gnosticism: ancient and modern' which examined Campbell's doctrine of immanence.[59]

New Theology became an issue for Evangelicals, however, when Charles Gore set himself to reply to Campbell's ideas. Gore gave a course of Lent lectures on the New Theology in 1907, and these were published as *The New Theology and the Old Religion*. The lectures provided a courteous, but thorough, demolition of Campbell's position, but in so doing Gore laid the blame for the development of New Theology at the door of nineteenth century Protestantism. According to Gore, 'what has given the New Theology its advantage is partly the fact that the type of "orthodoxy" which prevailed in England – the Protestant orthodoxy of the earlier nineteenth century – in certain important respects had given an expression of Christian truth quite inferior to that of the ancient Church. Thus we have been suffering from a largely legitimate reaction against the defects of this Protestant orthodoxy.'[60] Gore went on to list three 'special defects' of traditional Protestant orthodoxy: a deist conception of an interventionist God, which provoked Campbell's corresponding over-emphasis on immanence; reliance on an infallible Bible, 'riddled by modern science and historical criticism and... no longer reasonably tenable'; and a doctrinal system based on the atonement rather than the incarnation, and on an interpretation of the atonement repulsive to the modern moral sense.[61]

This challenge to Evangelical Protestantism was taken up by W.H. Griffith Thomas in the *Churchman* for May 1907. Griffith Thomas rejected the charge that the Protestant doctrine of God was akin to Deism, noting that Evangelicals taught intimate fellowship with God and the indwelling of the Holy Spirit in the believer. Immanence was important, he claimed, but less significant than divine transcendence, which was essential to a properly scriptural doctrine of sin. Griffith Thomas found Gore's understanding of sin to be inadequate, and accused the bishop of semi-Pelagianism. On Scripture, Griffith Thomas affirmed that the issue was authority, not infallibility. Protestants, he claimed, were loyal to the Articles, whereas Gore exalted tradition to a false position of equality with the Bible. As for the atonement, Griffith Thomas was quite prepared to concede that it was the central Evangelical doctrine, but he held that this simply reflected the balance of New Testament teaching. He concluded by declaring that the points singled out for criticism by Gore were really the safeguards of orthodoxy against the New Theology: transcendence, providing an adequate estimate of sin; scriptural authority, to ward off erroneous teaching; and atonement to make Christianity a gospel rather than a version of mysticism teaching either a glorified humanity in the sacraments or an ideal Christ evolved from human consciousness.[62]

Gore did not reply, but he was clearly unpersuaded, because he continued to ascribe the unsettlement of belief to the inadequacies of Protestant orthodoxy – for instance, a Cambridge University sermon of May 1909 repeated the points made in *The New Theology and the Old Religion*. Evangelical Churchmen, likewise, also continued to repudiate the accusation of responsibility for Campbell's errors.[63] As Gore held Evangelical doctrine partly responsible for liberalism, so Evangelicals underscored the connection between liberalism and higher criticism and reminded Gore of his espousal of critical theories in *Lux Mundi*.

Conflict over the Creeds, 1902-12

While Nonconformity debated the New Theology, the Church of England in the first decades of the twentieth century engaged in a protracted internal quarrel about the Gospel miracles and the creeds. This issue had been raised in the late nineteenth century with Abbott's *The Kernel and the Husk* (1886) and in a clash between Gore and W.H. Fremantle in 1887,[64] but from 1902 onwards the battle was almost continuous. In the account which follows an attempt will be made to concentrate on the main developments and on the role of Evangelical Churchmen in the controversy.

The question of the creeds arose in 1902 in the collection of essays *Contentio Veritatis*, written by 'Six Oxford Tutors'. In his essay on 'The person of Christ', W.R. Inge wrote with respect to the virgin birth and the resurrection: 'We should not now expect, *a priori*, that the Incarnate *Logos* would be born without a human father, that He would suspend His own laws during His sojourn on earth, or that He would resuscitate His earthly body, and remove it to the sky, nor do we see that those events, however well proved, are of any value as evidences of His Divinity.'[65] This cautious statement of doubt aroused less controversy than a paper on 'Natural Christianity' read to the Churchmen's Union by W.H. Fremantle, dean of Ripon. Fremantle's paper was reported in the *Times* of 31 October 1902 and the report suggested that the dean had rejected the virgin birth and bodily resurrection of Christ. Fremantle accused the *Times* of misrepresenting his words; the reporter denied the charge; Bishop Boyd Carpenter of Ripon published a correspondence with the dean to reassure people of Fremantle's orthodoxy, and High Churchmen tabled a resolution in the Lower House of the Northern Convocation reaffirming 'the primitive faith of the undivided Church in our Lord's Virgin Birth and in His Resurrection.'[66]

The Evangelical response to the Fremantle controversy was one of firm opposition to the dean. Canon Tristram spoke and voted for the resolution in Convocation and Wace took the chair at a conference of Churchmen which asked the bishops for reassurance about the Church's commitment to the virgin birth and resurrection.[67] Captain Cobham, the chairman of the Church Association, wrote to Boyd Carpenter demanding an episcopal censure of the dean and comparing Fremantle to Charles Voysey, the mid-nineteenth century heterodox Anglican and founder of the 'Theistic' church.[68]

A series of incidents exacerbated the controversy over the next two years. In May 1903 a motion on the virgin birth and resurrection was debated in Canterbury Convocation and although reporters were excluded from the session, it became known that Hensley Henson, canon of Westminster, had made a strong speech asserting that faith in the incarnation and resurrection could be separated from the virgin birth and the empty tomb.[69] Henson repeated this claim in a sermon to the Churchmen's Union, later published as *Sincerity and Subscription*. The *Record* noted Henson's Convocation speech, and commented with regard to the secrecy of the meeting, 'The "unrest"... caused by recent [ritual] controversies is small in comparison with that which will be provoked throughout the country if the Lower House of Convocation gives an uncertain sound on the Virgin Birth.'[70] In the event, Archbishop Davidson was able to resist conservative pressure for an episcopal declaration, mainly because of the timely publication of Armitage Robinson's *Some Thoughts on the Incarnation* which, although impeccably orthodox, emphasized that the incarnation, not the virgin birth, was the primary focus of Catholic faith.[71]

High Churchmen, however, were not satisfied with this. Towards the end of 1903 Gore, now bishop of Worcester, rebuked one of his clergy, the Revd C.E. Beeby, for an article in the Unitarian *Hibbert Journal* casting doubt on miracles, especially the virgin birth. Beeby resigned his living, much to the satisfaction of the Evangelical press, but Rashdall and Henson accused Gore of overbearing behaviour.[72] Handley Moule, on the other hand, took the opportunity afforded by his primary visitation to affirm his belief that the virgin birth was 'a question not of interpretation... but of ultimate fact.'[73]

At Easter 1904 Henson preached a controversial sermon on the resurrection, reinforced by articles in the *Contemporary Review* and the *Hibbert Journal*. These provoked angry editorials in the *Record*, a rebuke from the *Churchman* and complaints from the Church Association. For once Bishop Winnington-Ingram was able to agree with Captain Cobham about the contents of a letter of protest, but the agitation had no more effect on Henson's preaching than had similar fulminations against ritualism.[74] A spate of articles appeared defending the traditional understanding of the resurrection[75] and at the Islington Meeting of 1905 Watts-Ditchfield attacked the beliefs of Fremantle and Henson, declaring 'What he felt was a great danger and a great hindrance to them in their work amongst the masses was the utterances of those who ought to be their leaders in the Church.' Significantly, Watts-Ditchfield included in his censure Bishop Gore for his teaching on the 'myths' of Genesis 1-3, while another Evangelical, Canon J. Harford Battersby, spoke in support of Fremantle as a fellow member of the chapter of Ripon.[76]

The final incident of this series was a declaration in April 1905 calling for free and unfettered study of the New Testament, and for the Church not to insist on belief in all the 'details' of the Gospel narrative. This appeal for the New Testament to be treated in the same way as the Old was signed by 101 influential clergymen, but it met with hostility from Evangelicals. The *Churchman* suspected an attempt 'to rationalize and reduce the supernatural element in Christianity',[77] while the *Record* predicted that it would be used by rationalists and Romanists to attack the Church of England.[78] The Upper House of Canterbury Convocation responded to the agitation on 10 May 1905 with a resolution 'that this House is resolved to maintain unimpaired the Catholic Faith in the Holy Trinity and the Incarnation as contained in the Apostles' and Nicene Creeds, and in the *Quicunque Vult*, and regards the faith there presented, both in statements of doctrine and in statements of fact, as the necessary basis on which the teaching of the Church reposes.' This was underlined by a resolution of the Lambeth Conference in 1908.[79]

The next controversy broke out precisely because a clergyman applied rigorous critical methods to the New Testament, in the manner advocated by the declaration of 1905. J.M. Thompson (1878-1956), nephew of Dean Paget of the *Lux Mundi* school, was an earnest High Churchman until he read Loisy's *The Gospel and the Church* and began to study the Synoptic Problem.[80] Thompson believed that a study of the earliest strata of the New Testament – Mark and 'Q' – indicated that the Gospel miracles could be separated into two categories. There were healings and exorcisms, well attested in the early sources and quite compatible with modern science, and there were bizarre 'nature miracles' like the feeding of the five thousand, irreconcileable with science and resting, Thompson believed, on slender textual evidence. Thompson's aim was to free Christianity from 'an incubus of error' by demonstrating that thorough critical scholarship removed the nature miracles unacceptable to the modern mind.[81] This position was worked out in his *Miracles in the New Testament*, published in 1911.[82]

Miracles in the New Testament attracted attention for two reasons. First, Thompson applied his principles not only to the lesser nature miracles, but also to the virgin birth and the resurrection, concluding that '*the positive evidence for the fact of a miraculous birth must be pronounced to be exceedingly weak*' and 'We may believe in the Resurrection without accepting the story of the Empty Tomb.'[83] Secondly, Thompson was an examining chaplain to the bishop of Gloucester and dean of divinity at Magdalen College, Oxford, responsible for the spiritual welfare of the undergraduates, and himself under the jurisdiction of the Visitor, Bishop E.S. Talbot of Winchester. 1911, moreover, saw the translation of Gore from Birmingham to Oxford, so placing Thompson in close proximity to the leading defender of credal orthodoxy on the episcopal bench.

Talbot soon took action, revoking Thompson's licence in August 1911.[84] Gore attacked *Miracles in the New Testament* in his diocesan magazine[85] and early in 1912 delivered a course of lectures on 'Reconstruction of belief'. The dispute continued throughout 1912, with papers on miracles at the Middlesbrough Church Congress and a trenchant defence of Thompson by Hensley Henson in the preface to his *The Creed in the Pulpit*.[86]

Evangelical Churchmen strongly opposed Thompson. In a leading article on 'Erroneous and strange doctrine' the *Record* denounced *Miracles in the New Testament* as a direct denial of the faith and called for an episcopal rebuke.[87] The *Churchman* characterised the book as 'not the effort of a man who is feeling after a full faith, but of one who is definitely breaking away from that faith,'[88] while Dean Wace welcomed Talbot's action.[89] Refutations of the book were produced by J.A. Harriss, vicar of St Andrew's, Oxford, in two published sermons delivered in November 1911 and in articles for the *Churchman*,[90] and by E. Digges La Touche in his Donnellan lectures for 1911-12.[91] Digges

La Touche concluded his case with the affirmation: 'Incarnate Deity without miracle would be almost unthinkable.'[92]

Thompson's principal defenders also incurred Evangelical criticism. Henson's *The Creed in the Pulpit* was afforded a lengthy review in the *Record* in December 1912, which ended by describing the author's view of Scripture as 'unsatisfactory and unsatisfying'.[93] Dr Sanday's Church Congress paper on 'Miracles', which attempted to draw a distinction between 'supernatural' and 'abnormal' events, with the implication that nature miracles in the latter category were the result of creative writing on the part of the Evangelists, was immediately challenged from the floor of the Congress by Webb-Peploe and was later dismissed as inadequate by Wace.[94] Evangelicals, from conservatives like Wace to liberals like Guy Warman and Dawson Walker, the editors of the *Churchman* in this period, stoutly defended the traditional view of New Testament miracles.

It should be noted, however, that the Evangelical position differed somewhat from that of Bishop Gore. Gore's defence of the New Testament was primarily one of weighing evidence and criticism: he maintained that sound critical scholarship supported the accuracy of the Gospel narratives. In this way, Gore was able to defend the integrity of the New Testament while continuing to support the higher criticism of the Old Testament. He was also prepared to allow that there were minor mistakes in the Gospels, although he claimed that these were unimportant. Dean Wace, on the other hand, declared that Gore's arguments tended to 'leave the door open... to such extravagances as those of Mr Thompson.' Wace rested his case on inspiration, which, he believed, guaranteed the accuracy of the Gospel narratives and meant that events were to be accepted even if they were recorded in only one Gospel. Wace also deprecated Gore's concessions to Old Testament criticism as likely to undermine the general authority of Scripture.[95]

A further significant point arising from the events of 1911-12 was the changing Evangelical attitude to Hensley Henson. Although the review of *The Creed in the Pulpit* quoted above was critical and although Wace continued to express considerable hostility to Henson's teaching on the creeds, the review of December 1912 also paid a warm tribute to Henson's advocacy of Home Reunion and outspoken opposition to sacerdotalism.[96] For the rest of the decade Evangelical Churchmen were to find

Henson difficult to come to terms with, since their suspicion of his liberalism was balanced by admiration for his stance on relations with Nonconformity. Further scope for admiration was provided by the debates over Kikuyu and *Foundations*, as will be seen below.

Foundations, 1912

Foundations: A Statement of Christian Belief in Terms of Modern Thought appeared in November 1912. The editor was B.H. Streeter, all the contributors were Oxford men and three of the seven were examining chaplains.[97] The initial reactions included parody and satire from R.A. Knox in *Absolute and Abitofhell* and *Some Loose Stones* (1913), and strong criticism from orthodox Evangelicals.[98] Two essays in particular provoked Evangelical opposition: W.H. Moberly on 'The atonement' and Streeter on 'The historic Christ'. Moberly set out a theory of the atonement in line with the 'vicarious penitence' interpretation associated with his father and with McLeod Campbell; Walker and Warman in the *Churchman* desribed it as unscriptural, irrational and 'absolutely unsound' in an editorial comment of February 1913.[99] Streeter's essay was more controversial, however, because it suggested a novel interpretation of the resurrection. Streeter sought a middle course between physical resurrection and simple imagination on the part of the disciples and produced a theory that the Risen Christ was an 'objective vision' given by God to assure the early Church that Christ had overcome death. The *Churchman* saw this as an attempt to overthrow the resurrection altogether, while Dean Wace dismissed the theory as 'Mr Streeter's fancy', continuing, 'to my mind it is lamentable that mere speculations like Mr Streeter's should be put forward as "foundations" to students at Oxford as well as to general readers.'[100]

The debate over *Foundations* took on a new vigour at the end of 1913 and this was due almost entirely to the action of Frank Weston, the bishop of Zanzibar. Weston was an Anglo-Catholic of flawless orthodoxy, a disciple of Gore's and a ritualist. Above all, however, he was a missionary statesman seeking to spread Christianity in East Africa in the face of strong competition from Islam. In 1913, three events occurred which made Weston believe that his efforts were being undermined. One was the

Kikuyu Conference, which seemed to place Protestant unity above Catholic order. Another was the inhibition of a clergyman in England for practising invocation of the saints. The third was the arrival in Zanzibar of a parcel of books including *Foundations* and *The Creed in the Pulpit*.[101] Weston's response was an open letter to the bishop of St Alban's entitled *Ecclesia Anglicana: For What does She Stand?* In the open letter, he identified the three problems facing the Church of England as 'Modernism, Pan-Protestantism and denial of Catholic practices,'[102] taking *Foundations* as an example of the first, not because it was extreme, but because so many of the contributors held official diocesan posts. The conclusions of *Foundations* were summarised in a series of propositions and the book was dismissed as irrational and heretical.[103]

Weston's open letter not only reinvigorated the theological debate over *Foundations* but it also gave that debate greater breadth by associating with it the issues of Kikuyu and extreme ritualism. High Churchmen basically supported the bishop of Zanzibar, although with some reservations.[104] Gore, in a letter to the *Times* in December 1913 and in his celebrated open letter to his diocese, *The Basis of Anglican Fellowship in Faith and Organization*, published at Easter 1914, desribed a trio of problems slightly, but significantly different from Weston's. The bishop of Oxford agreed that liberalism and Pan-Protestantism were dangers to the Church of England, but his third fear concerned Romanising on the part of 'Catholic' extremists. Gore reiterated the point which he had been making for several decades, that it was immoral for a clergyman to repeat the creeds when he no longer accepted the truth of the propositions which they contained.[105] Liberal Churchmen replied to the Gore-Weston onslaught with pamphlets of their own. J.F. Bethune-Baker addressed his *The Miracle of Christianity: A Plea for 'The Critical School' in regard to the use of the Creeds* to Gore, while Sanday wrote *Bishop Gore's Challenge to Criticism* in order to explain and defend his own position on New Testament miracles.

The controversy came to a head in Canterbury Convocation in April and May 1914, when Bishop Winnington-Ingram of London moved a series of resolutions reaffirming the decisions of 1905 and 1908 with respect to the creeds. These resolutions were supported by petitions from many dioceses, and although opposed by the Council of the Churchmen's Union, eventually passed *nemine contradicente.*[106]

The Evangelical position during these debates might perhaps best be described as independent conservatism, in that the Evangelicals broadly supported the attack on liberalism, but did not wish to associate themselves with Weston and Gore's hostility to the Kikuyu Conference, which, after all, included an attempt to indict two CMS missionary bishops for heresy and schism. Thus Wace entirely agreed with Weston that *Foundations* went beyond the true and legitimate limits of the Church of England, but also maintained that the practices advocated by the bishop of Zanzibar had no real place in *Ecclesia Anglicana*: 'the voice of the Reformed Church of England is equally opposed to the rationalistic views which the bishop justly denounces, and to the ultra-Catholic and anti-Protestant views which he himself represents.'[107] Similarly, the *Churchman* welcomed Gore's criticisms of liberalism and published a critique of Sanday's reply by H.J.R. Marston, but described the rest of the bishop's open letter as painful reading.[108] W.H. Griffith Thomas wrote an article on *The Basis of Anglican Fellowship* in July 1914, accusing Gore of liberal opinions on biblical criticism and making scathing comments on the illogicality of his churchmanship. According to Griffith Thomas, the best way for Gore to follow up his own call for the Church of England to return to fundamental principles would be by seceding.[109] When Convocation debated the creeds, among the petitions was one from the National Church League which combined fidelity to the traditional symbols of the virgin birth and resurrection with a firm repudiation of exclusive episcopacy and of proposals to revise the Prayer Book in a 'Catholic' direction.[110] While Weston, Gore, Sanday and Bethune-Baker were debating clerical subscription and the creeds, Evangelicals like A.J. Tait, Guy Warman and Handley Moule were producing pamphlets on Kikuyu and applauding the pro-Kikuyu statements of Hensley Henson, whom Weston regarded as an arch-heretic.[111] Watts-Ditchfield spoke and voted for the Convocation resolutions of 1914,[112] but at the same time Evangelical Churchmen were wary of High Church attempts to entice them to support a campaign which might turn against Kikuyu. Evangelicals, counselled the *Churchman*, should stand aloof from alliances, whether with Gore against the liberals or with the Churchmen's Union against the ritualists.[113]

Hensley Henson and the Bishopric of Hereford, 1917

Three years after the *Foundations* controversy the Prime Minister, Lloyd George, precipitated another ecclesiastical crisis by nominating Henson to the bishopric of Hereford, vacated by the Broad Churchman John Percival.[114] Lloyd George wanted to make Henson a bishop because he was a gifted preacher, and the Prime Minister overruled the hesitation of Archbishop Davidson at the appointment of a man likely to prove unpopular in many quarters. Davidson warned Lloyd George in November 1917 'that his appointment would cause something of a storm,'[115] and the prediction proved to be a mild understatement.

The *Times* announced the nomination on 13 December 1917.[116] On the following day, the clergy of the diocese of Oxford, meeting to elect a proctor for Convocation, passed a resolution urging the dean and chapter of Hereford not to elect Henson.[117] On the 20 December Lord Halifax wrote to the *Times* calling the nomination a 'scandal'.[118] By this time Gore had called at Lambeth to protest, Henson was writing of 'some prospect of my figuring as the centre-piece in an Anglican *auto da fé*' and local opposition in Hereford was being orchestrated by the ECU and the Revd E. Hermitage Day, editor of the *Church Times*.[119] Henson was duly elected by the chapter on 4 January, and then the pressure moved from Hereford to Lambeth, as the ECU tried to persuade Davidson not to consecrate, while Watts-Ditchfield and other bishops urged Henson to produce a form of words which would satisfy the critics as to his orthodoxy.[120] Gore published a formal protest, but on 18 January the *Times* carried an exchange of letters between Davidson and Henson which reassured most of the critics, and Gore withdrew his protest.[121] Henson was consecrated on 2 February, with many High Church bishops conspicuous by their absence. Later that year resolutions were proposed in the House of Laymen and in Convocation regarding the creeds and the new bishop took these as a continuation of the opposition to his appointment.[122]

Hensley Henson suspected that his nomination to the see of Hereford provided an opportunity for many enemies to strike at him.[123] It is certainly true that his outspoken attitudes had aroused opposition: he had pleaded for liberty of interpretation with respect to the creeds; he had advocated Home Reunion and preached in Nonconformist chapels in the teeth of episcopal admonitions; he had criticised the popular myth of the 'Angels of Mons'.[124] As Herbert Ryle wrote to Davidson, 'numbers of clergy who only know Henson through the *Church Times* regard him as a self-seeking Deist who has no belief in the Deity of our Lord, and whose cleverness and wit are not balanced by reverence or sincerity.'[125]

The leading figures in the opposition to the Henson appointment were High Churchmen and the central organisation was provided by the ECU. Of the hundreds of letters received by Davidson on the subject, few were from Evangelical Churchmen, but those which did originate from that school varied in attitude. Canon Lillingston, who knew Henson as dean of Durham, welcomed the appointment and said that it would render a great service to Church and State.[126] Bishop Nickson of Bristol, while disagreeing with some of Henson's opinions, deprecated the agitation against him as unfair and wrote in this vein to his archdeacons and rural deans.[127] The National Church League portrayed the ECU campaign as an attack on the Royal Prerogative and circulated a petition paying tribute to Henson's 'high character, great learning, and generous sympathies.'[128]

Some Evangelicals, however, were alarmed by Henson's initial refusal to make any conciliatory statement in reply to his critics. Watts-Ditchfield wrote to ask, 'Can you see your way to affirm that what you have written does not imply that you have departed from the traditional and almost universal meaning which is attached to the words of the Creed, "Born of the Virgin Mary," "The third day He rose from the dead"?'[129] On 5 January the *Times* printed a letter from Sanday, replying to one from Darwell Stone. Sanday claimed that his position was 'so similar to Dr Henson's that I believe he will accept me as an advocate,' and went on to claim Henson's support for the statement that 'the Virgin Birth, the physical Resurrection and physical Ascension, are all realistic expressions, adapted to the thought of the time, of ineffable truths which the thought of the time could not express in any other way. To conceive of them realistically was natural and right in the age in which they took shape. Speaking for myself and for those who agree with me, I should say that it was no longer natural and therefore no longer to be enforced as right.'[130] Henson noted in his diary that this letter would be damaging,[131] and so it proved, for it led Dean Wace to withdraw his former support and to join Darwell Stone's opposition to the consecration.[132] On 16 January Watts-Ditchfield told Davidson that he would not attend the consecration.[133] Sir Robert Lighton, a leading figure in the NCL, was active in the local campaign against Henson, which circulated vitriolic leaflets likening the new bishop to Judas Iscariot.[134]

After Henson clarified his views, Wace withdrew his opposition. Watts-Ditchfield did not attend the consecration, although Moule, H.E. Ryle, Nickson, Theodore Woods of Peterborough and Bishop Taylor Smith, the Chaplain General, were there, representing the Evangelical school and providing examples of most shades of opinion within it.[135]

The aftermath of the controversy was a resolution in the House of Laymen in February 1918 on the subject of the virgin birth, which came to the bishops in May, and a petition on the miraculous birth and resurrection, presented to the Upper House in July. Watts-Ditchfield introduced the petition, which was signed by fifty four thousand communicants representing 'every school of thought in the Church except those against whom it is worded.' In his speech the bishop of Chelmsford referred to Sanday and Glazebrook as exponents of the views against which the petition was directed, but Henson took the affair to be 'a gross and repeated attack on himself, ' and Davidson had to intervene to calm the situation.[136]

The Girton Conference, 1921

The final example of theological controversy within the Established Church in this period was the storm provoked by the Modern Churchmen's Conference of 1921.[137] The Churchmen's Union began holding annual conferences in 1914, and the conference of 1921 took place at Girton College, Cambridge. The subject was 'Christ and the Creeds', prompted by the publication of the first volume of *The Beginnings of Christianity*, edited by F.J. Foakes-Jackson and Kirsopp Lake. Most English Modernists opposed the extreme liberal position adopted by Foakes-Jackson and Lake and before the Girton Conference, Broad Churchmen like Bishop Henson expected that controversy would focus on the former's paper on 'Christ and the Creeds'; indeed, Henson's alarm prompted Glazebrook, the conference organiser, to attempt to remove Foakes-Jackson from the programme.[138]

In the event, however, popular attention concentrated not on Foakes-Jackson but on two other speakers, Hastings Rashdall on 'Christ as *Logos* and Son of God' and Bethune-Baker on 'Jesus: human and divine'. Both papers were summarised inaccurately in the press – thus, for example, the *Daily Express* claimed that Rashdall denied Christ's divinity.[139] The *Church Times* printed criticisms of the conference by Gore and by Peter Green, and the situation was exacerbated when the full Conference report appeared in the *Modern Churchman*, complete with an inflammatory preface by H.D.A. Major challenging 'Traditionalists' to answer two questions: 'Will they accept the affirmation "God was in Christ", with the practical recognition in daily life that "Jesus is Lord" as constituting the irreducible minimum for modernist membership in the Church and in the teaching and ministerial offices?' and 'Will they concede to modern churchmen the right to modify the use of the Creeds?'[140] It has been suggested that Major's preface was the most provocative statement to emerge from the Girton Conference, and subsequent correspondence led to a formal charge of heresy submitted to Bishop Burge of Oxford by the High Churchman C.E. Douglas. Burge referred the charge to the Oxford divinity professors, who concluded that there was no case to answer, but the issue continued to cause trouble in Convocation into 1922 as the Anglo-Catholics campaigned for a synodical condemnation of the Girton papers. The conference had a more positive consequence, moreover, in encouraging Davidson to appoint a Doctrine Commission at the end of 1922.[141]

The stages of the response to the Girton Conference were faithfully recorded in successive issues of the *Modern Churchman*. The reactions of Anglo-Catholics, Methodists, Roman Catholics and Nonconformists were described in some detail, but very little mention was made of Evangelical Churchmen.[142] The initial response of the Evangelicals, however, may be seen in the *Record* and it was, perhaps predictably, hostile to the Modernists. A front page note on 18 August commented: 'There seems only too much reason to fear that a stage was reached at the Cambridge Conference which is diametrically opposed to the Truth as revealed in Holy Scripture, and is frankly inconsistent with the teaching of the Church of England.' The same issue, however, carried a favourable report on the reverent atmosphere of the conference, and this was echoed by the

Churchman, which reported that 'There were some papers read at the conference which by no stretch of charity could be regarded as Christian in the commonly accepted meaning of the word, but these were excrescences and were as stoutly resisted by other members of the conference as they would be by the most orthodox believers outside its borders.'[143] Correspondence in the *Record* was less certain that the Modernists were orthodox, and C.H.E. Freeman of St Silas's, Blackburn, proposed an alliance with the Anglo-Catholics against Modernism.[144] Others challenged the Christology of the Modernists, and Wace wrote an article in November 1921 pointing out that dialogue between Evangelicals and Modernists could not take place while Modernists refused to listen to those who regarded the Gospels as inspired, authoritative and trustworthy.[145] Evangelicals did not co-operate in the attempt to prosecute Henry Major for heresy, but some of them did produce a solemn protest against the violation of ordination vows by ritualists and Modernists. This protest, organised by Wace, Clarke, Joynson-Hicks, T.W.H. Inskip, Russell Howden and other Evangelical leaders, was signed by 1300 laity and 500 clergy, and was delivered to Davidson in May 1922.[146]

Against this, it should be noted that two Modernists were invited to address the Cheltenham Conference in 1921 and that the *Modern Churchman* had high hopes of greater co-operation between liberals and Evangelicals.[147] These hopes seem to have been over-optimistic, since the Cheltenham 'Findings' reaffirmed traditional beliefs respecting Christology, inspiration and the atonement.[148] An attempt will be made later to estimate the similarity between Modern Churchmen and Liberal Evangelicals, but it would seem that the Modernists underestimated the strength of Evangelical conservatism when they described the 'Solemn Protest' as the work of 'only a fragment of the Evangelical School.'[149]

Before turning to other aspects of the Evangelical response to theological liberalism, a few general points may be made about the part played by Evangelical Churchmen in the controversies of the period 1889-1922.

First, the staunch conservatism of the Evangelicals may be registered. There was a consistent rejection of liberal theology and a firm adherence to the doctrinal statements of the creeds, and this applied to the whole Evangelical school, from Henry

Wace to H.E. Ryle, who declared his commitment to 'the literal and historical resurrection from the tomb on the third day.'[150] As Handley Moule observed in his primary Charge, for the Evangelicals, the creeds were matters of fact, not mere interpretation.

Given this conservatism, it may be asked why historians' attention has concentrated on Gore and the High Churchmen as the leading defenders of orthodoxy. It would seem that this was due partly to the lack of Evangelical bishops in Canterbury Convocation – there was a phalanx of able High Churchmen in the Upper House throughout this period, whereas the only prominent Evangelical was J.E. Watts-Ditchfield, and he could certainly not match Gore's theological erudition. It was also the case that some Evangelicals were suspicious of synodical action and episcopal declarations – hence their failure to support Denison's call for a committee of enquiry into *Lux Mundi*. Furthermore, while High Churchmen devoted their energy and organisation to attacking Modernism, Evangelicals reserved their greatest efforts for the ritual controversy. Evangelicals often said that rationalism was a more serious threat to the Church than ritualism, but this rhetoric was seldom translated into practical action.

The ritual controversy also served to hamper co-operation between the two conservative parties in the Church. As has been seen, there were a number of joint declarations and protests, ranging from the 'Declaration on the Truth of Holy Scripture' in 1891 to the approach to Convocation on the creeds in 1918. This co-operation, however, was rarely whole-hearted. Anglo-Catholics liked petitions to emphasize the authority of the Church behind credal formulae, whereas Evangelicals held to the principle of *sola Scriptura*. For Evangelicals, Gore's readiness to accept Old Testament criticism fatally undermined his defence of the Gospels. Evangelicals were also suspicious, moreover, that the Anglo-Catholics would not rest content with a Church free of Modernism. They recalled the statement that 'When the Catholic influence prevails in the Church, there will be no more toleration for Modernists, and the extreme Evangelical will be far happier with his Free Church brethren.'[151] As Wace observed, the Evangelical ideal of *Ecclesia Anglicana* was very different to that advocated by Bishop Weston. Nor should it be forgotten that liberal Churchmen could be useful allies against Anglo-Catholicism, since ritualism was the antithesis of the critical and scientific outlook promoted by the English Modernists.

Evangelicals therefore preferred to make independent protests against liberalism, and sometimes they linked what they regarded as liberal and ritual irregularities. The *Rock*'s response to *Lux Mundi* took this line, and twenty years later the *Record* was pleased to note the bishop of Norwich's rebuke to a group of High Churchmen who protested about *Miracles in the New Testament*: 'My old experience as a schoolmaster has taught me that the difficulty of asserting discipline in some special case becomes enhanced in circumstances in which toleration has been allowed or claimed for other irregularities.'[152] The logical culmination of this policy was the statement of 1922 accusing both ritualists and Modernists of breaking their ordination vows.

The Evangelical opposition to liberalism therefore added to the complicated ecclesiastical situation of the early twentieth century. The three Church parties preserved their independence and were often in controversy with each other, although on many issues different co-operative combinations could be formed. By the end of the period, the Doctrine Commission was attempting to reconcile liberals, Evangelicals and Anglo-Catholics. It did not report until the late 1930s, but it might be suggested that its prospects of success were hampered from the outset by its failure to include conservative Evangelicals among its membership.[153] Mutual toleration within the Church of England continued to prove elusive.

European Theology

The concluding section of this chapter will be devoted to 'Liberal Evangelicalism'. First, however, some attention should be given to the Evangelical response to the major developments in European theology in the early twentieth century. Three schools will be considered briefly: Harnack and liberal Protestantism; the Roman Catholic Modernism of Loisy and Tyrrell; and the 'eschatological' school of Weiss and Schweitzer. The treatment offered here will be brief, largely because few Evangelicals engaged in dialogue with these European currents of theological thought, beyond dismissing them as exotic, unorthodox and unscriptural.

Liberal Protestantism

Nineteenth century liberal Protestantism was a multi-faceted and international phenomenon whose history has been the subject of considerable and acrimonious debate, not least among the theological heirs of the various contending schools of thought.[154] At the turn of the century, few scholars enjoyed a higher reputation than Adolf Harnack (1851-1930), professor at the University of Berlin, editor of the prestigious *Theologische Literaturzeitung* and author of a magisterial three volume *History of Dogma*.[155] In the winter of 1899-1900 Harnack gave a course of lectures in Berlin which were published from a student transcript as *Das Wesen des Christentums* (1900). An English translation, *What is Christianity?*, appeared the following year.

Harnack sought, by means of careful historical research, to recover the essence of Christianity from the accretions of later dogma, and he was confident of the ability of scientific history to give access to the historical Jesus. In *What is Christianity?* Harnack described what happened when 'the Gospel was detached from the mother soil of Judaism and placed upon the broad field of the Graeco-Roman empire.' He traced the development of Greek and Roman Catholicism, describing the former as 'foreign to the Gospel' and the latter as a 'total perversion' of the message of Jesus. For Harnack, the essence of religion was 'the love of God and neighbour' and the heart of the message of Jesus, 'the Kingdom of God and its coming', 'God the Father and the infinite value of the human soul' and 'the higher righteousness and the commandment of love'. The birth narratives in the Gospels were swept aside as later additions and readers were warned about the 'fanaticism' attendant on Christological debates. Harnack's exposition of Christianity emphasized that rather than being saved from sin, human beings need to be shown an example of how to live. Jesus – the Jesus of history, not the Christ of dogma – was this example, and his teaching was primarily an ethical message. Harnack therefore advocated a religion which was moral rather than mystical.[156]

Harnack's views were very influential – *What is Christianity?* had reached its fourteenth edition by 1927[157] – but his opinions were not likely to be well received by Evangelicals, for whom the gospel was about sin and salvation, not mere morality, and who would be highly suspicious of attempts to find a Jesus behind the text of the New Testament. Evangelical references to

Harnack were not frequent, but they were usually critical. The Revd B.R.V. Mills wrote a series of articles for the *Churchman* in 1906 on 'What is Christianity?' and he sought to show that the dogmas of Christianity rested on historical facts, not Greek speculation.[157] S.N. Rostron, in his Hulsean Prize essay *The Christology of St Paul* (1912) pointed out the gulf between Pauline Christology and that of liberal Protestantism.[159] Digges La Touche wrote that 'the Christ of the Liberal critic is a benevolent and morally earnest University Professor who stands for the bare minimum of fact and belief consistent with the existence of a moralized religion, with a spiritual interpretation of life. He is little more than the T.H. Green or, better still, the Rudolf Eucken of the first century.' He went on to attack the Jesus of the liberals as subjective, unhistorical and unconvincing, the incarnation of weak saintliness.[160] T.J. Pulvertaft echoed this criticism when he claimed, in response to Harnack's advocacy of foreign missions, that a Christianity without an atonement could not succeed in the mission field. Jesus as redeemer rather than simply as teacher and example was the consistent Evangelical emphasis.[161]

Roman Catholic Modernism

Like liberal Protestantism, Modernism in the Roman Catholic Church was a diverse and international movement. Generally it sought to bring traditional beliefs into closer relation with the modern outlook in philosophy, history, science and social ideas. The Modernists accepted the conclusions of biblical criticism and also adopted a theory of doctrinal development which allowed them to maintain that the fullness of the gospel reposed in the modern Roman system rather than in the simpler belief and practice of the early Church. For some Modernists the historical roots of Christianity were relatively unimportant; what really mattered was the developed system of the present day. Although tolerated by Leo XIII, Modernism was regarded with suspicion by Pope Pius X and was condemned by the decree *Lamentabili* and the encyclical *Pascendi* of 1907. Most of the clerical leaders of Modernism were excommunicated.[162]

Three points may be made about the Evangelical attitude to Modernism. First, they viewed some aspects of the movement with interest and sympathy, mainly because it was seen as an attempt to reform the Roman Catholic Church from within.

Articles explaining Modernism appeared in the *Record* in 1909, and the *Churchman* welcomed Tyrrell's *Lex Credendi* in 1906.[163] Second, sympathy was soon succeeded by disappointment as the doctrinal position of the Modernists became clearer. Both Rostron and Digges La Touche rejected Modernist Christology, while the *Record* noted with approval Rome's condemnation of A.L. Lilley's *Modernism* in 1908.[164] The third point was that Evangelicals, while supporting the repudiation of Modernism, also criticised Rome's method of meeting modern thought by excommunication and prohibition. This was the reaction to the excommunication of Loisy and Tyrrell and to the decree *Lamentabili*.[165] It might be suggested that these events allowed Evangelicals to reaffirm their own orthodoxy while also registering a criticism of the illiberal and un-English methods of the Roman hierarchy.

Weiss and Schweitzer

If the Jesus of liberal Protestantism inaugurated a kingdom of moral righteousness and the Modernist Christ began a process which led to the doctrinal system of Rome, the Jesus of the eschatologists came preaching an apocalypse which never took place. The eschatological school began with Johannes Weiss, whose *Die Predigt Jesu vom Reiche Gottes* (1892) attempted to set out a consistently eschatological interpretation of the ministry of Jesus. A more significant work, however, was Albert Schweitzer's *Von Reimarus zu Wrede* (1906). Schweitzer held that Jesus expected the imminent arrival of an other-worldly kingdom of God and went to his death believing that the crucifixion would precipitate the end of the world.[166] Schweitzer's book was introduced to English readers by Sanday in *The Life of Christ in Recent Research* (1907) and was translated as *The Quest of the Historical Jesus* in 1910. It caused an immediate storm and was criticised by several speakers at the Cambridge Church Congress.[167] It should be noted here that despite the criticism, Schweitzer's ideas were influential in some quarters – R.A. Knox, for example, detected eschatological tendencies in *Foundations*.[168]

Evangelical Churchmen responded to the eschatologists on two levels. The first level was simple denunciation. W. St. Clair Tisdall, reviewing *The Quest of the Historical Jesus* for the *Record*, wrote that 'The author applies the term "the historical Jesus" to the will-of-the-wisp which he and his party fancy they see flying over the quagmire of error in which they are fast embedded.' In the same way, the *Churchman* described consistent eschatology as 'baseless and illusory.'[169]

On a second and deeper level, attempts were made to offer a critique of Schweitzer's arguments. This was done by J.R. Darbyshire in the *Churchman* for January 1911, by Rostron and Digges La Touche in their general works on Christology,[170] and especially by E.C. Dewick in his *Primitive Christian Eschatology* (1912). Dewick's book was the Hulsean Prize essay for 1908, and it consisted of a thorough examination of eschatology in the Old Testament, in later Judaism, in the New Testament and in the sub-apostolic Church. His conclusions were that Schweitzer was mistaken in claiming that Jesus's contemporaries expected a transcendental kingdom of God and wrong also to maintain that Jesus taught only a future kingdom.[171] Dewick criticised the eschatologists for their arbitrary handling of the text of the New Testament and for pursuing consistency at the expense of accuracy :

> 'Not a few of the most influential heresies of old time may be traced to the desire of their advocates to be at all costs consistent. With faultless arguments their tenets were deduced from data which were often true as far as they went, but were only a part of the whole truth. It may perhaps be pardonable to surmise that among the number of the above, future ages will reckon the "Consistent Eschatological Theory" of Albert Schweitzer.'[172]

Liberal Evangelicalism

It has been seen that Evangelical Churchmen adopted a conservative position in the theological controversies of the early twentieth century and that they rejected the radical ideas of European liberals and Modernists. It may be asked, therefore, in what sense 'Liberal Evangelicalism' deserved its title and how it differed from the conservative wing of the Evangelical school.[173]

A preliminary consideration concerns the sources for 'Liberal Evangelical' thought. In the section which follows, most of the material has been drawn from the two collections of essays edited by Guy Rogers, *Liberal Evangelicalism: An Interpretation by Members of the Church of England* (1923) and *The Inner Life. Essays in Liberal Evangelicalism* (1925), from the Blue pamphlets produced by the AEGM and from the works of V.F. Storr. It should be noted that Liberal Evangelicalism was not monolithic, for the position of the AEGM in the 1920s was somewhat more liberal than that of its predecessor, the Group Brotherhood, in the 1900s. Harold Smith addressed the problem of terminology soon after the publication of the first volume of essays when he wrote to the *Record* : 'We have called ourselves "liberal Evangelicals" from the beginning of our clerical life; now we find the term appropriated by those whose opinions are far more "liberal" than our own, and we are not too anxious to be identified with them.'[174] The justification for using the AEGM material for this section is that it represents the most liberal position which Churchmen could occupy while still wishing to call themselves Evangelicals. Those who moved beyond the beliefs marked out here, like E.W. Barnes and J.W. Hunkin, both AEGM members in the 1920s, also moved from Evangelicalism to Modernism.[175] It is not disputed, therefore, that V.F. Storr, the AEGM's leading theologian, was more liberal than some early members of the Group Brotherhood,[176] but his significance is that he combined those views with a claim still to be an Evangelical Churchman.

Compared to many of those whose opinions have been reviewed in this chapter, the Liberal Evangelicals were extremely conservative. Despite criticisms from the conservative Fellowship of Evangelical Churchmen, which suggested that the Christology of *Liberal Evangelicalism* was shaky with regard to the Chalcedonian definitions,[177] the AEGM seems to have been firmly orthodox on the person of Christ. Storr's essay on this subject, while supporting the kenosis theory, defended Christ's pre-existence and rejected Adoptionism, and also upheld the virgin birth, the resurrection and the Gospel miracles.[178] E.W. Barnes, writing in *The Inner Life* on 'The rise and growth of man's spiritual consciousness', declared his belief in the full deity of Jesus Christ.[179] The great statements of the creeds were not at risk from Liberal Evangelicalism.

V.F. Storr, in particular, demonstrated a firmly Evangelical emphasis on the doctrines of sin and salvation. In *My Faith* (1927), described as 'a simple statement of the Christian Faith, as a Liberal Evangelical views it', he described sin as 'a poison... which infects our whole nature' and which incurs God's judgment.[180] Storr referred elsewhere to the traditional Evangelical characteristics of pastoral zeal and concern for individual souls, and he regarded these as important marks of continuity between the eighteenth century Revival and the AEGM.[181]

Unlike the Modernists, therefore, Liberal Evangelicals confidently upheld the virgin birth, bodily resurrection, Gospel miracles and deity of Christ in traditional terms. Unlike other liberal Protestants they emphasized the 'sinfulness of sin' and did not preach mere morality. Unlike the Anglo-Catholics, they kept the Cross and the atonement at the centre of their doctrinal system.[182] Theologically, however, they differed from traditional Evangelicalism in four main respects: in their openness to new knowledge; in their attitude to biblical criticism; in their interpretation of the atonement; and in their doctrine of the Second Advent.

A case could be made for suggesting that by the late nineteenth century Anglican Evangelicalism had adopted a broadly suspicious attitude to modern thought and that it adhered to a doctrinal system which was static rather than progressive. This position had several components and causes. On the one hand, the Evangelical preoccupation with personal salvation and holiness, combined with hostility to 'worldliness' produced a form of religion limited in scope, but very clear-cut within those limits: Evangelicals, as G.W.E. Russell recalled, knew the details of the 'Gospel plan' of sin, atonement and conversion, but were not really interested in other aspects of social or intellectual life.[183] On the other hand, where new knowledge was encountered, it was often perceived to be hostile to Evangelical religion. As has already been seen, scientific history, biblical criticism and Darwinian evolution all challenged aspects of the Evangelical world-view. Furthermore, Evangelicals also tended to be conservative in churchmanship in this period, as they sought to defend the status quo against Anglo-Catholic innovations. Although this conservatism should not be exaggerated, it would be fair to say that many Evangelicals were content with their system of doctrine and view of Scripture and were not anxious to change. This spirit was captured in J.C. Ryle's Charges of 1890 and 1893, entitled respectively *'Hold Fast'* and *Stand Firm!* There was much talk of old doctrines and old paths, and a reluctance to assimilate new ideas.

The Liberal Evangelical outlook was very different. They positively welcomed modern thought and criticised the conservatives for their fears and suspicions. Writing on 'The development of Evangelicalism', H.A. Wilson observed that:

> 'Evangelicalism, it was found, had not staked out a claim wide enough to include all her many children... The Liberal Evangelical is saddened and troubled by all this. He is assured that it is God Himself who has been teaching the world, not only by His Church, but also by men of science and critical scholars, and he is resolved... to follow fearlessly the Spirit of Truth and to claim all knowledge as part of God's Revelation.'[184]

This attitude was echoed by E.W. Barnes and Edward Woods[185] and by V.F. Storr, who saw the key theological development of the nineteenth century as the challenge to Christians to adopt an organic view of knowledge, one which welcomed new light, whatever its source, and which found a place for it in the doctrinal scheme.[186]

Several corollaries followed from this attitude. One was great faith in the progress of truth. In *The Development of English Theology in the Nineteenth Century* (1913), Storr reflected on the period 1800-1860 in these words: 'all the while the cause of truth was winning; and today we accept without demur much which our grandfathers resisted to the utmost... *magna est veritas et praevalebit*. "The Spirit of Truth... shall guide you into all the truth."'[187] Another implication was commitment to reason, so that Storr began *Development and Divine Purpose* (1906) by asserting that reason must be 'free and unfettered', a point which he repeated over thirty years later in *Freedom and Tradition* (1940).[187] Commitment to reason and faith in the progress of truth, moreover, meant that doctrine could not be static and absolute. E.A. Burroughs saw the essence of Liberal Evangelicalism as a religion which valued 'spirit' above 'form' and which appealed to those who 'are mainly interested in the *élan vital*, and believe in a true creative evolution under the auspices of that "Creator Spirit" who is the spirit of the Perfect Man.' He continued:

> 'The real line of cleavage is between those who... stand for the binding force of a system, an authority, a formula, based explicitly on the past, and those who think of the Church as an ever-growing Divine Adventure, of its successive movements of what St Paul calls "the increasing of God", and of the Christian attitude as one of "faith", not in the sense of submission to what is, because it always has been, but in that of resourceful expectancy of what new thing is coming out of

the treasures of Providence.'[189]

Storr wrote in *Freedom and Tradition* that Liberal Evangelicals could not have a rigid doctrinal system, and he expounded the last part of the AEGM's title as signifying the importance of progress under the guidance of the Spirit of Truth.[190]

One area in which the Liberal Evangelical openness to new knowledge marked them off from other members of the Evangelical school was that of biblical criticism. This issue has been considered at length in an earlier chapter and it need only be noted here that the AEGM welcomed and accepted the higher criticism of the Old Testament. The Blue pamphlets *The Bible: What it is and what it is not, Old Testament Prophecy* and *Jesus Christ and the Old Testament*, all published in 1924, all upheld the main conclusions of the critics and adopted a kenotic Christology to deal with the question of Christ's testimony to the Hebrew Scriptures. A simple statement of the liberal position may be quoted from Storr's *My Faith* (1927):

> 'The Bible teaches us *religious* truth. Its writers knew no more science or history than was generally known at that time. We need not, therefore, be surprised if we find that the account of Creation in Genesis does not agree with modern science, or if it can be shown that there are some historical mistakes in the Bible. Nor need we be troubled, if we find out that there are legends in the Bible which are not historically accurate.'[191]

Another cause of sharp division between Liberal and conservative Evangelicals was the doctrine of the atonement. The traditional Evangelical interpretation of the atonement was that of penal substitution – the belief that Christ died in the place of sinful humanity, bearing the guilt and punishment attributable to human beings for their disobedience to God. This position was set out at length by Handley Moule in his *Outlines of Christian Doctrine* (1889) – Moule described the doctrine in terms of sacrifice, propitiation, ransom and penalty – and it was also held by such representative Evangelicals as E.A. Litton, J.C. Ryle, Henry Wace, Nathaniel Dimock and Stuart Holden.[192] At the London Meeting of Lay Churchmen in 1915 Albert Mitchell, a leading member of the NCL, declared that the chief ground of personal religion rested 'in the fact that our Lord Jesus Christ... has... made, by His death upon the Cross, a full, perfect, and sufficient sacrifice, oblation, and satisfaction for the sins of the whole world... such sacrifice being made by Him as our Substitute in our stead and place, and also, as a distinct and separate truth, as our Representative and Vicar.'[193] Evangelicals in this period, moreover, were particularly anxious to defend their doctrine of the atonement in the face of a perceived threat to the finished work of Christ from Anglo-Catholic eucharistic theology.

Liberal Evangelicals accepted the centrality of the atonement, but often rejected penal substitution. Some qualification is necessary, because the doctrinal statement produced for discussion by the Group Brotherhood in 1907 did not contain anything unacceptable to conservatives.[194] By the 1920s, however, some leading Liberal Evangelicals were clearly rejecting the forensic interpretation of the atonement. R.T. Howard's essay 'The work of Christ' in *Liberal Evangelicalism* emphasized the love of God and made no reference to the ransom idea in connection with atonement, an omission for which he was criticised by the *Record*'s reviewer.[195] Storr's *My Faith* explicitly repudiated the appeasement of a wrathful God by the punishment of Christ, and seemed to suggest that the Cross served to draw people to God by showing the extent of his love.[196] In *The Problem of the Cross* (1919), Storr set out his views more fully, discussing the strengths and weaknesses of traditional atonement theories before concluding that divine immanence helped towards a new understanding of the Cross whereby God suffered with his world and Calvary was an expression in time of God's eternal self-giving love.[197] Some Liberal Evangelicals still used the language of substitution, but rejected the penal or forensic element of the doctrine, and this was the position adopted by H.A. Wilson at the Cheltenham Conference of 1925 when he appealed for mutual toleration on the basis of the centrality of the Cross.[198]

Controversy over the atonement also appeared in Evangelical reactions to the report of the Archbishops' Committee on the Evangelistic Work of the Church, one of the committees established in the aftermath of the National Mission of Repentance and Hope in 1916. The report was the subject of a letter headed 'A new gospel', sent to the *Record* in July 1918 by five Birmingham incumbents who accused the committee of neglecting the gospel of salvation and of emphasizing instead a call to service.[199] E.S. Woods, a member of the committee, defended the report, claiming that it achieved a balance between the need to repent and the challenge to serve God, but some Evangelicals continued to complain that the presentation of the gospel by the

Archbishops' Committee was defective and that it underplayed the atonement.[200]

For Liberal Evangelicals like E.S. Woods 'service' was a key idea, and it was linked to an interpretation of the kingdom of God which formed another contrast between the AEGM and the stance of traditional Evangelicalism.

Eschatology and the Second Advent were subjects of great interest to many conservative Evangelicals. It has already been seen that the study of prophecy was keenly pursued, not merely by the 'retired army officers' mocked by Elliott-Binns, but also by scholars like C.H.H. Wright.[201] The Prophecy Investigation Society numbered Canons Garratt and Girdlestone among its leading members, and the Balkan and First World Wars stimulated interest in the 'signs of the times'.[202] Attempts were made to calculate the date of the fall of the Turkish Empire; the significance of Allenby's capture of Jerusalem was trumpeted; Revelation was scoured for comments relevant to the present day.[203] There was little agreement on the precise details of prophetic interpretation, but traditionalist Evangelicals were united in believing the subject to be important. The Second Coming of Christ in a literal, physical form was maintained as a cardinal doctrine; it was discussed at the Islington Meeting of 1901, urged as a vital topic for sermons by Bishop Moule in 1913 and described as the greatest subject of all by C.H. Titterton and Charles Neill in *Scriptural Evangelicalism* (1925).[204] When the Advent Testimony Movement was launched in November 1917, Stuart Holden, Webb-Peploe and F.S. Webster were among the signatories to the initial letter, and Evangelical Churchmen were fully involved in the subsequent interdenominational testimony meetings.[205]

Transcendental eschatology and an emphasis on the Second Coming were not hallmarks of Liberal Evangelicalism. V.F. Storr rejected the traditional parousia in *Christianity and Immortality* (1918), suggesting that the doctrine simply underlined the sovereignty of Christ.[206] While conservative volumes like Titterton and Neill's *Scriptural Evangelicalism* or *Evangelicalism by Members of the FEC* (1925) included chapters on the Second Advent, neither of the Liberal Evangelical collections did, and none of the AEGM pamphlets were devoted to this subject. Liberal Evangelicals stressed a this-worldly kingdom of God and the need to work for social improvement. This was particularly clear in the works of E.S. Woods, from *Modern Discipleship and what it means* (1907) to *What is this Christianity?* (1934). The idea of the Christian as 'an adventurer for the kingdom'[207] was very different to that of the believer as an earnest student of prophecy. Not all Liberal Evangelicals rejected a literal Second Coming and they did not uphold an entirely this-worldly eschatology, but their emphasis was clearly far removed from the millennialist debates of the nineteenth century. As the Revd F. Mellows wrote, describing 'Neo-Evangelicalism' in the *Record* in March 1921, the liberals preached more about the kingdom of God on earth than the glories of heaven, and this may be linked to a more optimistic or life-affirming outlook which sought to save people in the world, rather than from the world. By 1931 the hymnbook of the AEGM's Cromer Convention had altered a verse of Caroline Noel's popular hymn from:

> 'Brothers, this Lord Jesus shall return again
> With his Father's glory, with his angel train.'

to:

> 'Brothers, this Lord Jesus dwells with us again
> In his Father's wisdom, o'er the earth to reign.':

a very different eschatology from that of traditional Evangelicalism.[208]

It remains to consider briefly the relationship between Liberal Evangelicalism and Modernism. Hensley Henson's tribute to V.F. Storr, written in October 1940, was that 'his attempt to effect a working harmony between Evangelicals and Modernists was far more successful than either faction imagined to be possible', and there was certainly an overlap between the AEGM and the Churchmen's Union.[209] E.S. Woods joined the Union as a result of the Girton Conference; E.W. Barnes, who spoke at Girton, described himself in 1921 as an Evangelical, but went on to be a prominent Modernist; Stephenson's list of the 'Dramatis Personae of English Modernism' includes E.A. Burroughs, E.C. Dewick, Elliott-Binns, J.W. Hunkin, Guy Rogers and H.A. Wilson, as well as Storr and Woods.[210] Since the list also includes Percy Dearmer and J.G. Adderley, however, it would not be accurate to call it a catalogue of fervent Modernists. Some figures defy classification – Charles Raven, for example, contributed to *The Inner Life* and to some Modernist publications, but was neither a committed member of the Churchmen's Union nor a consistent Liberal Evangelical.[211] Some general conclusions about Modernism and the AEGM may be made, however. In the period before 1930, at least, Liberal Evangelicals were far more orthodox than the leading Modernists: there were no speculative Christologies like those of Rashdall and Bethune-Baker. Liberal Evangelicals also lacked the donnish air of the Churchmen's Union – E.A. Knox commented that only two of the Girton speakers were parochial clergymen, while the AEGM consisted predominantly of ordinary incumbents.[212] Moreover, as Storr wrote in *Freedom and Tradition*, Liberal Evangelicalism retained a pastoral zeal and valued its legacy from the eighteenth century Revival, and this produced a 'difference in flavour' between the two movements.[213]

Conclusion

With regard to credal orthodoxy, therefore, Evangelicalism in this period was generally conservative. There were doctrinal conflicts between Liberal and conservative Evangelicals, but the liberalism of the AEGM was very mild compared to that of the Churchmen's Union. The existence of differences of opinion on Scripture, the atonement and the Second Advent, however, was not unimportant, especially when taken in conjunction with other examples of 'Liberal' Evangelicalism, like a readiness to adopt a degree of ceremonial in worship which the conservatives regarded as too close to ritualism. The pressures of modern thought, growing diversity of practice in public worship, different emphases in theology, varying attitudes to biblical criticism and opposing strategies for the assimilation of scientific knowledge imposed a considerable strain on the Evangelical school. In the first three decades of the twentieth century that strain led to the fragmentation of Anglican Evangelicalism, and the next chapter will examine its impact with particular reference to some Evangelical societies and organisations.

Notes

1 General accounts of the controversies may be found in R. Lloyd, *The Church of England 1900-65* (London, 1966), chapter 5; G.K.A. Bell, *Randall Davidson* (London, 1935), chapters 41, 42, 53, 72; and K.W. Clements, *Lovers of Discord: Twentieth Century Theological Controversies in England* (London, 1988). The definition of 'liberalism', is, of course, itself contentious!

2 A complete history of the Churchmen's Union appears in A.M.G. Stephenson, *The Rise and Decline of English Modernism* (London, 1984).
3 See V. Momerie, *Dr Momerie: His Life and Work.Written and edited by his Wife* (Edinburgh, 1905). The description of Momerie's background as ultra-orthodox is his own, ibid., 9.
4 F.J.C. Hearnshaw, *The Centenary History of King's College, London, 1828-1928* (London, 1929), 340-1.
5 Momerie, *Dr Momerie*, 131-2.
6 A.W. Momerie, *'Inspiration' and other Sermons* (Edinburgh, 1889), chapter 2 and 13, 201, 277.
7 *R*, 4 January 1889, 9.
8 KCA, minutes of the Council, 15 March 1889; 5 April 1889; 19 July 1889. Peter Hinchliff, *Frederick Temple, Archbishop of Canterbury. A Life* (Oxford, 1998), 237, attributes the compromise to Temple.
9 *Pall Mall Gazette*, 12 December 1890, 2, 6.
10 KCA, minutes of the Council, 9 January 1891.
11 KCA, M114, Momerie to the Council, 7 February 1891.
12 A.W. Momerie, 'Theology at King's College', *Contemporary Review*, 59 (London, 1891), 571.
13 *R*, 10 April 1891, 349-50.
14 *G*, 1 April 1891, 500-1.
15 A handbill advertising the 'Oration' is preserved in the KCA.
16 *T*, 27 May 1891, 4.
17 KCA, minutes of the Council, 12 June 1891.
18 Ibid., 26 June 1891.
19 *R*, 3 July 1891, 641; *G*, 1 July 1891, 1068; *BW*, 2 July 1891, 147.
20 C. Gore (ed.), *Lux Mundi* (London, 1889), citing the twelfth edition (1891), vii.
21 Ibid., 263, 259, 265.
22 H.D. McDonald, *Theories of Revelation: An Historical Study 1860-1960* (London, 1963), chapter 3. The phrase was coined by Principal Cave.
23 See cuttings from the *CT* in Liddon's scrapbook on *Lux Mundi*, Liddon Papers, Pusey House, Oxford.
24 J.G. Lockhart, *Charles Lindley, Viscount Halifax* (London), ii (1936), 32-4; O. Chadwick, *The Victorian Church*, (London, 1972[2]), ii, 102-3.
25 Liddon to D.C. Lathbury, 24 November 1889, Liddon Papers.
26 *Pall Mall Gazette*, 26 May 1890, 4.
27 *C*, November 1890, 111-2.
28 *R*, 13 December 1889, 1215.
29 *C*, September 1890, 658-61; S. Leathes, '*Lux Mundi*', *Theological Monthly* (London), August 1890, 73-85.
30 *Rock*, 27 December 1889, 4.
31 *Rock*, 6 December 1889, 9-10.
32 *Rock*, 30 May 1890, 8-9.
33 *Rock*, 27 December 1889, 4.

34 *R*, 15 August 1890, 801, expressed regret that Gore's essay had not been published separately.
35 *R*, 21 March 1890, 277.
36 *R*, 18 April 1890, 373.
37 *R*, 16 January 1891, 50-1.
38 *R*, 6 June 1890, 562.
39 Chadwick, *Victorian Church*, ii, 102.
40 Ellicott was conservative, but not Evangelical, as indicated by *DNB Twentieth Century 1901-11*, 618-9.
41 J.C. Ryle, *Visitation Charges, Diocesan Addresses, and Special Sermons* (London, 1903), 18-21 (1890 Charge) and 17 (1893 Charge).
42 *R*, 12 September 1890, 897.
43 *CC*, 3-4 February 1891, 23, 70-71.
44 *R*, 15 January 1892, 75.
45 *T*, 18 December 1891, 5.
46 *R*, 24 December 1891, 1269.
47 *R*, 8 January 1892, 31-2; 15 January 1892, 75.
48 Although Lyttelton's essay was often quoted, e.g. by V.F. Storr in *The Problem of the Cross* (London, 1919), 57.
49 *R*, 10 January 1902, 22, 42; 9 May 1902, 455.
50 *R*, 26 October 1916, 841.
51 Campbell's career is described in Clements, *Lovers of Discord*, 25-28 and in R.J. Campbell, *A Spiritual Pilgrimage* (London, 1916).
52 Clements, *Lovers of Discord*, 29-34; Campbell, *Spiritual Pilgrimage*, chapter 7.
53 *Daily Mail*, 12 January 1907, 7.
54 Clements, *Lovers of Discord*, 33-43.
55 *R*, 16 November 1906, 1005; 18 January 1907, 42.
56 *R*, 25 January 1907, 82-3.
57 *R*, 22 March 1907, 246.
58 *R*, 15 February 1907, 135-6; 12 April 1907, 306; 22 March 1907, 242.
59 R.B. Girdlestone, 'Gnosticism: ancient and modern', *C*, May 1907, 264-73.
60 C. Gore, *The New Theology and the Old Religion* (London, 1907), 150-1.
61 Ibid., 151-5.
62 W.H. Griffith Thomas, 'The New Theology and Protestant orthodoxy', *C*, May 1907, 299-308.
63 *R*, 11 June 1909, 613-4.
64 G.L. Prestige, *The Life of Charles Gore* (London, 1935), 81-5.
65 *Contentio Veritatis, essays in constructive theology by six Oxford tutors* (London, 1902), 88. The other contributors were H. Rashdall, H.L. Wild, C.F. Burney, W.C. Allen and A.J. Carlyle.
66 *T*, 31 October 1902, 10; 17 November 1902, 10; R, 14 November 1902, 1096; 28 November 1902, 1135; 20 February 1903, 176; H.D.A. Major, *The Life and Letters of William Boyd Carpenter* (London, 1925), 50-58.

W.H. Draper (ed.), *Recollections of Dean Fremantle* (London, 1921) contains no reference to the controversy.

67 Bell, *Davidson*, i, 395-6; *R*, 27 February 1903, 218.

68 *R*, 5 December 1902, 1162.For Voysey, see *ODCC*, 1451.

69 *CC*, 13-14 May 1903, 106, 149; H.H. Henson, *Retrospect of an Unimportant Life* (London), i, (1942), 73-4.

70 *R*, 22 May 1903, 527.

71 Bell, *Davidson*, i, 397.

72 Prestige, *Gore*, 243-7; *C*, February 1904, 270-1; *R*, 18 December 1903, 1225; Henson, *Retrospect*, i, 78.

73 J.B. Harford and F.C. MacDonald, *H.C.G. Moule, Bishop of Durham: A Biography* (London, 1923), 293-4.

74 Henson, *Retrospect*, i, 80-2; *R*, 27 May 1904, 568; 20 May 1904, 537; *C*, May 1904, 441.

75 *R*, 19 August 1904, 845-6; 26 August 1904, 866.

76 *R*, 13 January 1905, 46.

77 *C*, June 1905, 489.

78 *R*, 19 May 1905, 485.

79 The resolutions of 1905 and 1908 are quoted in full in *CC*, 29 April 1914, 260.

80 Thompson's career is described in *DNB 1951-60*, 972-3 and in J.M.T.[hompson], *My Apologia* (Oxford, 1940).

81 Ibid., 85.

82 J.M. Thompson, *Miracles in the New Testament* (London, 1911), v.

83 Ibid., 160, 206.

84 *R*, 4 August 1911, 718.

85 *R*, 14 July 1911, 661.

86 H.H. Henson, *The Creed in the Pulpit* (London, 1912), xiii-v.

87 *R*, 21 July 1911, 676-7.

88 C, August 1911, 561.

89 H. Wace, *Some Questions of the Day: Biblical, National and Ecclesiastical* (London, 1912), 26.

90 J.A. Harriss, *The Place of Miracles in Christianity. Two Sermons* (Oxford, 1911); J.A. Harriss, 'Some considerations on the Revd J.M.Thompson's book, *Miracles in the New Testament*', *C*, January 1912, 9-16; February 1912, 100-07.

91 E. Digges La Touche, *The Person of Christ in Modern Thought* (London, 1912).

92 Ibid., 306.

93 *R*, 13 December 1912, 1201.

94 *Official Report of the Church Congress held at Middlesbrough* (London, 1912), 181-4, 199-200; H. Wace, *Some Questions of the Day; National, Ecclesiastical and Religious* (London, 1914), 266-9.

95 Wace, *Questions: Biblical*, 67-75.

96 *R*, 13 December 1912, 1201.

97 The background to *Foundations* is described by F.A. Iremonger in *William Temple, Archbishop of Canterbury. His Life and Letters* (London, 1948), chapter 9.
98 Clements, *Lovers of Discord*, 58.
99 *C*, February 1913, 87.
100 Ibid.; Wace, *Questions:National*, 257.
101 H. Maynard Smith, *Frank, Bishop of Zanzibar* (London, 1926), especially 145-6. For an Evangelical view of Kikuyu, see Eugene Stock, *History of the Church Missionary Society* (London), iv (1916), 409-24.
102 F. Weston, *Ecclesia Anglicana: For what does she stand?* (London, 1913), 28.
103 Ibid., 9, 10, 13.
104 Clements, *Lovers of Discord*, 63-4.
105 *T*, 29 December 1913, 3; C. Gore, *The Basis of Anglican Fellowship in Faith and Organisation* (London, 1914), 10-15.
106 *CC*, 29 April 1914, 258-95; 30 April 1914, 333-61, and Appendix for the petitions.
107 Wace, *Questions: National*, 59-62.
108 *C*, May 1914, 323-4; H.J.R. Marston, 'Dr Sanday's position and some of its effects on the Anglican Communion', *C*, July 1914, 501-08.
109 W.H. Griffith Thomas, 'Bishop Gore's open letter', *C*, July 1914, 487-500.
110 *CC*, 29 April 1914, 413-4.
111 Maynard Smith, *Frank, Bishop of Zanzibar*, 181.
112 *CC*, 29 April 1914, 288-90.
113 *C*, June 1914, 407.
114 The Henson controversy is described in Clements, *Lovers of Discord*, chapter 4; Bell, *Davidson*, chapter 53; Prestige, *Gore*, 394-402; O. Chadwick, *Hensley Henson: A Study in the Friction between Church and State* (Oxford, 1983); Henson, *Retrospect*, i. The Davidson MSS at Lambeth Palace include three volumes of letters, memoranda and press cuttings on this issue (volumes 380-82).
115 Davidson to Lloyd George, 28 November 1917, DP, 380.
116 *T*, 13 December 1917, 5.
117 *T*, 15 December 1917, 3.
118 *T*, 20 December 1917, 10.
119 Bell, *Davidson*, ii, 857; E.F. Braley, *Letters of Herbert Hensley Henson* (London, 1950), 15; Clements, *Lovers of Discord*, 80.
120 Henson, *Retrospect*, i, 233-4.
121 *T*, 18 January 1918, 8.
122 Henson, *Retrospect*, i, 257.
123 Ibid., 212.
124 Clements, *Lovers of Discord*, 78-80.
125 H.E. Ryle to Davidson, 18 January 1918, DP, 381.
126 Lillingston to Davidson, 18 January 1918, DP, 381.

127 Nickson to Davidson, 25 January 1918, DP, 380.
128 NCL circular, DP, 381.
129 Henson, *Retrospect*, i, 233.
130 *T*, 5 January 1918, 9.
131 Henson, *Retrospect*, i, 240.
132 Wace to Davidson, 9 January 1918, DP, 382.
133 Watts-Ditchfield to Davidson, 16 January 1918, DP, 380.
134 W.J. Nelson to Davidson, DP, 381.
135 Henson, *Retrospect*, i, 257.
136 *CC*, 2 May 1918, 373-6; 10 July 1918, 482-3. See also J.E. Watts-Ditchfield, *The Creed. Speech by the Bishop of Chelmsford* (London, 1918).
137 See Stephenson, *Modernism*, chapters 5 and 6; Clements, *Lovers of Discord*, 85-104.
138 Stephenson, *Modernism*, 110-13.
139 Clements, *Lovers of Discord*, 94.
140 *MC*, September 1921, 193-200.
141 Stephenson, *Modernism*, 129-36; Bell, *Davidson*, ii, 1139.
142 *MC*, October 1921, 349-70.
143 *R*, 18 August 1921, 533; *C*, October 1921, 231.
144 *R*, 1 September 1921, 568.
145 *R*, 29 September 1921, 618; 3 November 1921, 721.
146 *R*, 11 May 1922, 324.
147 W.A. Cunningham Craig, 'The Cheltenham conference', *MC*, October 1921, 373. The speakers were Glazebrook and Emmet.
148 Ibid., 377.
149 *MC*, March 1922, 616-9.
150 M.H. Fitzgerald, *A Memoir of Herbert Edward Ryle* (London, 1928), 130.
151 *C*, April 1926, 84 (unattributed quotation).
152 *R*, 14 July 1911, 661.
153 *Doctrine in the Church of England* (London, 1938), 19-20; Stephenson, *Modernism*, 137-8. The Commission did include the Liberal Evangelicals E.A. Burroughs, V.F. Storr and H.A. Wilson. Dean Matthews said that it represented all hues 'except the orange of Fundamentalist Protestantism': W.R. Matthews, *Memories and Meanings* (London, 1969), 144.
154 See, for example, Claude Welch, *Protestant Thought in the Nineteenth Century* (New Haven, 1972, 1985).
155 M. Rumscheidt (ed.), *Adolf von Harnack* (London, 1989), 9-33; *ODCC*, 629; W.H.C. Frend, 'Adolf von Harnack (1851-1930)', *JEH* 52 (Cambridge, 2001), 83-102.
156 Welch, *Protestant Thought*, ii, 146-50; A. Harnack, *What is Christianity?* (London, 1901), citing the second edition, 204, 261, 281, 321, 55, 33, 135; Horton Davies, *Worship and Theology in England 1900-65* (Princeton, 1965), 124-5; S. Neill, *The Interpretation of the New Testament, 1861-1961* (Oxford, 1964), citing 1966 edition, 130-5.

157 Neill, *Interpretation*, 131.
158 B.R.V. Mills, 'What is Christianity?', *C*, April 1906, 227-35; May 1906, 303-10; June 1906, 340-8; July 1906, 403-12; August 1906, 472-80.
159 S.N. Rostron, *The Christology of St Paul* (London, 1912), 209-11.
160 Digges La Touche, *Person of Christ*, 134-8.
161 T.J. Pulvertaft, 'Professor Harnack on foreign missions', *C*, November 1905, 749-54; A.R. Whately, 'Dogmatic theology', " in C.H.H. Wright and C. Neil (eds), *A Protestant Dictionary* (London, 1904), 179-81.
162 *ODCC*, 926-7.
163 *R*, 30 July 1909, 794; 6 August 1909, 809; 13 August 1909, 839; 20 August 1909, 859; *C*, September 1906, 573.
164 *R*, 24 April 1908, 356.
165 *C*, December 1907, 706 (Tyrrell); April 1908, 201 (Loisy); July 1908, 409 (*Lamentabili*).
166 Welch, *Protestant Thought*, ii, 161-3; *ODCC*, 1248-9 (Schweitzer), 1464-5 (Weiss). N.T. Wright, *Jesus and the Victory of God* (London, 1996), 16-21, sets Weiss and Schweitzer in theological context.
167 Lloyd, *Church of England*, 86-7;
168 Iremonger, *William Temple*, 163.
169 *R*, 8 July 1910, 669; *C*, October 1910, 727.
170 J.R. Darbyshire, 'Present-day ideas and the hope of immortality', *C*, January 1911, 52-60; Rostron, *Christology of St Paul*, 213; Digges La Touche, *Person of Christ*, 172-208.
171 E.C. Dewick, *Primitive Christian Eschatology* (Cambridge, 1912), 131-5.
172 Ibid., 150, 230-1.
173 On the Liberal Evangelicals, see A. Eric Smith, *Another Anglican Angle. The History of the AEGM* (Oxford, 1991) and Ian M. Randall, *Evangelical Experiences. A Study in the Spirituality of English Evangelicalism 1918-1939* (Carlisle, 1999), chapter 3.
174 *R*, 31 May 1923, 353.
175 Their theological development may be seen in E.J.W. Barnes, *Ahead of his Age: Bishop Barnes of Birmingham* (London, 1979) and A. Dunstan and J.S. Peart-Binns, *Cornish Bishop* (London, 1977).
176 Notice a criticism of Storr's views in F.S.G. Warman, *The Evangelical Movement: Its Message and Its Achievements* (London, 1916), 20.
177 I. Siviter, 'The incarnation', in J.R. Howden (ed.), *Evangelicalism by Members of the FEC* (London, 1925), 27.
178 V.F. Storr, 'The person of Jesus Christ', in T. Guy Rogers (ed.), *Liberal Evangelicalism* (London, 1923), 113-7, 118-9.
179 E.W. Barnes, 'The rise and growth of man's spiritual consciousness', in T. Guy Rogers (ed.), *The Inner Life* (London, 1925), 35.
180 V.F. Storr, *My Faith* (London, 1927), v, 56, 58-63.
181 V.F. Storr, *Freedom and Tradition* (London, 1940), 111. Compare the evangelistic zeal of E.A. Burroughs, in H.G. Mulliner, *Arthur Burroughs, A Memoir* (London, 1936), 6.

182 V.F. Storr, *The Problem of the Cross* (London, 1919), 128-37; 'X', 'Liberal Evangelicalism: what it is and what it stands for, ' *C*, March 1915, 193-200.
183 M. Hennell, 'Evangelicalism and worldliness, 1770-1870', *SCH* 8 (1972), 229-36; J.H.S. Kent, *Holding the Fort* (London, 1978), chapter 5; G.W.E. Russell, *The Household of Faith* (London, 1902), 231-45.
184 H.A. Wilson, 'The development of Evangelicalism', in Rogers, *Liberal Evangelicalism*, 26-7.
185 Barnes, *Ahead of his Age*, 87; E.S. Woods, *Modern Discipleship and what it means* (London, 1910), chapter 10.
186 V.F. Storr, *The Development of English Theology in the Nineteenth Century, 1800-60* (London, 1913), 11-16.
187 Ibid., 2.
188 V.F. Storr, *Development and Divine Purpose* (London, 1906), 8; Storr, *Freedom and Tradition*, 98.
189 E.A. Burroughs, 'Evangelicalism and personality', in Rogers, *Liberal Evangelicalism*, 71-2.
190 Storr, *Freedom and Tradition*, 168, xiii.
191 Storr, *My Faith*, 49-50.
192 H.C.G. Moule, *Outlines of Christian Doctrine* (London, 1889), 70-87; E.A. Litton, *Introduction to Dogmatic Theology* (London, 1882, 1892), citing 1912 edition, section 55; J.C. Ryle, *The Upper Room* (London, 1888), 98; *Protestantism in Answer to Anglo-Catholicism, Romanism and Modernism* (London, 1922), 9; N. Dimock, 'The death of Christ', *C*, January 1890, 203-11; February 1890, 250-64; March 1890, 305-15; April 1890, 368-79; May 1890, 425-31; June 1890, 473-88; *R*, 19 January 1906, 71.
193 *R*, 21 January 1915, 81.
194 See the Minute Book of the Liverpool Six, AEGM Papers, University of Hull, DEM 1/14.
195 R.T. Howard, 'The work of Christ', in Rogers, *Liberal Evangelicalism*, 121-44; *R*, 5 April 1923, 217.
196 Storr, *My Faith*, 33-5.
197 Storr, *Problem of the Cross*, especially chapter 8.
198 H.A. Wilson, 'The need for Evangelical unity', *C*, April 1925, 95; H.A. Wilson, 'The atonement', *C*, July 1925, 208-14.
199 *R*, 11 July 1918, 434.
200 *R*, 25 July 1918, 464; 1 August 1918, 478; 8 August 1918, 493; J.T. Inskip, 'The present phase in the movement for evangelisation', *C*, April 1919, 181-8.
201 On millennialism generally, see E.R. Sandeen, *The Roots of Fundamentalism* (Chicago, 1970), which, although unreliable in its interpretation of attitudes, shows clearly how strong interest in the Second Advent was in the nineteenth century. For particular individuals, see E.R. Garratt, *Life and Personal Recollections of Samuel Garratt* (London, 1908), 23, 49, 50, and J. Silvester, *A Champion of the Faith; A*

Memoir of the Revd C.H.H. Wright (London, 1917), 150, 177, 190-1, 212-3. Elliott-Binns' comment appears in *English Thought 1860-1900; The Theological Aspect* (London, 1956), 189. D.W. Bebbington, *Evangelicalism in Modern Britain. A History from the 1730s to the 1980s* (London, 1989), 191-4, maps the diverging Evangelical positions in this period.

202 Garratt, *Samuel Garratt*, chapter 7; *R*, 5 January 1912, 22. Edward Hoare's *Rome, Turkey and Jerusalem* (London, 1876) was reissued in 1913.

203 *R*, 30 March 1916, 274; 20 December 1917, 880.

204 Moule, *Outlines*, 107; Harford and MacDonald, *H.C.G. Moule*, 296; *R*, 18 January 1901, 98-9; 14 November 1913, 1046; C.H. Titterton and C. Neill, *Scriptural Evangelicalism* (London, 1925), 140.

205 *R*, 8 November 1917, 750; recollections of Revd W. Stott.

206 V.F. Storr, *Christianity and Immortality* (London, 1918), 148-50.

207 E.S. Woods, *What is this Christianity?* (London, 1934), citing second edition (1947), 120.

208 *R*, 3 March 1921, 149; 3 July 1931, 441. I owe this reference to Bebbington, *Evangelicalism*, 191.

209 Braley, *Letters of H.H. Henson*, 125.

210 Stephenson, *Modernism*, 124, 19, 262-71; Barnes, *Ahead of his Age*, 133.

211 C. Raven, *A Wanderer's Way* (London, 1928), 147-9; F.W. Dillistone, *Charles Raven* (London, 1975).

212 E.A. Knox, *On What Authority?* (London, 1922), 223.

213 Storr, *Freedom and Tradition*, 112.

CHAPTER 7

Evangelicals Divided, 1890-1928

'Can two walk together, except they be agreed?'
(Amos 3:3)

The preceding chapters have explored the diversity of Evangelical Churchmanship in response to the challenges of ritualism, higher criticism, evolutionary biology and theological liberalism. This diversity placed considerable strain on the unity of the Evangelical school, and during the first three decades of the twentieth century differences of opinion found expression in conflicts within Evangelical institutions. This chapter seeks to illustrate the tensions of the period by examining four examples of Evangelical division. The first two are institutional: the secession of conservative Evangelicals from the Student Christian Movement and the Church Missionary Society, leading to the formation of the Inter-Varsity Fellowship and the Bible Churchmen's Missionary Society respectively. The third describes the development of two partisan bodies, the liberal Group Brotherhood (later the Anglican Evangelical Group Movement) and the conservative Fellowship of Evangelical Churchmen. Finally, an attempt is made to set out the different reactions shown by Evangelicals to the proposals for Prayer Book revision, culminating in the parliamentary debates of 1927-8. In this way, this chapter serves as an introduction to the fuller consideration of Evangelical diversity which concludes the present work.

The Parting of the Ways: The SCM and the IVF

Controversy within Evangelicalism was usually acrimonious and nowhere has the bitterness endured longer than in the sphere of student Christianity. Conservative evangelicals are still told the cautionary tale of the fall of the SCM from doctrinal purity into Modernist error and the weight of history still controls the response of Christian Unions to invitations to co-operate in mission with non-evangelical groups.[1] As a result of this lasting antagonism, the histories of the SCM and the IVF are less than fully impartial. *The Story of the Student Christian Movement* (1933) was written by the SCM's secretary, Tissington Tatlow, and it portrays conservative evangelicals as ignorant obscurantists, whereas Douglas Johnson's *Contending for the Faith* (1979) sets out the case for the IVF in similarly trenchant terms. Tatlow and Johnson, antagonists in the 1920s, continued their mutual hostility in print, abetted by local histories like O.R. Barclay's *Whatever happened to the Jesus Lane lot?* (1977) and J.S. Reynolds' *Born Anew* (1979). An attempt will be made here to go behind the façade of hagiography and denigration and to explain why a rift developed within the student movement in the early twentieth century.[2]

The origins of the SCM are themselves a subject of controversy. The conservatives have always been keen to emphasize that the movement was firmly evangelical at first, while Tatlow was equally anxious to demonstrate that breadth and inclusiveness were hallmarks of the SCM from the beginning.[3] It would seem that Tatlow read the situation of the 1910s back into the 1890s, for the impetus behind student Christian work came almost entirely from Evangelical sources. The forerunner of the Cambridge Inter-Collegiate Christian Union (CICCU), founded in 1877, was a prayer meeting initiated in the late 1840s by A.A. Isaacs, an unflinching Evangelical. The CICCU itself was established after a mission to undergraduates conducted by another Evangelical clergyman, Sholto Douglas.[4] Oxford followed suit in 1879, due to the enthusiasm of F.S. Webster, later curate to A.M.W. Christopher at St. Aldate's.[5] Webster's colleagues as founder-members of the OICCU included G.A. King, the first president, A.R. Buckland, later editor of the *Record*, D.J. Stather Hunt and W. Talbot Rice, all of whom were prominent Anglican Evangelicals in later life.[6] In the next decade student Christian work was encouraged by Moody and Sankey's mission to Cambridge (1882) and by the offer of the 'Cambridge Seven' to serve abroad with the China Inland Mission (1884).[7] Support was provided by H.C.G. Moule at Cambridge and by A.M.W. Christopher and F.J. Chavasse at Oxford.

The next stage in the creation of the student movement came in 1891, when R.P. Wilder, the founder of the American Student Volunteer Band, visited England. Wilder was a protegé of

Moody and arrived in London with letters of introduction to Eugene Stock and H.W. Webb-Peploe. He went on to address the Missionary Meeting at the Keswick Convention, where the CICCU leaders heard him speak and invited him to Cambridge. In 1892 they established the Student Volunteer Missionary Union and it was the SVMU summer conference at Keswick in 1893 which decided to set up Christian unions in the new universities and university colleges, thus giving rise to the Inter-University Christian Union, which became the British Colleges Christian Union in 1895 and the SCM ten years later.[8]

Within fifteen years a flourishing organisation had been formed. Local Christian unions were established and supported by the regular visits of salaried travelling secretaries. As well as the annual summer conferences, the SVMU held quadrennial missionary conferences from 1896 onwards, and the movement had both a regular magazine and a publications department for missionary textbooks.

Three important features of the SCM in its first decade should be noted. First, as has already been seen, its roots were almost entirely evangelical, drawing on the Evangelical traditions of the CICCU, on Keswick and on the American revivalism of Moody, Wilder and the Northfield Student Summer School. In his account of the later history of the SCM Tatlow acknowledged that the movement was initially seen as narrowly evangelical, a fact reflected in the lists of conference speakers and 'senior friends' who advised the student leadership.[9]

The SCM was, secondly, an interdenominational body, as were its component Christian unions. Thus, for example, the first executive committee of the SVMU, appointed in 1892, included the Presbyterian J.H. Maclean, and the 1893 summer conference was estimated to have an attendance of 40% Anglicans, 30% Scottish Presbyterians and 30% Free Churchmen.[10] It was the Presbyterian and Free Church element which went some way to justify Tatlow's claim that the SCM was never exclusively evangelical, for some of the Scots and the Nonconformists were more favourable to biblical criticism than were Evangelical Churchmen.

The third important point was the missionary zeal of the student movement. Membership of the SVMU involved signing a declaration stating that 'I am willing and desirous, God permitting, to become a foreign missionary.' In 1896 the first missionary conference adopted as the SVMU watchword 'The evangelisation of the world in this generation.'[11] The influence of the Watchword on the student movement and its early leadership should not be underestimated. G.T. Manley recalled, 'That watchword was in our hearts, and moved and shaped our lives,' and Douglas Thornton, hailed by Tatlow as 'the greatest prophet the student movement has ever had,' spoke in the same terms of 'this glorious watchword which has become our own, and now dominates our lives.'[12] The SVMU was born at a time of great optimism about missions, a time when the CMS was expanding its work rapidly and when missionary statesmen like John Mott spoke of the present age as 'the hour of setting sun' in which commitment to world evangelism could hasten the Second Advent. Christianity seemed to be in the ascendant and there was a constant call for new recruits, so that Handley Moule had to exert all his influence to keep some Ridley Hall ordinands for work at home.[13] In this atmosphere it may be seen how easy it was for the SCM to adopt a more inclusive policy in the interests of more effective recruitment. The pressing needs of the mission field could make domestic doctrinal differences seem comparatively unimportant.

From the late 1890s, therefore, the SCM made a vigorous attempt to broaden its appeal to the Church of England beyond the confines of the Evangelical school. Thornton and Temple Gairdner secured a letter from Bishop Creighton in December 1898 confirming that Anglican ordinands could join the movement without risk of compromising their churchmanship through association with Nonconformists.[14] The summer conference moved away from Keswick, with its undenominational and panevangelical connections,[15] and in 1899 a round table meeting took place between a delegation of student leaders and members of the SPG's Junior Clergy Missionary Association. As a result of this, the SPG sent representatives to the SVMU London Conference of 1900, at which Creighton was one speaker.[16] Contacts made through the SPG enabled the SCM to approach Anglican theological colleges and to secure High Church support for the summer conferences.[17] The 1906 conference was commended by J.O.F. Murray, dean of Emmanuel, Cambridge, and the speakers included Canons C.F.G. Masterman and C.H. Robinson of the SPG. Scott Holland addressed the conference of 1907, while Winnington-Ingram and Gore appeared in 1909 and

1910 respectively.[18] By 1908 W.H. Frere had endorsed the SCM and Herbert Kelly had affiliated the House of the Sacred Mission at Kelham to the movement.[19] Between about 1900 and 1910, therefore, the SCM made a very successful approach to the High Anglicans, bringing Kelham, Cuddesdon and other colleges into association with the movement and substantially broadening the platform of summer conference speakers. When Tatlow delivered a paper to the Manchester Church Congress of 1908 on 'The Student Volunteer Missionary Movement' Churchmen as diverse as Canon Kempthorne, Bishop E.S. Talbot and Bishop Ingham of the CMS praised the work of the SCM.[20]

As the SCM extended its appeal to include High Churchmen, so it also began to take a greater interest in theology and biblical criticism. This was due partly to a desire to be as inclusive as possible, partly to the sympathy for critical studies displayed by Nonconformists and by many ordinands in the 1890s and partly also to a growing awareness of the need for effective apologetics in evangelism among students at home. From 1905 the movement began to produce text books for study groups addressing questions of higher criticism and of the relationship between science and religion.[21] These books reflected the broadening outlook of the SCM leadership and were sympathetic to critical scholarship and to Darwinism. Thus a memorandum on a projected series of books on the Old Testament, planned in 1911 under the direction of E.S. Woods, stated that the scope of the works 'will necessitate the adoption of the modern critical position, at least in outline.'[22]

In the first decade of the twentieth century, therefore, the SCM developed in significant ways. It won the support of High Churchmen and was able to add Anglo-Catholics to its conference platform and to its secretariat. It sought to grapple with the intellectual problems facing Christianity and took a positive view of modern biblical studies. The social implications of the faith were raised at the Matlock conference of 1900 and the SCM began to adopt an understanding of the kingdom of God akin to that of the Liberal Evangelicals.[23] As the movement grew, so it became anxious to welcome enquirers in the hope that they would become committed Christians through membership of the SCM, rather than vice-versa. To this end, there was a readiness to relax doctrinal tests. All these broadening tendencies continued and accelerated through the 1910s and 1920s.[24]

While Tatlow, Edward Woods and other leaders welcomed these developments and watched the SCM become a powerful interdenominational movement, others observed the changes with mounting disquiet. Lord Kinnaird complained when the SVMU invited 'a ritualist like the bishop of London' to address the 1900 conference, while H.W. Webb-Peploe was horrified to find himself sharing the platform at Conishead in 1907 with higher critics.[25] Others regretted the move from devotional Bible study aids to text books endorsing higher criticism, a regret dismissed by Tatlow as the product of a desire 'to eliminate the intellectual grind in Bible study and substitute for it the finding of "best thoughts" and emotional appeal.'[26] A correspondent signing himself 'Puzzled' drew attention to the High Church predominance at SCM meetings in letters to the *Record* in February 1909, while later in the same year, 'A Friend of Students' claimed that 'students, not a few, are complaining that the text books are full of Harnack teaching, and that the Bible Circles are too much occupied with discussions which tend to lower one's reverence for the old Book.'[27] By this time, conflict between the SCM leadership and the conservative evangelicals was moving towards an open breach, and the centre of the controversy was the position of the CICCU.

Both sides in the controversy agreed that the CICCU did not follow the policy of the SCM in welcoming Anglo-Catholics and endorsing higher criticism. Tatlow wrote scornfully of 'the CICCU type' of Christian as one who was 'keen and sentimental', wedded to 'the theology of a day which had passed',[28] while for its part, the CICCU held aloof from the changes in the SCM in the early 1900s. The problem was that the CICCU was the Cambridge branch of the SCM and so the national leadership wanted it to reflect the policy of the movement as a whole. This problem was exacerbated by the presence of students and dons in Cambridge who were involved with the SCM, but who were not prepared to join the CICCU. This group, led by C.F. Angus of Trinity Hall, urged Tatlow either to broaden the CICCU or else to allow them to establish a separate SCM branch including High Churchmen, Nonconformists and Liberal Evangelicals. From 1907 the former policy was pursued, but without success since the CICCU resisted Tatlow's pressure. Early in 1910 a final attempt was made to change the outlook of the CICCU, but its General Committee voted instead to disaffiliate from the SCM.[29] A year later the CICCU also broke its connection with the SVMU.[30]

By 1910 enthusiasm for compromise had dwindled to a few Liberal Evangelicals within the CICCU. Tatlow had little sympathy for the CICCU attitude and before his visit to the General Committee in February 1910 he had been warned by R.L. Pelly that he had 'the quite hopeless task of unconvincing the convinced.' On the other hand, the conservative student leadership, G.F.B. Morris and H.W.K. Mowll, was quite content to disaffiliate from a movement which was seen as 'the opponent.'[31]

O.R. Barclay suggests that Tatlow believed that the CICCU would not survive, particularly in competition with a vigorous SCM group in Cambridge.[32] In fact the CICCU maintained its position until 1914 and in the aftermath of the First World War extended the influence of conservative evangelicalism to London and Oxford through an annual Inter-Varsity Conference. The Oxford University Bible Union and the London Inter-Faculty Christian Union were formed and evangelical unions were gradually established in other universities. The first full-time travelling secretary was appointed in 1925 and in 1928 the Inter-Varsity Fellowship of Evangelical Christian Unions (IVF) was created as a national federation of the new groups. Far from withering away, conservative evangelicalism had repeated the pattern of the rise of the SCM, although the IVF took steps to avoid any broadening of its platform by creating a firmly evangelical basis of faith to be subscribed by all officeholders.[33]

True to its policy of inclusiveness, the SCM made a number of attempts to absorb the conservative groups, so that the history of the evangelical unions is a bewildering story of negotiation, amalgamation and secession. The Bible Union at Oxford became a devotional wing of the SCM for a few years in the 1920s before the conservatives broke away again in 1927-8.[34] The CICCU refused a similar arrangement in 1919, although it did co-operate in the University Missions of 1920 and 1926.[35] Pressure was also exerted by the SCM on the London groups, leading to a confrontation between Tatlow and the LIFCU leaders.[36] Given Tatlow's increasing impatience with conservative evangelicalism, the real doctrinal differences between the IVF and the SCM on biblical inspiration, the Second Advent and the atonement, and the legacy of conservative suspicion and distrust of the SCM, it was hardly surprising that lasting co-operation proved elusive.[37] The two movements maintained their separate existence and their mutual hostility.

It may be asked how Evangelical Churchmen responded to the disputes within the SCM and to the creation of the IVF. Many Evangelicals continued to be enthusiastic supporters of the older movement, not least because of its role in providing missionary volunteers. The *Record* regularly carried articles commending the SCM's annual day of prayer and the movement received a glowing tribute in the CMS's *Church Missionary Review* in 1917.[38] As Tatlow noted, Eugene Stock played an important part in reassuring Evangelical Churchmen that the SCM was still orthodox despite its internal problems.[39] Liberal Evangelicals like E.S. Woods and R.L. Pelly were heavily involved in the movement in an official capacity and naturally supported the SCM against the CICCU. Indeed, some CICCU members felt that the Evangelical establishment in Cambridge was unnecessarily hostile to their cause and H.W.K. Mowll, while a student at Ridley Hall, rebuked Principal Tait for this.[40] With Tait at Ridley and Edward Woods at Holy Trinity after the First World War, there was little sympathy for the CICCU among the senior Evangelicals in the town and the university.

On the other hand, some Evangelical Churchmen did share the conservative suspicions of SCM inclusiveness. Tatlow attributed the CICCU's persistent conservatism to the continuing influence of old members, and certainly H.E. Fox was one Cambridge man who felt strongly enough about the impact of biblical criticism in the university to draw it to the attention of the ultra-conservative Bible League early in 1911. The League had already been active in Oxford and Cambridge for some years, sponsoring conferences in 1902-3.[41] Fox also wrote an appreciative review of the CICCU's account of the 1910 controversy, *Old Paths in Perilous Times*, for the *Record*.[42] The IVF conference of 1922 had at least two Evangelical Churchmen, W. Talbot Rice and H. Earnshaw Smith, among the speakers, and the Advisory Committee ten years later included Stuart Holden, Earnshaw Smith and J. Russell Howden. Bishop Taylor Smith was the IVF president in 1931-2 and Sir Thomas Inskip was one of the vice-presidents.[43]

Involvement in the IVF, however, did not imply automatic hostility to the SCM. Harrington Lees was a vice-president of the CICCU, but he wrote to the Evangelical press in 1913 repudiating conservative attacks on the SCM.[44] He wrote to Tatlow in the same vein, enclosing a donation to the student movement.[45] Stuart Holden took a similar position, combining involvement with the IVF with sympathy towards the SCM. In a letter of January 1912 he told Tatlow: 'I am entirely in accord with what you say as to their [CICCU's] need of wise guidance, and it is solely on this account that I am trying to hold on to them.'[46] Significantly, the CICCU did not wholly trust Stuart Holden and regarded his absence from the mission of 1926 as providential.[47]

Within the student world the SCM-IVF division was not absolute. Even in the 1920s Evangelicals like Max Warren could belong to both movements, although it was recognised that this was becoming increasingly difficult.[48] It would be fair to say that by this time the SCM was no longer regarded as an evangelical organisation, so that Evangelicals who supported it did so in full recognition of its inclusiveness and could therefore justify supporting the IVF too as a distinctively evangelical body. Liberal and moderate Evangelicals continued to work with the SCM or with both SCM and IVF, and it was only the staunchest conservatives who adhered solely to the newer organisation.

Schism in the CMS[49]

The Church Missionary Society was the acknowledged heart of the Evangelical school and support for the CMS has been used as one test for identifying Evangelical Churchmen.[50] Commenting on the May Meetings in June 1912, the *Churchman* affirmed 'In many ways the CMS is, for good or ill – we believe wholly for good – the visible centre of Evangelicalism... Sometimes we differ a little amongst ourselves – sometimes we are apt to feel that our differences are greater than in reality they are. But in the atmosphere of the CMS, with the Divine call sounding in our ears, and the appalling need of heathenism before our eyes, our unity becomes closer and more real than any external bonds can make it.'[51] Scarcely five years later the same periodical noted sadly that the CMS had become 'the stormcentre in the struggle between the representatives of the Older and the Newer Order among Evangelicals;'[52] by the end of 1922 a strong body of conservative Evangelicals had left the CMS and formed the Bible Churchmen's Missionary Society. It may be asked how this situation arose.

The CMS was no stranger to controversy. Given the position occupied by the Society within Evangelicalism, it was hardly surprising that differences of opinion on many subjects should find expression in the committee room at Salisbury Square, especially since under the CMS constitution, all clerical subscribers of a guinea or more were automatically members of the General Committee. Thus in the late nineteenth century there was a series of major disputes in the CMS: over relations with Bishop Copleston of Colombo in the early 1880s; over support for colonial bishoprics; and, most seriously, over a service held in St Paul's Cathedral in 1888 shortly after the unveiling of a controversial new reredos. In the latter case a circular criticising the CMS was sent to the press by a group of ultra-Protestant Evangelicals and there were rumours of an impending secession or the formation of a new Protestant missionary society.[53]

As well as these disputes, there were regular complaints about aspects of CMS policy, mostly from Protestants who feared that the CMS was working too closely with the SPG. By the early twentieth century many Evangelicals regarded the SPG as tainted with sacerdotalism – Canon Christopher, for example, was opposing joint missionary meetings with the SPG by 1904 for this reason[54] – and some were afraid that the contagion might spread to the CMS. Suspicion was heightened by the creation of diocesan Boards of Mission, which brought CMS and SPG speakers together and fed persistent rumours of an impending amalgamation of the two societies. A long correspondence on this subject appeared in the *Record* in 1902, provoked by a leading article in the *English Churchman* and including a strong attack by C.T. Porter on Eugene Stock's 'policy of "friendly relations" with sacerdotal missions.'[55] The issue arose again in 1903, with more vitriolic letters from Dr Porter and some more temperate warnings about the risks of co-operation with the SPG from G.T. Manley.[56] In December 1903 the General Committee approved a memorandum on joint meetings which affirmed a policy of co-operation with diocesan Boards but of avoiding other joint activities.[57] The SPG-CMS merger rumour reappeared in 1913,[58] while in 1915 a Joint Convention with the SPG seriously alarmed the *Record* and Bishop Ingham, as well as the ultra-Protestants, and provoked angry complaints to Salisbury Square.[59] The perceived menace of sacerdotalism, therefore, was a constant source of anxiety to some CMS supporters, even when the fervent Protestant H.E. Fox was honorary secretary.[60] It is interesting to note that some Evangelicals saw the main threat of the Liberal Evangelicals' West Ham memorial of 1917 to be its appeal for toleration of the eastward position – Stanton Jones wrote to Cyril Bardsley, Fox's successor as honorary secretary, that Bishop Knox thought this would 'create a tremendous cleavage.'[61]

Until the late 1910s biblical criticism was not a source of controversy within the CMS constituency. The spread of higher criticism and its effect in the mission field were certainly matters of concern to Evangelicals – witness the activities of the Bible League[62] and the publication of Fox's *Rationalism or the Gospel? with special reference to their relative influence on Christian missions* (1912) – but there was little suggestion that the CMS was anything other than soundly conservative. Indeed, when a series of pamphlets *'Bible Sceptics and "SPG"':A Correspondence* appeared in 1904, complaining of the SPG's endorsement of critical opinions, the *Church of England League Gazette* commented, somewhat smugly, 'it may be observed that no such questions have so far brought even a ripple to the surface of the other great Missionary Society of the Church.'[63]

The calm surface of the CMS, however, was violently disturbed in 1917 when a memorial was sent to the General Committee by an influential group headed by six bishops (including Watts-Ditchfield, Theodore Woods and Denton Thompson) and sixty eight other Evangelicals, mostly younger members of the school, like Guy Rogers, Arthur Burroughs, J.G. McCormick, Edward Woods and Guy Warman. The memorial called on the Society to demonstrate its comprehensiveness by welcoming a variety of spiritualities, working more closely with other Anglican missionary societies and repudiating any attempts to impose definitions of biblical inspiration beyond those laid down by the formularies of the Church of England.[64] The memorial represented the outlook of the Liberal Evangelicals and was produced by a group meeting at Guy Rogers' vicarage at West Ham.

When Archbishop Davidson heard of the liberal memorial he predicted 'This document will split the Society asunder.'[65] H.E. Fox had secured a copy of it before the Committee meeting and dispatched it to the Matlock Bath Clerical Society, a body of ultra-conservatives, which delegated D.H.C. Bartlett to organise a counter memorial.[66] Bartlett collected nearly one thousand signatures to a statement deploring doctrinal laxity in the CMS and attacking the eastward position for its allegedly sacerdotal implications. When the General Committee met on 11 December it was faced by three memorials: the West Ham document, presented by Watts-Ditchfield, Bartlett's conservative reply and an appeal for avoidance of controversy signed by a group of influential laymen including T.W.H. Inskip, Joynson-Hicks and the CMS treasurer S.H. Gladstone.[67] According to Watts-Ditchfield, the meeting was tense and acrimonious. The Church Association had sent out a whip and Bishop Knox made 'a great Protestant debating speech.'[68] It was eventually resolved to submit the memorials to a sub-committee nominated equally by Knox, Watts-Ditchfield and the CMS Patronage Committee, under the chairmanship of F.J. Chavasse. This committee met in January 1918 and produced a report, subsequently referred to as the 'Concordat', which was accepted by all the members and endorsed with great rejoicing by the General Committee early in February.[69] The Concordat affirmed that the CMS was loyal to the traditional Protestant practice of celebrating Holy Communion from the north side of the table, although courtesy might encourage a CMS delegation to take the eastward position when visiting another church; that the Bible was to be regarded as inspired and that Christ's attitude to Scripture should be authoritative. The committee also called for greater attention to the recruitment of students and noted that the young could not be expected to meet standards of doctrinal knowledge appropriate only to the more mature.[70]

It may be seen that the Concordat was ambiguous on several vital points, especially those concerning biblical inspiration. For the next few years, therefore, desperate attempts were made to defend it against criticism from all sides. E.N. Coulthard complained to Cyril Bardsley that it suggested that Evangelicals like himself who took the eastward position were no longer welcome in the CMS,[71] while Bartlett had to reply to a Liverpool protest, signed by over two hundred clergymen, denouncing the Concordat's 'vagueness and ambiguity' on the issues at stake, particularly with respect to the eastward position and the concessions to modern thought.[72] For the liberals, the *Challenge* called the Concordat disappointing, thereby provoking Rogers, Edward Woods and R.L. Pelly to defend it for giving the liberals all they wanted. This defence, of course, did not endear the Concordat to the conservatives.[73]

A series of events after 1918 placed increasing strain on the fragile compromise achieved by the Concordat. Towards the end of 1919 the Revd E.W.L. Martin, a CMS missionary, preached a series of sermons in Hong Kong entitled 'New Light on the Old Testament'. According to the conservatives, these sermons fully endorsed the most extreme conclusions of modern biblical criticism, dismissing Genesis 1-11 as Babylonian myths and likening the translation of Elijah to that of the Taoist sage Ke Hung. The sermons were widely reported and caused considerable disquiet among the conservatives. At the same time it became known that some CMS students in Japan were attending an institution whose staff included Father Kelly and this also provoked complaints to the CMS secretariat. Pressure from conservative missionaries was given added impetus in 1921 when the Bible Union of China was formed and a vigorous campaign began to regulate the orthodoxy of missionary candidates. At home, moreover, the Llandudno summer school of 1921 fuelled the controversy, because one of the speakers, Hume Campbell, criticised conservative views on the Old Testament.[74]

As early as April 1921 Fox was pressing for more action against the liberals. At the end of that year Bartlett and the FEC agreed to move resolutions designed to clarify the position of the CMS and to prevent what they regarded as liberal abuses of the Concordat.[75] In March 1922, therefore, Bartlett moved that 'Whereas the authority of Holy Scripture as the Word of God necessarily involves the trustworthiness of its historical records and the validity of its teachings; and whereas Holy Scripture claims this authority for itself, and our Lord, whose utterances are true, endorses this claim; we, the committee of the CMS, ... hereby undertake neither to send out as missionaries nor to appoint as teachers or responsible officials any who do not thus wholeheartedly believe and teach.'[76] Dean Wace secured the postponement of Bartlett's resolution until July and an attempt was made to reach a compromise at a conference convened by Watts-Ditchfield at Coleshill, Birmingham, in June.[77] Although that conference produced an agreed statement, hailed by the *Record* as a great achievement,[78] Bartlett and the conservatives were not wholly satisfied. The General Committee declined Bartlett's resolution, preferring an amendment by Knox and

Chavasse which, although conservative, did not meet the demands of the FEC on what they regarded as the crucial issues of the truth of biblical history and the Christological case for infallibility.[79] As a result of this, while another sub-committee laboured to produce a new formula to satisfy all sides, Wace resigned from the CMS[80] and the FEC set in train the formation of a new society. The Bible Churchmen's Missionary Society was duly established in October 1922 and although Wace withdrew his resignation after the November General Committee amended the July resolutions, a body of conservatives persisted in their plan to leave the CMS.[81]

It is important to recognise that the schism in the CMS did not result in a wholesale abandonment of the older society by conservative Evangelicals. The formation of the BCMS was a source of continuing controversy within the conservative ranks, and even within the FEC. Although H.E. Fox left the CMS, Wace, Ingham, Chavasse and Webb-Peploe remained in it, as did younger conservatives like G.T. Manley. FEC members like H.C. Tiarks wrote to the *Record* deploring the secession[82] and in February 1923 an influential letter appeared over the signatures of E.L. Langston, H.M. Foyl and W. Talbot Hindley, entitled 'Why we stand by the CMS'.[83] Foyl, who had seconded Bartlett's resolution in March 1922, wrote again later in the following year to point out that the FEC and the BCMS were not coterminous and that the honorary secretary and treasurer of the Birmingham CMS Auxiliary were FEC members.[84] Many conservatives were satisfied with the 1922 resolutions and regarded Bartlett's objections as ill-founded. The Evangelical rank and file felt that they could trust an organisation commended by Knox, Chavasse, Wace, Webb-Peploe, Taylor Smith and other well known leaders of the traditional section of the party. Others agreed with Lieutenant Colonel Seton Churchill that the bulk of the missionaries were sound and that it was folly to abandon them to the semi-modernists in the home secretariat.[85] As Albert Mitchell pointed out, moreover, at a time of crisis in the ritual controversy, Evangelical Churchmen could not afford to fight among themselves.[86] Finally, the spiritual and moral priority of mission helped to persuade many Evangelicals to refrain from any steps which might cripple the CMS, especially since the Society was already under great financial pressure. Appeals from colonial bishops and missionaries, endorsed by editorials in the *Record*, urged

Evangelicals not to desert the CMS and painted a graphic picture of the effects of domestic controversy on the work overseas.[87]

Given the depth of loyalty to the CMS, it may be asked why the controversy of 1917 provoked a secession at all, when the Society had weathered debates of apparently equal virulence on other subjects. Several reasons may be suggested. First, there were two clearly antagonistic groups, each committed to its own point of view and each resolutely opposed to compromise. The Liberal Evangelicals were determined to broaden the CMS; Bartlett and his allies were equally resolved to keep the Society within the 'old paths'. The CMS archives contain not only conservative complaints against the liberals, but also letters from Guy Rogers urging Bardsley to stand firm against Bartlett.[88] The two points of view, moreover, were backed by organisation in the shape of the Group Brotherhood and the FEC. Secondly, the subject of debate in 1917-22 was one of fundamental importance to all Evangelicals and, unlike the oft-repeated issue of co-operation with the SPG, one in which niceties of definition were crucial. The failure to reach agreement in November 1922, for example, turned partly on the deletion of the phrase 'and utterances' from a resolution designed to guarantee the infallibility of Christ's words with respect to the Old Testament. The deletion was proposed by Manley, a conservative, who later claimed that it made no difference to the resolution. Bartlett and the BCMS, however, maintained that it was a loophole allowing the liberals to reject Christ's endorsement of controversial points like the Davidic authorship of Psalm 110 by drawing a distinction between formal 'teaching' and informal, unauthoritative 'utterances'.[89] It has been seen in an earlier chapter that Evangelical Churchmen did not subscribe to one precise formula or definition of inspiration; the conservatives in the CMS controversy sought to press beyond basic agreement on the fact of inspiration to uniformity on points of detail and this was not attainable.

A third cause of the schism, and one which helps to account for the failure of attempts at compromise, was the steady development of an atmosphere of suspicion. Many conservatives did not trust the CMS leadership, especially after Fox left Salisbury Square in 1910, and therefore rumours of surrender to sacerdotalism or to modernism were always given credence in some quarters. As early as 1913 Theodore Woods was collecting signatures to a letter affirming confidence in the new honorary secretary, Cyril Bardsley, and this was presented to the General Committee in 1914.[90] With organisations like the Bible League and the Church Association scrutinising CMS activities for signs of deviation from Evangelical traditions, and with the liberals meeting in secret conclave at West Ham, an atmosphere of distrust was fostered in which each group was prepared to believe the worst of the others. It was this basic distrust, fed by one-sided reports of the notorious Hong Kong sermons of 1919, which led Bartlett to insist on a rigorous definition of the doctrine of inspiration.[91] Goodwill and mutual confidence were things of the past.

The creation of the BCMS exacerbated this situation, for the seceding conservatives sought to justify their action by claiming that they represented the authentic position of the founders of the CMS. Pamphlets like Bartlett's *BCMS: Why a New Society?* and *Evangelical Missions: Their Principles during the Nineteenth Century* described the controversy from the BCMS point of view and came close to accusing the CMS of apostasy. Bartlett's version of the November 1922 decision was that 'The historical trustworthiness of the Bible was rejected by 210-130,'[92] a statement which may have prompted the perplexed Evangelical who wrote to Bardsley, 'I am informed there are two secretaries for the CMS, one for the Bible as it is and one for alteration of the same.'[93] Wilson Cash, who succeeded Bardsley at Salisbury Square, wrote many letters to reassure conservative Evangelicals that the CMS had not repudiated biblical inspiration or the divinity of Christ, both of which were claimed in the mid 1920s.[94] The BCMS, for its part, accused the CMS constituency of misrepresentation and hostility, citing clergymen who had called the BCMS 'the new schismatical society', 'agents of the "Enemy of Truth"' and 'wholly the work of the Devil'.[95] A small, but significant indication that suspicions about the orthodoxy of the CMS continued was that when Murray Webb-Peploe offered for medical work in China in 1926, he specified a particular hospital where he knew the doctor to be a committed conservative: he was not prepared to make a general offer, because he did not trust the collective orthodoxy of the CMS medical staff.[96]

The effects of the BCMS secession on the CMS are difficult to gauge. The CMS lost 78 clerical subscribers and 37 of its 1300

Missionary Service League branches. A few missionaries left the Society, as did three vice-presidents and four honorary life governors.[97] Some churches transferred their financial support to the new Society – by 1928 the BCMS had nearly 400 local auxiliaries and an income of £44, 000[98] – and at a time of rapidly rising expenditure and constant deficits, any loss of income was serious. The secession certainly did not cripple the CMS. It did, however, drive an institutional wedge into the Evangelical school. Before 1922 Evangelicals had quarrelled within the framework of one society, for amidst the bewildering mass of leagues, associations and councils they had been united by adherence to the CMS. After 1922 a body of conservatives carried on their battle against sacerdotalism and modernism from without, secure in their own enclave and protected by a rigid basis of faith. The BCMS, with its own college providing training not only for missionaries but also for clergy for home parishes,[99] represented a triumph for Evangelical insularity and separatism, and for those whose reaction to the challenge of twentieth century developments was a determination to stand firmly in the 'old paths'.

Separate Structures: The AEGM and the FEC[100]

Reference has already been made in the account of the schism in the CMS to the role of two organisations which co-ordinated the activities of the Liberal and conservative Evangelicals. These two bodies were the Group Brotherhood (AEGM from 1923) and the Fellowship of Evangelical Churchmen. They helped to crystallize the division which developed in the Evangelical school and a brief description of their origins and policies is given to show further how the conservative-liberal conflict became institutionalized in the early 1920s.

The Group Brotherhood was the elder of the two movements. It began in 1906[101] and owed its origins to the dissatisfaction felt by a group of younger Evangelicals towards what they regarded as the narrow and negative policy adopted by the leadership of the party. It was held that Evangelicals spent too much time attacking Anglo-Catholicism, instead of winning support by presenting the positive virtues of Evangelical Churchmanship. There was criticism too of a perceived tendency to ignore all aspects of modern thought and to avoid the challenges presented by biblical criticism, science and the study of social problems. These disgruntled Evangelicals were not necessarily advocates of higher criticism or liberal theology, but they were concerned that the Evangelical school was failing to give a considered response to modern trends and that even in its concentration on the ritual controversy it was using the wrong weapons by carping at Anglo-Catholicism rather than commending the Evangelical gospel.[102]

This dissatisfaction led to action in 1906, probably on the initiative of Douglas Thornton. Thornton was on furlough from Egypt and discussed the condition of the Evangelical school with A.J. Tait, then principal of St Aidan's College, Birkenhead. Tait voiced his criticisms of the situation and Thornton urged him to act.[103] As a result, four and then six Liverpool Evangelicals began to meet regularly for discussion. The 'Liverpool Six' – Tait, Lisle Carr, H.E.H. Probyn, B.C. Jackson, A.F. Thornhill and Guy Warman – produced a list of doctrinal 'points' and resolved to take advantage of Warman's invitation to address the Islington Meeting of 1907 to present their case for a new Evangelical policy.[104] Warman duly delivered a paper calling for a new commitment to positive teaching as a response to ritualism, urging that Evangelicals must agree on their doctrines, preferably through local conferences, and then use all the resources of the press to convey them to the general public.[105] Meanwhile, the Six convened a meeting after Islington, produced a plan of campaign and established groups on the Liverpool model in Norwich, Oxford, Cambridge and other centres. Several conferences took place during the summer, including one at Woolton where Canon J.C. Wright gave the movement its name by calling it a 'band of brothers'. For the next few years the Brotherhood concentrated on discussing doctrine and on promoting the publication of the *English Church Manuals* and *Anglican Church Handbooks* as positive expressions of Evangelical opinion on a wide variety of subjects.[106]

It must be emphasized again that the Brotherhood was not particularly 'liberal' at this stage. The 1907 'points' were firmly Protestant in their understanding of the ministry and the sacraments and called Scripture 'the true, full and final revelation of God's will and the ultimate source of doctrine.' The 1908 conference was held at Wycliffe Hall, and the principal, W.H. Griffith Thomas, a staunch conservative, was a member of the

Brotherhood until he went to Canada in 1910.[107] The main features of the Brotherhood were its concern for a positive policy and its rule of secrecy. Membership was by election and prospective members had to be vetted by the Six before admission. As a result, what began as a movement of younger Evangelicals gradually became one of younger Liberal Evangelicals, since those who were deemed to be out of sympathy with an increasingly liberal leadership could be excluded from the organisation.[108] There were still conservative members, like Sydney Carter, but the policy of the Brotherhood as a whole moved towards a clearer espousal of the aim of broadening the Evangelical school. This was seen, for example, in Guy Rogers' paper 'The limits of Evangelical unity', published in the *Record* in July 1917, which called for a frank recognition of the right of Evangelicals to hold views on biblical criticism and on ceremonial which were anathema to the traditionalists.[109] It was hardly surprising that most of the signatories of the West Ham memorial to the CMS were members of the Brotherhood, nor that the leading liberal protagonists in the ensuing controversy belonged to the movement. Fox wrote to Cyril Bardsley in January 1918 that most of the memorialists 'were members of a private society known as "The Groups"... an eclectic body, consisting of about 250 clergy and having for their object the adaptation of Evangelical principles to "modern thought".'[110] It is not clear whether Fox knew that Bardsley himself was a member of the Brotherhood, but it may be surmised that he did not.

The next step in the development of the movement was the decision to abandon secrecy. In April 1923 the committee decided that 'the Brotherhood must "come out into the open"' and invite all sympathetic clergymen to join.[111] It would seem that one of the most important reasons behind this decision was the belief that a vigorous Evangelical organisation was needed to check the advance of Anglo-Catholicism – as Storr wrote in the *Record*, 'they are confessedly anxious lest the official machinery of the Church should fall into the hands of one party; and there is danger of this unless moderate opinion organises itself and becomes vocal.'[112] After much debate, the name Anglican Evangelical Group Movement was chosen, in order to emphasize the movement's loyalty to the Church of England and to Evangelical principles, to reflect the importance of the local groups and to indicate that the AEGM intended to be progressive rather than static.[113]

1923 witnessed the publication of a set of essays by AEGM members entitled *Liberal Evangelicalism*. Over the next two years a series of pamphlets appeared, as did a second book, *The Inner Life*. Membership of the movement expanded from 300 in 1923 to 900 in 1927 and 1500 by 1935, organised into 61 groups. Liberal Evangelical Congresses were organised and, as Keswick became more thoroughly conservative, so a convention was held at Cromer from 1928 onwards.[114] As will be seen later, the AEGM played a significant role in the disputes over the revision of the Prayer Book in the late 1920s.

By 1923 the membership of the AEGM was largely composed of Liberal Evangelicals, although Sydney Carter retained his membership even after appointment as the principal of the BCMS college at Bristol.[115] The leadership was also firmly liberal, including Guy Rogers, H.A. Wilson and especially V.F. Storr. According to Rogers, Storr joined the Brotherhood because he was asked to contribute to *Liberal Evangelicalism*.[116] He became the movement's leading spokesman and author, writing many of the Blue pamphlets, serving as honorary organising secretary and then as president from 1930 until his death ten years later.[117] It was Storr who shaped the creed of the AEGM, producing a simple exposition in *My Faith* (1927) and a fuller account of the movement in *Freedom and Tradition* (1940), an attempt to place Liberal Evangelicalism in its historical and theological context. More than anyone else, Storr ensured that the Brotherhood not only paid attention to modern thought, but also accepted many of its conclusions, a significant shift from the open-minded, yet cautious approach of the Liverpool Six.

The conservative Fellowship of Evangelical Churchmen came into being twelve years after the Group Brotherhood. It was inaugurated at a meeting held at Sion College in November 1918 and, according to an early circular, the first supporters included Ingham, Fox, Webb-Peploe, J.B. Barraclough, E.L. Langston and D.H.C. Bartlett. S.H. Gladstone was the chairman and the honorary secretaries were the Revds W. Dodgson Sykes and H.E. Boultbee. By 1921 Bartlett had become the hon. Secretary, Albert Mitchell was a vice-president and Manley was on the Executive Committee.[118] The Fellowship claimed 500 clerical members,[119] united by a 'Terms of Basis' affirming the infallibility of all Christ's utterances and explicitly repudiating the eastward position.[120]

In the course of 1920 there was a certain amount of controversy about the existence of the FEC, with some Evangelicals wondering whether it would merely duplicate the work of the National Church League.[121] George Denyer wrote to the *Record* to justify the new society and to explain its purpose: it was a 'fellowship that shall bind together for prayer, study, sympathy and discussion men and women who cannot accept the higher critical positions, and who are genuinely anxious as to the modernist views which seem to find acceptance with so many of our Evangelical brethren.'[122] Bartlett wrote in similar vein, calling the FEC 'the latest attempt to rally and conserve within the Church of England the old Evangelical School which is well-nigh threatened with extinction by Modernism and Indefinitism.'[123] The annual Report of 1921 underlined this concern, declaring that the purpose of the FEC was 'not to entrench upon other Evangelical societies nor to enter into competition with them in their respective spheres, but simply to link up and unify for study and prayer, conference and united action, the distinctive Evangelicals scattered throughout the country who are deeply attached to the "old paths" and the principles of the founders of the CMS, CPAS etc.' At a time when 'compromising propositions and practices are constantly being urged upon Evangelicals, ' the report continued, '...the need of common counsel is very urgent, and the advantage of common action most desirable.'[124]

In fulfilment of this purpose, as has already been seen, the FEC was active in the disputes leading to the formation of the BCMS. It also promoted petitions on Prayer Book revision, campaigning indefatigably against any concessions to Anglo-Catholicism or Modernism. Regular meetings and conferences were held and the Fellowship produced both a series of booklets on aspects of doctrine and a more solid volume of essays, *Evangelicalism by Members of the FEC* (1925). The latter, edited by Russell Howden, might be seen as a counterblast to *Liberal Evangelicalism* and it concluded several weighty essays, notably those by G.T. Manley and T.C. Hammond on the authority of Scripture. By February 1928 the FEC was claiming to 'express and represent the mind of the great body of Evangelical Churchmen in the country, '[125] a somewhat ambitious boast, despite its sizeable membership and busy programme.

The AEGM and the FEC were important for at least two reasons. First, their very existence demonstrated that mutually incompatible interpretations of Evangelical Churchmanship were held within the school and that these interpretations were strong enough to be represented formally by organised bodies. The move from individual disagreement in the context, for example, of a clerical and lay association, to debate between rival societies over what constituted Evangelicalism was a serious one. Secondly, moreover, organisation exacerbated conflict by providing the machinery for the formulation of policies, propaganda and concerted action. As was noted above, one reason why the unrest in the CMS in the 1910s led to a secession when earlier disputes had been resolved was that both sides in the later conflict were backed by party organisation. Thus the Groups pressed for liberalisation and began the quarrel with the 1917 memorial, while the FEC supported Bartlett's response and took steps to set up the BCMS. Differences of opinion first found expression in the AEGM and FEC and then they in turn fostered further polarization.

This division was deeply worrying to bodies like the National Church League, which were anxious to preserve Evangelical unity in the face of the debate on Prayer Book revision. The Cheltenham Conferences of 1922 and 1925 were devoted to the search for common ground, with T.W. Gilbert, a leading figure in the NCL, placing particular emphasis on the need for mutual toleration.[126] Likewise, the *Churchman* constantly urged co-operation in the paramount duty of resisting Anglo-Catholicism on the Prayer Book question. Despite the best endeavours of the NCL, however, it proved impossible to maintain a united front on this issue, as the next section will demonstrate.

Prayer Book Revision[127]

The revision of the Book of Common Prayer was one of the major sources of controversy in the Church of England in the first decades of the twentieth century. It took over twenty years to produce a scheme of revision and some of the proposals contained in that scheme were highly contentious. This section will examine Evangelical attitudes to the revision question between 1906 and 1928. Before turning to the proposals under discussion in that period, however, it may be asked how Evangelical

Churchmen regarded the Prayer Book as it stood before the revisers set to work on it.

As an earlier chapter observed, by the late nineteenth century Evangelical Churchmen had overcome much of their former uncertainty about the doctrinal purity of the Prayer Book.[128] The change from Tractarian Churchmanship, with its deep respect for the Anglican liturgy, to ritualism, with its desire to return to the first Edwardian Prayer Book or even to interpolate prayers from the Roman Catholic Canon of the Mass, was followed by a corresponding change as Evangelicals ceased to criticise the Book of Common Prayer as insufficiently Reformed and instead hailed it as a bulwark of Protestantism. A.E. Barnes-Lawrence in *A Churchman and His Church* (1917) called the Prayer Book a priceless treasure and quoted a glowing tribute from Dean Burgon,[129] while Henry Wace constantly maintained that the Prayer Book expressed the true nature of the Church of England as Catholic, Apostolic, Reformed and Protestant. Most Evangelicals, therefore, were not enthusiastically advocating further revision in a Protestant direction by this period, although the Protestant Reformation Society did submit some proposals to the archbishop of Canterbury in 1911, including the substitution of the word 'presbyter' for 'priest' and the omission of all Lessons from the Apocrypha. Davidson called these suggestions 'drastic' and they were not widely supported.[130]

Despite their admiration for the Prayer Book, some influential Evangelicals were convinced of the need for revision to align the liturgy more closely with modern conditions. F.J. Chavasse told the Church Congress of 1906, 'There is no doubt we need a revision of our Prayer Book', a call backed four years later by T.W. Drury and J.E. Watts-Ditchfield, and by H.J.R. Marston, who advocated 'a thorough revision.'[131] In March 1904 the *Churchman* published an article on 'Prayer Book amendment' by Bishop Samuel Thornton, which set out some of the changes desired by Evangelicals: a relaxation of the rubrics to give more opportunities for special services (like Watts-Ditchfield's Sunday afternoon mens' services); greater variety in the prayers, including intercessions for overseas missions; permission to shorten the Communion service by saying the words of administration to a whole rail of communicants, rather than to each individual; changes to avoid the length and repetition of the standard morning service of Morning Prayer, Litany and Holy Communion.[132] Evangelicals wanted the Book of Common Prayer to be enriched by the addition of new prayers and to be made more flexible, especially for the benefit of clergymen working in populous parishes or among the unchurched, where simple, brief services would make more impact than the Church's 'incomparable liturgy' in all its sixteenth century splendour. Elasticity and modernisation were the goals of those like Chavasse and Dean Lefroy who commended Prayer Book revision.

When the work of revision was undertaken, however, modernisation was only one of the aims in mind. The process which led to the parliamentary debates of 1927 and 1928 began with the 1906 Report of the Royal Commission on Ecclesiastical Discipline, which recommended that 'Letters of Business should be issued to the Convocations with instructions: (a) to consider the preparation of a new rubric regulating the ornaments (that is to say, the vesture) of the ministers of the Church, at the times of their ministrations, with a view to its enactment by Parliament; and (b) to frame, with a view to their enactment by Parliament, such modifications in the existing law relating to the conduct of Divine Service and to the ornaments and fittings of churches as may tend to secure the greater elasticity which a reasonable recognition of the comprehensiveness of the Church of England and of its present needs seems to demand.'[133] The Commissioners were trying to deal with the ritual question and chose to do so by advocating a combination of greater elasticity with firm enforcement of the new standards. From the first, therefore, Prayer Book revision was a tool for solving the 'crisis in the Church' by a mixture of concession and discipline.[134]

Letters of Business were duly issued to the Convocations and the revision process began. The four houses of Convocation worked separately at first, sometimes reaching opposing conclusions. By October 1918, however, most of the proposals had been agreed by both Provinces, although suggestions for a revised Order of Holy Communion still proved contentious and a compromise, drawn up by Drury and W.H. Frere, was rejected by the York Synod in 1920. The Convocations were still able to make their reply to the Letters of Business, although by the time they did so the mechanism for Church reform had been transformed by the Enabling Act, which had set up a National Assembly to debate ecclesiastical legislation. The Convocations therefore submitted their work to the Assembly, which proceeded to produce its own revision scheme, revealed in its final form early in 1927. It was this scheme, embodied in the Prayer Book Measure, which was rejected by the House of Commons in December 1927 and again in June 1928.

The course of the revision was lengthy and tortuous, but it is possible to draw out a number of decisions which were of particular importance to Evangelical Churchmen. In 1907 the Canterbury House of Bishops set up a sub-committee to investigate the Ornaments Rubric, one of the disputed points which the Royal Commission had been especially anxious to clarify.[135] This sub-committee produced a lengthy report early in 1908, supporting the Anglo-Catholic contention that the Rubric ordered the use of the vestments.[136] In 1909 Canterbury Convocation adopted a resolution stating that the Ornaments Rubric should remain unchanged and that both forms of clerical dress currently in use should be permitted. Wace called this resolution 'nonsensical' and resigned from the revision committee.[137] At the same time the York bishops were debating the possibility of allowing a white vestment for the celebration of Holy Communion as a compromise between the surplice and the full Roman vestments. By 1911 Canterbury Convocation had approved reservation of the elements for the communion of the sick and the abbreviation of the words of administration to the first half ('The Body of our Lord Jesus Christ, which was given for thee, preserve thy body and soul unto everlasting life') only.[138] In 1914 the Canterbury Lower House proposed to rearrange the Communion Office to make it more like the 1549 Canon, and this was agreed by the bishops in 1918.[139] In the 1920s it was agreed that the revised book would be an alternative to the Book of Common Prayer, not a replacement for it, and, as debates on the Canon continued, the House of Clergy in the National Assembly voted in favour of two new Canons, one derived from the ECU's 'Green Book' and the other from the 'Grey Book' supported by Bishop Temple and the 'Life and Liberty' movement.[140] By 1927, therefore, the Assembly had amended the original scheme (NA 60 and NA 84) and produced the so-called 'Composite Book',[141] containing the 1662 Prayer Book and all the revision proposals. These proposals had modernised and simplified the traditional services in some ways, but they also endorsed the vestments, permitted reservation, introduced prayers for the departed, added All Souls and Corpus Christi to the Calendar (the latter albeit thinly disguised as 'Thanksgiving for Holy Communion') and gave the clergy the choice of an Order of Holy Communion closer to medieval models than the 1662 form, although with the addition of an invocation of the Holy Spirit on the elements (*epiklesis*) derived from the Eastern rites.

Evangelical Churchmen were by no means uncompromising and indiscriminate opponents of Prayer Book revision throughout this period. It has been seen already that many of them were advocates of revision in the early 1900s and this continued right through the 1910s, despite their objections to some of the specific proposals advanced by the Convocations. Indeed, a constant refrain in Evangelical speeches, pamphlets and publications was that they supported revision in principle, but nonetheless could not accept changes in the doctrinal position of the Church of England. At the very beginning of the revision process, Lady Wimborne in the *Nineteenth Century and After* for August 1906 welcomed the Royal Commission's recommendations on greater elasticity, but sounded an alarm that revision might take the Church in a Romeward direction.[142] Guy Johnson made the same point in the *Twentieth Century Quarterly*,[143] while when the *Modern Churchman* of 1911 accused Evangelicals of general hostility to revision, W.J. Sommerville wrote a sharp reply affirming that most Evangelicals supported 'a very drastic revision of the Church's formularies.'[144] The General Committee for Promoting Prayer Book Revision, set up in 1910, included A.J. Tait, Lisle Carr and the conservative R.B. Girdlestone, as well as other Evangelicals.[145] Even in the 1920s the National Church League and the Church Association issued statements favourable to modernisation, as long as controversial questions of doctrine were left undisturbed, and the *Record* reiterated this point in January 1927.[146] When T.W. Gilbert wrote that 'Evangelicals have as great a desire for constructive Revision as any other school of thought in the Church of England, provided that the Revision does not alter the doctrinal basis of the present Prayer Book,'[147] he was speaking for all shades of opinion, from Bishop Knox to the AEGM. Differences only arose when it came to weighing up the gains of revision against the estimated doctrinal changes and then deciding on a policy with respect to the Composite Book.

Some Evangelical advocates of revision criticised the official proposals for failing to meet modern needs. In an address to the 1921 Church Congress, Watts-Ditchfield complained that the Prayer Book had become an issue for liturgical experts to debate and that in the party warfare the aim of reaching the unchurched had been overlooked. Modernisation and simplification – the Evangelical priorities for revision – had been given insufficient attention compared to technical questions on the wording of the Canon.[148]

Another general objection was to the whole principle of an alternative Prayer Book. Wace made a strong case against it on the grounds that the worship of the Church was an expression of its doctrine and therefore for the Church to endorse mutually contradictory forms of worship was to abdicate entirely from any teaching role. The proposal for two Canons was, he said, 'a positive monstrosity',[149] and this was echoed by Russell Howden in his *The Proposed New Prayer Book. The Evangelical Standpoint and Objections* (1927).[150] Others observed that to sanction an alternative was to stereotype division and to introduce a new source of bitterness into parochial life.[151]

Much of the disquiet, however, centred on issues of doctrine. In the first years of revision, the vestments were the most controversial subject, particularly after Darwell Stone told the 1908 Church Congress that Anglo-Catholics used the vestments explicitly in order to demonstrate their doctrinal unity with the Roman Catholic and Greek Orthodox communions.[152] At this stage and on into the 1910s many Evangelicals agreed that there was no prospect of compromise on this question. Speaking for the Liberal Evangelicals, Guy Warman repudiated the permissive use of the vestments in an address to the Devon and Cornwall Clerical and Lay Conference in 1908, while in 1915 H.A. Wilson affirmed that on this issue the 'broader Evangelicals' were firmly behind Dean Wace.[153] The Church Association, the National Church League and the *Record* sustained their implacable opposition to vestments until the end of the controversy, but the Liberal Evangelicals modified their position, so that Henry de Candole's Blue pamphlet *Ritual and Ceremonial* (1924) applauded Dearmer's 'English Use'.[154]

By this time, however, vestments had been replaced as the central issue by two other points. One was the rearrangement of the Communion Office. The original suggestion was to add between the prayers of consecration and oblation a new prayer referring to 'making a memorial' of the crucifixion in the eucharist.[155] As has already been seen,[156] Evangelical Churchmen were deeply hostile to any implication that the eucharist was a memorial sacrifice, because they regarded this as detracting from the finished work of Christ. This proposal was subsequently dropped and, after the different schools failed to agree on a single form of words for a new Canon, the National Assembly approved two Canons instead, one following the ECU model and the other close to the Liberal 'Grey Book'.[157] Albert Mitchell, the leading lay Evangelical liturgiologist, described both Canons as 'doctrinally defective and liturgically inept'; Wace, while denouncing the 'Grey Book' Canon in passing as unsound, concentrated his fire on the 'Green Book', approval of which, he claimed, meant that 'the Roman doctrine of the Eucharist has now effected an official lodgment in the ramparts of the English Church.'[158] The most prolific critic of the new Canon, however, as of all the various attempts to alter the Communion Office, was Bishop Knox, who devoted many articles and speeches to this, attacking particularly the invocation (*epiklesis*) and the act of remembrance (*anamnesis*), which, he alleged, gave scope for false teaching on the real presence and the eucharistic sacrifice.[159] Knox, whose opposition to the *epiklesis* was not shared by Wace and other Evangelicals,[160] wrote a book, *Spiritual Objections to the Alternative Communion Service* (1923), which was a full scale treatise on the theological consequences of the doctrine of the eucharistic sacrifice for the understanding of the character of God.

The second point which preoccupied Evangelical Churchmen in the 1920s was that of reservation. The revision proposals allowed reservation for the communion of the sick and Evangelicals feared that this would lead to perpetual reservation and to the development of the cultus of the blessed sacrament, complete with exposition and benediction. Like the vestments question in the 1910s, this fear united all shades of Evangelical opinion, from the Church Association to the AEGM. The Protestants, from T.W. Gilbert and the NCL to the Kensitites, would not approve of reservation under any circumstances.[161] The Liberal Evangelicals were in regular contact with the bishops on the safeguards which they deemed necessary to ensure that reservation remained solely for the communion of the sick, and the AEGM arranged a meeting with sympathetic bishops after the

1927 defeat to seek further restrictions on the practice.[162] Both F.J. and C.M. Chavasse opposed all forms of reservation after 1920[163] – largely, it may be suspected, because of the rapid growth in the number of churches practising benediction or encouraging devotions before the reserved sacrament during the First World War. Five Evangelical laymen, including the usually broad-minded Eugene Stock, appended a protest against reservation to the National Assembly's report on revision (N.A. 60) in 1922;[164] A.J. Tait, who was usually identified with the Liberal wing of the Evangelical school, spoke strongly against reservation at the Farnham Conference on the subject in 1925;[165] Bishop Denton Thompson declared it to be unacceptable in 1923;[166] and a year later Guy Rogers, Arthur Burroughs and J.T. Inskip joined Bishop Ingham in opposing it in the House of Clergy.[167] When the Assembly approved the addition of Corpus Christi to the Calendar, fears about adoration of the blessed sacrament provoked 'A Call to Action' which had Storr as its secretary and which was subscribed not only by Evangelicals of all types but also by Modernists like Inge, Glazebrook and Streeter.[168]

Other doctrinal worries may be mentioned more briefly. The Protestants were concerned that the revised Burial Office gave scope for prayers for the dead, as did the reintroduction of All Souls into the Calendar.[169] Conservative Evangelicals also deprecated the removal of Old Testament references from the Baptism and Marriage services, regarding these as concessions to higher criticism. Dean Wace voiced this objection at an early stage in an article on 'Rationalistic Revision',[170] and it was taken up by the Church Association, by Russell Howden and by the BCMS.[171] The conservatives were also opposed to the revision of the Psalter and to the liberal tendencies which they detected in the 'Grey Book', with its apparent anxiety to omit references to divine wrath. Some were anxious lest the modified Declaration of Assent to the new book committed all clergymen to approve of its doctrine, a situation which would force Protestants to choose between condoning what they regarded as error and leaving the Church.[172]

Some of the opposition to the proposals came from simple conservatism.[173] Some arose because the Revisers omitted the prayer for the King from Morning Prayer, making it optional.[174] Some was provoked by concern about the effect on Home Reunion, especially after the Baptist Union passed resolutions criticising the Composite Book in the summer of 1927.[175] Two other non-doctrinal issues, however, formed the main stumbling blocks to Evangelical acceptance of the Prayer Book Measure, and these were the finality of the revision and the rigour with which the new book would be enforced.

A significant number of Evangelical Churchmen were concerned that the Composite Book was merely the first step in a process designed to take the Church of England back to obedience to Rome, and these fears were heightened by the reports of the Malines Conversations.[176] Implacable opponents of the scheme, like the Revd L.D. Griffith, a frequent correspondent to the *Record*, called it 'the first installment of Anglo-Catholicism';[177] Russell Howden doubted the finality of the Composite Book;[178] and Evangelicals sympathetic to the revision like Watts-Ditchfield, H.A. Wilson and Arthur Burroughs wrote to the archbishop expressing anxiety on this score.[179] In an astute analysis of Evangelical attitudes, Wilson informed Davidson in February 1927 that 'If the concessions... made are to be regarded as merely an instalment by those in whose interests they are offered, we feel that we are simply presenting them with a salient in our position as a *point d'appui* for further advance. If, on the other hand, the concessions will be accepted as a final settlement by those for whose sakes they are framed and if the authorities will rigourously [sic] enforce discipline on those lines, then I am *perfectly certain* that the vast majority of us would strain every nerve to achieve general acceptance of the new book.'[180]

The importance of enforcement was pointed out by Hensley Henson in 1922, when he told the National Assembly that 'the real issue... behind Prayer Book revision was Prayer Book enforcement.'[181] As the Measure proceeded towards Parliament this problem not only aroused the anxiety of supporters like Burroughs, but also made a powerful weapon in the hands of Knox and Joynson-Hicks. Knox's output of pamphlets included one entitled *Will the Deposited Book restore order in the Church?* (1927), while Joynson-Hicks raised the question of enforcement in correspondence with the archbishop, in the House of Commons on 15 December 1927 and in his *The Prayer Book Crisis*, which appeared just before the vote on the revised Measure in summer 1928.[182]

Protestant alarm was increased and propaganda apparently

vindicated by the activities of the more extreme Anglo-Catholics, led by Darwell Stone.[183] They opposed the Prayer Book Measure as a betrayal of Catholic principles[184] and mustered 700 signatures on a petition from priests hostile to the Composite Book. In November 1927 1400 members of the Federation of Catholic Priests pledged to continue perpetual reservation even if ordered to desist by the bishops.[185] This, combined with Davidson's failure to give clear information as to precisely how the book would be enforced, helped to swing opinion away from the Measure. It is noteworthy that one pamphlet on enforcement came from the pen of the Evangelical MP Lord Sandon, who was clearly undecided in the autumn of 1927 as to how to vote. Like H.A. Wilson, he was prepared to support the Measure, but only if it promised a final settlement. Unlike Wilson, he was unconvinced by episcopal assurances, so while the rector of Cheltenham supported the Measure in the Assembly, Sandon voted against it in the House of Commons in 1927 and 1928. It was evidently a finely balanced decision, for he took the trouble to write to the archbishop afterwards, explaining that he saw his choice as the lesser of two evils.[186]

There was substantial agreement among Evangelical Churchmen as to the points at issue in the revision debate. In terms of doctrine, the new Communion Office, permission for reservation, changes in the Burial Office and, for some, formal recognition of vestments, were the main causes of Evangelical anxiety. The apparently Romeward tendency of the revision and the danger of a further drift away from the Reformation if the new book was not firmly enforced were the other principal preoccupations of most sections of the school. When it came to voting on the Measure, however, this unity dissolved, and the Evangelical party divided, first into three camps and then, as the parliamentary debates drew closer, into two.

For much of the period of Prayer Book revision the most popular option was to support revision in principle while opposing certain specific proposals. It has been seen that this was the general attitude of most Evangelicals towards the whole process from 1906 onwards. Once suggestions began to be embodied in particular schemes, this point of view expressed itself in attempts to promote non-controversial revision or to obstruct changes objectionable to Evangelicals. Resolutions deprecating doctrinal change were passed, for instance, and attention was drawn to the revision of the Canadian Prayer Book, which was concerned entirely with modernisation and enrichment and which explicitly avoided all points of doctrinal controversy.[187]

Another technique was to press for the exclusion of some parts of the Prayer Book from the revision process. Bishop Knox promoted a memorial to the episcopate in 1924 opposing any changes in the Communion Office and it secured over 300,000 signatures.[188] H.W. Hinde, vicar of Islington, stood for election to Convocation in 1923 on the slogan 'No alternative to and no alteration in our Holy Communion Office' and this was warmly endorsed by the *Record*.[189] Since most of the disputed doctrinal points related to Holy Communion, it was hoped that if this service could be left untouched, wide support could be secured for uncontentious but necessary reforms elsewhere in the Prayer Book. Once the Measure had been published and submitted to the National Assembly for discussion, Evangelicals campaigned to divide it, separating the proposals relating to Holy Communion and reservation from the rest. A resolution to this effect was moved in the House of Clergy in July 1923 by the Evangelical leaders Canon Grose Hodge and Prebendary Sharpe, and in the House of Laity by Sir Thomas Inskip and Albert Mitchell, but both attempts failed, as did subsequent motions on the same lines.[190] There was some episcopal support for this policy – in October 1925 Bishop Pollock of Norwich's proposal to divide the Measure secured the votes of eight other bishops, including the Evangelicals Perowne of Bradford, Nickson of Bristol and Denton Thompson of Sodor and Man.[191] Pollock continued to advocate this as a solution to the controversy, but without success. There were numerous ideas for compromise, including Watts-Ditchfield's plan for a conference and retreat to seek spiritual guidance on the points at issue and Theodore Woods' meeting at Farnham Castle to discuss reservation.[192] These ventures were unable to bring the controversy to an end, however, and although the Prayer Book Measure passed both the Assembly and the Convocations with large majorities, a significant body of Churchmen was not reconciled to the scheme. It should be remembered, moreover, that under the Enabling Act, Parliament could not amend a Measure, but had to accept or reject it as a whole. Once the Measure had received final approval from the Assembly, therefore, Evangelicals had to decide whether to support it in its entirety or to oppose it wholesale.

Faced with this choice, a strong body of Evangelicals gave their adherence to the Measure. Some did so with great enthusiasm – E.S. Woods wrote to Archbishop Davidson in February 1927 'to say how profoundly thankful I am about the Bishops' Prayer Book proposals. If I may say so, they do seem to me to reveal the guidance of the Spirit in all the long deliberations, and if anything would bring peace to the Church, they ought to. I for one am prepared to accept them *con amore* and I propose to use whatever influence I may possess to induce others to do the same.'[193] Guy Warman, bishop of Chelmsford, was heavily involved in the business of revision, so much so that he was chosen to draft the reply of the Parliamentary Ecclesiastical Committee to the various objections levelled against the Measure.[194] Warman also appealed to the AEGM to support the proposals,[195] which it did, but with much less enthusiasm than Woods. Bishop Burroughs' doubts have already been noted – he saw the Composite Book as a regrettable concession to Anglo-Catholicism, but one which was necessary in the interests of peace and discipline in the Church.[196] Other moderates like Storr, Guy Rogers and H.A. Wilson supported the book for the sake of its positive reforms and because it promised an end to anarchy. Garfield Williams, secretary of the Assembly's Missionary Council, wrote to the *Record* that the Measure should be passed so that the Church could turn its attention to the call of mission.[197] In June 1927 a group of Evangelical proctors in Convocation issued a statement commending the Measure, justifying its doctrine as capable of an Evangelical interpretation and, above all, declaring their confidence in the bishops' ability and will to enforce the new standards.[198] The call to 'trust the bishops' was powerful and some felt, moreover, that they should accept the decision of the Assembly. A combination of obedience, satisfaction with episcopal assurances, desire for peace and support for the non-controversial proposals induced many Evangelicals to give their assent to the Composite Book.

If many Evangelicals supported the Prayer Book Measure, more opposed it and they did so with a vigour that was unquenched by the active disapproval of most English diocesans, including all the Evangelicals on the bench. The Evangelical press was unanimously against the Book, and all the channels of protest used during the ritual controversy were deployed against the Measure, from public meetings to pamphlets and from petitions to cartoons. Very effective pressure was brought to bear on MPs – the archbishop was informed that Ramsay Macdonald was 'snowed under with letters and post-cards from Protestants' – and he was not the only MP to experience the Protestant campaign.[199] Some novel techniques were used to arouse public feeling, like the 'Protestant Parsons' Pilgrimage' launched in 1926 by the Revds F.M. Cundy and George Denyer, who proposed to travel through England alerting people to the dangers of the revision scheme.[200]

Perhaps the most remarkable features of the Evangelical opposition to the Prayer Book Measure were its breadth and coherence, both largely due to the Committee for the Maintenance of Truth and Faith, established as a co-ordinating body in 1927. Its first members were mainly NCL stalwarts – Inskip, Joynson-Hicks, Knox, F.J. Chavasse, Mitchell and H.W. Hinde – but it was soon joined by more Liberal Evangelicals like H.E.H. Probyn and G.F. Graham-Brown, the principal of Wycliffe Hall.[201] Moreover, the Committee also incorporated Protestant and conservative Evangelicals beyond the reach of the NCL. The Northern Council of the Committee, for example, included representatives of the Church Association, the FEC, the Protestant Reformation Society and the Protestant Truth Society.[202] This co-operation spread, so that when the United Protestant Council organised a demonstration at Central Hall, Westminster, Captain Barron (Church Association), the Revd W.A. Limbrick (PRS) and J.A. Kensit were joined on the platform by the bishop of Norwich,[203] while later that year Hinde also addressed the Council.[204] After the defeat of the Measure in December 1927, the Committee for the Maintenance of Truth and Faith organised a meeting of thanksgiving at the Albert Hall at which the participants included Archdeacon Thorpe, Bishop Knox, Mitchell, Hinde, J.A. Kensit, E.L. Langston and the FEC stalwart the Revd I. Siviter.[205] Through the World's Evangelical Alliance an appeal was made to evangelical Nonconformity to support the campaign. The Prayer Book crisis, therefore, brought an unprecedented degree of Evangelical unity. The Committee for the Maintenance of Truth and Faith was able to achieve what the Church Association, the NPCU and the NCL had attempted and failed. It may be suggested that this was partly because all Evangelicals could recognise the importance of the issue and partly because the parliamentary procedure made it so simple. There was no scope for Evangelical opponents of the Measure to disagree on amendments or compromises, because Parliament had no power to do other than accept or reject it. All the Protestant groups, therefore, were able to concentrate their energies on a simple campaign for rejection.

This is not the place to enter into an analysis of the parliamentary defeat of Prayer Book revision in 1927-8.[206] It may be observed, however, that many of the points made in debate in the House of Commons were ones emphasized by Evangelical propaganda, particularly with regard to reservation and the doctrinal position of the Church of England. Nor should it be forgotten that two of the most effective speeches against the Measure were made by Evangelical Churchmen – Joynson-Hicks moving the rejection in perhaps the best speech of his career and Inskip winding up the debate for the opposition.[207]

Prayer Book revision therefore both divided and united Evangelicals. The need to decide for or against the Measure drove a wedge into the party, with the bulk of the AEGM on one side and the conservatives and Protestants on the other. At the same time, the issues of 1927-8 produced a remarkable unity among opponents of the Composite Book. Seldom, if ever, had a vicar of Islington shared a platform with a Kensit, while at one stage of his career Bishop Knox had seriously considered sueing the Church Association for libel.[208] The revision question brought together not only representatives of what Henson called the 'Protestant underworld', but also respected and moderate Evangelicals desperately worried that the Composite Book was merely another step on the road to Rome. In this way the Prayer Book crisis was the outcome of decades of conflict with ritualism, of Protestant propaganda and of deep distrust of the bishops. Cyril Bardsley, bishop of Leicester, was present for the second parliamentary defeat and as he left the Palace of Westminster, he heard a man shout, 'The bishops are beaten, Alleluia!' and the crowd cheered.[209] In the eyes of many Evangelicals, Parliament had saved the Church of England and at long last checked the Romeward drift.

Conclusion

This chapter has examined only four expressions of conflict within the Evangelical school. Others could be added – for instance, the unrest within the Keswick movement over higher criticism at the end of the 1910s or the dispute between the Bible League and the Evangelical Alliance on the same issue.[210] These four studies, however, have emphasized that Evangelicalism was not monolithic. Individual Evangelicals responded in different ways to the pressures of modern thought and contemporary controversy.

In the case of the first situation considered, that of the conservative secession from the SCM, the period witnessed the steady transformation of what had been basically an evangelical organisation into a far broader movement. Evangelical Churchmen recognised this fact; many continued to support the student movement as an interdenominational and non-partisan society. It was really only within the student world that SCM and IVF were regarded as rivals and only there that the SCM's more recent and broader outlook was denounced as a fall from original righteousness by the conservatives.

The dispute within the CMS was different because the CMS was fundamental to the identity of the Evangelical school in a way that the SCM was not. 'Is he CMS?' could be a test of Evangelical Churchmanship, and so any threat to the Society's orthodoxy struck at the heart of the party. For this reason, perhaps, the debate was bitter and protracted, lasting for over a decade.

It has been seen that one reason why the conflict in the CMS was pressed to the extent of a secession was that behind the liberal and conservative groups stood the machinery of party organisation, at once the expression and the cause of division. The formation of the AEGM and the FEC demonstrated how far Evangelicals differed from one another on vital doctrinal issues. An easy equation of FEC with BCMS and AEGM with CMS should be avoided, however, for some FEC members, along with other conservatives, remained loyal to the CMS, while the staunchly conservative Sydney Carter was a longstanding member of the AEGM.

The long process of Prayer Book revision also revealed differences among Evangelicals. Ultimately, however, the procedure prescribed by the Enabling Act forced them to make a simple choice and so succeeded not only in separating the Liberal Evangelicals from the rest, but also in assembling a broad coalition in opposition to the Measure.

The simple picture of Evangelical Churchmanship as solidly

conservative and unflinchingly Protestant therefore needs heavy qualification. This chapter has provided some examples of Evangelical diversity; the next will attempt to review the complexities revealed by this book as a whole in the response of Evangelical Anglicans to some of the issues facing the Church of England in the late nineteenth and early twentieth centuries.

Notes

1 See, for example, R.M. Horn, *Student Witness and Christian Truth* (London, 1971), especially chapter 10.

2 D. Johnson, *Contending for the Faith: A History of the Evangelical Movement in the Universities and Colleges* (Leicester, 1979), 131. Compare the dissection of the history and historiography of the student movement in David M. Thompson, *Same Difference? Liberals and Conservatives in the Student Movement* (Birmingham, 1990), esp. 2-10.

3 Johnson, *Contending for the Faith*, 72; T. Tatlow, *The Story of the Student Christian Movement* (London, 1935), 272.

4 Johnson, *Contending for the Faith*, 39-40, 50; J.C. Pollock, *A Cambridge Movement* (London, 1953), chapter 3; O.R. Barclay, *Whatever happened to the Jesus Lane lot?* (Leicester, 1977), chapter 1.

5 Johnson, *Contending for the Faith*, 52.

6 J.S. Reynolds, *Born Anew. Historical Outlines of the OICCU 1879-1979* (Oxford, 1979), 3.

7 Pollock, *Cambridge Movement*, chapter 6.

8 Tatlow, *SCM*, chapters 2-4; 149.

9 Ibid., 115.

10 Ibid., 31, 43.

11 Ibid., 29-30, 75.

12 W.H.T. Gairdner, *D.M. Thornton: A Study in Missionary Ideals and Methods* (London, 1908), 39 (Manley) and 30 (Thornton); Tatlow, *SCM*, 91.

13 The Cambridge atmosphere of the 1890s is captured in E.S. Woods and F.B. Macnutt, *Theodore, Bishop of Winchester* (London, 1933), chapter 2.

14 Gairdner, *D.M. Thornton*, chapter 3.

15 Tatlow, *SCM*, 137.

16 Ibid., 138-42.

17 Ibid., 144-51.

18 Summer conference programmes, SCM archives, boxes A8 and A19.

19 Tatlow, *SCM*, 157.

20 *Official Report of the Church Congress held at Manchester, October 1908* (London, 1908), 350-79.

21 Tatlow, *SCM*, 261-2.

22 Bible Study 1910-15, SCM archives, box A31.

23 Tatlow, *SCM*, chapter 18.

24 Ibid., chapter 33.
25 Ibid., 180, 273-4.
26 Ibid., 261.
27 *R*, 5 February 1909, 132; 10 December 1909, 1258.
28 Tatlow, *SCM*, 261, 213; chapter 20.
29 SCM archives, box A20 contains material on the events leading up to the 1910 secession, including letters between Tatlow and C.F. Angus. See also Barclay, *Jesus Lane lot*, chapter 4.
30 M.L. Loane, *Archbishop Mowll* (London, 1960), 52.
31 Pelly to Tatlow, 18 February 1910, SCM archives, box A20.
32 Barclay, *Jesus Lane lot*, 68.
33 Johnson, *Contending for the Faith*, chapters 6-8.
34 Reynolds, *Born Anew*, 13-15.
35 N.P. Grubb, *Once caught, no escape. My life story* (London, 1969), 55-7; Barclay, *Jesus Lane lot*, 88-95; C.E. Raven (ed.), *The Mission to Cambridge University 1919-20* (London, 1920).
36 Johnson, *Contending for the Faith*, 131.
37 Memorandum on the Relations between the SCM and Evangelical Groups in the Colleges (February 1924), SCM archives, box A20.
38 *Church Missionary Review*, May 1917, 210.
39 Tatlow, *SCM*, 385-6.
40 Loane, *Archbishop Mowll*, 59-60.
41 Bible League Minutes of Council, 7 February 1911; 10 September 1901; 11 November 1901; 10 December 1901; 10 March 1902; 8 December 1902; 27 February 1903; D.W. Bebbington, *Evangelicalism in Modern Britain. A History from the 1730s to the 1980s* (London, 1989), 188.
42 *R*, 25 July 1913, 699.
43 *R*, 19 January 1922, 39; F.D. Coggan (ed.), *Christ and the Colleges* (London, 1934), 208, 211. Inskip was secretary of CICCU in Michaelmas term 1896, according to a termcard in the Cambridge University Library, Add. Mss. 8545.
44 *R*, 8 August 1913, 738.
45 Lees to Tatlow (n.d.), SCM archives, box A20.
46 Holden to Tatlow, 12 January 1912, SCM archives, box A20.
47 Barclay, *Jesus Lane lot*, 93.
48 M.A.C. Warren, *Crowded Canvas* (London, 1974), 40.
49 Apart from the extensive archives of the CMS, accounts of this controversy may be found in G. Hewitt, *The Problems of Success. A History of the Church Missionary Society 1910-42* (London, 1971), i, part 4; W.S. Hooton and J. Stafford Wright, *The First Twenty Five Years of the Bible Churchmen's Missionary Society, 1922-47* (London, 1947), chapters 1-4; G.W. Bromiley, *Daniel Henry Charles Bartlett: A Memoir* (Burnham on Sea, 1959), chapter 3, and Joan Bayldon, *Cyril Bardsley: Evangelist* (London, 1942), chapter 3.
50 W.J.C. Ervine, 'Doctrine and diplomacy: some aspects of the life and

thought of the Anglican Evangelical clergy, 1797-1837', Cambridge PhD thesis, 1979, 6.

51 *C*, June1912, 402.

52 *C*, December 1917, 706.

53 A. Bentley, 'The transformation of the Evangelical party in the Church of England in the later nineteenth century', Durham PhD thesis, 1971, 455-70.

54 J.S. Reynolds, *Canon Christopher of St Aldate's* (Abingdon, 1967), chapter 15.

55 *R*, 2 May 1902, 425.

56 *R*, 20 November 1903, 1141.

57 *R*, 18 December 1903, 1235.

58 *R*, 25 April 1913, 369.

59 *R*, 12 August 1915, 734; 9 September 1915, 396.

60 See, for example, a letter from Fox to a Miss __, 8 June 1899, CMS archives, G/C 13, repudiating the charge of consorting with ritualists.

61 Stanton Jones to C.C. Bardsley, 4 November 1917, CMS archives, G/C 13.

62 Bible League Minutes of Council, 5 May 1909, 29 June 1909.

63 *'Bible Sceptics and "SPG"': A Correspondence* (Oxford, 1904), citing second edition (1905), 83-4.

64 *R*, 15 November 1917, 768.

65 E.A. Knox, *Reminiscences of an Octogenarian* (London, 1935), 329.

66 Bromiley, *D.H.C. Bartlett*, 22.

67 *R*, 13 December 1917, 856-7.

68 Watts-Ditchfield to Davidson, 20 December 1917, DP, 380.

69 *R*, 14 February 1918, 109.

70 *Church Missionary Review*, March 1918, 104-11.

71 Coulthard to Bardsley, 2 February 1918; Bardsley to Coulthard, 5 February 1918; Coulthard to Bardsley, 6 February 1918, CMS archives, G/C 13.

72 *English Churchman*, 3 October 1918; *R*, 16 April 1919, 330.

73 *Challenge*, 22 February 1918, 280; 1 March 1918, 292-3; *R*, 15 May 1919, 413.

74 Bromiley, *D.H.C. Bartlett*, 25-6; (Anon.) *Evangelical Missions: Their Principles during the Nineteenth Century* (London, n.d.), 10; CMS archives G/C 13 (Fr Kelly) and G/AX 17 (Bible Union of China).

75 Bromiley, *D.H.C. Bartlett*, 26.

76 Ibid., 28.

77 Programme for Coleshill, AEGM archives, DEM 1/15.

78 *R*, 22 June 1922, 421.

79 Hooton and Stafford Wright, *BCMS*, 6-10.

80 *R*, 27 July 1922, 505.

81 *R*, 30 November 1922, 804.

82 *R*, 9 November 1922, 754.

83 *R*, 1 February 1923, 74.
84 *R*, 22 February 1923, 123.
85 *R*, 7 September 1922, 591; 2 November 1922, 738.
86 *R*, 28 September 1922, 632.
87 *R*, 13 July 1922, 472 (Bishop Lasbrey); 16 November 1922, 730 (Uganda); 5 October 1922, 645 (editorial).
88 Rogers to Bardsley, 30 September 1922, CMS archives G/AX 19.
89 Hooton and Stafford Wright, *BCMS*, 12-14; Memorandum by G.T. Manley, 5 February 1923, CMS archives G/AX 21.
90 Woods to Bardsley, 6 November 1913, CMS archives G/C 13.
91 Manley to Wilson Cash, 24 April 1925. Manley writes of 'a complete travesty of the facts.' CMS archives G/AX 21.
92 D.H.C. Bartlett, *BCMS: Why a new Society?* (London, n.d.), 11.
93 Bayldon, *Cyril Bardsley*, 75.
94 See CMS archives G/AX 21 for examples.
95 *Bible Churchmen's Missionary Messenger*, February 1924, 16; *Evangelical Missions*, 33.
96 K. Makower, *Follow my leader: A biography of Murray Webb-Peploe* (Eastbourne, 1984), 73.
97 Hewitt, *Problems of Success*, i, 471.
98 Hooton and Stafford Wright, *BCMS*, 231; *BCMS Report* (1928), 133-4.
99 Hooton and Stafford Wright, *BCMS*, chapter 4.
100 L. Hickin, 'Liberal Evangelicals in the Church of England', *Church Quarterly Review* 169 (London, 1968); A. Eric Smith, *Another Anglican Angle. The History of the AEGM* (Oxford, 1991); Ian M. Randall, *Evangelical Experiences. A Study in the Spirituality of English Evangelicalism 1918-1939* (Carlisle, 1999), chapter 3, map the history of the AEGM; no history of the FEC has yet been published.
101 Not 1905, as L.E. Elliott-Binns claims in *The Evangelical Movement in the English Church* (London, 1928), 69, followed by Smith, *Another Anglican Angle*, 5.
102 Hickin, 'Liberal Evangelicals', 44; Randall, *Evangelical Experiences*, 46-7.
103 Hickin, 'Liberal Evangelicals', 44.
104 Minute Book of the Liverpool Six, with account of its origins by Warman, AEGM archives, DEM 1/14.
105 *R*, 18 January 1907, 64-5.
106 AEGM archives, DEM 1/14.
107 Ibid., including Committee Minutes 3 June 1910. J.W. Walmsley, 'The history of the Evangelical party in the Church of England between 1906 and 1928', Hull PhD thesis, 1980, consistently (and mistakenly) reads the Liberal Evangelicalism of the AEGM back into the origins of the Group Brotherhood: e.g. 152, 311-2.
108 AEGM archives, DEM 1/15. The committee vetoed applications from the Revds W. Bothamley and B. Herklots on 8 January 1924.

109 *R*, 12 July 1917, 489.
110 Fox to Bardsley, 28 January 1918, CMS archives G/C 13.
111 Committee minutes, 25 April 1923, AEGM archives, DEM 1/15.
112 *R*, 19 July 1923, 464.
113 V.F. Storr, *Freedom and Tradition. A Study of Liberal Evangelicalism* (London, 1940), ix-xiii.
114 *R*, 19 July 1923, 464; Storr et al. to Davidson, 14 January 1927, DP 450, 23; Hickin, 'Liberal Evangelicals', 50.
115 Committee minutes, 26 March 1926, AEGM archives, DEM 1/16. The Bristol Group of the AEGM refused to invite Carter to its meetings and he complained to the central committee.
116 T. Guy Rogers, *A Rebel at Heart. The Autobiography of a Nonconforming Churchman* (London, 1956), 166-7.
117 G.H. Harris, *Vernon Faithfull Storr: A Memoir* (London, 1943), chapter 7.
118 A circular about the FEC is preserved in the CMS archives, G/C 13. See also the FEC's *Second Report*, for the period 1919-21. I am grateful to the Revd Dr Wilfrid Stott for the loan of this document.
119 *R*, 26 February 1920, 176.
120 *Second Report*, 4.
121 *R*, 22 April 1920, 322.
122 *R*, 29 April 1920, 346.
123 *R*, 6 May 1920, 367.
124 *Second Report*, 3.
125 A.E. Hughes to Davidson, 27 June 1928, DP 458, 121.
126 *C*, October 1922, 253-96; July 1925, 199-252.
127 General accounts of the Prayer Book controversy may be found in G.K.A. Bell, *Randall Davidson* (London, 1935), chapters 39 and 82; Knox, *Reminiscences*, chapter 16; Horton Davies, *Worship and Theology in England V: The Ecumenical Century 1900-65* (Princeton, 1965), 290-306; H.H. Henson, *Retrospect of an Unimportant Life*, ii (London, 1943), chapter 15; A.R. Vidler, *The Church in an Age of Revolution* (1974[3]), chapter 14; G.I.T. Machin, 'Parliament, the Church of England and the Prayer Book crisis', in J.P. Parry and Stephen Taylor (eds.), *Parliament and the Church 1529-1960* (Edinburgh, 2000). Volumes 444 to 456 of the Davidson Papers are devoted to this subject and there are many references in the printed *Church Assembly Report of Proceedings* (London, 1921-28).
128 See above, chapter 2.
129 A.E. Barnes-Lawrence, *A Churchman and His Church* (London, 1917), 103.
130 *R*, 28 July 1911, 705.
131 *Official Report of the Church Congress* (London, 1906), 90; *Official Report of the Church Congress* (London, 1910), 202-29.
132 Samuel Thornton, 'Prayer Book amendment', *C*, March 1904, 291-302.
133 W. Joynson-Hicks, *The Prayer Book Crisis* (London, 1928), 108; *RCED*

Report.

134 According to Vidler, *Age of Revolution*, 167, this approach was a major cause of the failure of the revision scheme; Machin, 'Parliament', 134.

135 DP, 444, 133.

136 *C*, March 1908, 129.

137 *R*, 14 May 1909, 517-20.

138 *R*, 12 May 1911, 448.

139 *R*, 27 February 1914, 198; 28 February 1918, 148.

140 *R*, 22 November 1923, 745-7.

141 The Composite Book became the 'Deposited Book' when a copy was deposited with the Clerk of the Parliaments. It is referred to throughout this chapter by its earlier title.

142 Lady Wimborne, 'The Report on Ecclesiastical Discipline', *Nineteenth Century and After* (London), August 1906, 173.

143 W. Guy Johnson, 'The Report of the Ritual Commission', *Twentieth Century Quarterly* (London), January 1906, 22-3.

144 W.A. Cunningham Craig, 'Liberal and Evangelicals – a plea for co-operation', *MC*, August 1911, 267; W.J. Sommerville, 'Co-operation of Evangelicals and Liberals – a reply', *MC*, September 1911, 336.

145 Pamphlet in DP, 445, 47, 51.

146 *R*, 26 April 1923, 265; 3 May 1923, 286; 13 January 1927, 28.

147 T.W. Gilbert, *Prayer Book Revision from an Evangelical Point of View* (London, 1923), 1.

148 *Official Report of the Church Congress* (London, 1921), 244.

149 *R*, 3 May 1923, 282-3.

150 J.R. Howden, *The Proposed New Prayer Book. The Evangelical Standpoint and Objections* (London, 1927), 21-2.

151 *R*, 5 October 1922, 646. Compare the resolutions of the 1923 AEGM Conference, AEGM archives, DEM 1/15.

152 *Official Report of the Church Congress* (London, 1908), 75-8.

153 *R*, 12 June 1908, 566; 18 March 1915, 261.

154 H.L.C. de Candole, *Ritual and Ceremonial* (London, 1924), 9. Contrast Gilbert, *Prayer Book Revision*, 1-2, and the Church Association pamphlet, *The Mass Vestments. Their Doctrinal Meaning and Threatened Restoration* (London, 1923).

155 *R*, 9 May 1918, 308.

156 See above, chapter 2.

157 *R*, 22 November 1923, 745-7.

158 *R*, 22 November 1923, 749.

159 E.A. Knox, 'Changes in the Communion service', *C*, April 1920, 181-92.

160 *C*, February 1920, 61; T.W. Drury, 'The epiclesis in the service of Holy Communion', *Church Quarterly Review* 97 (London, 1923-4), 1-13.

161 Gilbert, *Prayer Book Revision*, 2; Church Association pamphlet, *Reservation; What? and Why?* (London, 1923).

162 Committee minutes, 10 January 1928, AEGM archives, DEM 1/15.

163 Knox and Chavasse to Davidson, 20 October 1926, DP, 449, 242; S. Gummer, *The Chavasse Twins* (London, 1963), 100-08. Contrast *R*, 21 November 1918, 730, where F.J. Chavasse was prepared to allow reservation for the communion of the sick.

164 *R*, 22 June 1922, 430.

165 *Reservation: Report of a Conference held at Farnham Castle on October 24-27, 1925* (London, 1925), especially 91-7.

166 *R*, 31 May 1923, 350.

167 *R*, 4 December 1924, 792.

168 Copy in DP, 448, 219-20.

169 Gilbert, *Prayer Book Revision*, 4; Church Association pamphlets, *Revision and Prayers for the Dead* (London, 1923); E.A. Knox, *Objections to the Prayer Book Measure 1928* (London, 1928), 14.

170 H. Wace, *Some Questions of the Day: Biblical, National, and Ecclesiastical* (London, 1912), 261-7.

171 Howden, *New Prayer Book*, 3; Church Association pamphlets, *Shall the Church stand by God's Word?* (London, 1923), *'Unfeigned Belief'* (London, 1923), *Suppression and Mutilation of the Ten Commandments* (London, 1923); *Bible Churchmen's Missionary Messenger*, January 1928.

172 *R*, 25 January 1923, 52.

173 Hugh Cecil to Davidson, 27 February 1927, on the attitude of Asquith and Churchill, DP, 450, 283-4.

174 Colonel Sir James Legard, *A Layman's Views of the New Prayer Book* (London, 1927), 10-11.

175 Noted in DP, 452, 34.

176 See, for example, E.A. Knox, *The Malines Conference and the Deposited Book* (London, 1928).

177 *R*, 10 May 1923, 307.

178 Howden, *New Prayer Book*, 31.

179 Watts-Ditchfield to Davidson, 4 October 1918, DP, 446, 292-3; Burroughs to Davidson, 4 February 1927, DP, 450, 126-7.

180 Wilson to Davidson, 24 February 1927, DP, 450, 255.

181 *Church Assembly Report of Proceedings*, 28 June 1922, 59 (London).

182 Joynson-Hicks to Davidson, 24 February 1927, DP, 450, 249-52; *Parliamentary Debates (211 HC Deb. 5s)*, cols 2540-50 (15 December 1927); Joynson-Hicks, *Prayer Book Crisis*, 124-7.

183 F.L. Cross, *Darwell Stone: Churchman and Counsellor* (Westminster, 1943), chapter 6.

184 Revd A.E. Cornibeer to Davidson, 29 June 1927, DP, 452, 154.

185 *R*, 3 November 1927, 773.

186 Viscount Sandon, *The Deposited Prayer Book* (London, 1927); *Parliamentary Debates*; Sandon to Davidson, 15 June 1928, DP, 455, 275.

187 *R*, 12 June 1914, 577; 12 April 1917, 248; C.S. Carter, '"A safe, sane and conservative revision"', *C*, October 1924, 293-9.

188 *R*, 31 January 1924, 74; E.A. Knox, *A Letter to.. the Lord Archbishop of*

Canterbury.. (London, 1924).
189 *R*, 6 December 1923, 781.
190 *Church Assembly Report of Proceedings*, 3 July 1923, 336, 371 (London, 1923).
191 E.J.W. Barnes, *Ahead of his Age: Bishop Barnes of Birmingham* (London, 1979), 185.
192 *R*, 31 May 1923, 349. Knox's retort was that 'even prayer and love cannot make twice two five', *R*, 14 June 1923, 381.
193 E.S. Woods to Davidson, 11 February 1927, DP, 450, 153-4.
194 Warman to Davidson, 21 October 1927, DP, 253, 253-74.
195 Committee minutes, 7 February 1927, AEGM archives, DEM 1/16.
196 H.G. Mulliner, *Arthur Burroughs: A Memoir* (London, 1936), 181.
197 *R*, 3 March 1927, 164.
198 *R*, 23 June 1927, 466.
199 Davidson to E.S. Woods, 18 February 1927, DP, 450, 157; Hugh Cecil to Davidson, 26 July 1927, DP, 452, 276.
200 *R*, 28 October 1926, 739.
201 *R*, 31 March 1927, 245; 7 April 1927, 266.
202 National Council of the Committee for the Maintenance of Truth and Faith to Davidson, DP, 454, 113.
203 *R*, 3 March 1927, 167.
204 *R*, 7 July 1927, 502.
205 *R*, 12 January 1928, 52.
206 See Machin, 'Parliament', 139-41;Vidler, *Age of Revolution*, 167-8; Davies, *Worship and Theology*, 301-04; Bell, *Davidson*, ii, 1354-8.
207 *Parliamentary Debates*, cols 2531-2655; H.A. Taylor, *Jix, Viscount Brentford* (London, 1933), 258.
208 Knox to Davidson, 15 December 1907, DP, 444, 225.
209 Henson, *Retrospect*, ii, 196; Bayldon, *Cyril Bardsley*, 130.
210 Bible League Minutes of Council, 4 November 1917; 4 December 1917; 1 January 1918; Bebbington, *Evangelicalism*, 219-20.

CHAPTER 8

Conclusion

'Let us hear the conclusion of the whole matter.' (Ecclesiastes 12:13)

In his novel *The Parson's Progress* (1923), Compton Mackenzie described an incident which encapsulated much of the ecclesiastical confusion of the early twentieth century Church of England. While Mackenzie's hero, Mark Lidderdale, is serving as curate at the ritualist church of St Chad's, Pimlico, an attempt is made to introduce the forty hours' service of exposition of the blessed sacrament. This provokes a series of stereotypical reactions: the bishop responds by forbidding benediction; the Latin party among the Anglo-Catholics protest; the advocates of the rival 'English Use' support the ban; the Broad Churchmen speak disparagingly of 'the degraded materialism of scholastic superstition'; the 'Low Churchmen' attack the Broad Churchmen for doubting the deity of Christ and the Anglo-Catholics for subverting the Reformation; and the secular press is utterly bewildered by the whole controversy.[1] Where Mackenzie's depiction of party warfare is inaccurate, however, is in its assumption that the 'Low Church' group was homogeneous. In reality, if not in fiction, the responses of the Evangelical school to ritualism and also to biblical criticism, Darwinian biology and new departures in theology were rather more variable and rather less predictable.

Evangelicals were united in their opposition to ritualism, an opposition prompted by a wide range of considerations from doctrine to the perceived consequences of Anglo-Catholicism in the life of the Church and the nation. It should be emphasized that there was far more to the ritual controversy than the vestiges of a dying 'No Popery' sentiment, and that those like Hensley Henson who spoke contemptuously of an ignorant 'Protestant underworld' misunderstood or chose to ignore the Evangelicals' belief that the gospel itself was at stake in the struggle to defend 'spiritual religion' against sacerdotalism. The ritual controversy was sustained by, and Prayer Book revision foundered on, the theological convictions of Evangelicals like E.A. Knox, F.J. Chavasse, Henry Wace and Sir Thomas Inskip, as much as on the iconoclasm of the Kensits and the campaigns of the Church Association. Knox and his colleagues were not ill-informed fanatics, but men whose belief that ritualism was a spiritual menace united all shades of Evangelical opinion.

Unity of opposition in principle, however, quickly dissolved when practical proposals were advanced for dealing with the spread of ritualism, and some policies, particularly the parliamentary and legal weapons employed by the Church Association and the direct action of the PTS, were energetically repudiated by many Evangelicals. Thus, while positive steps were taken to pursue the ritual controversy by promoting Evangelicalism in the spheres of education, literature and patronage, more aggressive methods never commanded the support of more than a section of the Evangelical school. Moderate Evangelicals failed to induce, and militants to compel, the bishops to take decisive action; the episcopal veto blocked access to the courts; and Protestantism was not strong enough as a single-issue political campaign to win parliamentary support for a change in the law. In this period, therefore, Evangelicals could do little more than watch the advance of Anglo-Catholicism while making largely futile and increasingly desperate protests to the Church hierarchy. The defeat of the proposals for Prayer Book revision in 1927-8 was the exception that proved the rule, because the perceived challenge to the Reformation produced an unusually broad Protestant coalition, while the machinery set up by the Enabling Act created ideal conditions for a single-issue campaign. In denying parliamentary endorsement to the Deposited Book, Evangelicals managed to maintain the uneasy legal *status quo* within the Church. This was the modest limit of their success against ritualism.

Biblical criticism, Darwinism and liberal theology were all aspects of the general phenomenon of 'modern thought' and Evangelical reactions to this phenomenon in all its manifestations were marked by several common features. One was simple ignorance: some clergymen and perhaps many lay people remained largely unaware of the challenge to traditional beliefs posed by the new ideas in science and theology. They continued to hold and teach a view of Scripture which took no account of Wellhausen, Darwin, Driver, Sanday or any other advocates of change. The existence of this group was revealed by the violent reactions which followed whenever the implications of Darwinian science or biblical criticism were clearly explained – for example, by E.W. Barnes in his notorious 'Monkey Sermon'. It then became apparent that ideas which had been assumed to be common knowledge had not in fact been assimilated by many Churchmen. This position, of course, was not occupied exclusively by Evangelicals: they had no monopoly on ignorance.

It cannot be denied, however, that Evangelicalism as a movement was basically conservative in this period in a way that the other Church parties were not. Some elements within the Evangelical outlook were conducive to such an attitude: a tendency to undervalue this world as sinful and fallen and a corresponding concentration on otherworldly concerns; a pessimistic premillennialism which was determined to stick to the 'old paths' and doggedly to 'hold the fort' until rescued by the Second Advent;[2] a commitment to an ideal of active parochial ministry which left little time or energy for academic work; and a suspicion that acquaintance with the wisdom of the world must indicate a shrinking loyalty to the folly of the Cross. Even the Liberal Evangelicals, who set out to cast off what they regarded as outmoded traditions and to bring Evangelicalism into line with the best insights of modern thought, were only relatively liberal. On the basic doctrines of the creeds the AEGM was as orthodox as the most stalwart conservative, so that in the Hereford controversy, for instance, the Liberal Evangelical J.E. Watts-Ditchfield was one of the bishops who refused to attend Henson's consecration.[3] The AEGM was not a Modernist organisation, and indeed it has been claimed that by the 1920s it represented 'a liberalism that was already in fact slightly outmoded.'[4]

To acknowledge Evangelical conservatism, however, is not to endorse the popular caricature of Evangelical Churchmen as ignorant obscurantists and proto-fundamentalists, although the movement had its fair share of both. Many Evangelicals recognised the need to face the questions raised by modern thought. In part, this was prompted by the demands of apologetics, but it also stemmed from fundamental Evangelical principles. The right and the duty of private judgment, the conviction that truth was a unity, and the belief that all truth must accord with God's revelation in Scripture drove Evangelicals to examine new ideas honestly and thoughtfully. The reconciliation of Scripture with science and historical criticism was a duty accepted by all, even if they differed in methods and conclusions. Some continued to uphold traditional views and to explain away modern objections as unscientific or unscholarly. Others welcomed higher criticism and Darwinism wholeheartedly and revised their doctrine of inspiration accordingly. Still more modified the traditional position, harmonising Genesis and geology, accepting a form of evolution which still allowed for divine intervention and contending for the 'substantial accuracy' of the Old Testament against the conclusions of the more radical critics. In these ways Evangelical Churchmen sought to give an honest appraisal of new ideas while remaining loyal to their basic convictions about biblical inspiration and the authority of Christ.

The process of adjusting Evangelicalism to modern thought, therefore, produced a variety of results and a spectrum of opinions. Evangelicals all rejected what they regarded as the excesses of biblical criticism, evolutionary science and liberal theology, but there were major disagreements as to what constituted excess. V.F. Storr, for example, could accept Darwinism, endorse Driver's conclusions on Old Testament criticism and reject a substitutionary atonement, while W.H. Griffith Thomas defended penal substitution, opposed Driver and advocated Orr's 'directed evolution', and others were more conservative still, opposing any evolutionary transmutation of species. The principle of accepting truth and rejecting excess, with the subsequent problem of separating the two, also applied to ceremonial in worship, where some Evangelicals were content to 'level up', claiming that moderate ritual and even the eastward position were acceptable, while others denounced these practices as the first stages of a drift into sacerdotalism.

Evangelical individualism, responding to the trends of late nineteenth and early twentieth century religious thought, produced many shades of belief and practice, so that it must be recognised that to speak of an Evangelical 'party' or even of a 'school' is only to suggest that its members had certain features in common and not to imply the existence of a rigid uniformity. Indeed, a succession of writers tried to subdivide Evangelicalism into more ideologically coherent groups. Henry Lewis, in the *Nineteenth Century and After* for 1907, suggested three: the

Keswick group, the CMS group and the ultra-Protestants.[5] Eleven years later Ronald Knox produced four: Active Protestants, Evangelicals, Neo-Evangelicals and Evangelical Liberals.[6] These classifications were perhaps more helpful than simple references to 'Evangelical Churchmen', but no system could hope to capture all the nuances of allegiance within the Evangelical body. Many articles were published on the 'essentials of Evangelicalism' and the Cheltenham Conferences of 1922 and 1925 were devoted to attempts to preserve Evangelical unity-in-diversity by insisting that Churchmen could differ on many points while still calling themselves Evangelicals.[7]

In many ways Evangelicalism had never been a 'party' with a unified creed and organisation. From the eighteenth century onwards it was called a 'rope of sand' and the movement was never free from internal controversies.[8] It would be misleading, therefore, to claim that the early twentieth century witnessed the destruction of Evangelical unity as if a monolithic party had existed and was then dismantled. Evangelical Churchmen remained in agreement on many fundamental truths: the Protestant nature of the Church of England; the centrality of the atonement; the inspiration of Scripture and its authority as the final standard of Christian doctrine and conduct; liberty of conscience and the right of private judgment; the direct access of every soul to God through Christ; the all-sufficiency of Christ as Saviour; the gift of the Holy Spirit to all believers, regardless of ecclesiastical rites.[9] Nonetheless, there were two important changes in this period which make it possible to speak of a fragmentation of Anglican Evangelicalism after the First World War. The first was that differences in the interpretation of the fundamentals were taken beyond previous limits, so that contradictory understandings of biblical inspiration and the atonement emerged. The second was that an institution which had formerly united Evangelicals – the CMS – ceased to do so, and that bodies representing confessional disagreements – the AEGM and the FEC – rose to prominence. Rather than claiming that Evangelicalism was united in 1890 and divided in 1930, it would be more accurate to say that the movement was even more diverse and even less united by 1930 than it had been at the end of the previous century. Anglican Evangelicalism thus interacted dynamically with the forces testing the comprehensiveness of the Church of England – and of the Church in England – in these years. Although Evangelicals set out to prevent a major extension of the boundaries of Anglicanism to embrace Anglo-Catholicism and Liberalism, in the struggle they found the margins of their own school of thought significantly enlarged. This experience was not unique to Evangelical Anglicans, for many of the same pressures affected fellow evangelicals in other denominations, and with comparable results.The debate over the identity of Anglican Evangelicals in the face of changing religious ideas was thus a reflection of the wider debate over the identity both of the Church of England and of the phenomenon of evangelicalism in the early twentieth century.

Notes

1 C. Mackenzie, *The Parson's Progress* (London, 1923), 193-6.

2 See J.H.S. Kent, *Holding the Fort* (London, 1978). 'Holding the Fort' was a popular revival hymn by Philip Bliss.

3 Watts-Ditchfield to Davidson, 16 January 1918, DP, 380.

4 C. Smyth, 'The Evangelical movement in perspective', *Cambridge Historical Journal* 7 (Cambridge, 1941-3), 172.

5 H. Lewis, 'The present condition of the Evangelicals', *Nineteenth Century and After* 19-20 (London, 1907), 228-32.

6 Ronald Knox, 'Tendencies of Anglicanism', *Dublin Review* 324 (London, 1918), 26.

7 W.H. Griffith Thomas, 'What is Evangelical Churchmanship?', *C*, April 1914, 295-309; W.N. Hudson, 'The position of the Evangelicals in the Church of England (2)', *C*, November 1915, 835-42; 'Cheltenham Conference papers', *C*, October 1922, 253-96; 'The Cheltenham Conference: unity among Evangelical Churchmen', *C*, July 1925, 199-252.

8 See, for example, W.J.C. Ervine, 'Doctrine and diplomacy: some aspects of the life and thought of the Anglican Evangelical clergy, 1797-1837', Cambridge PhD thesis, 1979, chapter 6.

9 F.S.G. Warman, 'The essentials of Evangelicalism', *C*, October 1910, 751-3.

10 D.W. Bebbington, *Evangelicalism in Modern Britain. A History from the 1730s to the 1980s* (London, 1989), 181-228.

Bibliography

I. Manuscript sources and locations.

BIBLE CHURCHMEN'S MISSIONARY SOCIETY, LONDON
Annual Reports.
Pamphlets on the new Society.

BIBLE LEAGUE, SALISBURY
Minutes of the Council, 1892-1928.

CAMBRIDGE UNIVERSITY LIBRARY
Simeon Trust Papers (CUL Add. MSS 8293).
Minute Books.
Papers on Liverpool Diocese.

CHURCH MISSIONARY SOCIETY, LONDON
CMS/BCMS material, G/AX 17, 19, 21, 22, 23, 24, 25.
General letters, 1899-1918, G/C 13.
Modernism in China, GIX CH 1/2.
Father Kelly, 1920, GIX J 1.

UNIVERSITY OF HULL
Anglican Evangelical Group Movement Papers.
Minute Book of the Liverpool Six, 1907-11, DEM 1/14.
Minute Book 1920-26, DEM 1/15.
Minute Book 1926-30, DEM 1/16.
Central Committee File 1927-8, DEM 2/1.
Miscellaneous Papers, DEM 10/1-2.

KING'S COLLEGE, LONDON
Minutes of the Council.
Letters from A.W. Momerie, Packet M 114.

LAMBETH PALACE LIBRARY, LONDON
Letters and Papers of Archbishop Davidson.
Hensley Henson, volumes 380-2.
Prayer Book Revision, volumes 444-56.
Davidson's Diaries and Memoranda, 1914-19.

PUSEY HOUSE, OXFORD
Liddon Papers.
H.P. Liddon's scrapbook on *Lux Mundi*.

CENTRAL LIBRARY OF THE SELLY OAK COLLEGES, BIRMINGHAM
Archives of the Student Christian Movement.
Summer Conferences, Boxes A8 and A19.
Fox-Tatlow correspondence, Box A12.
The CICCU, 1906-16, Box A20.
Bible study, 1910-15, Box A31.
SCM and Evangelical groups, Box A95.

II. Printed Sources.

1. *Reference Works and Printed Reports.*

Chronicle of Convocation (London).
Church Assembly Report of Proceedings (London).
Crockford's Clerical Directory (London).
Cross, F.L. and Livingstone, E.A., (eds), *The Oxford Dictionary of the Christian Church* (Oxford, 1983[2]).
Douglas, J.D. (ed.), *The New International Dictionary of the Christian Church* (Exeter, 1978[2]).
Lewis, D.M., (ed.), *Dictionary of Evangelical Biography* (Oxford, 1995).
Official Report of the Church Congress (London).
Parliamentary Debates (London).
Stephen, L., and Lee, S., (eds), *The Dictionary of National Biography* (Oxford, 1885-90, and *Supplements*).
Who was Who (London).

2. *Newspapers and Periodicals.*

Bible Churchmen's Missionary Messenger (London).
Bibliotheca Sacra (Andover).
The British Weekly (London).
The Challenge (London).
The Church Gazette (London).
The Church Missionary Review (London).
The Church Times (London).
The Churchman (London).
The English Churchman (London).
The Expositor (London).
The Expository Times (Edinburgh).
The Guardian (London).
Journal of Transactions of the Victoria Institute (London).
The Modern Churchman (Knaresborough).
Pall Mall Gazette (London).
The Record (London).

The Rock (London).
The Times (London).
Word and Work (London).

3. *Primary Sources and Biographies.*

Abbott, W., et al., *Four Foundation Truths: A Message to Churchmen of Today* (London, 1895).

Adami, J.G., *The Unity of Faith and Science* (London, 1924).

Aglionby, F.K., *Life of Edward Henry Bickersteth* (London, 1907).

Aitken, W.H.M.H., *The Mechanical versus the Spiritual: Two Contrasted Conceptions of the Christian Religion. A Word for the Times* (London, 1899).

- *The Doctrine of Baptism: Mechanical or Spiritual* (London, 1901).
- *Apostolical Succession* (London, 1903).
- *Apostolical Succession considered in the light of the facts of the history of the Primitive Church* (London, 1903).

Alford, C.R., *'Stand Fast'; or, Contention for the Common Salvation against the inroads of Ritualism a Christian Duty* (London, 1895).

Anon., 'Darwin on the origin of species', *Christian Observer* (London), 1860.

- *Evangelical Missions: Their Principles during the Nineteenth Century* (London, n.d.).
- *'Bible Sceptics and "SPG": A Correspondence* (Oxford, 1904).

Babington, A.M., (ed.), *Memorials, Journal and Botanical Correspondence of Charles Cardale Babington* (Cambridge, 1897).

Balleine, G.R., *A History of the Evangelical Party in the Church of England* (London, 1908).

Barlow, M, (ed.), *Life of William Haggar Barlow* (London, 1910).

Barnes, E.J.W., *Ahead of his age: Bishop Barnes of Birmingham* (London, 1979).

Barnes, E.W., *Religion and Science* (London, 1924).

Barnes-Lawrence, A.E., *A Churchman to Churchmen* (London, 1893).

- *A Churchman and His Church* (London, 1917).

Bartlett, D.H.C., *BCMS: Why a New Society?* (London, n.d.).

Bartlett, R.E, 'The Church of England and the Evangelical party', *Contemporary Review* 47 (London, 1885).

- *The Limits of Ritual in the Church of England* (Chelmsford, 1890).

Barton, C.E., *John Barton: A Memoir* (London, 1910).

Bayldon, J., *Cyril Bardsley: Evangelist* (London, 1942).

Bebbington, D.W., *William Ewart Gladstone* (Grand Rapids, 1993).

Bell, G.K.A., *Randall Davidson* (London, 1935).

Bennett, W.H., and Adeney, W.F., *Biblical Introduction* (London, 1899).

Berney, T., *An Address presented to.. Parliament* (n.p., 1895)

Bethune-Baker, J.F., *The Miracle of Christianity. A Plea for 'the Critical School' in regard to the use of the Creeds. A letter to the Rt Revd Charles Gore* (London, 1914).

Binns, L.E. Elliott-, *The Book of Exodus* (Cambridge, 1924).

- *The Evangelical Movement in the English Church* (London, 1928).

Birks, T.R., *The Scripture Doctrine of Creation* (London, 1872).
- *The Difficulties of Belief in connexion with the Creation and the Fall, Redemption and Judgment* (1876^2).
- *Modern Physical Fatalism and the Doctrine of Evolution* (London, 1882^2).

Bishop, T.B., *Evolution Criticised* (London, 1918).
Braley, E.F., *Letters of Herbert Hensley Henson* (London, 1950).
Britten, J., *A Prominent Protestant (Mr John Kensit)* (London, 1898).
- *A School for Slander; or, 'The Soul of Dominic Wildthorne'* (London, 1909).

Bromiley, G.W., *Daniel Henry Charles Bartlett: A Memoir* (Burnham-on-Sea, 1959).
Broomhall, M., (ed.), *John Stuart Holden: A Book of Remembrance* (London, 1935).
Brown, A.J., *Prayer Book Revision: What will it mean? Questions and Answers about the Composite Book* (London, 1927).
Buckland, A.R. (ed.), *Words of Help on Belief and Conduct* (London, 1905).
Bulkeley, O., *Scripture and Science not at variance in the statements of Genesis 1* (Ryde, 1903).
Campbell, R.J., *The New Theology* (London, 1907).
- *A Spiritual Pilgrimage* (London, 1916).

Carbery, Victoria, Lady, *The Revised Prayer Book. "Sound an Alarm" (Joel II:1). A Few Words on a Serious and Critical Question to the Laity of the Church of England* (London, 1923).
Carpenter, S.C., *Winnington-Ingram* (London, 1949).
Carter, A.H., *God's Word Supreme* (London, 1914).
Carter, C.S., *The English Church and the Reformation* (London, 1912).
The Case against the proposed Appeal to the first Six Centuries (London, 1905).
Chadwick, O., *Hensley Henson: A Study in the Friction between Church and State* (Oxford, 1983).
Chavasse, F.J., *Plain Words on some Present Day Questions* (London, 1898).
Cheyne, T.K., and Black, J.S., (eds), *Encyclopaedia Biblica* (London, 1899-1903).
Christopher, A.M.W., and Sharpe, J.C., *Quousque? Whereunto are we drifting?* (Oxford, 1908).
The Church and Her Doctrine (London, 1891).
Church Association, *Scheme of Future Policy* (London, 1892).
- *Enabling Bill Leaflets* (London, 1919).
- *Prayer Book Revision Papers* (London, 1923).

Churchill, Lt Col S., *Can we trust the Bishops?* (London, 1928).
Clarke, A.H.T., *The Revised Prayer Book: Its Danger* (London, 1927).
Close, A., *The Hand of God and Satan in Modern History* (London, 1912).
Coggan, F.D., (ed.), *Christ and the Colleges: A History of the Inter-Varsity Fellowship of Evangelical Unions* (London, 1934).
The Conference of Churchmen (London, 1899).
Contentio Veritatis: Essays in Constructive Theology by Six Oxford Tutors (London, 1902).

Creighton, L., *Life and Letters of Mandell Creighton* (London, 1904).
Cross, F.L., *Darwell Stone: Churchman and Counsellor* (Westminster, 1943).
Dale, H.M., *Evangelicals and the Green Book* (London, 1924).
Dale, R.W., *The Old Evangelicalism and the New* (London, 1889).
De Candole, H.L.C., *Ritual and Ceremonial* (London, 1924).
- *Prayer Book Revision* (London, 1924).
Denison, G.A., *A Letter to the Revd Charles Gore* (London, 1890).
- *The Speech of Archdeacon Denison in the Lower House of the Convocation of Canterbury* (London, 1891).
Dewick, E.C., *Primitive Christian Eschatology* (Cambridge, 1912).
Digges La Touche, E., *The Person of Christ in Modern Thought* (London, 1912).
Dillistone, F.W., *Charles Raven* (London, 1975).
Dimock, N., *The Crisis in the Church of England: Its History and Present Position* (London, 1899).
Draper, W.H., (ed.), *Recollections of Dean Fremantle, chiefly by himself* (London, 1921).
Driver, S.R., *The Book of Genesis with Introduction and Notes* (London, 1926[12]).
Drury, T.W., *Two Studies in the Book of Common Prayer* (London, 1901).
- *Confession and Absolution* (London, 1903).
- *Elevation in the Eucharist: Its History and Rationale* (Cambridge, 1907).
- 'The *Epiclesis* in the service of Holy Communion', *Church Quarterly Review* 193 (London, 1923).
Dunstan, A., and Peart-Binns, J.S., *Cornish Bishop* (London, 1977).
Ellicott, C.J., *Christus Comprobator; or, The Testimony of Christ to the Old Testament* (London, 1891).
Ensor, G., *Bishop Ryle and Genesis: Being an Examination of his 'Early Narratives of Genesis'* (London, 1904).
Evangelical Church Schools Annual Report (London, 1907).
Evangelical Layman, An, 'Divorçons!', *Hibbert Journal* (London) 1909-10.
Falloon, H., *The Blessed Dead: Do they need our prayers?* (London, 1905).
Farley, I.D., *J.C. Ryle, first Bishop of Liverpool*, (Carlisle, 2000).
Farrar, F.W., *Protestantism: It Peril and Its Duty* (London, 1893).
Farrar, R., *The Life of Frederic William Farrar* (London, 1904).
Fausset, A.R., *True Science confirming Genesis* (London, 1884).
Fellowship of Evangelical Churchmen, *Second Report* (London, 1921).
Fielder, T., *The Truth of the Bible* (London, 1912).
Filleul, P.V.M., *The Limits of Toleration* (London, 1898).
- *Considerations regarding the Bishop of Salisbury's recent letter to his clergy, chiefly on the subjects of 'Eucharist' and 'Confession'* (London, 1899).
- *The Catholic Revival: What is it doing for England?* (London, 1900).
Finlayson, A.R.M., *Life of Canon Fleming* (London, 1909).
Fitzgerald, M.H., *A Memoir of Herbert Edward Ryle* (London, 1928).
Fleming, J.A., *Evolution and Revelation: A Vindication of the Divine Origin of the Bible* (London, 1926).

- *Evolution or Creation?* (London, 1933).
Foundation Truths of the Gospel (London, 1901).
Fox, H.E., *Our Lord and His Bible; or, What did Jesus Christ think of the Old Testament?* (London, 1905).
- *Rationalism or the Gospel? with special reference to their relative influence on Christian missions* (London, 1912).
French, R.V., (ed.), *Lex Mosaica; or, the Law of Moses and the Higher Criticism* (London, 1894).
Gairdner, W.H.T., *D.M. Thornton: A Study in Missionary Ideals and Methods* (London, 1908).
Garratt, E.R., *Life and Personal Recollections of Samuel Garratt* (London, 1908).
Gilbert, T.W., *Prayer Book Revision from an Evangelical point of view* (London, 1923).
Girdlestone, R.B., *The Foundations of the Bible: Studies in Old Testament Criticism* (London, 1891[2]).
- *Doctor Doctorum: The Teacher and the Book. With some remarks on Old Testament criticism* (London, 1892).
- *The Student's Deuteronomy* (London, 1899).
- *Old Testament Theology and Modern Ideas* (London, 1909).
- *The Building Up of the Old Testament* (London, 1912).
- (et al.), *English Church Teaching on Faith Life and Order* (London, 1897).
Gooding, H.B., *Bible Study* (London, 1924).
Gore, C., (ed.), *Lux Mundi: A Series of Studies in the Religion of the Incarnation* (London, 1889).
- *The New Theology and the Old Religion* (London, 1907).
- *The Basis of Anglican Fellowship in Faith and Organisation. An Open Letter..* (London, 1914).
Gowing, E.N., *John Edwin Watts-Ditchfield, First Bishop of Chelmsford* (London, 1926).
Gregory, J.G., *Idolatry, Ancient and Modern* (London, 1891).
Grensted, L.W., *The Making of the New Testament* (London, 1924).
Grubb, N.P., *Once Caught, No escape* (London, 1969).
Guest, H.J., *A Layman to Laymen on Prayer Book Revision* (London, 1927).
Gummer, S., *The Chavasse Twins* (London, 1963).
Gurney, T.A., *The Church of the First Three Centuries* (London, 1911).
Gwatkin, H.M., *The Bishop of Oxford's Open Letter. An Open Letter in reply* (London, 1914).
Hammond, T.C., *In Understanding be Men* (London, 1936).
Hardy, T., *Tess of the D'Urbervilles* (London, 1891).
Harford, J.B., *Since Wellhausen: A Brief Survey of Recent Pentateuchal Criticism* (London, 1926).
Harford, J.B., and Macdonald, F.C., *H.C.G. Moule, Bishop of Durham: A Biography* (London, 1923).
Harnack, A., *What is Christianity?* (London, 1901).
Harris, G.H., *Vernon Faithfull Storr: A Memoir* (London, 1943).

Harriss, J.A., *The Place of Miracles in Christianity: Two Sermons* (Oxford, 1911).

Heitland, L., *Ritualism in Town and Country: A Volume of Evidence* (London, 1902).

Henson, H.H., *Cui Bono? An Open Letter to Lord Halifax on the Present Crisis in the Church of England* (London, 1898).

- 'Letters of Business', *Contemporary Review* 90 (London, 1906).
- *The Creed in the Pulpit* (London, 1912).
- *Retrospect of an Unimportant Life* (London, 1942-43).

Herklots, B., *The Future of the Evangelical Party in the Church of England* (London, 1913).

Heurtley, C.A., *The Inspiration of Holy Scripture. Constancy in Prayer.. Two Sermons preached before the University of Oxford* (Oxford, 1861).

- *Wholesome Words: Sermons on some important points of Christian doctrine preached before the University of Oxford* (London, 1896).

Hinchliff, P., *Frederick Temple, Archbishop of Canterbury. A Life* (Oxford, 1998).

Hocking, J., *The Soul of Dominic Wildthorne* (London, 1908).

Holden, J.S., *Chapter by Chapter through the Bible: Expository and Devotional Comments* (London, 1920).

Horsefield, F.J., *The Bible, our only standard of truth* (London, 1894).

Howard, R.T., *Evangelicals and the Grey Book* (London, 1924).

Howden, J.R., *The Old Paths in the Light of ModernThought* (London, 1921).

- *The Proposed New Prayer Book. The Evangelical Standpoint and Objections* (London, 1927).
- *The Composite Prayer Book. The Evangelical Standpoint and Objections* (London, 1927).
- (ed.), *Evangelicalism by members of the FEC* (London, 1925).

Hughes-Games, J., *The Duty of Evangelical Churchmen under Possible Eventualities. A Paper* (London, 1900).

Inskip, J.T., *A Man's Job: Reminiscences* (London, 1948).

Iremonger, F.A., *William Temple, Archbishop of Canterbury. His Life and Letters* (London, 1948).

Isaacs, A.A., *The New Vicar: A Descriptive Tale of Modern Church Doctrine and Practice* (London, n.d. [1904]).

Joynson-Hicks, W., *The Prayer Book Crisis* (London, 1928).

Kelway, A.C., *George Rundle Prynne* (London, 1905).

Kennedy, E.J., *Old Theology Restated* (London, 1907).

Kirkpatrick, A.F., *Old Testament Prophecy* (London, 1924).

Knowling, R.J., *Literary Criticism and the New Testament* (London, 1907).

Knox, E.A., *The Glad Tidings of Reconciliation* (London, 1916).

- *On What Authority? A Review of the Foundations of Christian Faith* (London, 1922).
- *An Open Letter concerning the provision of an Alternative Prayer Book* (London, 1923).
- *Spiritual Objections to the Alternative Communion Service* (London, 1923).

- 'Prayer Book Revision and the National Church', *Nineteenth Century and After* (London, 1923).
- *A Letter to.. the Archbishop of Canterbury* (London, 1924).
- *Wake up England ! The Reformation is at stake* (London, 1925).
- *'A Pillar of Salt'; or, The Peril to England of hankering after Rome* (London, 1926).
- *Does the Deposited Book change the doctrine of the Church of England on the Lord's Supper?* (London, 1927).
- *The Unscriptural character of the alternative Consecration Prayer.. A Reply..* (London, 1927).
- *Will the Deposited Book restore order in the Church? Some startling facts* (London, 1927).
- *The Malines Conversations and the Deposited Book* (London, 1928).
- *Objections to the Prayer Book Measure 1928* (London, 1928).
- *The Tractarian Movement 1833-45* (London, 1933).
- *Reminiscences of an Octogenarian* (London, 1935).

Knox, Ronald, 'Tendencies of Anglicanism', *Dublin Review* 324 (London, 1918).

Lancelot, J.B., *Francis James Chavasse* (Oxford, 1929).

Langston, E.L., *Bishop Taylor Smith* (London, 1939).

Leeds, H., *Life of Dean Lefroy* (Norwich, 1909).

Lees, H.C., *The Joy of Bible Study* (London, 1909).

Lefroy, W., *The Christian Ministry: Its Origin, Constitution, Nature and Work* (London, 1890).
- (ed.), *Lectures on Ecclesiastical History, delivered in Norwich Cathedral* (London, 1896).

Lewis, H., 'The present condition of the Evangelicals', *Nineteenth Century and After* 19-20 (London, 1907).

Litton, E.A., *Introduction to Dogmatic Theology on the Basis of the Thirty Nine Articles* (London, 1912[3]).

Loane, M.L., *Archbishop Mowll* (London, 1960).

Lockhart, J.G., *Charles Lindley, Viscount Halifax* (London, 1935, 1936).

Mackenzie, C., *The Altar Steps* (London, 1922).
- *The Parson's Progress* (London, 1923).
- *The Heavenly Ladder* (London, 1924).
- *My Life and Times* (London, 1963-67).

Madden, T.J., *The Book of Common Prayer: Scriptural, Catholic, Protestant* (London, 1896).

Major, H.D.A., *The Life and Letters of William Boyd Carpenter* (London, 1925).

Makower, K., *Follow My Leader: A Biography of Murray Webb-Peploe* (Eastbourne, 1984).

Matthew, H.C.G., *Gladstone 1809-98* (Oxford, 1999).

McKay, R., *John Leonard Wilson, Confessor for the Faith* (London, 1973).

Miller, H., *A Guide to Ecclesiastical Law. For Churchwardens and Parishioners* (London, 1912[10]).

Moberly, R., *Ministerial Priesthood* (London, 1897).

Momerie, A.W., *'Inspiration' and other sermons delivered in the chapel of the Foundling Hospital* (Edinburgh, 1889).

- 'Theology at King's College', *Contemporary Review* 59 (London, 1891).

[Momerie, V.,] *Dr Momerie: His Life and Work* (Edinburgh, 1905).

[Moore, A.L.,] *Darwinism and the Christian Faith* (London, 1888).

Moule, H.C.G., *The New Birth: A Brief Enquiry and Statement* (London, 1888).

- *Outlines of Christian Doctrine* (London, 1889).
- *Veni Creator* (London, 1890).
- *The Evangelical School in the Church of England: Its Men and Its Work in the Nineteenth Century* (London, 1901).
- (ed.), *A Brief Declaration of the Lord's Supper, by Nicholas Ridley* (London, 1895).

Moule, Henry, *More than one universal deluge recorded in the Scriptures* (London, 1869).

- *Scripture interpreted on Scripture Principles. An Exposition of Genesis 1* (London, 1874).

Mulliner, H.G., *Arthur Burroughs: A Memoir* (London, 1936).

National Church League, *The Proposed Revision of the Prayer Book* (London, n.d.).

Neil, J., *Musical Service: Is it right?* (London, 1903[2]).

Newman, J.H., *Lectures on the Prophetical Office of the Church* (London, 1837).

- *Apologia pro Vita Sua* (London, 1864).

Nunn, H.P.V., *What is Modernism?* (London, 1932).

Objects of the Victoria Institute (London, n.d.).

Orr, J., *God's Image in Man and Its Defacement in the light of modern denials* (London, 1905).

- *Sin as a problem of today* (London, 1910).

Percival, J., *A Charge* (London, 1915)

- (et al.), *Church and Faith, Being Essays on the Teaching of the Church of England* (London, 1899).

Perowne, J.J.S., 'Dr Pusey on Daniel the Prophet', *Contemporary Review* (London), 1866.

- 'The age of the Pentateuch', *Contemporary Review* (London), 1888.
- 'The inspiration of the Bible and modern criticism', *Expository Times* (Edinburgh), 1890.
- *The Relation of Old Testament Criticism to the Christian Faith* (Edinburgh, 1890).
- 'Notes on Genesis', *Expositor* (London), 1890.
- 'Genesis and Science', *Expositor* (London), 1891.
- *A Charge* (London, 1895).

Phillips, W.A., *The Protestant Reformed Church of England: An Historical Retrospect* (London, 1928).

Pollock, B., *Speech by the Bishop of Norwich delivered in.. Convocation* (London, 1927).

Pratt, J.H., *Scripture and Science not at Variance* (London, 1872[7]).
Prestige, G.L., *The Life of Charles Gore* (London, 1935).
Proby, W.H.B., *Annals of the 'Low Church' party in England, down to the death of Archbishop Tait* (London, 1888).
Protestant Truth Society Report for the year 1896-7 (London, n.d.).
Protestantism in answer to Anglo-Catholicism, Romanism and Modernism (London, 1922).
Raven, C.E., (ed.), *The Mission to Cambridge University 1919-20* (London, 1920).
Reservation: Report of a Conference held at Farnham Castle on October 24-27, 1925 (London, 1926).
Reynolds, J.S., *Canon Christopher of St Aldate's* (Abingdon, 1967).
Rogers, T.G., (ed.), *Liberal Evangelicalism: An Interpretation by Members of the Church of England* (London, 1923).
- *The Inner Life. Essays in Liberal Evangelicalism* (London, 1925).
- *A Rebel at Heart. The Autobiography of a Nonconforming Churchman* (London, 1956).
Rostron, S.N., *The Christology of St Paul* (London, 1912).
Royal Commission on Ecclesiastical Discipline, Minutes of Evidence and Report (London, 1906).
Rumscheidt, M., (ed.), *Adolf von Harnack* (London, 1989).
Russell, G.W.E., *The Household of Faith* (London, 1902).
- *A Short History of the Evangelical Movement* (London, 1915).
Ryle, H.E., *The Early Narratives of Genesis* (London, 1892).
- *Physical Science and the first chapter of Genesis* (London, 1896).
- *On Holy Scripture and Criticism* (London, 1904).
- *On the Church of England* (London, 1904).
- *The Book of Genesis in the Revised Version* (Cambridge, 1914).
Ryle, J.C., *Knots Untied* (London, 1874).
- *Old Paths* (London, 1877).
- *What do we owe to the Reformation?* (London, 1877).
- *Facts and Men: Being Pages from English Church History.. with a Preface for the Times* (London, 1882).
- *'The Oracles of God'. A Paper for the Times on the Inspiration of the Bible* (London, 1882).
- *The Upper Room* (London, 1888).
- *Is all Scripture inspired? An attempt to answer the question* (London, 1891).
- *Have you a priest?* (1896).
- *Visitation Charges, Diocesan Addresses and Special Sermons* (London, 1903).
Salvidge, S., *Salvidge of Liverpool* (London, 1934).
Sanday, W., *Bishop Gore's Challenge to Criticism. A Reply* (London, 1914).
Sandon, Viscount, *The Deposited Prayer Book* (London, 1927).
Sangar, J.M., *A Curate's Protestant Speech and Subsequent Forfeiture of his Cure* (London, 1892).
- *No Surrender of our Protestant Rights. A Lecture* (London, 1897).

- *England's Privilege and Curse; or, Sixty Years of Government by a Gracious and Beloved Queen, yet of Progressive National Apostasy* (London, 1897).
- *The Protestant Crisis* (London, 1899).

Short, A.R., *The Bible and Modern Research* (London, 1931).

Silvester, J., *A Champion of the Faith: A Memoir of the Revd C.H.H. Wright* (London, 1917).

Simpkinson, C.H., *The Life and Work of Bishop Thorold* (London, 1896).

Sinclair, W., *The Prospects of the Principles of the Reformation in the Church of England* (London, 1893).

Sinker, R., *'Higher Criticism': What is it and where does it lead us?* (London, 1899).

Smellie, A., *Evan Henry Hopkins: A Memoir* (London, 1920).

Smith, G., *Successive Creation or Progressive Evolution. A Paper* (London, 1880).

Smith, H. Maynard, *Frank, Bishop of Zanzibar* (London, 1926).

Smith, R. Payne, *Science and Revelation. A Lecture* (London, 1871).
- *The First Book of Moses, called Genesis* (London, 1885).

Smith, S., *'The Ascent of Man' by Professor Henry Drummond. A Review* (London, 1894).
- *Ritualism in the Church of England in 1900* (London, 1901).

[Smith, Sydney,] 'Strictures on two critiques in the *Edinburgh Review* on the subject of Methodism and Missions', *Edinburgh Review* 14 (Edinburgh, 1809).

Smyth, W. Woods, *Facts and Fallacies regarding the Bible* (London, 1910).

Soames, W.H.K., *Is Sacerdotalism Scriptural? What saith the Scripture?* (London, 1903).

Speeches of Samuel Smith, Esq., MP, and the Rt.Hon. Sir William Harcourt, MP, in the House of Commons, June 16th and 21st 1898, and an Address by Samuel Smith, Esq., MP, on Ritualism and Elementary Education (London, 1898).

Spencer, F.E., *Did Moses write the Pentateuch after all?* (London, 1892).
- *Present Day Problems* (London, 1904).
- *Old Testament History* (London, 1909).
- *A Short Introduction to the Old Testament* (London, 1912).

S[tanton], A.H., *Catholic Prayers for Church of England People* (London, 1897).

Stephen, L., *The Life of Sir James Fitzjames Stephen* (London, 1895).

Stock, E., *Lesson Studies from the Book of Genesis* (London, 1885).
- *The History of the Church Missionary Society* (London, 1899, 1916).
- *My Recollections* (London, 1909).

Stokes, Sir G., *Natural Theology* (London, 1891, 1893).

Storr, V.F., *Development and Divine Purpose* (London, 1906).
- *The Inspiration of the Bible* (Winchester, 1908).
- *The Development of English Theology in the Nineteenth Century, 1800-60* (London, 1913).
- *Christianity and Immortality* (London, 1918).
- *The Problem of the Cross* (London, 1919).

- *The Bible: What it is and what it is not* (London, 1924).
- *Inspiration* (London, 1924).
- *Jesus Christ and the Old Testament* (London, 1924).
- *My Faith* (London, 1927).
- *Freedom and Tradition: A Study of Liberal Evangelicalism* (London, 1940).

Streeter, B.H. et al., *Foundations. A Statement of Christian Belief in Terms of Modern Thought* (London, 1912).

Tait, A.J., *Lecture Outlines on the Thirty Nine Articles* (London, 1910).
- *The Heavenly Session of our Lord: An Introduction to the History of the Doctrine* (London, 1912).
- *What is our deposit?* (London, 1914).
- *The Nature and Functions of the Sacraments* (London, 1917).

Taylor, H.A., *Jix, Viscount Brentford* (London, 1933).

Temple, W., *The Prayer Book Crisis. A Reply to the Rt Hon Sir William Joynson-Hicks* (London, 1928).

Tennant, F.R, 'The influences of Darwinism upon theology', *Quarterly Review*(London), 1909.

Thomas, W.H. Griffith, *Priest or Prophet? A Question for the Day* (London, 1900).
- *The Catholic Faith* (London, 1904).
- *A Sacrament of our Redemption* (London, 1905).
- *Old Testament Criticism and New Testament Christianity* (Stirling, 1905).
- *Genesis: A Devotional Commentary* (London, 1907-08).

Thompson, J. Denton, *Central Churchmanship; or, the Position, Principles and Policy of Evangelical Churchmen in relation to Modern Thought and Work* (London, 1911).

Thompson, J.M., *Miracles in the New Testament* (London, 1911).
- *My Apologia, by J.M.T.* (Oxford, 1940).

Titterton, C.H., and Neill, C., *Scriptural Evangelicalism: Fundamental Truths of the Word of God* (London, 1925).

Tomkins, O., *The Life of Edward Woods* (London, 1957).

Toon, P., (ed.), *J.C. Ryle: A Self-Portrait* (Swenger, Pa., 1975).

Toon, P., and Smout, M., *John Charles Ryle* (Cambridge, 1976).

Townsend, J.H., *A Sling Stone for the Critics* (London, n.d.).

Trevelyan, G.M., *An Autobiography and Other Essays* (London, 1949).

Tristram, H.B., 'Recent geographical and historical progress in zoology', *Contemporary Review* (London), 1866.

Upton, W.P., *The Proposed Revision of the Prayer Book. A Review of its Principal Features* (London, 1923[2]).

Urquhart, J., *Roger's Reasons* (London, 1898).

Verbatim Report of Speeches delivered at the Great Demonstration held in the Queen's Hall, Langham Place on Tuesday Evening, May 3rd 1898 (London, 1898).

Wace, H., *The Evangelical Pastorate for Undergraduates at Oxford* (Oxford, 1898).

- *English Religion: An Address on the Decision of the Archbishops in regard to Incense, Lights and the Reservation of the Sacrament* (London, 1900).
- *The Bible and Modern Investigation* (London, 1903).
- *Some Questions of the Day: Biblical, National and Ecclesiastical* (London, 1912).
- *Some Questions of the Day: National, Ecclesiastical and Religious* (London, 1914).
- *Prayer Book Revision.. A Statementand an Appeal* (London, n.d.).
- 'The revision of the Prayer Book', *Church Quarterly Review* 193 (London, 1923).

Wace, H., and Meyrick, F., *An Appeal from the New to the True Catholics; or, The Faith and Practice of the first Six Centuries* (London, 1904).

Wakeman, H.O., *An Introduction to the History of the Church of England from the Earliest Times to the Present Day* (London, 1896).

Waller, C.H., *The Authoritative Inspiration of Holy Scripture* (London, 1887).
- *The Word of God and the Testimony of Jesus Christ* (London, 1904).
- *Moses and the Prophets* (London, 1907).

Walsh, W., *The Secret Work of the Ritualists* (London, 1894).
- *The Secret History of the Oxford Movement* (London, 1897).

Warman, F.S.G., *The Ministry and Unity* (London, 1914).
- *The Evangelical Movement: Its Message and Its Achievement* (London, 1916).

Warren, M.A.C., *Crowded Canvas* (London, 1974).

Watts-Ditchfield, J.E., *The Creed. Speech by the Bishop of Chelmsford* (London, 1918).

Webster, F.S., *Jonah: Patriot and Revivalist* (London, 1906).

Weston, F., *Ecclesia Anglicana: For what does she stand?* (London, 1913).

Wilcox, J.C., *John Kensit, Reformer and Martyr. A Popular Life* (London, 1903).

Williams, C., *Flecker of Dean Close* (London, 1946).

Wilson, J.M., *Evolution and the Christian Faith* (London, 1924).

Wimborne, Cornelia, Lady, *The Ritualist Conspiracy* (London, 1898).
- 'The report on ecclesiastical discipline', *Nineteenth Century and After* (London) 1906.

Wisdom, H.C., *The Proposed Changes in the Prayer Book of the Church of England* (Stirling, 1925).

Woods, C.E., *Memoirs and Letters of Canon Hay Aitken* (London, 1928).

Woods, E.S., *Modern Discipleship and what it means* (London, 1910).
- *What is this Christianity?* (London, 1934).

Woods, E.S., and Macnutt, F.B., *Theodore, Bishop of Winchester* (London, 1933).

Woods, F.T., *The Prayer Book Revised* (London, 1927).

Woods, F.T., et al., *The Creed of a Churchman* (London, 1916).

World's Evangelical Alliance Pamphlets: Addresses on 'The Reformation' (London, 1925).

Wright, C.H.H., *An Introduction to the Old Testament* (London, 1890).

- *Daniel and His Prophecies* (London, 1906).
- *Daniel and Its Critics* (London, 1906).

Wright, C.H.H., and Neil, C., (eds), *A Protestant Dictionary* (London, 1904).

Wright, M., *Home Idolatry and Home Missions* (London, 1892).

4. Secondary Sources.

Anson, P.F., *Fashions in Church Furnishings 1840-1940* (London, 1965^2).

Arnstein, W.L., *Protestant versus Catholic in mid-Victorian England. Mr Newdegate and the Nuns* (Columbia, 1982).

Barbour, I.G., *Issues in Science and Religion* (London, 1966).

Barclay, O.R., *Whatever happened to the Jesus Lane Lot?* (Leicester, 1977).

Bebbington, D.W., *Evangelicalism in Modern Britain. A History from the 1730s to the 1980s* (London, 1989).

- *The Nonconformist Conscience: Chapel and Politics, 1870-1914* (London, 1982).
- *Holiness in Nineteenth Century England* (Carlisle, 2000).

Bell, P.M.H., *Disestablishment in Ireland and Wales* (London, 1969).

Bentley, James, *Ritualism and Politics in Victorian Britain. The Attempt to legislate for belief* (Oxford, 1978).

Binns, L.E. Elliott-, *Religion in the Victorian Era* (London, 1946^2).

- *English Thought 1860-1960: The Theological Aspect* (London, 1956).

Brake, G. Thompson, *Policy and Politics in British Methodism 1932-1982* (London, 1984).

Bullock, F.W.B., *The History of Ridley Hall, Cambridge* (Cambridge, 1941, 1953).

- *A History of Training for the Ministry of the Church of England in England and Wales 1800-74* (St. Leonard's-on-Sea, 1955).
- *A History of Training for the Ministry of the Church of England in England and Wales 1875-1974* (London, 1976).

Cameron, N.M. De S., *Evolution and the Authority of the Bible* (Exeter, 1983).

Carter, Grayson, *Anglican Evangelicals. Protestant Secessions from the Via Media, c. 1800- 1850* (Oxford, 2001).

Chadwick, O., *The Victorian Church*, ii, (London, 1972^2).

Church, R.W., *The Oxford Movement 1833-45* (London, 1891).

Clements, K.W., *Lovers of Discord: Twentieth Century Theological Controversies in England* (London, 1988).

Clements, R.E., *A Century of Old Testament Study* (Guildford, 1983^2).

Cohen, I.B., *Revolution in Science* (London, 1985).

Colley, L., *Britons. Forging the Nation, 1707-1837* (London, 1992).

Cox, J., *The English Churches in a Secular Society: Lambeth, 1870-1930* (New York, 1982).

Cupitt, D., 'Darwinism and English religious thought', *Theology* 78 (London, 1975).

Davies, H., *Worship and Theology in England 1850-1900: From Newman to Martineau* (Princeton, 1962).

- *Worship and Theology in England. The Ecumenical Century 1900-65* (Princeton, 1965).

Desmond, A., and Moore, J., *Darwin* (London, 1991).

Doctrine in the Church of England (London, 1938).

Edwards, D.L., *Leaders of the Church of England 1828-1944* (London, 1971).

Ellegård, A., *Darwin and the General Reader. The Reception of Darwin's Theory of Evolution in the British Periodical Press 1859-72* (Goteborg, 1958).

Gillispie, C.C., *Genesis and Geology* (Cambridge, Mass., 1951).

Glover, W.B., *Evangelical Nonconformists and Higher Criticism in the Nineteenth Century* (London, 1954).

Harris, H., *The Tübingen School* (Oxford, 1975).

Hastings, A., *A History of English Christianity 1920-2000* (London, 2001).

Hearnshaw, F.J.C., *The Centenary History of King's College, London, 1828-1928* (London, 1929).

Heeney, B., *Mission to the Middle Classes: The Woodard Schools 1848-91* (London, 1969).

Heiser, F.B., *The Story of St Aidan's College, Birkenhead 1847-1947* (Chester, 1947).

Hennell, M., 'Evangelicalism and worldliness, 1770-1870', *SCH* 8 (London, 1972).

Hewitt, G., *The Problems of Success. A History of the Church Missionary Society 1910-42*, I (London, 1971).

Hickin, L., 'Liberal Evangelicals in the Church of England', *Church Quarterly Review* 169 (London, 1968).

Hilliard, D., 'Unenglish and unmanly:Anglo-Catholicism and homosexuality', *Victorian Studies* 25, (Bloomington, Indiana, 1982).

Hooton, W.S., and Wright, J. Stafford, *The First Twenty Five Years of the BCMS (1922-47)* (London, 1947).

Horn, R.M., *Student Witness and Christian Truth* (London, 1971).

Jasper, R.C.D., *Prayer Book Revision in England 1800-1900* (London, 1954).

Johnson, D., *Contending for the Faith: A History of the Evangelical Movement in the Universities and Colleges* (Leicester, 1979).

Kent, J.H.S., *From Darwin to Blatchford. The Role of Darwinism in ChristianApologetic 1875-1910* (London, 1966).

- *Holding the Fort* (London, 1978).

Larsen, T., *Friends of Religious Equality. Nonconformist Politics in Mid-Victorian England* (Woodbridge, 1999).

Livingston, J.C., *The Ethics of Belief. An Essay on the Victorian Religious Conscience* (Tallahasee, Florida, 1974).

Livingstone, D.N., 'Preadamites: the history of an idea from heresy to orthodoxy', *Scottish Journal of Theology* 40 (Edinburgh, 1987).

- *Darwin's Forgotten Defenders: The Encounter between Evangelical Theology and Evolutionary Thought* (Edinburgh, 1987).

Lloyd, R., *The Church of England 1900-65* (London, 1966).

Machin, G.I.T., 'The last Victorian anti-ritualist campaign 1895-1906',

Victorian Studies 25 (Bloomington, Indiana, 1982).
- *Politics and the Churches in Great Britain, 1869-1921* (Oxford, 1987).
- 'Parliament, the Church of England and the Prayer Book crisis, 1927-8', in Parry, J.P., and Taylor, S., (eds), *Parliament and the Church 1529-1960* (Edinburgh, 2000).

Manwaring, R., *From Contoversy to Co-existence: Evangelicals in the Church of England 1914-80* (Cambridge, 1985).

Marsden, G., 'Fundamentalism as an American phenomenon, a comparison with English Evangelicalism', *Church History* 46 (Chicago, 1977).
- *Fundamentalism and American Culture. The Shaping of Twentieth Century Evangelicalism 1870-1925* (New York, 1980).

Marshall, I.H., (ed.), *New Testament Interpretation* (Exeter, 1979[2]).

McDonald, H.D., *Ideas of Revelation: An Historical Study 1700-1860* (London, 1959).
- *Theories of Revelation: An Historical Study 1860-1960* (London, 1963).

McGrath, A., *Iustitia Dei. A History of the Christian Doctrine of Justification* (Cambridge, 1986).
- *Evangelicalism and the Future of Christianity* (London, n.d. [?1994]).

Meacham, S., 'The Evangelical inheritance', *Journal of British Studies* 3 (Hartford, Conn., 1963).

Moore, J.R., *The Post-Darwinian Controversies* (Cambridge, 1979).

Morgan, R., '*Non Angli, sed Angeli*: some Anglican reactions to German Gospel criticism', in S. Sykes and D. Holmes (eds), *New Studies in Theology*, 1 (London, 1980).

Morrell, J.B., and Thackray, A., *Gentlemen of Science: Early Years of the British Association for the Advancement of Science* (Oxford, 1981).

Morris, J., *Religion and Urban Change. Croydon, 1840-1914* (Woodbridge, 1992).

Munson, J.E.B., 'The London School Board election of 1894: a study in Victorian religious controversy', *British Journal of Educational Studies* 23 (London, 1975).
- 'The Oxford Movement by the end of the nineteenth century: The Anglo-Catholic clergy', *Church History* 44 (Chicago, 1975).

Murphy, H.R., 'The ethical revolt against Christian orthodoxy in early Victorian England', *American Historical Review* 50 (Washington, 1955)

Neill, S., *The Interpretation of the New Testament, 1861-1961* (Oxford, 1964).
- *A History of Christian Missions* (Harmondsworth, 1986).

Nias, J.C.S., *Gorham and the Bishop of Exeter* (London, 1951).

Nockles, P.B., *The Oxford Movement in Context. Anglican High Churchmanship, 1760-1857* (Cambridge, 1994).

Norman, E.R., *Anti-Catholicism in Victorian England* (London, 1968).

Packer, J.I., *'Fundamentalism' and the Word of God* (London, 1958).

Pickering, W.S.F., *Anglo-Catholicism. A Study in Religious Ambiguity* (London, 1989).

Pollard, A., 'Anglican Evangelical views of the Bible, 1800-50', *Churchman* 74 (London, July-September 1960).
Pollock, J.C., *A Cambridge Movement* (London, 1953).
Ramsey, A.M., *From Gore to Temple* (London, 1960).
Randall, I.M., *Evangelical Experiences. A Study in the Spirituality of English Evangelicalism 1918-1939* (Carlisle, 1999).
Reynolds, J.S., *Born Anew. Historical Outlines of the Oxford Inter-Collegiate Christian Union 1879-1979* (Oxford, 1979).
Rogerson, J., *Old Testament Criticism in the Nineteenth Century: England and Germany* (London, 1984).
Rosman, D., *Evangelicals and Culture* (London, 1984).
Rouse, R., and Neill, S., *A History of the Ecumenical Movement 1517-1948* (London, 1967).
Rowell, G., *The Vision Glorious. Themes and Personalities of the Catholic Revival in Anglicanism* (Oxford, 1983).
Royle, E., *Victorian Infidels* (Manchester, 1974).
- (ed.), *The Infidel Tradition from Paine to Bradlaugh* (London, 1976).
Ruse, M., 'The relationship between science and religion in Britain, 1830-70', *Church History* 44 (Chicago, 1975).
Sandeen, E.R., *The Roots of Fundamentalism: British and American Millenarianism 1800-1930* (Chicago, 1970).
Smith, A.E., *Another Anglican Angle. The History of the AEGM* (Oxford, 1991).
Smith, K. Hylson-, *Evangelicals in the Church of England 1734-1984* (Edinburgh, 1988).
Smith, J.T., *Methodism and Education 1849-1902* (Oxford, 1998).
Smyth, C., 'The Evangelical Movement in perspective', *Cambridge Historical Journal* 7 (Cambridge, 1941-43).
Stephenson, A.M.G., *The Rise and Decline of English Modernism* (London, 1984).
Symondson, A., (ed.), *The Victorian Crisis of Faith* (London, 1970).
Tarver, M.A.J., *Trent College 1868-1927* (London, 1929).
Tatlow, T., *The Story of the Student Christian Movement* (London, 1933).
Thompson, David M., *Same Difference? Liberals and Conservatives in the Student Movement* (Birmingham, 1990).
Thomson, G.I.F., *The Oxford Pastorate: The First Half Century* (London, 1946).
Toon, P., *Evangelical Theology 1833-1856. A Response to Tractarianism* (London, 1979).
Vidler, A.R., *The Church in an Age of Revolution* (Harmondsworth, 1974[3]).
Voll, D., *Catholic Evangelicalism: The Acceptance of Evangelical Traditions by the Oxford Movement during the second half of the Nineteenth Century* (Munich, 1960; E.T. London, 1963).
Waller, P.J., *Democracy and Sectarianism: A Political and Social History of Liverpool 1868- 1939* (Liverpool, 1981).
Welch, C., *Protestant Thought in the Nineteenth Century* (New Haven, 1972, 1985).

Wellings, M., 'Anglo-Catholicism, the "crisis in the Church" and the Cavalier case of 1899', *JEH* 42 (Cambridge, 1992).

- 'The first Protestant martyr of the twentieth century: the life and significance of John Kensit (1853-1902)', *SCH* 30 (Oxford, 1993).
- 'What is an evangelical?', *Epworth Review* 21 (Peterborough, 1994).
- 'The Oxford Movement in late nineteenth century retrospect: R.W. Church, J.H. Rigg and Walter Walsh', *SCH* 33 (Woodbridge, 1997).

Whale, J., *One Church, One Lord* (London, 1979).

White, J.F., *The Cambridge Movement* (Cambridge, 1962).

Wilson, D.B., 'A physicist's alternative to materialism: the religious thought of George Gabriel Stokes', *Victorian Studies* 28 (Bloomington, Indiana, 1984).

Wolffe, J., *The Protestant Crusade in Great Britain, 1829-1860* (Oxford, 1991).

Wright, N.T., *Jesus and the Victory of God* (London, 1996).

Yates, N., *Anglican Ritualism in Victorian Britain, 1830-1910* (Oxford, 1999).

5. Unpublished Theses and Papers

Balda, W., 'Spheres of influence: Simeon's Trust and its implications for Evangelical patronage', Cambridge PhD, 1981.

Bentley, A., 'The transformation of the Evangelical party in the Church of England in the later nineteenth century', Durham PhD, 1971.

Ervine, W.J.C., 'Doctrine and diplomacy: some aspects of the life and thought of the Anglican Evangelical clergy 1797-1837', Cambridge PhD, 1979.

Evershed, W.A., 'Party and patronage in the Church of England 1800-1945: a study of patronage trusts and patronage reform', Oxford DPhil, 1985.

Hardman, B.E., 'The Evangelical party in the Church of England 1855-65', Cambridge PhD, 1964.

Herring, G.W., 'Tractarianism to ritualism: a study of some aspects of Tractarianism outside Oxford from the time of Newman's conversion in 1845 until the first Ritual Commission in 1867', Oxford DPhil, 1984.

Jay, E.J., 'Anglican Evangelicalism and the nineteenth century novel', Oxford DPhil, 1975.

Morris, J.N., 'Religion and urban change in Victorian England: a case study of the borough of Croydon 1840-1914', Oxford DPhil, 1986.

Walmsley, J.W., 'The history of the Evangelical party in the Church of England between 1906 and 1928', Hull PhD, 1980.

Whisenant, James C., 'Anti-ritualism and the division of the Evangelical party in the second half of the nineteenth century', Vanderbilt PhD, 1998.

White, J.W., 'The influence of North American evangelism in Great Britain between 1830 and 1914 on the origin and development of the Ecumenical Movement', Oxford DPhil, 1963.

Wilson, Alan T.L., 'The authority of Church and party among London Anglo-Catholics, 1880- 1914, with special reference to the Church crisis of 1898-1904', Oxford DPhil, 1988.

Index

Studies in Evangelical History and Thought

(All titles uniform with this volume)
Dates in bold are of projected publication

Clyde Binfield
The Country a Little Thickened and Congested?
Nonconformity in Eastern England 1840–1885

Studies of Victorian religion and society often concentrate on cities, suburbs, and industrialisation. This study provides a contrast. Victorian Eastern England—Essex, Suffolk, Norfolk, Cambridgeshire, and Huntingdonshire—was rural, traditional, relatively unchanging. That is nonetheless a caricature which discounts the industry in Norwich and Ipswich (as well as in Haverhill, Stowmarket, and Leiston) and ignores the impact of London on Essex, of railways throughout the region, and of an ancient but changing university (Cambridge) on the county town which housed it. It also entirely ignores the political implications of such changes in a region noted for the variety of its religious Dissent since the seventeenth century. This book explores Victorian Eastern England and its Nonconformity. It brings to a wider readership a pioneering thesis which has made a major contribution to a fresh evolution of English religion and society.

***2005** / 1-84227-216-0 / approx. 274pp*

John Brencher
Martyn Lloyd-Jones (1899–1981) and Twentieth-Century Evangelicalism

This study critically demonstrates the significance of the life and ministry of Martyn Lloyd-Jones for post-war British evangelicalism and demonstrates that his preaching was his greatest influence on twentieth-century Christianity. The factors which shaped his view of the church are examined, as is the way his reformed evangelicalism led to a separatist ecclesiology which divided evangelicals.

2002 / 1-84227-051-6 / xvi + 268pp

Jonathan D. Burnham
A Story of Conflict
The Controversial Relationship between Benjamin Wills Newton and John Nelson Darby

Burnham explores the controversial relationship between the two principal leaders of the early Brethren movement. In many ways Newton and Darby were products of their times, and this study of their relationship provides insight not only into the dynamics of early Brethrenism, but also into the progress of nineteenth-century English and Irish evangelicalism.

2004 / 1-84227-191-1 / xxiv + 268pp

J.N. Ian Dickson

Beyond Religious Discourse

Sermons, Preaching and Evangelical Protestants in Nineteenth-Century Irish Society

Drawing extensively on primary sources, this pioneer work in modern religious history explores the training of preachers, the construction of sermons and how Irish evangelicalism and the wider movement in Great Britain and the United States shaped the preaching event. Evangelical preaching and politics, sectarianism, denominations, education, class, social reform, gender, and revival are examined to advance the argument that evangelical sermons and preaching went significantly beyond religious discourse. The result is a book for those with interests in Irish history, culture and belief, popular religion and society, evangelicalism, preaching and communication.

***2005** / 1-84227-217-9 / approx. 324pp*

Neil T.R. Dickson

Brethren in Scotland 1838–2000

A Social Study of an Evangelical Movement

The Brethren were remarkably pervasive throughout Scottish society. This study of the Open Brethren in Scotland places them in their social context and examines their growth, development and relationship to society.

2003 / 1-84227-113-X / xxviii + 510pp

Crawford Gribben and Timothy C.F. Stunt (eds)

Prisoners of Hope?

Aspects of Evangelical Millennialism in Britain and Ireland, 1800–1880

This volume of essays offers a comprehensive account of the impact of evangelical millennialism in nineteenth-century Britain and Ireland.

2004 / 1-84227-224-1 / xiv + 208pp

Khim Harris

Evangelicals and Education

Evangelical Anglicans and Middle-Class Education in Nineteenth-Century England

This ground breaking study investigates the history of English public schools founded by nineteenth-century Evangelicals. It documents the rise of middle-class education and Evangelical societies such as the influential Church Association, and includes a useful biographical survey of prominent Evangelicals of the period.

2004 / 1-84227-250-0 / xviii + 422pp

Mark Hopkins
Nonconformity's Romantic Generation
Evangelical and Liberal Theologies in Victorian England

A study of the theological development of key leaders of the Baptist and Congregational denominations at their period of greatest influence, including C.H. Spurgeon and R.W. Dale, and of the controversies in which those among them who embraced and rejected the liberal transformation of their evangelical heritage opposed each other.

2004 / 1-84227-150-4 / xvi + 284pp

Don Horrocks
Laws of the Spiritual Order
Innovation and Reconstruction in the Soteriology of Thomas Erskine of Linlathen

Don Horrocks argues that Thomas Erskine's unique historical and theological significance as a soteriological innovator has been neglected. This timely reassessment reveals Erskine as a creative, radical theologian of central and enduring importance in Scottish nineteenth-century theology, perhaps equivalent in significance to that of S.T. Coleridge in England.

2004 / 1-84227-192-X / xx + 362pp

Kenneth S. Jeffrey
When the Lord Walked the Land
The 1858–62 Revival in the North East of Scotland

Previous studies of revivals have tended to approach religious movements from either a broad, national or a strictly local level. This study of the multifaceted nature of the 1859 revival as it appeared in three distinct social contexts within a single region reveals the heterogeneous nature of simultaneous religious movements in the same vicinity.

2002 / 1-84227-057-5 / xxiv + 304pp

John Kenneth Lander
Itinerant Temples
Tent Methodism, 1814–1832

Tent preaching began in 1814 and the Tent Methodist sect resulted from disputes with Bristol Wesleyan Methodists in 1820. The movement spread to parts of Gloucestershire, Wiltshire, London and Liverpool, among other places. Its demise started in 1826 after which one leader returned to the Wesleyans and others became ministers in the Congregational and Baptist denominations.

2003 / 1-84227-151-2 / xx + 268pp

Donald M. Lewis

Lighten Their Darkness

The Evangelical Mission to Working-Class London, 1828–1860

This is a comprehensive and compelling study of the Church and the complexities of nineteenth-century London. Challenging our understanding of the culture in working London at this time, Lewis presents a well-structured and illustrated work that contributes substantially to the study of evangelicalism and mission in nineteenth-century Britain.

2001 / 1-84227-074-5 / xviii + 372pp

Herbert McGonigle

'Sufficient Saving Grace'

John Wesley's Evangelical Arminianism

A thorough investigation of the theological roots of John Wesley's evangelical Arminianism and how these convictions were hammered out in controversies on predestination, limited atonement and the perseverance of the saints.

2001 / 1-84227-045-1 / xvi + 350pp

Lisa S. Nolland

A Victorian Feminist Christian

Josephine Butler, the Prostitutes and God

Josephine Butler was an unlikely candidate for taking up the cause of prostitutes, as she did, with a fierce and self-disregarding passion. This book explores the particular mix of perspectives and experiences that came together to envision and empower her remarkable achievements. It highlights the vital role of her spirituality and the tragic loss of her daughter.

2004 / 1-84227-225-X / approx. 360pp

Ian M. Randall

Evangelical Experiences

A Study in the Spirituality of English Evangelicalism 1918–1939

This book makes a detailed historical examination of evangelical spirituality between the First and Second World Wars. It shows how patterns of devotion led to tensions and divisions. In a wide-ranging study, Anglican, Wesleyan, Reformed and Pentecostal-charismatic spiritualities are analysed.

1999 / 0-85364-919-7 / xii + 310pp

Ian M. Randall

Spirituality and Social Change

The Contribution of F.B. Meyer (1847–1929)

This is a fresh appraisal of F.B. Meyer (1847–1929), a leading Free Church minister. Having been deeply affected by holiness spirituality, Meyer became the Keswick Convention's foremost international speaker. He combined spirituality with effective evangelism and socio-political activity. This study shows Meyer's significant contribution to spiritual renewal and social change.

2003 / 1-84227-195-4 / xx + 184pp

James Robinson

Pentecostal Origins (1907–c.1925): A Regional Study

Early Pentecostalism in Ulster within its British Context

Harvey Cox describes Pentecostalism as 'the fascinating spiritual child of our time' that has the potential, at the global scale, to contribute to the 'reshaping of religion in the twenty-first century'. This study grounds such sentiments by examining at the local scale the origin, development and nature of Pentecostalism in the north of Ireland in its first twenty years. Illustrative, in a paradigmatic way, of how Pentecostalism became established within one region of the British Isles, it sets the story within the wider context of formative influences emanating from America, Europe and, in particular, other parts of the British Isles. As a synoptic regional study in Pentecostal history it is the first survey of its kind.

***2005** / 1-84227-329-9 / approx. 424pp*

Geoffrey Robson

Dark Satanic Mills?

Religion and Irreligion in Birmingham and the Black Country

This book analyses and interprets the nature and extent of popular Christian belief and practice in Birmingham and the Black Country during the first half of the nineteenth century, with particular reference to the impact of cholera epidemics and evangelism on church extension programmes.

2002 / 1-84227-102-4 / xiv + 294pp

Roger Shuff

Searching for the True Church

Brethren and Evangelicals in Mid-Twentieth-Century England

Roger Shuff holds that the influence of the Brethren movement on wider evangelical life in England in the twentieth century is often underrated. This book records and accounts for the fact that Brethren reached the peak of their strength at the time when evangelicalism was at it lowest ebb, immediately before World War II. However, the movement then moved into persistent decline as evangelicalism regained ground in the post war period. Accompanying this downward trend has been a sharp accentuation of the contrast between Brethren congregations who engage constructively with the non-Brethren scene and, at the other end of the spectrum, the isolationist group commonly referred to as 'Exclusive Brethren'.

***2005** / 1-84227-254-3 / approx. 318pp*

James H.S. Steven

Worship in the Spirit

Charismatic Worship in the Church of England

This book explores the nature and function of worship in six Church of England churches influenced by the Charismatic Movement, focusing on congregational singing and public prayer ministry. The theological adequacy of such ritual is discussed in relation to pneumatological and christological understandings in Christian worship.

2002 / 1-84227-103-2 / xvi + 238pp

Peter K. Stevenson

God in Our Nature

The Incarnational Theology of John McLeod Campbell

This radical reassessment of Campbell's thought arises from a comprehensive study of his preaching and theology. Previous accounts have overlooked both his sermons and his Christology. This study examines the distinctive Christology evident in his sermons and shows that it sheds new light on Campbell's much debated views about atonement.

2004 / 1-84227-218-7 / xxiv + 458pp

Martin Wellings

Evangelicals Embattled

Responses of Evangelicals in the Church of England to Ritualism, Darwinism and Theological Liberalism 1890–1930

In the closing years of the nineteenth century and the first decades of the twentieth century Anglican Evangelicals faced a series of challenges. In responding to Anglo-Catholicism, liberal theology, Darwinism and biblical criticism, the unity and identity of the Evangelical school were severely tested.

2003 / 1-84227-049-4 / xviii + 352pp

James Whisenant

A Fragile Unity

Anti-Ritualism and the Division of Anglican Evangelicalism in the Nineteenth Century

This book deals with the ritualist controversy (approximately 1850–1900) from the perspective of its evangelical participants and considers the divisive effects it had on the party.

2003 / 1-84227-105-9 / xvi + 530pp

Haddon Willmer

Evangelicalism 1785–1835: An Essay (1962) and Reflections (2004)

Awarded the Hulsean Prize in the University of Cambridge in 1962, this interpretation of a classic period of English Evangelicalism, by a young church historian, is now supplemented by reflections on Evangelicalism from the vantage point of a retired Professor of Theology.

***2005** / 1-84227-219-5*

Linda Wilson

Constrained by Zeal

Female Spirituality amongst Nonconformists 1825–1875

Constrained by Zeal investigates the neglected area of Nonconformist female spirituality. Against the background of separate spheres, it analyses the experience of women from four denominations, and argues that the churches provided a 'third sphere' in which they could find opportunities for participation.

2000 / 0-85364-972-3 / xvi + 294pp

Paternoster
9 Holdom Avenue
Bletchley
Milton Keynes MK1 1QR
United Kingdom

Web: www.authenticmedia.co.uk/paternoster

November 2004